Women of Power

WOMEN OF POWER

Laurel King

CELESTIALARTS

Berkeley, California

CELESTIAL ARTS
P.O. Box 7327
Berkeley, California 94707

Cover design by Ken Scott
Text design by David Charlsen
Author photo by C. C. Berger
Composition by Auto-Graphics

Library of Congress Cataloging-in-Publication Data

King, Laurel.
    Women of power / Laurel King.
        p.   cm.
    ISBN 0–89087–579–0. — ISBN 0–89087–580–4 (pbk.)
    1. Women in public life—United States—Biography.   2. Helping
behavior—Case studies.   3. Mental healing—Case studies
I. Title.
HQ1391.U5K54   1989
305.4—dc20   89–38149
                                                                              CIP

First Printing, 1989

0 9 8 7 6 5 4 3 2 1   89 90 91 92 93

Manufactured in the United States of America

For Nancy Terry,
whose heart is as big and warm
as the desert she dwells in.

Acknowledgments

I have been blessed with tremendous support during the writing of this book. I thank my husband, Chris, for his constant love and encouragement, my friend Alison Keye for her editing, and my typist and transcriber Lynn Walsh for her long hours of work. I also thank typists Deborah Hamilton, Anne De Chenne, and Robert Denchy.

I want to thank Susan King for the inspired title, Marty Raphael for her marketing skills, and my agent Peter Beren for his support and knowledge. I am also grateful to designer David Charlsen for his creative input, and for the support and encouragement of publisher David Hinds at Celestial Arts.

My thanks to Rochelle Ford, director of Avanta Network, for her time and assistance in gathering valuable information regarding Virginia Satir.

I want to thank my friends for their love and faith in me and their ongoing encouragement.

My special thanks go to the women interviewed in this book and to their office staffs. Thank you again for sharing your life stories with me.

Table of Contents

Afterword

Women of Power

WOMEN OF POWER

Each time I listened to one of these women's stories I was offered a great gift: the gift of her experience, joys, sorrows, and successes. I could see my life in their stories—what I had done differently, what I may or may not do in the future. I saw the support and encouragement we can receive from one another.

Taking the risk of following your inner voice while listening to your heart and intuition is the theme that runs throughout this book. These are stories of women who live their truths. Trusting themselves has not always been easy, and many times they have doubted, been afraid, and been criticized. But they have still moved forward, through adversity into healing, for themselves and others.

Virginia Satir, often called the "Columbus of Family Therapy," was one of the first therapists to reach across years of conventional practice by simply touching her client's hand, using a gesture of human warmth as a way to heal. She again breached conventional rules by involving the family in an individual's therapy. She knew that the family environment affected her clients.

Following her instincts, Claudia Black began to invite the adult children of her alcoholic clients into her office. Nobody had done that before. People invited the spouses of the alcoholic, and perhaps the children living at home, but not the adult children. She began to see behavioral similarities in these adult children, and out of that developed a therapeutic philosophy for this previously ignored population.

As a psychiatrist at the University of Chicago, Elisabeth Kubler-Ross began a series of lectures on death and dying. To the chagrin of many of her colleagues, she began to ask how dying clients felt. From her work with the terminally ill she

conceptualized the five stages of death and dying. She began
to talk about some of the mystical experiences she was having,
and then, to the horror of the scientific community, began
speaking on life after death. She says she has a new assignment awaiting her and is anxious to find out what it is.

These women have been active in their own spiritual and
emotional growth for years. The majority of them were not born
into supportive family environments; they had to develop that
trust and faith in themselves. They have been through painful,
emotional, and life-threatening experiences, they have sought
answers for themselves, and now others are learning from their
experience.

They are well-known authors, lecturers, and teachers in
the areas of metaphysics, addiction, rebirthing, incest, family
therapy, shamanism, death and life after death, and the promotion of world peace. They are all healers of one form or another.

They have endured. Their life stories reveal how they arrived at what they are doing today. They are healing or have
healed from incest, alcoholic parents and partners, and other
forms of physical and emotional abuse. In some cases their
own pain caused them to seek answers for themselves and created the desire to work with others.

Time has proven that when people do their own healing,
that healing spirals out to those around them. As these women
began to grow and discover answers, they shared these with
friends and colleagues and word of their teaching spread. They
wrote books that became, for all these women, teachings on a
worldwide level.

I titled this book *Women of Power* because I feel these
women are connected in some way to a spiritual source of inspiration and knowledge. To me, spirit comes through one's
heart and intuition. I believe they have learned to honor their
own wisdom, and therein lies their power.

The way these women connect to that source of inspiration
is an individual thing. They connect through people, their
writing, their work, alone time, and meditation. The word
spiritual has a different meaning to each of them. Some are
comfortable with the word. Others don't like the word at all:
for them it brings up images of an ungrounded, head-in-the-
clouds approach to life or a "holier-than-thou" type of person.

Regardless of those images, I believe they would all agree that they listen to their own souls.

I have always wanted to write a book about influential women. More and more, people are acknowledging the need for the rise of the feminine voice. By this I refer not only to the female form, but also to the knowledge of the intuitive voice within us. This knowledge is not just cognitive. It is born of the inner transformation I feel these women personify. It is through that voice that positive change is being made on the planet today.

Lynn Andrews points out that aborigines have been living on this planet successfully for hundreds of thousands of years; yet we who have not been in touch with the feminine nature of Mother Earth have made great progress in destroying the planet in less than a hundred years. She encourages us to reconnect with the earth, our God-selves, and to heed the information we are receiving.

The idea for this book came to me one day while I was doing some writing at a friend's beach house. I had been reflecting on my last year, wondering why it had been so difficult for me to be in the public eye. After writing *Living in the Light* with Shakti Gawain, I had agreed to give a series of workshops and lectures around the country. But when it came time to do the workshops, I was terrified. I always felt something would go wrong. Before each event I heard a voice inside me screaming, Please don't make me do it!

I remember one night before a lecture in Chicago. I was sitting on the motel bed sobbing, asking for help. Somehow the courage I needed came to me, and I was able to show up for the lecture. Also, the courage came to make a commitment to myself that I would no longer accept public-speaking engagements unless I felt better about them.

I knew that I might never be one for public life, yet I wondered about the women who were. I wanted to know how Terry Cole-Whittaker, Anne Wilson Schaef, and Sondra Ray could be teachers on an international level. Had they healed something I hadn't? What made them more at ease with the public? I wondered what their childhoods had been like and what their journeys had been, and the book began to take form in my mind.

I spontaneously made a list of eight or ten women I was

interested in interviewing and later added names that friends recommended. I chose public women, since the issue of a public life was something I was dealing with myself. There was nothing analytical or scientific about my approach. I took the first names that came to me and wavered only slightly from them.

The interviews lasted anywhere from three to seven hours. Many of the women told their life stories from birth until the present time. I asked questions that interested me and those I felt a reader would be curious about. It was particularly important for me to have a personal experience with each woman and to ask questions about their friendships, their daily lives, and their childhoods. That gave me a foundation for knowing them and more faith in what they write and teach. The best teachers, I believe, are those who are trying to live what they teach.

One of the pitfalls in becoming an author is that suddenly one can be seen as an "authority figure," or perhaps even as "better than others." Many of these women shared the discomfort of being seen as separate from those around them. Laura Davis said that suddenly people treated her differently, thinking she knew it all. Yes, these women are leaders in their respective fields, may have more knowledge, and may even have been in the process of healing longer. But they would be the last to say that they are better than others.

Elisabeth Kubler-Ross shared her sadness and loneliness in being seen as a demigod. She has come to resent it. I remember hearing her speak in San Francisco in December 1988. Three previous speakers had introduced her, and with each speaker she became bigger in my eyes. I became anxious at the thought of really meeting this woman and having to interview her. After all, how could I interview a legend? I was amazed when this five-foot-tall, slight woman came on stage. After graciously thanking her introducers, she remarked, "What they forgot to tell you is I drink coffee and smoke cigarettes." Since then she has quit coffee, and her guides have urged her to give up cigarettes. The point is, she wanted to say, "I am not perfect. I am human."

This book is about real people with real lives. That is what inspires me. The perfect person is an illusion, just one more way to compare ourselves falsely and end up less than equal. By asking the questions I did, I wanted to open more

room for common ground. There is always a place of common-
ality if we look for it.

As the interviews progressed I began to see similarities
and differences. These women have specializations that lie in
different areas but are not limited to those areas. Some of the
women have studied and worked with each other.

Louise Hay believes that self-love is the foundation for
healing ourselves. Though primarily known for her work with
persons with AIDS and cancer, she says her teachings apply to
anyone who wants to have more compassion for him- or herself. Her best-selling book *You Can Heal Your Life* reaches all
people who want to know more about healing. She, like Terry
Cole-Whittaker, has a metaphysical background. Both have
ministerial doctorates from the Church of Religious Science.

Terry Cole-Whittaker's television ministry was said to
reach over two million viewers. After a change of heart and
financial problems, she gave her last sermon on Easter Sunday
1985. The foundation of her work continues to be a metaphysi-
cally based belief that by changing our thoughts about ourselves we can heal ourselves and our environment. She writes
of the ascendancy of feminine consciousness and the planetary
need for it.

Sondra Ray is the leading authority on rebirthing and how
birth affects our relationships. She is founding director of The
Loving Relationships Training. She too believes in the power of
the word and uses affirmations in her work. In Sondra's ten
books about diet, health, birth, relationships, and immortality,
she recommends breath as a way to clear out the old and allow
vitality, limitless energy, and God-realization to enter your
body.

Anne Wilson Schaef and Claudia Black are both authori-
ties in the field of addiction. Claudia's seminal book *It Will
Never Happen to Me* identified the adult child of the alcoholic.
A grassroots movement has since developed with groups of
Adult Children of Alcoholics forming throughout the country
and other nations. Anne's *When Society Becomes an Addict* was
the first book to assert that the society in which we live oper-
ates like an addict. Prior to her work in addiction she was
widely known for *Women's Reality.* She developed and teaches
the Living in Process System.

Both Claudia and Anne knew, and once were influenced
by, the ground-breaking work of Virginia Satir. They, like

Virginia, recognize the importance of the family in the individual's psychology. Virginia was one of the first therapists to see the need to bring the family of a client into the therapist's office. She believed peace began at home, and looked for and encouraged the health of a family system. Her books *Conjoint Family Therapy* and *Peoplemaking* are considered classics in family therapy.

Laura Davis, joint author of *The Courage to Heal: A Guide for Women Survivors of Child Sexual Abuse*, educates people nationwide on that issue. She and coauthor Ellen Bass were the first to write that healing from incest is possible. Her own recovery serves as hope and inspiration for survivors.

Barbara Marx Hubbard has devoted over twenty-five years to the goal of planetary peace through positive social change. In *The Hunger of Eve Fulfilled* she writes of her personal journey toward self-actualization and beyond, to a point where she chose to be a co-creator with God. She sees herself as a social architect creating forms in which people can become involved in activities that promote peace and planetary harmony.

Shaman Lynn Andrews encourages us to recontact the Earth's feminine energy in order to restore our planet to health. Beginning with her first book, *Medicine Woman*, Lynn describes her meeting with shaman women Agnes Whistling Elk and Ruby Plenty Chiefs and what she learned from them. More than sixteen years and six bestsellers later, she continues to chronicle her apprenticeship with these women and her membership in the ancient Sisterhood of the Shields.

Elisabeth Kubler-Ross is world renowned for her book *On Death and Dying*, her work with the terminally ill, and her teachings on life after death. She is a psychiatrist, scientist, and mystic.

Each woman discovered her work in different ways. Knowing what they were going to be when they grew up was easy for some; others discovered it later in life. Anne Wilson Schaef knew from the fifth grade on that she would work with people's feelings and motivations. Virginia Satir knew from age five that she would be a detective of parents. Louise Hay was thinking only about surviving: Would she live to see her twenties? Would she escape the molestation at home? It was later in life, after her career as a model and fourteen years of marriage, that Louise found metaphysics.

Four of these women's lives were affected by near-death

experiences in their childhoods. Anne Wilson Schaef almost died at birth. When she was born, her mother had a systemic infection that she caught through breastfeeding. It was uncertain for the first two months of life whether she would live or die. As an adult she would be declared clinically dead, travel out of her body, and come back again. Laura Davis and Elisabeth Kubler-Ross both weighed two pounds at birth. Laura, a twin, was kept in an isolation unit and touched by no one for her first six weeks of life. Her sister died twenty-four hours after birth. Elisabeth was whisked home by her mother and nurtured night and day for nine months. She was born as one of triplets, and all three girls survived. At age five Elisabeth caught pneumonia and was kept at the hospital in physical isolation for weeks. She's never forgotten the dehumanization of that experience or the treatment she received when she nearly died of typhoid in her early twenties. The wartime hospital staff thought she was Polish, not Swiss, and was unwilling to do anything for her. And at age five, Virginia Satir was rushed to the hospital with peritonitis. She spent many months in the hospital, was deaf for two years, and wore leg braces for many more years. Perhaps these women were asked to choose life and living early in their journeys, and that decision would influence their teachings.

They all appear to be high-energy people. They run businesses, write, lecture, travel, entertain friends, garden, farm, and play, sometimes all in the same day. Do they overwork? Do they take time out to rest? Some do and some don't.

Elisabeth Kubler-Ross says she never learned how to rest or play and that she is a workaholic. In 1988 she suffered a stroke and clearly got the message that she has to rest, but she really doesn't want to. It was also difficult for Virginia Satir to make time for herself and to let anyone help her. In my last interview with Virginia, just before she died, she said, "I need more time for myself" and "There is so much to be done."

The generation of healers that is following them—women in their thirties, forties, and fifties—are just as excited and devoted to their work, yet they recognize that people who care for others often do so at a cost to themselves, and many are seeking more balance in their lives.

Anne Wilson Schaef and Claudia Black have both addressed the symptoms of such "caretakers" in their books. Anne learned that caretaking can be life threatening. Her heart literally stopped when she found herself in a situation in which she was trying to "save" people. When she came "back from death," she knew things had to change. She entered treatment for codependence and became less interested in saving the world and more interested in doing what she loves to do. This still includes teaching and lecturing and gives her more time for writing. She simply lives and speaks her truth.

Claudia Black says she was "clearly scripted for the helping professions." As an adult child of an alcoholic, she had two of the common symptoms: an overdeveloped sense of responsibility and a need to care for others in order to gain some sense of self-meaning or importance. It was easy for Claudia to find herself in social work. But through her own emotional recovery and her development of adult-child concepts, she became increasingly aware of the importance of self-limits and of meeting her own needs.

Barbara Marx Hubbard, who at fifty-nine has been working toward planetary peace for over twenty-five years, has more energy and more enthusiasm than she did in her early thirties. She credits this to being able to co-create with the universe. The task is not hers alone. She and Sondra Ray both feel that they have a mission to fulfill. Both are devoted to planetary peace, and neither seems to be suffering from her singlemindedness. They say they have found a way to tap into limitless amounts of energy. Sondra, Barbara, and Terry believe in immortality—the belief that the body can regenerate itself. For them, this belief shows in continual energy and a sense of agelessness.

It is exciting to see the work of these women spiraling outward. They are becoming more widely known on an international level. Their books have been translated into as many as twenty-two foreign languages. Many of the women give workshops in foreign countries. I found it interesting that many of the women had traveled to the Soviet Union in their work. They took time in their interviews to reflect positively on the leadership of that nation. Barbara Marx Hubbard, a diplomat for The Center for Soviet-American Dialogue, says that Soviets in high political office are very interested in the transformative ideas and the spiritual movement in the United States. She told the audience at a San Francisco conference that Gorbachev's *perestroika* team is initiating transformation from the top and is having trouble getting down through the bureaucratic layers to the people, whereas in the United States the spiritual movement—the movement toward planetary peace—is a grass-roots movement that is having trouble finding its way to the top.

Sondra Ray accompanied the Center for Soviet-American Dialogue to the Soviet Union in 1988 and was immediately invited by the government to speak to the populace. She appeared on Russian national television and spoke on rebirthing and immortality.

During her last trip to the Soviet Union, Virginia Satir taught her concepts of peace, new possibilities, and family therapy at four universities. She commented, "For me, Gorbachev is representing something the world hasn't seen since George Washington. We've got to have democracy, and while in Russia I saw that he's taking steps to do this."

These are interesting and inspiring life stories, rich with challenges and successes. For me, these are our modern-day success stories—women who are motivated by health, growth, and healing. Listening to their stories has taught me more about trust. These women have been able to honor their own wisdom, and their faith has led them to new teachings for themselves and others. As they continue to make discoveries about themselves, what they learn will bring new growth to their lives and to the lives of those around them. The expression of their thoughts and feelings is contributing to a new world.

Virginia Satir

Virginia Satir, M.A., D.S.S., *spent her life in the promotion of peace. Known as the "Columbus of Family Therapy," she saw a need for bringing the family into the therapist's office and from there developed concepts and techniques to improve communication among family members, the community, and the world. She taught the importance of building self-esteem, seeing this as a foundation for honest communication.*

She is the author and coauthor of twelve books. Her landmark books Conjoint Family Therapy *and* Peoplemaking *have been translated into twenty-two languages. A world-renowned lecturer and trainer, she cofounded the Mental Research Institute in 1959 and founded the Avanta Network in 1977.*

She was a Diplomate of the Academy of Certified Social Workers, and she has been honored with the 1975 Gold Medal for Service to Humankind from the University of Chicago and the Distinguished Service Award from the American Association for Marriage and Family Therapy. In February 1987 she was appointed to the California State Commission to Promote Self-Esteem and Personal and Social Responsibility.

She received an M.A. in 1948 from the School of Social Service Administration at the University of Chicago. The University of Wisconsin awarded her an honorary Ph.D. in 1973.

Extraordinary events led to my interview with Virginia Satir. The phrase divine intervention *comes to mind when I think of it. In fact, it was the circumstances around meeting her that led me to believe thoroughly that whoever was supposed to be in the book would be.*

Although her name was well known to me, I did not think of Virginia Satir when I was planning this book. It was in interviewing Anne Wilson Schaef and Claudia Black, both of whom mentioned her in their stories, that I knew I needed to contact her.

11

As I went off to my desert retreat to write for the months of February and March I planned to try later in the year. Near the end of my stay I had a powerful dream in which I saw a woman speaking to a large group of people. When I awoke I knew that the woman in the dream was Virginia Satir. To confirm it I found a picture of her, and it matched the woman in my dream. I am always startled by events like this, even though they are becoming more common to me.

As I wandered the desert I couldn't get her out of my mind, so I thought I should try to reach her sooner rather than later. Her schedule was completely booked, but she agreed to give me two interviews, one before her trip to the Soviet Union in May and June and one after. The most surprising thing to me was that when I arrived at her Menlo Park home for the interview, the woman who opened the door seemed to be over six feet tall (she was acutally a couple of inches less), whereas the woman in my dream was short. I stared up into her face for a few moments before I adjusted to the surprise.

The first interview, in May 1988, was warm, open, and loving. Virginia Satir was famous for her warmth and her ability to make contact with people. The second interview, about two months later, was difficult. I woke up on the day of the interview in a miserable mood bordering on physical illness. Up to the last moment I wanted to pick up the phone and cancel, but this voice in my head said, Do it now; you won't get another chance. Although I resented that voice, I drove south for the interview. When Virginia opened the door, it was clear that she wasn't feeling like being interviewed any more than I felt like interviewing her. (I still wonder why neither of us canceled.) She was polite and courteous, yet I missed her warmth. She was obviously distracted and hurried. She wanted to talk about her trip to the Soviet Union and the world situation; I wanted answers to questions about the specifics of her life—her friendships, her romances, what she did when she wasn't working. Even so, the interview was successful in that her story continued to unfold. When I was leaving, she invited me to Crested Butte, Colorado, where she was doing a month-long training.

I did not get a chance to observe her work in Crested Butte. Several days later I heard that Virginia was in the hospital. I knew then why she had been so distracted. She died September 10, 1988, of pancreatic cancer.

I did not expect the level of grief I felt about her death, especially because it seemed I had been with her so briefly. I con-

tinued to grieve for her throughout the writing of her story. It was as if through the interviews and her books and tapes she had become a part of my life. It gave me an understanding of the grief that those who were close to her, who had studied and worked with her, were feeling throughout the world.

Virginia Satir always said that she wanted to "go even further in knowing the magnificence of a human being." She believed that within each of us is the capacity for health and peace, and that no matter how things look there are new possibilities for the individual, for humanity, and for the world.

She was born on June 26, 1916. "My grandparents were born in Germany and came here as pioneers. My grandfather, on my father's side, homesteaded and built the house that all his children but one were born in. The farmhouse was in a little town called Neillsville, Wisconsin, which is about seventy miles from Eau Claire. In that part of the country dairy products were very important. There were a lot of Swiss cheesemakers there, as well as a lot of Poles and a lot of Germans. I grew up with first-generation Americans because my parents were born here.

"My father was the youngest of thirteen, and in those days you didn't go to school much, you worked on the farm; I think my father always felt a little cheated because of that. He was a big man, a large man. I am said to look a lot like him.

"My mother was a beautiful, red-headed woman who I don't think knew she was beautiful. They lived together until my mother died, which was in 1968. My father lived seven years longer.

"Those years of my childhood really were very nice for me. I had the run of the farm and lots of pets. I loved them. Our chief babysitter was a large dog, a cross between a Newfoundland and a collie. My mother said she could never have brought us up without him. There was me, my twin brothers, my sister, and my brother. I was the oldest. My twin brothers came when I was eighteen months old, so actually I started growing up then, because my mother had so much work to do and my father didn't like farming all that much and often spent too much time in town.

"I learned to read when I was three, by myself. I don't know how I ever did it but I did. By the time I was nine years

old I had read all the volumes in our school library and a
great many in the public library. I got my first library card
when I was six years old. My mother and father supported
every bit of education their children could get even though
they themselves had very little formal education beyond reading and writing.

"One of the things my father did was work in a forge. He
could look at a tool or at a keyhole, go to the forge and make
a key for it. He was really a genius at that. My mother was
another kind of genius. She took old clothes her sister-in-law
sent her from the city and made absolutely exquisite clothes. I
was always the best-dressed person because she was so good at
it. There wasn't much money anywhere because this was during the depression. I remember her getting men's suits, taking
them apart and cleaning them in gasoline, and then making us
clothes with embroidery and different kinds of braid. We always looked first class. I think my feeling about looking well
and having good clothes came from that.

"My parents had strong moral values. The only time I
ever got disciplined by my father was when he brought home
some candy and it was in his pocket and I knew it was there
and I took a piece. He asked me if I did and I lied to him. I
only lied once to him. I think all of us felt terribly guilty if we
did something that was immoral, and so we never did because
of those strong values, ethics, and honesty.

"Both of these people had a high, high commitment to
standards. You make a promise and you keep it. Both my parents on those levels were very ethical and moral, so they were
wonderful role models. I've thought about that over the years
because it was so easy for me to be clear about what I could
say yes or no to. It was very clear that ethics came before
anything else—if I made a promise I kept it. I was never limited.

"I could examine anything and I did. I concocted all
kinds of stuff, but I never got criticized when it didn't come
out. My mother would show me how it could be better. In fact,
I remember once wanting to surprise my mother and dad by
making a chocolate cake, and I must have been six years old.
So I made a chocolate cake from cocoa and flour. Then I
baked it, and when my mother got home it was as hard as a
board because I didn't put in any leavening or eggs. My
mother said, 'Well, I think we can do something with that.'

She then made a lemon sauce pudding and added it to that. That was the way my mother was. Always, 'Well, how can we fix it?' I think that is probably one of the reasons I am successful with people who nobody else wanted to have anything to do with. I saw the potential. She taught me that."

Virginia's curiosity came from her parents. She learned that it was okay to question anything, that just because someone said it was so didn't make it that way. "I remember very clearly when I was five years old, saying to myself, when I grow up I am going to be a children's detective of parents. I had no idea what it would be, but it had to do with puzzles. I didn't know why my parents treated each other as they did. My father was helpful, but he obviously drank a little bit too much every now and then. So there was a lot of trouble between my parents on that level, but he was never without work, ever. My mother would obviously feel bad and I would ask her how she felt and she said she was all right, but I knew she wasn't all right. I never questioned the love of either of my parents for me, but I didn't understand how adults worked. There was a young woman across the road from us who was pregnant and she didn't want a baby, so she rolled around on the grass and the baby came and was mentally retarded. I don't know if it had anything to do with that or not, but adults didn't make much sense to me."

Virginia remembers her parents arguing over her illness when she was five and a half and came down with appendicitis. Her mother, a Christian Scientist, did not believe in medical care, so Virginia did not receive immediate attention. Her parents argued for three weeks over whether or not to have her hospitalized. "The idea was that I was nearly dead. Peritonitis had set in by the time my father took me to a hospital, and they said I was dead anyway so why try, but he said, 'She can't be dead, she has got to live!' They got somebody to do surgery, but I was in the hospital a long time—several months.

"What is interesting is I have never looked upon myself, even when I was ill, as an ill person. One of the things which I know a lot about is that when things get too heavy I somatize. I know that my peritonitis had someting to do with my parents."

When Virginia came home from the hospital her father burned her mother's religious books, and in retaliation her

mother cut off her "gorgeous red wavy" hair. Shortly after that
Virginia got an ear infection. "It rendered me totally deaf
within a matter of weeks. I did go back to school, and very
few people knew I was deaf because I developed such a keen
ability to observe people. I think it is one of the things I do
so well today. I really observe people. I learned to lip-read,
and I spelled out all the words because in those days they
didn't have sign. I didn't have any professional help. I made
up my own way of communicating with people because I
wanted to connect with them, and that is true today. I make
up whatever I need to do to talk with people who can't talk—
the blind, the deaf, people of different languages. I was deaf
for two years. Then my mother said she'd had a faith healing,
and the hearing was restored in one ear. That whole time from
about five to eight was really a tough time for me. I also had
braces on my legs from what they called weak ankles, and
shortly after that I was diagnosed as having astigmatic eyes,
and they put glasses on me. At the same time that all this was
going on I was acting like a totally normal child. I think that
was interesting as I look back. I never had a normal life, and
I guess I don't have one today."

Virginia learned the value of work early in her life. Her
first job came from her father. "I must have been seven and a
half or eight years old at that time and wanted to earn some
money, and he said, 'Well, I'll give you some rows to plant
some beans. If you will plant, weed, water, and pick them, we
can take them to the bean factory and you can get some
money.' I had wonderful beans because I cared for them very
well. I made nine dollars—that was a lot of money. Every
year I did something. I picked strawberries for two cents a
quart, and I got nine dollars for that. That was my summer's
wage which I would use to buy school clothes. What I wanted
I was willing to work for, and my father was always helpful in
that. We all learned how to work and take care of ourselves.
My brothers can keep a house and take care of themselves.
That personal competence was very important.

"The love of beauty and the love affair with growing
things was very strong with me. I haven't really changed that
much. I am still involved with the most important growing
things in the world, which are people. I started out with people whom others said you couldn't do anything with, and I

proceeded to show that that was nonsense and that I could do it.

"The seasons were wonderful in Wisconsin. The autumns were beautiful; the winters were freezing cold! It would get to forty degrees below zero without wind chill. The summers were simply gorgeous! The springs were magnificent! I remember walking to school through a place of green moss, grass, flowers, and little violets. One of the things I miss in this kind of climate is the seasons. We lived three miles from the school, and most of the time we walked, but when it was very cold my father would take the sled and the team of horses and gather the children from the other farmhouses, about ten of us, and take us to school. He made fur robes that we would all huddle under, and I always remember the squeak of the sled, of the runners on the snow. Every once in a while I get very lonely for the snow. I would love to take a horse and go out with a cutter or a sled and do something.

"We had a consolidated school, a little country one-room school. There would be eighteen or twenty kids covering all grades. I had a ball because I loved everything. I only went to school for seven years before I went to college because it was easy to learn and I loved to learn. The teachers who taught us might have been seventeen years old. I remember one, in particular, who loved art and music. I got the greatest love of these from her. 'The Perguian Suite' was the first piece of classical music I ever heard.

"I was a very thoughtful child, and I was also very perfectionistic. Maybe *perfectionistic* isn't the right word; maybe *excellence* is the right word. I was always striving for excellence and I still do today. For me, I don't want anything shoddy or second class, in my work or anyone else's work."

Virginia finished the eighth grade, and now that it was time for her to enter high school the family moved to Milwaukee. "My mother had told me, and I knew from the time I was six or seven years old, that when I got old enough for high school, we were going to move to the city and never mind if the depression came. My mother was definitely the motivator. I went into high school, and the high school was huge, but I never really had problems adjusting."

Her main focus was getting educated, so she says she did

few social things. She loved archery, though, and won a couple of tournaments the year she graduated.

"When I was in high school, because we were in the middle of a depression, I carried extra credits so that I could get out of school faster. I had to work. Part of what I did was clean houses for people to earn money. I did a lot of that; in fact, I did so much work on my knees they became infected. But you know, if I wanted something, like education or whatever, I went for it. I don't think I have ever said, 'I can't do it because I can't afford it.' For example, I had just graduated from high school in 1932 and I hadn't yet turned sixteen. I went to Milwaukee State Teacher's College to see the registrar of admissions. I will never forget him. I showed him my diploma and told him I wanted to register as a college student. He said to me, 'Well, how much money do you have?' I said, 'I've got three dollars.' He said, 'How are you going to go to college on that?' I replied, 'Well, I always can do what I am going to do.' He registered me, and when I left, he called my mother and told her, 'Your daughter is here and she has only three dollars in her pocket and I have already registered her in school. What about that?' My mother said, 'Look, if Virginia says she's going to do it, she will do it.'

"I wanted to go to a teacher's college because I wanted to work with children. I lived at home and went to college by streetcar and I did all that on three dollars per week." Virginia worked for the WPA (Work Projects Administration) and at Gimbel's department store. On the weekends she took care of children to earn lunch money.

"I paid for my books. I paid for my transportation. I could buy a lunch for twenty cents. I had good teachers and I loved school and I had great energy. I worked at half-time jobs while I was carrying extra units, and I graduated third-highest in the class." Ranking third in her class assured her a job upon graduation. "I was lucky because not more than 10 percent of the graduates were placed. So I went out to Williams Bay, Wisconsin, and taught in a consolidated school. But I knew at that time that I never wanted to be an armchair expert—I wanted some experience. I also remember something else: in my senior year of college the instructor asked us to write a paper on crippled children, and I said to her, 'I can't do that; I have to write a paper on children with crippling conditions.' I often wish I had that paper. I wasn't going to label people."

She stayed two years at her first job and was offered tenure but knew she wanted to experience different settings. She eventually took positions in Ann Arbor, Michigan; Shreveport, Louisiana; St. Louis; and Miami. Virginia's workdays always continued into the evenings, when she would visit a student's family. She felt that in order to really know and help her students, she needed to discover what their families were like and what they learned at home.

"Thank goodness for me that I didn't go into my students' homes with a condemning attitude. I was often horrified at what I saw, but I was not condemning because I knew there was something else.

"Then I realized how powerful the findings of Freud were when he discovered that what moves us stems from our consciousness. To bring our thoughts and actions into consciousness becomes very important. Like, I'm beating my kid now, and I feel forced to do it. Then I find out I was beaten as a child, so that modeling is there, and it's as though it's all in my consciousness and that's what's driving me. That was an important piece.

"I know that somewhere along the line I gave my left brain permission not to inhibit the rest of me. I had an idea that the last word has never been spoken. I realized that whatever is now only represents discoveries as of now. It doesn't say anything about what else will happen. And the next piece is that whatever is now, there is more. So I was always free to look. Well, I knew what I wanted to look for—the puzzles that had to do with why people behave toward one another the way they do. I know the pain has been in the world because people haven't known they're driven by things other than their conscious awareness."

As Virginia began to make discoveries for herself, she began to look around for people who thought as she did and for a place where she could learn more about what she was seeing.

"I heard of something called psychiatric social work and thought, well, maybe that will help me, so I went to graduate school. I went there to learn about people. What I learned was a highly developed set of ideas that describe pathology, but it did nothing for prescribing health. Nothing. And it was this funny idea that if you learned about pathology, then you would know something about health, and nothing is further from the truth.

"And the other awful thing was that I saw people telling people what was wrong without giving them solutions. Now in social work you're supposed to be able to help people, and I couldn't help them with that stuff, but I wanted to help them and I did.

"I had to develop solutions. If I can't find it, I'll develop it. That's really how I did it, because the world didn't have that much. I came back to some things I knew very well. The first thing was, you don't help anybody by scolding them, by finding negatives. I also had so much experience showing me that each one of us has the potential for growth, and that whatever anybody is doing, the organism is trying to work toward growth. The symptoms are an effort to do that. Even if they can't make what's happening a growth-producing outcome, they're still going to try.

"It was easier for me then to think of things like courtesy and love, like helping people to see the relationship of what they had learned as children to what they were doing now. To get in touch with how they learned and things of that sort, and I realized I was a model for that.

"I worked a long time in a home for delinquent girls called the Chicago Home for Girls. These kids had run away, stolen, prostituted, participated in bank holdups—and they were thirteen and fourteen years of age. What they needed was to feel some connection with themselves and with life and with family, and they had horrible feelings about themselves. One of the things I did was to develop some puppets. Then I had them use those—one puppet for themselves and some for their parents—and I had these puppets talk to each other. I don't know why I left that, but anyway that was an innovation. I suppose the adaptation I made of that is the role playing I do now in the simulated family. That was something I did because I knew that all seeds have to grow from something. You know, if there's no rain and no nurturing, the seed's going to die. I saw this behavior as saying to the world: Look, this seed is dying; it needs help. The way we used to help it was to beat it up or to talk it to death. We'd talk about how things were, instead of, okay, so that's what your feelings are right now, so let's see what we want to do with that.

"When somebody would tell me that they were so angry they wanted to kill their mother, I would say, well, that says something to me about something you want from her. What is it? I would go off the killing and into the wanting. Very simple things, like somebody comes in my office and they're depressed and I touch their hand and . . . right away you can feel something, and then they tell me they're depressed, and I say, well, what would you like to be? Let's work on that and already it's changed. Now that wasn't the usual way of treating someone. Somebody comes in, they sit in a chair, and the therapist sits behind the desk and looks at them.

"I knew that there were possibilities within the self. Things would come to me, like once upon a time everybody in the world thought the world was flat. Then one day these characters went around and said, 'We'll sail and we'll find out.' It gradually began to dawn on people that the world is an ellipsis. But what do *you* have to do? You change it. That for me is what is so important now. We're in the process of finding out that people are not flat; they are an ellipsis, so to speak. They are capable of growth.

"Then, just as people thought the world was flat, we looked only at behavior; the inner part of the self didn't matter, and the only other thing we had for the inner part of self until we started working it was religion, and religions became dogmatic. But that world of social work I went into, at that time, was highly psychoanalytic, and we looked at problems in relation to those ideas."

Virginia trusted the discoveries she was making and knew that what she had working for her was the health of people. At a workshop at the Professional School of Psychological Studies in San Diego she told students how she learned this and how this belief affected her work with people:

"In 1946 a lot of people came to the U.S. who had been in concentration camps. I couldn't help them because I felt so awful about what happened, that human beings could torture and maim and do what they did to those people. I felt bad that I couldn't help them, but I realized that I identified too much. Then I realized that these people were still alive and that whatever happened to them was the past, and therefore they had come through that past. So when I was at that state of awareness I knew I could help these people, because they wouldn't be here if they didn't have health. This was something I could ally with.

"When I went to Israel and worked there for seventeen years, I had to face the same thing. I knew that if they were alive, they had come through whatever is there. That is a manifestation of their health. At first I began to feel there was something wrong with me because I didn't have compassion. Actually, I had plenty of compassion. But when compassion turned to identification, I couldn't do anything.

"One of the first cases I had was to work with a woman who burned up two children in a furnace. She took a big shovel and put each kid on a shovel and shoved them in and burned them to death. I couldn't stand to work with that woman. I was supposed to see her. I couldn't stand to behave as though this woman hadn't done what she'd done, and to pretend I didn't feel the way I felt. So I said to her the next time I saw her, 'Every time I look at you, I see you shoving those kids in the furnace.' She looked at me and said, 'That's all I see too.' We fell on each other and cried.

"There is awful stuff in the world, and human beings are capable of horrible things. Torture, rape—yet there still is within that somebody the capacity for health. One thing I say to therapists is if you can't stomach it, don't do it. If you have to lie to yourself that things aren't as they are, don't do it because there's no reason to make yourself sick. I have found that if a person is in front of me, they have strength because they're living and therefore I work with the strength.

"The problem is never the problem; it's the coping with the problem that makes the problem. Working with health is the only place to get anywhere. I don't spend any time on getting people to unlearn anything. If we add new possibilities, we don't have to worry about getting rid of unwanted behavior or compulsions. What we no longer use will atrophy and fall away. Where I spend time is in helping people to get new possibilities. I wanted to mention that because it flies in the face of what everybody has learned. Remember, we're mostly all trained as ill-health specialists. The thing that separated me for a long time was that I was working on health.

"That doesn't mean you overlook anything. For example, any person with a client who has had the experience of sexual abuse as a child, you can expect that there would be some dents in their self-esteem, fears in the sexual relationship, and undue dependencies. So what I want to do is raise the self-esteem, to let them be in touch with what can happen, with a clear idea of how they came to be that way. That's why I do so much work in family reconstruction. That's why very often when there's a problem in the present, I say, 'Where did you learn that?' "[1]

After eight years of working with children in homes and guidance clinics, Virginia knew that she could not continue in that environment. She needed to be where she could freely use the discoveries she was making, so in 1951 she went into private practice.

"Now I gave myself a challenge that very few therapists would take. I was in a heavy medical-psychoanalytical context and was drawn toward those people who nobody wanted. There was no insurance coverage, so if I was going to make my living, I had to do good work and I couldn't have casualties. I was taking as clients the highest-risk people there were. One doctor told me he wouldn't have the patients I had for anything." Virginia worked with a small group of physicians she trusted. She would ask for their expertise when needed, and they referred clients to her.

She worked in private practice in Chicago from 1951 to 1958 and then moved to California. "When I left Chicago, I had two offices filled to the brim. I was consulting with the school system, I was consulting with some factories, and I was working about seventy-five hours a week. I wanted to work forty hours when I came out here. Well, within a short time somebody from a mental hospital spotted me at a meeting and asked me to come do something. I said, well, I'll do it just once. That meant I worked in all the mental hospitals in California."

Soon after she met colleagues Don Jackson, a psychologist, and Jules Riskin, a physician, and they cofounded the Mental Research Institute in Palo Alto, California. She had read a paper that Don Jackson wrote on the family. "It was a tremendously moving paper. I saw him talking about the same things I had seen. I called him, and he asked me to come and

1. Virginia Satir, *Making Contact with Virginia Satir* (Crested Butte, Colo.: Blue Moon Cassette Services, 1988). Audio cassette.

make a presentation. Then, in the middle of the presentation, he said, 'Would you help me start an institute?' The three of us did that—Jules Riskin, Don Jackson, and I. We had a paltry amount of money and that was all there was: $6,000 to do everything."

Their goal was to do further research on the relationship between family interaction and the development of health and illness in its various members. They had become aware of a connection between schizophrenia and family interaction: a client would work with a psychologist for three hours a week, make progress, and then go home to a dysfunctional family the other 165 hours. Early on Virginia began teaching family therapy, gathering people around her on an informal basis and interviewing families. Several experienced therapists were interested in learning this new approach, watching her behind a one-way window in the evening until quite late at night. Jules Riskin recalls: "She was extremely creative, forceful, and charismatic. She was gifted in developing new ideas but not interested in the details of doing research. She was an inspirer. I had my first experience in family therapy working as a co-therapist with Virginia. The experience was somewhat like, although I've never done it, sitting on the outside of a fast-moving jet airplane. It was quite thrilling."

The Mental Research Institute, like many of the organizations Virginia cofounded, continues to pursue the study of the family as its primary interest. Riskin's main research today at the institute is in family interaction, stress, and nuclear war. Virginia's primary interest was in doing and training others to do family therapy. She started a family-therapy training program in September 1959 with a private grant, which turned out to be the first family-therapy grant in the world.

"Then I was in the world and that's where I've been ever since. I presented my first paper abroad in 1961. There were eight people there. It was the first meeting of the International Association of Social Psychiatry, of which I am now an honorary member. In 1964 I went back for another presentation. The room was so full that there was only standing room."

That year Virginia published *Conjoint Family Therapy*, which developed from a class she taught in family dynamics at Illinois State Psychiatric Institute in Chicago and the work that followed at the Mental Research Institute. It has since become a classic in the family-treatment field. In *Conjoint Family*

Therapy she identifies the dynamics that can happen in a family and describes the role the therapist can play in them. Stressing the importance of clear communication among family members, which she saw as a vital treatment goal, she explains how she models honest and direct communication in her contact with each family member. The book describes techniques she found most useful in practicing family therapy, including the use of a family life chronology, a history of events for three generations that helps the therapist and clients see the parents as children growing up with their parents. Later editions of *Conjoint Family Therapy* include an in-depth interview with a family and discuss Virginia's approach and interventions with them. They also include a look at the greater picture of the family within the context of its community.

In 1964 Virginia also began visiting the Esalen Institute in Big Sur, California, and became one of its directors. Esalen was becoming widely known as a center where people could come to teach, learn, and practice the latest work being done in the transpersonal field. Enjoying what she was experiencing at Esalen and deciding she needed a change, she left the Mental Research Institute in 1966 and went to live at Esalen. "I started the first week-long, and then I started the first month-long training session there. I saw that there were whole areas that I didn't know anything about—what we called the 'effective domain' at that time. There were practices represented by different people who were outside the mainstream, things about sleep research, drug research, the LSD stuff and research in altered states. I became acquainted with people from all over the world. People like Elmer and Alyce Green, Ida Rolf and all the body people, Charlotte Selver, Fritz Perls—all people I knew well. For many of us the stimulation that we had at Esalen fit. We were into a different place than the rest of the world. For me it was like opening up a whole level of resources. I was very impressed with what happened with body therapy, massage, and therapeutic massage, because this was getting close to health. That also coincided with the development of the flower children in the sixties. I saw this as an outcome of trying to make the world a better place, and Esalen was a center of a new freedom, in a way. The responsibility hadn't quite sunk in yet, but freedom was there. I also saw excesses of some things, but you know, a lot of times when you have something new you go through a lot of chaff to get to the real wheat."

The growth that was happening around Virginia was also happening inside of her. "I don't think people do anything that their insides aren't receptive to. Think of your inside and outside as two radios: one has to have a receptor and the other one a sender. The inside sends something to be received outside, and vice versa. I was very much aware of all that. When we did the early research on LSD I was a subject. I couldn't have done that unless there was a receptor for it. I think this is true for everyone. But the levels of receiving from the outside are dependent on the persons involved. You could have the most wonderful treatment in the world, but if you're not receptive to it you can't get it, so a big part of treatment is helping people to be receptive. Now there are more receptors for health than there have previously been in the world.

"I was responsible for putting life into therapy. Nobody thought, How does this relate to health?—we were still in a negative attitude. But it also had to be the right time, because if it wasn't the right time there wouldn't have been anyone to receive me. I think that each era of life brings people in who are needed to do certain things. I often think about classical music. We've not done anything since that could compare to the classical music of Bach, Beethoven, and Mozart. They were all within two hundred years. The classics are there, and there'll probably never be any more. There might be something else but not the classics. Then there was a time when we had these certain kinds of paintings. I don't think we'll ever again have the beautiful icons that were made then. The world is bringing in new things."

As Virginia sought to discover how what she was learning was related to health, she still suffered her own bouts with physical illness. Neither she nor her associates saw her as ill, yet she suffered from pneumonia, gall bladder problems, and cancer. "I had a lot of illness, and I knew that illness had something to do with how I was. I know that I had a lot of worries as a child. That's what caused some of it. I kept them in. I didn't want to bother or talk to anybody, so in a way it's amazing that I even grew up; yet I grew up with the help of physical illness. You know, you get a headache and then somebody gives you medicine and it goes away. Well, maybe that headache had something to tell you. I'm not for people having pain, but the idea is that we need to see what something is telling us. There's a draft in the room. What is that telling you? That something is open. You better go find out what is open.

"It is interesting, too, because I had such a strong belief in God. I never questioned why God was doing this to me. I would think, Gee whiz, I got this. Can you help me with it somehow or another?"

Virginia left Esalen in 1969 and shortly thereafter founded the International Human Learning Resource Network, where she started to bring together innovative thinkers from around the world to share what they knew with one another. In 1972 she founded and directed the Satir Family Camp. Having always loved nature, Virginia brought families into the mountains of Big Sur to cook, hike, and camp in the wilderness. While exploring the outdoors the families also explored their communication and interpersonal dynamics.

Virginia was becoming well known, and demand for her training and knowledge was worldwide. By 1972 *Conjoint Family Therapy* had been published in several foreign languages, and her second book, *Peoplemaking*, was published in that year. Also a landmark in the family-treatment field, *Peoplemaking* shares her family-therapy concepts and techniques with lay people as well as professionals. Drawing on her thousands of experiences all over the world, it was a book that supported, educated, and empowered the family by emphasizing the need for self-worth and congruent communication in the family. In the *New Peoplemaking* (1988), in response to readers' requests, she added chapters on adolescence, life in the later years, spirituality, and peace in the world.

Five more books followed in the seventies. *Helping Families to Change* (1975), with James Stachowiak and Harvey Taschman, and *Changing with Families* (1976), with Richard Bandler and John Grinder, share the authors' experiences in the family-therapy field. They offer techniques, insights, and choices for developing communication skills within the family.

Much of Virginia's work emphasizes the importance of enhancing and preserving self-esteem. In *Making Contact* (1976) she writes that whenever self-esteem is injured, the chance to make contact is reduced. Four forms of communication that

injure self-esteem are placating, blaming, being super-reason-
able, and speaking irrevelancies. She discusses ways to be
emotionally honest and strengthen self-worth.

Self Esteem: A Declaration, published in 1975, includes
her poem "I Am Me," which answered for her the questions
What is life all about, anyway? and What is the meaning of it
all? It is a strong statement of self-worth:

> I am me
> In all the world.
> there is no one else like me.
> There are persons who have some parts like me,
> but no one adds up exactly like me.
> Therefore everything that comes
> out of me
> is authentically mine
> because I alone chose it.[2]

Virginia did not like being boxed in as a person or as an
author: she wrote and published poetry, meditations, and innovative self-growth books, as well as professional psychological
studies. Virginia's colleagues John Banmen and Jane Gerber
later edited Virginia's most popular meditations and inspirational pieces and collected them in the book *Meditations and
Inspirations*, which they published in 1985.

Your Many Faces (1978) presents Virginia's therapeutic
techniques in the form of a play. The "Theater of the Inside"
has readers identify their cast of internal characters—the faces
of power, fear, love, joy, and anger. It demonstrates that the
key to opening the door to new possibilities in your life rests
first in recognizing and accepting that you need all the many
faces making up your inner self.

In the eighties Virginia coauthored several books that
continued to define her expanding beliefs and models. *Satir
Step by Step* was coauthored with colleague Michele Baldwin,
Ph.D. Part I of the book contains a verbatim transcript of a
family interview with Virginia, including in-depth comments
and observations from both authors explaining her interventions
and techniques.

---

2. Virginia Satir, *Self Esteem: A Declaration* (Berkeley, Calif.: Celestial Arts,
1975).

Part II of the book, written by Baldwin, presents Virginia's philosophy and therapeutic approach, defining the goals and beliefs underlying them. Baldwin describes major elements in Virginia's approach—the use of metaphor, drama, touch, and humor—and explains simulated family,[3] parts parties,[4] and other techniques.

Although Virginia was world famous for her concepts and techniques, she always stressed it was not what a therapist did, but who they were, that was important. "What I've really been talking about is that what I do rests on what I see and what I am. In a general, overall way, I saw people who hated themselves, who felt deprived, who felt helpless. Then I connected with them through courteousness."

With such an approach, she writes in *The Use of Self in Therapy* (with Michele Baldwin and other therapists),

> the treatment context becomes a life-learning and life-giving context between the patient and a therapist, who responds personally and humanly. The therapist is clearly identified as a self interacting with another self. Within this context the therapist's use of self is the main tool for change. Using self, the therapist builds trust and rapport so more risks can be taken. Use of the self by the therapist is an integral part of the therapeutic process and it should be used consciously for treatment purposes.
>
> I have learned that when I am fully present with the patient or family, I can move therapeutically with much greater ease. I can simultaneously reach the depth to which I need to go, and at the same time honor the fragility, the power and the sacredness of life in the other. When I am in touch with myself, my feelings, my thoughts, with what I see and hear, I am growing toward becoming a more integrated self. I am more congruent, I am

---

3. In a simulated family, workshop participants form a family and assume the roles of its members.
4. In parts parties, a person discovers the different personality parts of oneself. For example, a person may identify an angry part, a helpless part, and a worker part. Different people are chosen from the audience to play those parts.

more 'whole' and I am able to make greater contact
with the other person.[5]

Virginia believed that close friend John Banmen (who, at
the time of this writing, is coauthoring her biography with Jane
Gerber) understood her therapeutic system more than she did.
Virginia recognized that everybody had a positive life energy
that needed to manifest itself in the right direction, Banmen
says, and one indication of that occurring was a person's self-
esteem. Virginia's chief goal was to help family members have
more self-esteem. "To achieve that purpose, she would often
use the techniques she developed. And being an innovator she
used what she needed at the moment, never limiting herself to
the use of set techniques for set situations. She saw the individual's needs and then used or developed what she needed to
make contact with that person."

Banmen continues: "In working with professionals she was
extremely professional. She would be the expert and provide
the expert role. She would play the role of the visiting star,
and people would treat her that way.

"At the personal level, she could accept ideas so readily
it was just amazing. For example, I would say, 'Have you ever
thought of doing it this way?' She would say, 'Oh, that's great.'
She was able to incorporate ideas, so you always thought you
were part of it.

"And the other extreme was if she really wanted something, nothing could move her. For example, she had this
graduation ceremony where she had a ritual of candles and she
wanted all of us to parade outside and it was windy, really
windy, and she had to do it. Even nature would not limit her
when she wanted something. Sometimes she would have very
strong views on how it should be done at the form level, and
then at the essence level she would be so open."

Banmen says Virginia had a hard time asking for favors.
"I would say to her, 'If you would just ask people to do something, they will do it.' And when others asked her to do something, she would do it completely." She once wanted to ask
him to film her with Elisabeth Kubler-Ross at a workshop in
Winnipeg, Canada, where Banmen lives, but she couldn't just

5. Michele Baldwin and Virginia Satir, eds., *The Use of Self in Therapy* (New
York: The Haworth Press, 1987), 23.

ask him. Instead, she tried to build up to it by taking him out to breakfast, readying him for the request. "Deep down," he says, "she was a pretty shy lady."

Michele Baldwin agrees that there was a shy, vulnerable part to Virginia's personality. As she writes in a profile of Virginia, "She is also a shy little girl who was always too big for her age and thought she was ugly. Through the years, Virginia has developed a solid appreciation of her worth and beauty, but occasionally at times of stress or weariness, her shy little girl will appear and need reassurance. Virginia can get hurt and is capable of the same range of negative feelings as others, but she always bounces back rapidly."

Baldwin also describes the different parts of Virginia: the complete professional, the master weaver, the actor/comedian, the stage director. In illustrating Virginia's artist-magician part, she writes: "When Virginia works with an individual, a family or a group, she has an uncanny ability to make connections which are not clear to others. Rather than knock down defenses, she seems to go right through them. She is extraordinarily skilled in reaching reluctant participants, people from different cultures or people who speak different languages. This all happens so rapidly and in such a seemingly effortless manner that it often assumes a magical quality.[6]

"She saw our children grow up. She was part of our extended family. We vacationed and worked together. She was an extremely creative individual. When I worked with her on the books, the brainstorming was very creative. Yet it could be frustrating sometimes, trying to catch her to work on them."

As Virginia's books were read, worldwide demand for her training and teaching expanded. She began doing seminars internationally on self-esteem, family therapy and personal growth, family reconstruction, and mental health. She worked with government agencies and taught at universities.

She was awarded four honorary doctorates, was a member of at least twenty-five organizations, served on twenty-seven boards, and was president of the Association for Humanistic Psychology from 1982 to 1983. She was appointed to the California State Commission to Promote Self-Esteem and Personal and Social Responsibility and a member of the Advisory Board for the National Council for Self-Esteem.

---

6. Michele Baldwin, *A Profile of Virginia Satir* (unpublished).

In 1977 she began working with the Sioux Indians to help
heal the scars left by Wounded Knee, becoming involved in
Tiyospaye, a network of people working to form bridges of understanding between Indian and non-Indian people. Offering a
nonviolent alternative to some of the polarization and racial
separateness in South Dakota, Tiyospaye embraces and encourages change, risk, and widely divergent opinions to bring the
two cultures together. The network sponsors an annual seminar,
which Virginia helped organize, and has started an outreach
program between conferences.

Also in 1977 she founded the Avanta Network, an educational, nonprofit organization whose purpose is to develop and
share ways of enhancing self-esteem and interpersonal communication skills, offer models for personal growth, and provide a
professional training network. Virginia was director of training.
Each summer professionals from around the world joined in
Crested Butte, Colorado, to study strategies for personal
change with her and her staff.

"Everybody had such a personal view of what it meant to
them," says Rochelle Ford, Executive Director of Avanta,
about the summer trainings. "Virginia always said it takes
training to become more fully human. The theory was that you
started with yourself and spiraled out from there to make the
world a better place. If everybody had good self-esteem, that
would spiral out to their friends, family, workplace, city or
town, and pretty soon the world would be at peace. She believed that everybody did the best they knew how on any given
day, and she was here to help people do better.

"Some people brought their notebooks and pads and
thought they were just going to take notes all day. People
really got physically, emotionally, and intellectually involved
in the process—it was a mind, body, and spirit experience.
Some thought they came to learn how to help others, and they
learned how to deal with all their stuff. Virginia's theory was
that you got better at helping other people by getting your own
agenda squared away, so you could clear yourself to be there
for other people.

"She was a pretty amazing lady, and I don't know if she
had any idea of what she did or how she did it; she just did
it. She put one foot in front of the other and it was like magic
when she did it. There are members of the Avanta organization
who have taken Virginia's teachings apart and put them back

together step by step, into a teachable form. But Virginia just did it; it was very intuitive on her part. If you asked her what she was doing, she would say she was just being with people," Ford says.

Virginia loved the outdoors, hiking and nature. Because she was in Crested Butte for the month-long training, she spent more time there than at home, and she loved her time outdoors. She also loved to cook. One of Virginia's favorite things was to pick rhubarb from her secret patch in the mountains of Crested Butte and make pies. As she got busier and the trainings got larger, she had to turn over the baking to a local baker, but she continued to pick the rhubarb herself. Whenever friends visited her home in California they were treated to her homemade bread and soup.

So much of her story is what she did because her life was her work. She had a beautiful home in Menlo Park filled with art that she collected throughout the world, but she was seldom there. She would spend only eighteen hours to three days home between her three-month-long training tours around the United States and in the Soviet Union, Japan, West Germany, and El Salvador. When she was home for those few hours or days, she would visit the office to see what decisions had to be made and have one or two interviews, a photo session, and perhaps a local seminar; go to the beauty parlor and get a facial; unpack and pack again; and she was off.

She was focused on helping the world both in the present and future. Her staff would pick her up at the airport, and there was no discussion about where she had been. It was, "What's happening now and what needs to be done?" Working for her was intense, focused time. For years she did not have a secretary because she thought she could do it all herself. Finally, at the insistence of board members, she hired one full-time person for her office and two staff people for Avanta.

She loved her work and had a lot of fun during her trainings. Afterward she would enjoy sight seeing and having dinner and conversing with friends. She had friends all around the world. When asked if she took any vacations, she delighted in saying that she hiked Machu Picchu the last Christmas (1987). "You know," she remarked, "I am going to be seventy-two on my next birthday and people say, 'How do you do it? How can you be there, work for months straight everyday, and still be bursting with energy?' What I arrived at was, first of all, if I know that the universe is friendly, I'm not going to fight it. I am not going to put my will against the universal will. So if I find that I want to go in a direction that I am not going in, I know I am going up the river, so I just let go. I don't push the universe. The second part of it is that the past is finished and the present is the place where I can make all the changes. So for me the present is very important. I don't spend any time holding grudges or worrying about the past. I don't even spend any time in worries about the future at this point, because I know that if the present is straight, the rest will come. I absolutely know that worrying hurts my body. The more time I spend in anger or pity or any of those things, without having an outlet to change something, it is erosive to my body. We know how the feelings affect the health of the body.

"When you have your energy available for growth, you are giving growth. Every time you worry you give yourself negative energy. You know, sometimes at night I think about some things. One evening at a talk I was giving a man was humiliatingly nasty. It took me a few hours to deal with that, but I wasn't going to be taken in by it. But you know, the important piece I found out was that you face whatever feeling is there. So I felt that I faced it and did what I needed to do with that and then I could let it go. It's not that you develop calluses. I can't do that because the full life is lived with vulnerability, not defense."

The area in which Virginia learned the most about "pushing" was with men. "I was still feeling that I might not be a complete person unless I had a man around, so therefore I based my survival on it—you see, you don't have any problems unless you are trying to aim for something that has a self-worth value for you. Then I was pushing against something and it didn't even fit. I would try to make a relationship be what it wasn't—that is what I am calling pushing. I was pretty realistic about a lot of things but not about that."

Virginia met her first husband at a train station and was married in 1941. "You see, in 1941 there was such anxiety in the air because we were mobilizing troops and we hadn't declared war, but you saw soldiers everywhere. Most of us, on some level, knew that there would be war coming—terrible things. So among the younger people there were all kinds of anxieties; women wanted husbands, and the men wanted to have somebody at home because it was kind of like having a link. I hadn't dated that many men, although I had done enough. So I was taking the train home for Thanksgiving and needed to leave my bag with someone at the station while I went to the washroom. There was this very handsome fellow sitting there in uniform, and I asked if he would watch my bags. Well, it turned out that his mother had just died and he had come home on a furlough for her funeral. He was kind of down, so we talked, and it turned out that he was at an air force base outside of St. Louis. I invited him to dinner because I was taught that you offered hospitality to these men. Well, he was twenty-two and I was twenty-five, and within a short time we decided that we would get married because he was going overseas. And we did. We got married at midnight and I will never forget it. I wore a black dress. He went off to the air force base right after the ceremony; I didn't see him for a week or so, but it was a war marriage. We were together, here and there, for two months when I got very ill. I had an ectopic pregnancy and almost died again, and then he went off and I didn't see him for almost five years. I didn't really know him at all. I wrote to him every single day, and he wrote as often as he could.

"You can see that that marriage was doomed even though I am still a romantic at heart. It was very hard for me to know that the marriage was not going to succeed. I adopted two teenage children while he was overseas. When he came back, we were strangers. We didn't know each other. And I didn't know anything about how to share. Had I known back then what I know today, we would have had a lot of different things happening. But I didn't know. You always look back with hindsight, and hindsight is wonderful for writing Ph.D. papers but not very good for life."

She was married to her first husband for nine years. In 1951 she married a second time, again for nine years.

By 1961, she says, she was done with marriage. "I made a choice at that point. I had to decide whether the bulk of my life was going toward what I perceived as a mission, or whether I was going to stop that. I had tried for about eight years to settle that thing, and about the time I was thinking of remarrying, I finally decided I couldn't stop my work. If I really were going to go on a mission, I had to give it most of what I had. Then I needed to find a way to live while I was doing that, and to live happily. So I think I've achieved that, although right now I don't have enough pauses in my life. It doesn't make much sense to come here three days and to leave again. It's hard to go so long without a break. But on the whole it's going to get better. I think I've got a better schedule for next year.

"The amount of requests for my time sometimes gets to be a burden because it's hard for me to say no. So I get other people interested. For example, we now have the beginning of a Satir Institute in Hong Kong. I went there five years ago, then people started to come to me for training, and then I sent some of my trainers over there, and the outcome was a center. There are other centers developing like that. The chief thing I'm doing now is to make my work synonymous with my name so people who know my work will be able to do this, and that's happening all over. I do not believe that anything dominated by an individual can live. We just had our annual Avanta meeting in Toronto where we discussed this. The question was, Do you want Avanta to live after you're gone? I said, Absolutely. And so then what you have to do is work that out so it can be done. I don't have any need to be on top of anything."

Virginia worked up until the day she went into the hospital. In July 1988 she went to the doctor complaining of stomach pains and was diagnosed with pancreatic cancer. Days before her death she wrote to her friends, colleagues, and family:

> I send you love. Please support me in my passage to a new life. I have no other way to thank you than this. You have all played a significant part in my development of loving.
> As a result, my life has been rich and full so I leave feeling very grateful.

She died Saturday, September 10, at home.

"Virginia left most of her worldly possessions to the Avanta organization," says Rochelle Ford, "so we do have a commitment to invest her money wisely in training people in her mission work and to learn how to be family therapists via better human beings. People are really committed to her and keeping the organization going. In the past the world chose to have her do most of the training. Even if they had to wait until 1993, we had workshops booked for her."

Memorial services were held worldwide. A year after her death a memorial service was held in Crested Butte, where her ashes were buried.

But to return to Virginia's words: "I realized that my whole career in the healing profession was to create a condition where people could have two things—health and peace.

"I want to go even further in knowing the magnificence of a human being and how we can live lives that are going to make that magnificence come forward. If anything gets done in this world, it's because human energy does it. More and more I think we in this world are getting the message that we don't have to wait for somebody to tell us it's okay. All you have to do is put one foot in front of the other. If we can send men to the moon, we can find ways to live happily with one another. I know that."[7]

"I know that peace is not the absence of war and that health is not the absence of illness—it's a whole other thing. This is an example: how can we go on trying to make peace when so much of our income comes from designing bombs and nuclear equipment? We can't. That's ridiculous. And to say we won't use them is another ridiculous thing, because it still means we're in the same space.

"And, for me, Gorbachev is representing something the world hasn't seen since George Washington. We've got to have democracy, and while in Russia I saw that he's taking steps to do this. They're worried about whether there are forces that will destroy what he is doing. He somehow has something that is going to make that work, I know. And I consider him to be the greatest statesman we've seen. We've had nobody here in this country, but they're there, they're there.

"What Gorbachev is doing and what other people are doing is looking for . . . the hunger, the hurt underneath. You look for how you can help it rather than put your time into trying to avoid it. Sure, if somebody wants to kill somebody, it has to do with what they want.

"We are in another place in the world. That place is one

---

7. Virginia Satir, *Peace Within, Peace Between, and Peace Among.* (Palo Alto, Calif.: Avanta Network, 1987). Audio cassette.

in which the human being can finally begin to take charge of itself, himself, and herself.

"More and more of my work is going into the planetary concept and into the realm of how to become more fully human.

"Maybe I've had so much success with people not because of what I know, but what I am and what I see others as being.

"Every time I am part of a transaction that ends in somebody getting healed, we are making peace."

PERSONAL TRUTHS

My own personal standard is that I will be courteous and truthful and that I will be congruent.

VIRGINIA SATIR
Author of

The Satir Approach to Communication. Coauthored with Johanna Schwab, Michele Baldwin, Jane Gerber, and Maria Gomori. Palo Alto, Calif.: Science and Behavior Books, 1989.

The New Peoplemaking. Palo Alto, Calif.: Science and Behavior Books, 1988.

The Use of Self in Therapy. Coauthored with Michele Baldwin. New York: The Haworth Press, 1987.

Meditations and Inspirations. Berkeley, Calif.: Celestial Arts, 1985.

Your Many Faces. Berkeley, Calif.: Celestial Arts, 1978.

Changing with Families. Coauthored with Richard Bandler and John Grinder. Palo Alto, Calif.: Science and Behavior Books, 1976.

Making Contact. Berkeley, Calif.: Celestial Arts, 1976.

Helping Families to Change. Coauthored with James Stachowiak and Harvey Taschman. Northvale N.J.: Jason Aronson, 1975.

Self-Esteem: A Declaration. Berkeley, Calif.: Celestial Arts, 1975.

Satir Step by Step. Coauthored with Michele Baldwin. Palo Alto, Calif.: Science and Behavior Books, 1964, 1967, 1983.

Conjoint Family Therapy. Palo Alto, Calif.: Science and Behavior Books, 1964, 1967, 1982.

Claudia Black

Claudia Black, Ph.D, M.S.W., *is the originator of the adult children of alcoholics (ACA) concept. She is a worldwide lecturer and trainer in the field. Her bestseller,* It Will Never Happen to Me, *identified what occurs for a child in an alcoholic home and the psychological suffering that can continue as the child progresses into adulthood. Her work offers people deep understanding of themselves and shares what can be done to both prevent and handle these problems. Her other books are* Repeat after Me *and* My Dad Loves Me, My Dad Has a Disease.

She is a recipient of the 1985 Marty Mann Award and holds a master's degree in social work and doctorate in social psychology.

Claudia Black's work has had a profound effect on my life. I was working as an addiction counselor at a women's hospital, in the chemical dependency wing, when I heard about her book It Will Never Happen to Me. *I began to ask my clients to read it, and within a few days they would come up to me and thank me for referring it to them and say, "This book explains everything." The problem was, I hadn't read the book. I've discovered that I can sometimes be a channel for things that I myself am not doing. Here I was seven years in recovery from chemical dependency, and I was unwilling to look at issues that might have begun in my childhood.*

I was the classic "looking-good kid" that Claudia talks about, and I was feeling increasingly depressed. I had just broken up with a recovering alcoholic man whom I had lived with for four years, my car was breaking down every other day, and I was worried about money. Then I'd show up at work to support others.

I fell apart a few months later, quit counseling others, and began to look at myself. A year later I ended up in an adult-child therapy group and read It Will Never Happen to Me. *Finally life began to make sense to me. I began to have compassion for the fear and terror that I had lived with, to understand their source, and to believe that healing was possible.*

Since I had been consistently nervous before each interview, I was surprised that I felt so calm when I went to talk to Claudia Black. This was probably because when we were on the phone setting up the interview, she offered to make me a sandwich so I wouldn't be hungry during our talk. Whenever someone offers to make me a sandwich, I feel extremely cared for (it must be a pleasant childhood memory).

We met at a hotel near the airport in Orange County. We sat on a sunlit patio for hours while she told her story. Although she takes her work very seriously, she joked about my seeing her as a "spiritual woman leader," as I had mentioned in my letter asking for the interview. She said that her office assistant had read the letter and asked, "Are you sure she's talking about you?" Then Claudia asked if she was dressed properly to uphold that image. She was wearing a navy blue and white striped T-shirt and comfortable white knit slacks, and while I'm sure she wasn't barefoot, I remember her that way.

Claudia Black believes it was her own childhood, its pain and confusion, that ultimately led her to the study of addiction and the development of adult children concepts. Today she is a leading authority on children from alcoholic homes, and her book *It Will Never Happen to Me* has appeared on the *New York Times* best-seller list.

Claudia Black was born October 26, 1951. She was raised in a small logging community in Washington State. Her parents owned the only tavern in town, and the family home was only yards away. "I was always comfortable in my parents' bar. It was sort of an extension of our home.

"Life was very slow in that little logging town when I was a child. A lot of what I remember about my childhood is walking from my house to my girlfriend's. She lived about two miles away, and we went from my house to her house and then from her house to mine."

Although life was calm in the community, it was anything but calm at home. Claudia, her brother, and her sister grew up amid all the pain and drama of an alcoholic home.

Some of that pain began when her dad broke his neck in a car accident and her mother went to work at their bar. Her mother's presence had been a stabilizing factor for Claudia, and she missed not having her at home.

Knowing her parents loved her gave Claudia a strength that she would draw upon later in her life. "When I was a little girl, my father had a wonderful ability to make me feel special. He let me know that he loved me. So I felt very, very special at a young age, and I always clung to that knowledge.

"I think my dad was probably always chemically dependent, but I can clearly remember the difference between his early-stage and middle-stage alcoholism. Later in his drinking career, his disease became such that he was no longer nice, he certainly was not fun, and he became very tyrannical and mean. Even as a young child I knew that something had happened to him. I didn't understand what, but I wasn't willing to see him as a bad person.

"Even though my father's alcoholism was blatant, I was

one of those kids who didn't realize that I was from an alcoholic home until I was in my twenties. I say it was blatant because by my teenage years my dad was experiencing visual
and auditory hallucinations. He drank on a daily basis, yet he
wasn't one of those people who appeared drunken. But, looking back, he was never really sober. He would start drinking
early in the morning and would drink until he went to bed,
which was often 2 o'clock in the morning. My family didn't
know about chemical dependency, and we had the same stereotypical beliefs that other people had: alcoholics were skid-
row old men who were not capable of holding down a job and
who had no families. To me 'alcoholics' looked ancient, and
they never bathed. They sat at my mom's tavern, where she
tried to help them not spend their social security checks too
quickly so they could pay their utility bills and have lights on
in their houses. So I knew things weren't right in my family,
but I didn't know that the problem was alcoholism.

"At a very young age, I was intuitively aware that something was wrong. People weren't talking openly. There was just
this sad sense and with that a lot of fear. I think fear became
a way of life for me, and I did what I could to bring some joy
into the lives of my family. I guess I truly understood that my
father was sad.

"I took on adult responsibilities at a young age. It's not
that I remember being asked to, but it made me feel better,
and it certainly helped to play a role in the family. I did a lot
of caretaking of my older brother and younger sister. Looking
back, I didn't have a whole lot of energy left for my sister,
who was four years younger; and it was all I could do to try
and make things easier for my mother, make my dad happy,
and take care of my brother.

"My brother had muscular dystrophy. I think that his illness influenced my life as much as my father's chemical dependency. I was particularly close to my brother; I loved him
very much, and we were close in age. I didn't know my sister
as well because she was still a toddler when my mother started
working and she spent time at a babysitter's.

"My father and I did a lot of things together, and I think
part of the reason for that was to compensate for my brother
being too ill to play the role of his son. Dad and I went fishing and hunting together. We went to ball games together.
Most of all, when I was very young, we went barhopping to-

gether. Oftentimes just he and I went, and other times I can
remember all three of us kids and maybe even my mom sitting
outside the taverns. Looking back, I think a lot of my need to
be with him was a need to protect him. Somehow I knew that
he might be in trouble, or that if I went with him, maybe he
would come home a little bit sooner."

Despite the burdens Claudia shouldered at home, she felt
it was her job to protect the family image. She did not talk
about her feelings, nor did she feel safe in telling anyone
about what was happening at home. She made friends at
school, was goal oriented, and did well in her studies. She
was a prime example of the "looking-good" kid she would
write about twenty years later.

"Being goal oriented was also a way of making my dad
feel good about who he was. My father always wanted me to be
a doctor. 'If you're a doctor, you're successful.'

"He told everybody, from the time I was six years of age,
that I was going to be a doctor. I don't know if this grandiosity
came from his chemical dependency as much as it was that he
was born in poverty in Appalachia and most people he was
around were not high school educated.

"I took on a leadership role in school. I was president of
my fifth-grade class. In high school I was a debater. I was a
student body officer and a cheerleader. The list could go on. I
have always liked doing physical things. I was probably not
the most graceful or the most coordinated, but I was well disciplined and I practiced."

She says she never thought of herself as having any musical talent, but in high school she played the piano, clarinet,
and timpani.

"I had a lot of friends, but they usually came to our
house. I didn't venture too far because my brother needed taking care of. I didn't have hobbies, but my parents were very
good about buying us games. In the fifties we watched a lot of
television. I spent years in front of a television set, partly because of my brother's lack of mobility. It was something we
could do together. I remember walking a lot, taking my brother
for walks and chasing snakes with his wheelchair. I also remember my pets. Animals have played an important part in
my life. We had a dog named Mac for sixteen years; a cocker
spaniel who was really my age; Sarge, a German shepherd, for
twelve years; and a cat, Twinkie, for ten years.

"In the fifth grade, as a project, I wrote a book about cats. I loved cats then, and today I have a seventeen-year-old cat named Bubbles LaRue who is the love of my life."

An important event in Claudia's adolescent years was her parents' decision to send her to an academically superior high school in the next town. Because of this decision, she lived with another family during the week and would return home only on weekends.

"One of the things that my mother told me later was that she knew things were not good at home and that she felt my father's desire for my 'better education' was actually giving me a way out, so I wouldn't have to be traumatized on a daily basis. At times I couldn't even go to school on Monday mornings because I was so shaken by what had gone on at home over the weekend.

"By that time things had gotten rather difficult. My father had very little control over his life, and he was no longer working because he really needed to drink.

"My dad wasn't a batterer in the traditional sense. His abuse was more in his threats. At times he ran around with guns and said he would shoot us. He would threaten to blow the house up, to blow the tavern up, to run us down in the car. There were times my mom and sister were crawling across the living-room floor, afraid he was going to pop the windows out. By then I was in college; thank God I had college to go to."

Because Claudia spent weekends at home and weekdays in another town during high school, she experienced a fragmentation in her friendships that led to a greater sense of feeling separate and alone.

"I can remember sitting on the school bus going to a ball game. I was a cheerleader and on the student council, yet I felt like I had no one to sit with, that I had no one I was really close to, that they all had their 'best friends,' and that somewhere I must have friends. I mean, after all, someone elected me. I was always in these elected positions. Somebody must have liked me or seen some value in me. I didn't feel as separate from the people I grew up with, but by high school and college I had less access to them. They were beginning to be married and to have babies and were doing a lot of drinking, drug use, and sexual activity that I wasn't involved in."

Claudia's sense of aloneness was heightened by her brother's death. Her friend and ally died of muscular dystrophy when she was sixteen. "Any control that my father had, he really lost at that point, and all my attention was on his violence. What that meant was that there was really no opportunity to grieve for my brother. Because of the everyday outside stresses, there was no way to mourn, no time, no appropriate outlet."

Violence and irregular behavior were a way of life for her family. Claudia learned early in her life not to question behavior but to adjust to it. She also was to learn that not everyone reacted to her family the way she did. Claudia recalls that when her high school boyfriend met her family, he said, " 'There is something very wrong with your dad.' He questioned why my family and I tolerated my dad's behavior. He was willing to say, 'You are normal. What your dad is doing is not normal.' My dad had a real negative reaction to this young man, understandably so. He was not directly confrontive with my dad, but he wouldn't buy into my dad's delusions." Her high school boyfriend played an important role in her life: "He was kind, he was nice, and he was not chemically dependent. One of the things I have always had is a fairly good ability to pick people in my life who were not, as we say in our field today, sick or hurtful."

Her grandmother was also a stabilizing factor in her life. "She lived a couple of hours away. She would come and visit a week or two at a time, and every summer, for years, I would go to my grandma's house. She made me feel special by baking cinnamon rolls and giving me little presents. I've always perceived my grandmother as a strong woman."

Following high school, Claudia left home to attend college at the University of Washington. People who frequented her family's bar paid for some of her tuition. A bottle labeled "Claudia's College Fund" was set on the counter for people to empty their change into. She received hundreds of dollars from that fund.

"I managed to get all *A*'s and *B*'s in my first four years of college, but I was afraid of flunking out the whole time. I was very preoccupied with my classes, and it was sort of a numbing-out period for me. It wasn't a fun time.

"During my freshman year in college a lot of violence occurred at home. I heard about it and felt that I had to respond to it. My parents were getting a divorce, and I wanted to lend support to my mom because I knew it was a very difficult time for her. My college years were a time of trying to get good grades and trying not to be traumatized by events at home."

Claudia had thought about going to medical school but was unsure of herself, so she enrolled in a nursing curriculum. Then, within the first two or three weeks of her sophomore year, she checked out of the nursing department and enrolled in the school of social work. Looking back, she says it seems as if this change was made without forethought, but now it is clear she was meant for the helping professions.

During her junior year in college she was married to her high school boyfriend. "I was twenty years old, married, and I felt old. He and I had a very caring relationship, but I knew so little about myself. I didn't know what I needed or what my feelings were. I wasn't very good at negotiating. I was good at caring, and I was beginning to learn how to play."

Upon graduation, Claudia went to work. She consciously knew that she was not interested in working with alcoholics or children, yet she accepted a job working with young delinquent girls in an inpatient treatment setting. "I loved it. I loved the kids. Probably for the first time I realized a sense of my strength that came from my work. I experienced a sense of command, and, interestingly enough, I was putting some distance between me and my home.

"I was starting to feel free and energetic about myself and realizing that life didn't have to be based around trauma. I was developing some real confidence in myself and making some nice women friends. I ended up leaving my husband although he is still someone I know and value.

"It was almost the first time in my life I felt like I was doing something that was totally for me. I was autonomous. I was not in a dysfunctional relationship with anybody. By then my mom was divorced and had a new person in her life, and my sister had more stability in her life. I was able to focus on me. For the first time I knew that I had needs and they were important, regardless of what other people's needs were."

Claudia returned to graduate school a few years later. "Graduate school was a wonderful time for me. I worked full time, went to school full time, had internships, and played a lot. My priority was working because that was how I was going to support my education. I was incredibly self-sufficient. I didn't want to live a life of school-like poverty anymore, cooking out of popcorn poppers, which I did my first four years. I was going to work, and I wasn't going to get loans."

Claudia continued to work with delinquent children to support herself through graduate school, in an agency that also worked with families. "My affinity for kids surfaced. I felt a fervor and compassion for each of them. I just loved them. Sometimes that's all you can do for kids in trouble, just love them. Sometimes society and the family system are such that people say, 'Does it really make a difference?' I knew it did.

"I worked on a team where our supervisor, at twenty-six, was older than the rest of us. We were young and we were excited about what we were doing professionally. We were an extremely creative team."

She also worked in the rape prevention field, which provided her first opportunity for professional public speaking. "I gave seminars to groups of women on trusting their perceptions, responding to their own cues, giving themselves the benefit of the doubt. This was important and empowering work. It reinforced my comfort level with audiences."

Claudia's first awareness of alcoholism in her family came in graduate school when she took a course in alcoholism, not because she was interested in the subject, but because she had heard the teacher was good. "In the first five minutes of this class I realized that there was a reason for the way we had experienced life in our family—the reason was called alcoholism. All somebody had to do was explain blackouts and personality changes, and it was like bells went off. I had always believed that our family life was so complex, and yet there was one word that could totally describe it: *alcoholism*."

It was also during this time that Claudia began what she refers to as the recovery process. With more time to focus on herself, she became increasingly aware of her own feelings. "There was a sense of energy. I was having a good time and yet there were clear signs of depression. My feelings were rampant. They were all over the place." At twenty-three she entered therapy.

"I worked with my therapist on issues of trust, control, and dependency. It was a nontraditional therapy. It was more bioenergetics and Gestalt, which was probably very good for me because I knew I could talk well and I knew it would take longer for me to break my defenses in a traditional form of therapy." Through this process her sense of self grew.

After she completed her master's in social work, Claudia took part of the summer off and went to visit her father in West Virginia. She saw then that he was chronically ill from his alcoholism.

The summer over, it was time for her to find a job. Again she surprised herself when she applied for a job in the alcoholism field. "I simply marched myself into an alcoholism treatment program and convinced them that they needed me." The professor from whom she had taken the alcoholism class gave her a recommendation and Claudia did the rest.

"I knew nothing about how to work with chemically dependent people. I rationalized that I knew how to work with a multi-interdisciplinary team approach. I liked inpatient work, and I had been doing it. I was interested in group models and wanted to work with families. I told them they needed someone under thirty, a female and a nonalcoholic, on their team. I knew they had none of the three. I convinced them that they needed me."

Claudia was there only six weeks when she was offered a position in Los Angeles. Having an adventuresome spirit, she accepted the job. She had never really wanted to go to Los Angeles, but when the opportunity presented itself, she said why not. Within two weeks she was in Los Angeles. It was a culture shock for a young woman from a small town in Washington.

"I was overwhelmed. It took me a long time to begin to like California. Really, it took three years and a move to Laguna Beach before I began to enjoy life in California." It was at this job that she first began to implement the discoveries that she would become widely known for. In the mid to late seventies she initiated the first Adult Children of Alcoholics groups.

"They asked me to start a family program, and at that time in the chemical dependency field, family programs did not include children. Treatment included one couples' group and then sending the spouse to Al-Anon. But I was twenty-six years old, I was very naive about the field, and I thought that 'family' meant to include the children. This wasn't expected, but nobody was really paying close attention to what I was doing. So I began to invite them to groups, from three and four years of age to eleven, twelve years of age. There was something else I quickly realized. Most of my clients were at the age where their kids were older than I was, and gut-level human sense said, 'You need to bring the kids in.' "

She didn't care if the children were five or fifty; she only knew that they needed to be seen and heard. She started groups for children, adolescents, and the first adult children groups. At that time, Claudia says, Stephanie Brown of Stanford was the only other person in the United States who was leading therapy groups for adult children. They would discover each other in the next ten months.

"I began to use the phrase *adult children* as my way of distinguishing what I was doing at my job. I'm working with the little kids, and now I'm working with my teenage kids, and what in the world do I call these people? They're not the spouses, they're not the partners; well, they're my adult kids.

"Most of the kids I was working with were what I call the 'looking-good kids.' " These were the children who had learned the coping mechanisms of adjusting, placating, and controlling to deal with the traumas of an alcoholic home. As they grew into adulthood, they tended to function well at their jobs while suffering emotional pain inside.

"I began to search the literature for anything about children of alcoholics and found little. I did not realize that what I was doing was unusual, different. I had been influenced by Virginia Satir's work, but in terms of chemical dependency, I could only find information about fetal alcohol syndrome and the genetic aspects. I found articles entitled 'Children of Alcoholics,' and after reading the whole article, maybe the last paragraph would mention them and only to say that the best thing you could do was to get Dad sober and Mom to Al-Anon. Nobody talked about the children.

"I quickly realized that I was flying by the seat of my pants and that there was no information. I also knew you couldn't be raised in an alcoholic home and have everything be fine."

It was at this point that Claudia identified and labeled the denial process. She recognized that children from alcoholic homes learned to distrust and deny their own feelings and those of others. "These children followed the spoken or unspoken rules: 'Don't talk, don't trust, and don't feel.' I realized that it wasn't safe for them to talk and that somehow it was my job to make it safe. I had worked with delinquent kids who were supposed to be hard to work with, and who are, but you give me a 'looking-good kid' with denial and that's a lot harder. At least angry kids give you something. When I began with the adult children, they came in saying, 'I'm here to help Mom or Dad.' I talked with them about what they could do in reference to Mom and Dad, what's appropriate and what's not. But I also told them there were some things about themselves they needed to know. These were things that might already be happening in their lives, or could happen."

Claudia says it was like telling their fortunes. She told them that they were probably experiencing difficulty in their relationships, that they could be involved with alcoholics or were becoming alcoholics themselves, and that their feelings were probably beginning to surface at inappropriate times. They might even be feeling that they were losing control or going crazy.

Claudia began by helping children of alcoholics feel safe. She began to put them into groups, so they could see they were not unique and so they could receive validation for their feelings. She began to use art therapy, play therapy, puppets, role playing and collages.

"I developed models for short-term educational and therapy groups using art and play techniques. What was significant about the models was that they were meant to work not only with acting-out children, but they also broke the denial systems of 'looking-good children.'

"What I found was that many of these people previously could have had clinical diagnoses or were treated for depression or even schizophrenia and personality disorders. As we focused on family-origin issues, the basis being a chemically dependent home, they began to respond to a more directive approach than the traditional theoretical process. It gave them hope, and they were willing to commit themselves to a treatment process.

"My artwork with young children was very significant in that it gave people a way in which to work with children from alcoholic homes that previously wasn't available."

Claudia developed much that wasn't done before. She developed the adult-child concept, identified the denial process, developed a 'looking-good' model, and described the emotional progression of children from this kind of background.

She was so busy making these discoveries that she hardly stopped to see the impact of what she was doing. Fortunately, she was not alone in her discoveries. By then she had become involved with a man named Jack Fahey who had the foresight to see what it all meant. It was he who finally pointed out that what she was doing with these adult children was important and that people needed to know about it.

"He had been in the educational arena, had done films with Father Martin and Joe Pursch [authorities in the chemical dependency field]; he knew the field. I had met him professionally; we started to date, and he just kept saying, 'This is important. You need to write about it, and you need to talk about it.' I kept thinking I didn't have time to write about it, much less to talk about it. I had groups to run, psychosocial assessments to do. I was working as a team member in an inpatient chemical dependency program. I wasn't just doing kids' work or family work. Jack clearly seemed to understand the magnitude of the need for the information to get out more than I did. My children's book was his idea. He said children need tools they can use. The children's book started out as a project because I didn't think of myself as a writer. I thought I didn't know how to write, but I knew how to put a children's book together."

Motivated by the need to give these children a tool, she wrote *My Dad Loves Me, My Dad Has a Disease* (1982). In the introduction and foreword she writes:

> *My Dad Loves Me, My Dad Has a Disease* is a workbook for the children of alcoholics. It is designed to help children better understand alcoholism and to better understand their own feelings. The basic premise of this book is that alcoholism is a disease, affecting not only the alcoholic but those who love him as well. This is a book that will help the "others" affected by the disease of alcoholism to become well.
>
> Although this workbook was designed for, and the illustrations created by, children through age fourteen, it may also hold insights for the now adult child, raised in an alcoholic home. Remember, this is a workbook; you will need colored pens or crayons as you read.
>
> In this book children between the ages of six and fourteen share what it is like for them to live

in an alcoholic family—how they see alcoholism. Working through this loneliness, fear, and frustration by expressing feelings is what this book is all about. This workbook gives children the opportunity to share their thoughts and feelings and to better understand the disease of alcoholism.

There is hope for the alcoholic and those affected by their alcoholism. We the children, don't have to remain confused and silent.

The world was hungry for the information Claudia was gathering, and suddenly she was exposed to national media coverage.

"In 1979 *Newsweek* magazine did a one-page article on Stephanie Brown's and my work. The *Newsweek* article immediately led to an appearance on the 'Donahue' show. It changed my career. Suddenly I was perceived as an expert, a specialist on children of alcoholics. I received hundreds and hundreds of letters from across the United States. I hadn't been in the field very long and I was very young, and suddenly I found myself on a lecture circuit.

"At this time Sharon Wegscheider-Cruse was making a strong impact in the field. She was talking more about families, not children. As I ran into her frequently on the road, people would often arrange the bill so it had Sharon talking about the family and Claudia talking about children, be they young, adolescent, or adults. That's the way it was for two or three years.

"I find it amusing in some ways that I speak professionally for a living. I was always pretty shy, and there is a strong introverted part of me. Professionally I'm not shy; personally I am."

In 1982 she published her second ground-breaking book, *It Will Never Happen to Me*. Focusing on the effects of alcoholism on children, she describes the coping mechanisms these children develop while growing up and the problems they face as adults. She addresses what can be done to help children of alcoholics begin the recovery process and restructure their lives.

Repeat after Me, a workbook for adult children of alcoholics, followed in 1985. Its purpose is to lead readers toward an understanding of their childhoods with the goals of greater self-awareness and self-love.

Claudia and her husband Jack have also produced several films, videos, and a game, all of which address the issues of children of alcoholics and the recovery process.

"I think that there are many aspects of the issue of children of alcoholics that I still have an interest in writing, speaking, and learning about. For example, I would like to say more for women and for the chemically dependent person who is an adult child. I'd like to give greater validation to those who had additional reasons to defend themselves, such as only children, those with two alcoholic parents, and the physically disabled in the alcoholic home. At this time I am actually working on three books to be published in 1989 and 1990. Obviously there is a lot yet to do. Fortunately I am young and I'm aware that this was meant to be.

"I still have difficulty perceiving myself as a writer. Today, when people ask me what I am, I grin and sometimes say, 'Well, I guess I am an author; I've written three books.' What I have written is mine. I write because I feel I have a need to say something."

As word spread of Claudia's findings and those of others in the field, the need for some solutions arose. In 1982 the National Association for Children of Alcoholics (NACOA) was established. Claudia was one of the central people involved in the founding of the organization, and she continues to be involved in its work. The head office is in her hometown of Laguna Beach.

"We felt organizations did things that individuals couldn't, such as impacting and networking to other organizations. There needed to be an advocate to represent the needs of children of alcoholics of all ages, and that is the direction and the work of NACOA. It began at a time when the self-help groups—Adult Children of Alcoholics—were beginning. So people sometimes confuse the two."

Claudia is happy to say that in recent years NACOA, with Director Gerry Myers, has obtained a grant for the National Elementary School Project. The funding was from the Pew Charitable Trusts, Metropolitan Life Foundation, the Federal Department of Education, the Federal Office of Substance Abuse Prevention, the National Committee for Prevention of Child Abuse, and the Marvel Entertainment Group. The project has placed packets of information and six large color posters in every public elementary school in the nation. Over 47,000 public elementary schools in the nation have received comic books, a resource booklet, and posters with Marvel comic characters—the Incredible Hulk, Ice Man—telling children, "If your mom or dad drinks too much, there is somebody in your school you can trust." Claudia says, "The message is you are not alone, you are not at fault, your feelings are valid, there is somebody you can trust."

Although Claudia is obviously fervent about her work, it is not the sole focus of her life. She has been in love with her husband, Jack, for eleven years, and married to him for five.

"I don't think I would have done what I have done without Jack. He has made a big difference in my work. He was the one, particularly in the beginning, who continued to push. Perhaps I would not have done it without that push, because I don't think I recognized the significance of what I was doing. He has a real passion for me and my work. We have a nice creative relationship together in terms of that work. He has been part of my books, the films, and the Stamp Game.[1]

"It is a nurturing and respectful relationship. After eleven years there are still polite thank-yous and pleases. If there are problems or disagreements, they tend to get resolved very quickly. Part of this is that both of us are uncomfortable with conflict for long periods of time. One of our real strengths in this relationship is that we are both willing to work at it. Jack has a great sense of humor. Sometimes I refer to it as a sick sense of humor, but it's a sense of humor I happen to enjoy.

"We take lots of trips together. We scuba dive. We have a weight room in our house where we work out together. He has hobbies—playing computer games, collecting stamps and coins. When he's busy with them, I go to the movies or see my own friends. So we certainly enjoy each other's company, and at the same time we have very different interests. I like to go to movies—he doesn't. I like to dance—he doesn't. Recently, I have got him taking dance lessons with me. We're having a wonderful time."

Claudia hesitates momentarily before she begins to talk

---

1. "The Stamp Game," by Claudia Black (Denver: MAC Publishing), is a game that helps people learn how to identify and express their feelings.

about a crisis that she and her husband have been through. "I don't tend to talk about it publicly, but at this point it seems to be okay to do so.

"Jack has leukemia and is only alive because of a research project. It was diagnosed by accident when he went in for some simple surgery, and they discovered something was wrong with his blood. We came out that day knowing he had a leukemia that was very rare, untreatable, and terminal.

"I remember walking out of the hospital after the diagnosis, feeling very young at thirty-one. My dad had just died from alcoholism and I thought, I've got to keep this separate from my issues with my dad—his dying and the issues with my brother and his illness and death. Somehow I knew I could become overwhelmed by it happening one more time. Now I had another man in my life who was going to have a chronic, terminal illness. I told myself that it was different—that as an adult, I could own my fears, my angers, and my sadness, and I could ask for help. I didn't have to walk through it alone, and I could pray for guidance.

"It took about a year before he really started to get sick, and clearly, within another year, he was in a dying stage where they could only keep him alive with transfusions. It was a very traumatic time—a very traumatic time because I was also very public.

"In what he thought were his last few months of life they put him in a research project, like they often do with terminal cancer patients, and it saved his life. For eighteen months he was in remission, and we no longer had to live with the certainty that he would die. He was able to go off the medication and was being watched. Recently, it appears to have progressed again, so treatment has begun again. At least the prognosis is no longer terminal. It's considered treatable without remission.

"We used a lot of denial, I have to say. Sometimes Jack and I actually laugh about some of the crazy things we did at the height of his illness. One of them was to buy a sailboat. We decided that if he was going to die, we were going to have a good time. We still own this fifty-two-foot sailboat and we sail a lot. He rode out the back end of a hurricane at the height of his illness. We didn't even recognize it. Denial can serve a purpose. We used it well."

Claudia says there have always been major issues in her life. Jack's illness and her fame are the latest. One way she has sought support for herself is through therapy.

"I'm always in therapy. I think everybody can benefit from therapy. I go in and out, but I have been there for quite a while. It helps to keep me honest.

"I try to pay attention to my own well-being, by doing my own Twelve Step programs; yet at the same time, because I'm well known, there are some things that I feel more comfortable talking about in an individual session in therapy. I don't find myself working on core issues from the past now. Therapy helps me stay clear with myself."

Describing her daily life, she says, "I don't really have a ritual to my day because sometimes I come home from a trip and have five days off and other times, ten. That affects what my day is about. When I'm not on the road, I have an office with staff and I go to work. When I have days at home, I like to be in my house."

The stability of having lived in the same community for seven years is important to her. When she's home she likes to open up the blinds, see the Pacific Ocean, and let the sunshine in. "I want to see the water. I run around barefoot in casual clothes. I often have music on too, jazz and popular. Jack and I have a little dinette in a wonderful corner of the house with a great view. Often we'll go downstairs in the morning. He'll have a cup of coffee, and we'll sit with our cat, Bubbles, and a newspaper, no TV. That has been a wonderful ritual for us. We just let Bubbles be the center of attention."

Claudia is vibrant and healthy. She has a lean body and a beach tan. "I try to do something physical every day, and I think about where that is going to fit into my day. I'm active, I'm a doer, I'm extremely high energy. Sometimes I don't really understand it myself. I can work all day, have a party for fifty people, and have five other things going that night as well. I'm afraid that is not exaggerating."

Claudia has two staff people who protect her from demands, but, she says, "I have had to learn to set limits, which is something that is difficult for us as adult children. I have had to learn to say no, and that means some people aren't going to like me as well because I am not attending to their needs. That is sometimes the price of being in the public eye.

I also have to realize that when I am out in public I am pretty accessible to people, and sometimes they will perceive that I can always be that accessible. I find when I am with my audiences I am with them, but I can't incorporate them into my life as they would often like.

"I have some very nice women friends—long-term relationships, three to fifteen years. I'm pretty good about bringing people into my life, not being as alone and feeling so separate anymore. I'm much better about knowing what my feelings are. I have friends all over the United States too. I see my family. My mom has gone on a couple of sailing vacations with me. I make a point to see my grandmother. I see my sister less, for geographic reasons, but she's very much a part of my life.

"If I have some drawbacks to my life, it seems they have to do with time.

"Sometimes I get too compulsive about my work and don't take care of me as well as I'd like. When I don't set enough limits and take care of my own needs, I can feel low. It isn't actually depression, but I can quickly get in touch with those old feelings of powerlessness and loneliness when I am busy taking care of other people's needs, responding to other people's demands instead of taking care of me."

If she had a second career, it would probably be acting. She also wanted to be a dancer but does not see that in her future. "I have absolutely no talent for singing, but sometimes I feel like I would just like to sing to those people I give talks to. Sing them songs instead of standing up and talking about things that can be so serious.

"I feel spiritual, and I feel like my work is very spiritual. I try to live it more than to verbalize it. I am relatively quiet about spirituality and hope I live my life in a manner that shows a love for all."

When asked to describe her personality, she says, "I am an extremely kind person and highly concerned about the welfare of people. I keep clear about boundaries and responsibilities—my own and others'. I like to make things happen. Sometimes I say to my husband, 'I don't think it is easy living with Claudia Black.' Sometimes I want things done now, I want them done in my time frame, but I also have a tendency to be harsh with myself.

"I am extremely practical. I am not just a dreamer. I try

to make things happen, and I try to make them practical enough and realistic enough so that they can happen for myself and other people.

"I feel good about my femaleness. I feel strong. I feel strength with a healthy kind of power, and at the same time there are some things about me that tend to have more masculine characteristics. I feel a positive sense of both femininity and masculinity. I am soft but I am firm. There are times when I get back into that stereotypical female, where I want someone to take care of me, but I think that is just human. You know, some days my husband wants someone to take care of him.

"I think that a lot of my ability, compassion, and fervor to speak for children of all ages certainly comes from my sense of my own vulnerability. I want to speak for those who can't speak for themselves. I want to help empower people and to give them a sense of their strength and to give them the safety in which to talk about it.

"My hope is that I will always stay connected to what the issues of children are. You can't change what is going to happen at home, but you can take away their sense of shame. You can take away their utter helplessness and powerlessness. You can lessen their loneliness.

"You can help to give them choices about how they live their lives. I'd like each and every person raised in a traumatic family to develop an empathy and a respect for their vulnerability as a child. I know they can reach through the fears and allow themselves a path of recovery. It's my hope that I and others will continue to advocate and speak for the young child who continues to live a painful childhood. The issue of children of alcoholics has moved into 'dysfunctional family issues' and 'codependency.' We've seen a social movement begin, a grassroots movement. We can see a fashion or trendiness develop that is possibly necessary. But the healthy and unhealthy aspects of the movement will sort themselves out. When they do, we will continue to have knowledge, resources, and recovery for millions of people who have previously never been identified or addressed."

PERSONAL TRUTHS

1. I believe everyone is truly very special and deserves to believe in that specialness.

2. Just as there is a lot of fear and hurt in the world for many children, there is the potential for incredible love and joy. We must address the pain and speak to the specialness of each child, be that child a three-year-old or the "child within" of a ninety-year-old.

3. Every child deserves a physically and psychologically safe environment in which to grow.

4. Each of us has the ability to make the world a better place.

CLAUDIA BLACK
Author of

Repeat after Me. Denver: MAC Publishing, 1985.

It Will Never Happen to Me. Denver: MAC Publishing, 1982; and New York: Ballantine Books, 1987.

My Dad Loves Me, My Dad Has a Disease. Denver: MAC Publishing, 1982.

Lynn Andrews

Lynn Andrews *is a shaman, a spiritual teacher, and a best-selling author who has apprenticed with Agnes Whistling Elk and Ruby Plenty Chiefs, Native American shaman women, for more than sixteen years. Through her training she has become the only non-native member of the Sisterhood of the Shields, the shamanistic society of forty-four women who practice and maintain the ancient wisdom of woman. Lynn teaches this knowledge through her writings and says her primary goal is to bring feminine consciousness back to Mother Earth. She is the author of six best-selling books:* Windhorse Woman, Crystal Woman, Star Woman, Jaguar Woman, Flight of the Seventh Moon, *and* Medicine Woman. *Lynn lectures, gives occasional workshops, counsels privately, and travels worldwide to study with members of the Sisterhood. She has homes in Los Angeles, and in Santa Fe, New Mexico.*

Lynn Andrews is one of my favorite writers. What she says, as well as the way she says it, is healing. Sometimes I am more fascinated with the way she weaves her words together than with what she is saying. She says she is a shaman and a writer, and I believe she sees both of those parts of herself as one and the same. When I attended her workshop "Into the Crystal Dreamtime,"[1] I saw how carefully she used her words to initiate people into a shamanistic experience. At first I could not understand why she read the meditations she was leading us through. Then, as her words took me farther and farther into this magical inner world, I saw how they are part of her shamanistic gift. She believes in the power of words and chooses them well.

Some people question what she says. They wonder how she could have experienced the things she writes about, like being cut

---

1. Sponsored by Whole Life Promotions, Santa Monica, Calif.

open and having crystals placed inside her body or bringing jewelry back from another level of consciousness. She writes of her apprenticeship with shaman women Agnes Whistling Elk and Ruby Plenty Chiefs and tells us, with certainty, that those things actually happened.

She invited me to her Los Angeles home for the interview. Even though we had an appointment, I kept wondering if she would be there when I arrived. Perhaps I thought she would be suddenly whisked away by Agnes and Ruby. When I arrived at her home she was there, but I'm not sure she was expecting me. I knocked on her door and was at first told to come back later. I explained who I was, and the door immediately swung open. I was greeted with warmth and invited in. She was smaller and more fragile looking than I expected, but Lynn has that wonderful blond hair that you see in all her photos and huge green eyes that almost fill her entire face.

She is both a private and public person. She makes herself available to large groups of people. She will hand out her business phone number to six hundred people at her workshop and invite people into her home for shamanistic counseling. Yet many things about her remain elusive. She does not want to talk publicly about some of her feelings or about personal friendships, family, or involvements. She was willing to do some, but I could sense how uncomfortable she was with the questions. She is more comfortable talking about her teachings than herself. She has a mysterious quality about her. One day she is at home, and the next she could be called away to a meeting of the Sisterhood of the Shields.

Lynn is the only woman in the book who identifies herself as a shaman, but given that she sees shamans as "wounded healers," she would probably say that many of the women in this book would fit that description.

Lynn, like Claudia Black and Anne Wilson Schaef, addresses the issue of addiction. In working with private clients, she says, she holds a mirror up to them so they can see how their addictions are causing them to lose their heat. She says addiction is a way for people to slow down their journeys to enlightenment.

I found it interesting to note that Lynn and Louise Hay reminded me of each other. Most of all it is their deep, clear, resounding voices, but they also have a certain levity that they can call on and an ability to laugh at themselves. I couldn't help imagining how Louise Hay would fare at a gathering of the Sisterhood of the Shields.

I think an unfortunate but good training for becoming a shaman is to be from a dysfunctional home. It is a great wound that must be healed and also an incredible teaching to enable you to understand and help people," says Lynn Andrews.

"I had both a wonderful and a very difficult childhood. I was very loved by my family. It was just that my father was really two different personalities. In one he was incredibly supportive and taught me how to be a powerful and successful woman, but in the other he went into rages and made it very difficult for me."

Lynn says that shamans are called wounded healers because they survive life-threatening situations. She says she did not go through an actual illness or death, but she sees the physical and emotional abuse she endured as a child as that death.

"When you've come out of a dysfunctional situation, you end up with a tremendous amount of endurance and stamina and an ability to sense trouble in the air. You have to sense trouble as a kid to survive, and if you take that trouble one step further, you begin to realize that you can actually heal and shift it. You look at a person and realize what they can become. You can see in their auras where they are losing their life force. You can become a healer. In fact, you are a healer. Most people who have lived through that situation are healers by the time they are nine or ten years old.

"Coming from dysfunctional homes also produces the *puer aeternus* or the *puella aeterna*, which is Latin for "the eternal child." If you have to act adult as a child, which is what that means, then when you grow up you want to be a child because you have been an adult all your life. On the one hand, never having had a childhood is a wonderful schoolhouse for being a healer or a teacher; but on the other, it robs you of that time of total spontaneity and creativity children have. You become an adult, and you don't really respect the adult world. You don't want to be a part of it.

"So the *puer* or *puella* sabotages his or her success and

tends not to want to have long-lasting relationships. They tend to find great difficulty in earning money, sticking with jobs, and so forth. It takes a tremendous amount of work to grow out of that syndrome. I think that is why I talk about the act of power so much. One of the great cures of being the *puella* is to work very, very hard because it is one of the things that inner child just doesn't want to do.

"I was certainly an adult as a child. I was taking care of everybody and trying to keep the peace. So it was a big struggle to become an adult and later to own what I had accomplished—to be able to say, yes, I have achieved something extraordinary—I have been able to write books. I have been able to pull my act together. It's important to own that and to give myself a pat on the back."

Lynn spent her first fourteen years on a horse ranch in eastern Washington on the Canadian border. She remembers riding horses from early in the morning to late in the day, which is something she still loves to do. "All my first friends were Indian. I didn't know they were Indian; they were just my friends. I spent many, many nights of my life staying with my girlfriend, Beverly, in her family's hogan. I loved that place."

Other happy times were those spent skiing and fishing with her Dad. "I did a lot of things outdoors. My father was a wonderful teacher in that regard, and so was my mother. I had a wonderful relationship with plants and trees, and I had a feeling for the harmony that we need to live with.

"I also had a tremendous interior life. I was always a writer. Whenever I wanted to feel good, I would go sit in the apple tree and write. I wrote a lot of poetry, animal stories, and stories about spirits. I even wrote a story about two spotted ponies for *Jack and Jill* magazine when I was a child.

"I have always been able to see auras around people, and I used to write about that to some degree. I love to study and have been studying all my life in one way or another, perhaps because my father was a great intellectual and we studied together from the time I was four years old. He was an engineer for General Electric. My mother was on the production end of radio and television for years—an incredibly beautiful, talented lady. My grandmother was an extraordinary woman too, and a great teacher. She taught me to play the piano and introduced me to the classics. I also played the clarinet.

"Another interesting thing about my childhood is that I went all through Catholic school, although I am not Catholic. It was a wonderful place to be because I could always go into the chapel and pray. I always liked prayer and communing with God in one way or another."

Lynn was taken from her Washington State home when she was fourteen. Her parents divorced, and she and her mother left for Los Angeles, her mother's hometown.

"By that time my father had moved to San Francisco, and I was to stay with him for the summer while Mother went down to find us a place to live in Los Angeles. That was a really difficult summer for my dad and me, and I ended up spending most of my summer with my godparents in Carmel.

"After the summer I came down to Los Angeles to live with my mom and go to school. It was terrible! I thought I had dropped straight into Hades when I moved here. It took me a long time to adjust. We had had a beautiful place on Lake Washington, and I missed the lake and the trees and the rhododendrons. I'd always had nature around me, and when I moved to Los Angeles the hills were brown and everything looked burnt.

"I missed everything in Washington. I missed my friends and my boyfriend. I was used to a small school, and I came to Los Angeles to find enormous schools with lots of people. Nobody knew me and I didn't know anybody. I hated it and I didn't have my horses. But I learned how to survive.

"I was a cheerleader and tried very hard to become one of the girls, which was difficult for me. To survive, I kept doing the things that I had always done. I studied and wrote all the time. I loved authors and writers of the past. I devoured people like Somerset Maugham and Anaïs Nin, and they became bibles for me. I got very involved with Shakespeare, Nietzsche, and Rainer Maria Rilke. I don't think that I was very good at revealing my inner life, and that may be why I became a writer.

"Perhaps having gone through all the things that I did in childhood made it possible for me to work with Agnes and Ruby, because they were really tough on me in the beginning and for a very good reason: I was a very slow learner."

Lynn studied English and philosophy at Marymount College. Immediately after finishing her studies she became a stockbroker and got married.

"We had a daughter, Vanessa. My husband was in the film business and a racecar driver for Porsche, so we lived in Los Angeles. It was an interesting marriage. I found myself in the wonderful housewife-and-mother syndrome. In my book *Jaguar Woman*, in the chapter on *Última Madre*, I talk about the Great Nurturing Mother as opposed to the Rainbow Mother. I am definitely a Rainbow Mother. I am a creative person who lives and feeds her children on ideas. My husband wasn't too thrilled about that. He wanted good German food, so I tried to become a gourmet cook. I really made an effort, but it just wasn't my bag. I wanted to write and to learn. I was so hungry for life in those days.

"I have just been looking through my old files and papers, and I came across some of my writings about being so hungry for life and wanting to understand what we are all doing here. I saw myself as being in a rut, which would only be a rut for a Rainbow Mother kind of person. If I had been the Great Nurturing Mother type of woman, I wouldn't have felt that way. My life would have been total fulfillment because there was nothing wrong with my first husband. He was a very nice man. It was simply that I didn't know myself and should never have been married at such an early age. I did not really want to live in that kind of life. I was not cut out to go to beauty parlors and get my nails done. I can't think of anything worse. Having lunches and just hanging out was not my thing. I am not saying that it isn't wonderful for millions of people, but for me it wasn't.

"Without the Great Nurturing Mother we would have no society anywhere in the world. She is really the pillar of our society, and it's a magnificent shield to hold up in the world. I tried to create that shield and I did it okay, but it wasn't me. I just felt an incredible drive. I knew that there was some kind of destiny in my life which I was wasting, so I got a divorce."

When Lynn left her first husband, she took Vanessa with her. "It was an incredible adventure into how to be a single parent, how to be mom and dad. When my first husband remarried, his wife didn't want him to see my daughter much and that was extremely difficult for her. Vanessa has a lot of scars from that. I never have fully understood what exactly happened, but it put me in the interesting position of feeling the need to be both parents for her. I don't know that that is even possible, but I tried, and maybe, in a sense, that helped me balance my male and female energies. I began to realize that, in fact, I was not a woman living in Europe like my father tried to teach me to be."

Lynn says she was raised to be the "classical wife," staying at home, playing tennis and some golf, and supporting the emotional needs of her husband. Suddenly she realized that she was going to have to support herself, and she wasn't sure of how to do that. She tried to produce and write children's television. Then, with several others she started a company called Chrysalis, which combined art and technology to create environments that were artistic and encouraged learning possibilities. The group received awards for making an environment that a toddler could crawl inside, and when the child pushed on the walls they changed color. The experience taught toddlers that they have an effect on their environment.

"Bucky Fuller was on the board of directors. A lot of really extraordinary people were involved. I was involved early on, and then I got married again and signed my part of the company over to someone else.

"I continued trying to do children's television. I knew I was going to be a writer, and I knew I wanted to write, but I didn't have anything that I really wanted to write about—not yet. It was then, right around the end of my second marriage, that I met Agnes and Ruby."

About her second marriage she says, "I shouldn't have gotten married as early as I did. I should have waited until now. I would be fine being married now, but in those days there was so much to learn. It was like suddenly leaving grade school and going out into the world and trying to work when you haven't had the education. I needed that time out in the world. I should have traveled. I should have done a lot of things I just didn't do. I don't know why I was compelled to get married but I just was—maybe because I always wanted a happy family more than anything."

During her marriage Lynn continued to find comfort and joy in writing, studying, and creating art.

"I love to work on wood. All these stained-glass windows and sculptures," she says about the art in her living room, "are made out of wood. There is no lead. I just started working on it one day. I knew a guy up in Santa Barbara who taught me how to do them and I kept it up. I was also a painter for years, but I've sold anything I ever did except for the picture up there," she says, pointing to a picture of two burros standing beneath a beautiful New Mexico sky.

"I have actually painted all my life. My dad was a painter, and we painted and drew pictures together. My mother is a very fine artist too. She was one of the top dress designers in Hollywood many years ago. My grandmother was an extraordinary artist and quite celebrated in Europe for her watercolors, so art runs in our family."

Following her heart's desire, she worked as a nontraditional art dealer for several years. "I was traveling a bit, and I found things for people that they couldn't find on their own, particularly in Guatemala and from American Indians. I was fascinated with power objects like those fetishes on the table there," she says.

It was during one of her trips to Guatemala, in search of a fertility sash, that the incredible journey described in her first book, *Medicine Woman*, begins. "I sensed that something was about to happen in my life, but I didn't have a clue about what it was. I had a feeling of excitement all the time, just a fluttering. Also at that time I was having very extended dreams, dreams like I had never had before. Agnes told me that they were just preparing me for dreamwork where I would really and truly be able to get messages—direct transmissions from her, because she and Ruby work with me a lot that way."

While in Guatemala searching for the fertility sash, she bumped into a tall Indian man who seemed to know her and insisted that she should be in the north. He said that she would revisit the city, but her journey was farther north. He also said he would send her two helpers within forty-four days, one male and one female. She thought the man was crazy.

A week later, back in southern California, she attended an art exhibit where she saw a photograph of an American Indian marriage basket. "I had seen the marriage basket before in my dreams, and seeing it in the gallery was almost superfluous at that point. It's a surprising thing to see something in your dreams that you have never seen before and then see it in the physical. Particularly something as beautiful as the marriage basket."

She returned home. That night she dreamed again of the marriage basket, and the next morning she called the gallery to purchase the photograph, only to be told there was no such photo. The dreams continued, and several weeks later, at a party, she met Hyemeyohsts Storm, an Indian medicine man and author of *Seven Arrows*. She told him of her dreams and her desire to find a marriage basket. He knew of only one such basket but doubted it was for sale. It was a sacred object, he said, and if she wanted to find it, she would have to locate a heyoka shaman woman, Agnes Whistling Elk. The person who could guide her to Agnes was Ruby Plenty Chiefs in Manitoba, Canada. Lynn, obsessed by the basket, jumped on a plane and flew to Manitoba. She met Ruby, who, she says, was a frightening sight. It was this visit that led her to Agnes, the woman in her dreams.

When she told Agnes that she wanted to purchase the marriage basket, the Indian woman said that it was a sacred object that could only be earned. The basket represented the balance of the male and female within us and the healing of Mother Earth.

Lynn stayed in Canada and began her extraordinary apprenticeship with Agnes and Ruby, which led to the retrieval of the marriage basket from sorcerer Red Dog and eventually to her initiation into the Sisterhood of the Shields, an ancient secret society of shaman women.

Living in the wilds of Canada came as an initial shock to Lynn. "I had grown up not far from there, just south of the Canadian border, but on the other hand, I did wonder what I was doing there now, particularly when I first laid eyes on Ruby. She scared me to death. If she walked in here now and she played her sweet self, you would think she was the dearest little old lady in the world and a beautiful and magnificent Indian woman. She is very beautiful. Then she can move her eyes sort of like this, toward you" (Lynn imitates Ruby's cold, piercing look), "and it turns you to ice, it's so scary. She uses that fear. I mention this because a lot of people have asked me, 'Why all this stuff about fear in the beginning of your apprenticeship?' The reason is that it stimulates your powerself. You immediately wake up. All your senses become alive, like being doused with a bucket of cold water. Most of us are half asleep all the time. That is why most people never feel alive unless they are in love. So one of the main reasons Ruby is in my life is to wake me up, to scare me half to death."

Lynn often tells people that the real changes in her life began with this apprenticeship. Prior to this she studied philosophy, religion, and psychology, yet she could not implement real change in her life. "I knew intellectually why I was doing things, but I couldn't do anything about it."

Her apprenticeship has put her in situations in which she needed to grow and change in order to survive. She grew physically strong, learning to live off the earth, walking, cutting wood, tracking and butchering prey, gathering food, climbing—all the things that were expected of her as an apprentice. At the same time she was shown, and experienced, spiritual truths because, she says, Agnes feels there must be a balance between spiritual learning and physical endurance.

After regaining the marriage basket, Lynn says, she was tricked into making an act of power in the world. She had always wanted to live on the reservation with Agnes but Agnes wouldn't let her, until one day she was invited to stay. Filled with joy and excitement, Lynn leased her Los Angeles home for two years, packed her bags, and returned to Agnes's cabin. She was surprised to find Agnes sitting outside her cabin in front of a blazing fire. When Lynn said hello, Agnes turned around and angrily asked what she was doing there. She told Lynn that she was not Indian and did not belong on the reservation; it was time for her to write of what she had learned. Lynn must bring sacred and ancient teachings of the power of woman to her people.

Agnes said she would not dream her or see her again until Lynn wrote what she knew. Angry and hurt, Lynn returned south, rented a sharecropper's cabin, and proceeded to write her first book, *Medicine Woman*. This was an exceedingly difficult task for her. Although she had always wanted to write her own books, she had never been able to. She found that talking about it was very different from doing it.

When she sat down to write, her brain would fog over. She experienced indecision and lack of focus. "I had created a mirror for myself. I could see all those terrible qualities I had done nothing about. I realized, actually quite late in life, that to make an act of power you have to really shut out the whole world for a while. At least that's what I had to do. Then balance comes back into your life.

"To do this I could not have the phone ringing or people coming in and out of the house. I couldn't run down to a restaurant and have lunch. As a result, people felt that I didn't have time for them anymore, but that wasn't really it. It was that I had to find time for me to accomplish something."

She also came up against language barriers. "There is a problem with the English language because there are so few words for describing the transformation into the spiritual. There are not many words for sacred, spiritual, medicine woman, or shaman. It means a hundred things to a hundred different people, and that's really unfortunate. So sometimes the words overlap. Sometimes I use Indian words or terms, just simply because there is no other way to do it unless I make up a new word. You have to talk around an enlightened experience."

She realized that she could only write about her journey as a white woman being initiated into the knowledge of indigenous cultures. She does not feel it is proper to write about traditional Indian medicine, so ancient Indian secrets are not revealed. "Agnes made it clear I needed to write about the power and the beauty of indigenous people. I don't talk about the sun dance or the ghost dance. I don't write about their religions. These women live in native cultures. A lot of the native people around the world want their cultures to be maintained, held very quietly by tribal elders and teachers, and I understand that. That is one of the reasons that I don't write about, or even learn about, very traditional things. It's not my world. If someone wants to learn about that, they should indeed go to an Indian, not to me, because I don't teach those things.

"An editor of one of the biggest papers in the country said, 'Lynn, you must be doing something right. If you are not being talked about or criticized somewhere, something is wrong.' Interestingly enough, the most difficulty I have had has been with native people. They don't understand because most of them haven't read my books. The old people are very close to me. The younger people have been so ripped off and have had difficulty integrating into the culture of the conquering nations that live around them, encircling them, strangling them, breaking all their treaties, and destroying their quality of life. They are finding it difficult not to be angry, and I don't blame them. I am angry about it too, and I have done everything that I can think of to help. Of course, the minute you say 'help,' you create a duality that is another problem right there. That's one of the reasons I stopped trying to raise money for the American Indian Movement [AIM]. I realized that I am not Indian. I raised money for AIM and was involved in Indian trials many years ago, but Agnes asked me to stop because, she said, 'You only have so much energy in a lifetime, and you can use your energy in a much more effective way.'

"When Agnes asked me to stop spreading my energy around, it was then she told me to write *Medicine Woman*. I wrote about the power of the female side of the native culture, which has been hidden, tromped on, denied, and all but forgotten." After two years of hard work, she completed the book, published in 1983.

"An act of power is a very difficult thing, and yet it is the one thing that raises you to another level in your spiritual search. An act of power is essential. What it does is provide mirrors that nothing else can give you. Those mirrors do not lie. You discover who you really are. Without that, I think, you kind of slide through life.

"An act of power is a hard thing to find. A lot of women and men come to me who have done incredible things in their lives. They are doctors, lawyers, and judges, very important anthropologists, or whatever. Then I really start talking to them and get into their hearts a little bit and find what they always wanted to be was a dancer or an artist.

"Your act of power is like a vertical thrust up through the sound barrier. You find something you always dreamed of doing. You take that dream, start focusing on it, and the other things in your life get taken care of."

Even after her first book was written, Lynn's journey had only begun. She did not fully realize the danger that she had put herself in when she retrieved the marriage basket from Red Dog. She had created a dangerous adversary who would willingly take her life to regain his powers. To protect herself, it was necessary for her to learn the ancient art of shielding.

In her second book, *Flight of the Seventh Moon* (1984), she describes what Agnes told her:

> To make a shield in the proper manner, you have
> to destroy the conflicting parts of yourself. A
> shield is protective medicine. It is also a mirror.
> There are shields with so much power they will
> bring victory in battle. There are shields that will

give you courage. There are shields that protect
you from a sorcerer's attack. There are shields that
bring the allies in time of need. But remember
that an ally can't fight for you—only with you.
There are truth shields, and if you hold up that
power no one can lie to you. Shields are not only
for defense. They stand as a record of who you
are in the world in all your aspects—mental, emotional, physical, and spiritual. They stand for your
sacredness within. They can be placed outside the
lodges to tell people who you are.[2]

To make a shield, the warrioress bends a piece of wood,
like a sapling from a willow tree, into the shape of a wheel
and stretches hide across it, much as one prepares a canvas
for painting. Then upon the hide she applies objects like
plants, beads, feathers, and horsehair to create the vision that
she sees for her shield. In *Flight of the Seventh Moon* Lynn
describes what each of her shields looked like and what they
meant to her. Looking back on that experience, she says, "The
shields were for my enlightenment. While building my shields
I saw different parts of myself—the child self, the wise
woman. It was one of the most important processes for me."
  With the completion of her shields Lynn was initiated into
the Sisterhood of the Shields. She is one of forty-four women
who represent different indigenous cultures in the world. Lynn
is the only non-native. Just as others have asked, Why you?,
she has asked herself again and again, Why was I chosen?
Her answer seems to have evolved over time.
  "I think my history of past lives is the reason I was
picked by the Sisterhood. The only way someone can become
initiated in the Sisterhood is when another member dies and
passes on. So there was a great, great woman who passed on,
which allowed me to be initiated. Up until then I had not believed that the Sisterhood was even real. I thought it was a fig-
ment of my imagination or my dream state. When I actually
met them in the flesh, it was quite a shock. Then I realized
that we are all from a circle—men, or women—and somehow
we have fallen out of that circle to be born onto this earth.

2. Lynn V. Andrews, *Flight of the Seventh Moon: The Teaching of the Shields*
(San Francisco: Harper & Row, 1984), 58.

This earth form has to do with finding our way back to that circle. When I saw the Sisterhood, I realized I had found my way back to one of my circles. That was my real reason for being there. The Sisterhood and I had been together in many lifetimes.

"The other part of it was that I am a shaman and a writer. I am what they needed at the time." Lynn explains that the teachings and history of the indigenous cultures these women represent are memorized and passed down over the centuries through an oral tradition. Now these cultures and their teachings are in danger of being wiped off the earth. She believes this history is applicable to twentieth-century life and we have a lot to learn from cultures that have lived at peace with the earth for hundreds of thousands of years.

"I'm spending my life writing about my work with the ancient women who are part of the Sisterhood. My work has to do with becoming a bridge between the primal mind and white consciousness. We, as a race—the White, the Black, the Indian, the Asian—all of us who have become a part of the mechanized, materialistic society, have lost our sense of Mother Earth and nature. We have lost that wilderness of the soul. My work has to do with bringing us back to Mother Earth, the feminine consciousness that is so lacking on this planet today.

"I talk so much about balancing the male and female. It is important, because the world is in danger of wobbling off and dying. We have to talk about what is missing, and that is feminine consciousness. My work is to try to help people hear the feminine voice within—whether they are men or women.

"Perhaps my being able to write about my experiences helps people in the cities of the world to bring balance back into their lives."

Lynn is the only publicly known member of the Sisterhood of the Shields.

"They have to remain anonymous, much to my chagrin. They have always told me that there is a real obvious reason for this." She explains that the Sisterhood must maintain a certain level of work, and that if they were not secretive they would be besieged by people. So Lynn has been the one selected to make their knowledge public. "It was an incredible mantle to put on, which I didn't fully realize, but that is okay because I am glad that I'm here and glad that I am doing what I'm doing. I wouldn't change my life for anything."

Lynn counsels private clients, does some lecturing, and occasionally gives seminars.

"I have never believed in giving seminars, and yet I am about to give some big ones. I am doing that because the energy on the earth has changed. When I was in the Himalayas, it was very clearly stated to me by the Sisterhood that it was important to teach what I've learned at a group level. Energy is moving so fast that everybody is feeling that they can't keep up with what is happening!

"One of the reasons we're falling behind is that we are holding onto the old. A lot of psychic debris is being formed by the energy trying to get through beings who are not clear. So in large gatherings we can avail ourselves of the group energy so it is not just you and me working one to one, but a whole group of people. We can avail ourselves of each other's power, and we can burst through those energy blocks much more effectively."

Regarding her workshop, Lynn says, "I am taking people through shamanistic initiations. A lot of people say, 'How can you take somebody through initiation in a group? How can you do this without a tribal situation?' Well, first of all, I don't teach tribal magic. I don't teach tribal ceremony and ritual. I am only talking about what I, as a Western woman, have learned from my teachers who happen to be from native cultures. Naturally, my initiations have been vastly different than, say, what an aborigine in Australia would experience, yet there are some similarities. But that does not mean that our initiations are anything like theirs. The Goowawa, for example, who are the little people of Australia, presented themselves to me and wanted to become friends with people on this continent. So I am going to bring people through an initiation to meet the little people from Australia, because they are brilliant and wonderful. They can become fabulous allies, and they want to reach across cultural boundaries."

Lynn's third book, *Jaguar Woman* (1985), chronicles her journey to the Yucatán to study with one of the Sisterhood. She writes of hiking down a spiral canyon, La Caldera, to a swamplike place where she learns about her addictive self. There she has another opportunity to confront Red Dog, who, in an attempt to capture the power of the Sisterhood, has stolen the Jaguar Mask.

Later books reveal other magical places. In *Star Woman* (1986) she meets Twin Dreamers, who is able to release her own ego so she can take on the physical shape and ego of others. Twin Dreamers makes it possible for Lynn to ride Arion, a beautiful white stallion that takes her into a world of visions where she learns more about her dark side, a suppressed wildness.

Crystal Woman (1987) tells of her journey to the wilderness of central Australia, about 150 miles west of Ayers Rock, where she studies with an aborigine and is guided into the crystal dreamtime of that woman's culture.

Of *Windhorse Woman* she says, "*Windhorse* is a Tibetan term, probably a shamanic term originally, that is essentially the state just before enlightenment. When you sit across from someone who is in this state a windhorse comes out of the top of the crown chakra. My experience was that you ride that windhorse into the plane of enlightenment. In the prayer flags of Tibet the horse is in the center of the flag, and, of course, the sound of the flags in the wind is the voice of God, the voice of Buddha, or your creator. But *windhorse* has a very strong meaning in my book."

Lynn docs spiritual counseling and teaching with private clients in various ways. "I don't know that *clients* is the right word—they are people who want to apprentice to me, and so I give them spiritual-shamanic teaching in one way or another. It depends on what people need. Ceremony is only as powerful as the person giving it, so you need to work with people's psychological health—otherwise, what's the point? If they are full of addictions or drugs, or cannot deal with addictive relationships or whatever, you are not going to have a very powerful ceremony. So you have to deal with all those things first. I handle things in a shamanic way, which is essentially spiritually based teaching.

"I always look at people as if they are icebergs floating on the sea of enlightenment and the whole process of enlightenment and self-realization is the experience of that iceberg melting into the sea. We melt into the sea of enlightenment by holding our powers, keeping that energy instead of giving it away through our addictions."

Lynn's addictions before her apprenticeships were books,

baths, and sadness, and she says they were due to low self-esteem, not feeling worthy as a woman, and to fears of dealing with her relationship with her father.

Some of her clients are people suffering from physical illnesses. "When someone who has cancer comes to me, I have to explain that they choose their disease like they choose their friends. People would rather give their pain to someone else and blame them. Disease is a teacher. It is an actual growth experience. If you refuse to learn lessons in life, your body will make you deal with those lessons. A lot of disease has to do with the war between the male and female projections you throw out into the world. Energy follows thought. What you imagine is real. We are all thought forms. We create health and we create illness. Choosing one's death is one of the gifts of becoming a more self-realized person."

Lynn's life and friends changed radically when she began her apprenticeship in the early 1970s. "I had a lot of social relationships with wonderful people, but people get used to a relationship with you in a certain way and they want you to stay there. It is hard to lose people in your life, but when I started working on all of this, obviously I changed a great deal. My needs were very different, and what I wanted to talk about was very different. Some of my friends were fascinated and loved every minute of it, and some were very threatened and kind of hurt. My two best friends in Los Angeles are friends I have had since before any of this began, even before my daughter, Vanessa, was born. I am close to them and grateful for them. Without your friends what do you have?"

She says that Agnes and Ruby, being her teachers, are her "dearest, dearest friends. Although I am always a little wary because they play so many tricks on me. It is like walking down the street and knowing that there is going to be a foot somewhere to trip you up." Agnes and Ruby contact her either by phone, or, more often, they come into her dreams. "It is not like you and I sitting here talking now; it is more like they get my attention and then I perceive their meaning. I understand what they are saying, but I don't necessarily hear a bunch of words."

Lynn does not offer any details of her current relationship, except to say, "I am involved with someone now. We have been together for a very long time. It is a good relationship."

A relationship that has had a profound effect on her was that of Zoila and Jose, which she writes about in *Jaguar Woman.* "Their relationship is so profound, in that they are really very different people, but they have been able to balance out their marriage so magnificently. The thing about them that was so wonderful to me was that he could be who he was and she could be who she was without any problem. Whatever he had to do to grow was perfectly wonderful with her, no matter what it was—absolutely no matter what—and the same thing for her. There were no rules. There was no anything, only the structure of their love, and that structure was very close and very well met. Very strong but not confining.

"In our society we tend to fall in love, and then we expect so very much from that other person and they expect so much from us, and it is the expecting that ruins everything. If you can just be who you are, you will fill that person's life with love. If you can't, the whole relationship is going to be destroyed.

"I get such a kick out of people saying, 'Oh, I gave him so much love!' You don't give someone love; you simply are love or you are not. You only give an overabundance of what you already have. You don't say, 'Well, now I am going to give you a little bit of love.' That's baloney, that's not love at all. That is some kind of manipulation. Zoila and Jose were full of so much abundance of energy and joy and love that there was no way that anybody around them could be anything but joyous.

"Your mate is your closest mirror in life. Sexuality is an important part of spiritual life. It is extra-important because it stimulates the root chakra and balances your spiritual endeavors and gives them energy. When sexual life is normal and flowing, then probably the rest of life is in balance. I often hear from women today who say they 'used to be sexual.' Perhaps this has to do with how hard we're working, so most of our energy is being taken up."

Lynn divides her time between her home in southern California, her Santa Fe adobe, and her travels with Agnes and Ruby. When she's with Agnes and Ruby, she says, she never knows what's going to happen next; it's always different. It's more predictable at home. She lives in what she calls a cabin on a quiet street in Los Angeles. The three-bedroom house sits up against a canyon wall and has a rustic feel to it—wooden floors, a large fireplace, books everywhere, and her collected artwork. A picture of her mother, herself, and her daughter is on the mantle. Lynn has lived there with her daughter for more than fifteen years.

"It's a very little house. It's 1500 square feet. I have to add an office or I am going to burst out of it. I love this street. It's quiet—you can't hear the freeways. Coyotes run up and down this street at night. There are foxes and deer. I don't know that I could survive here otherwise. Everybody says, 'What are you doing in Los Angeles?' I say, 'Well, where do you think people need to be healed but in the cities of the world? Unfortunately, they don't need me in the wilderness of Canada.'"

Lynn keeps to a routine while in Los Angeles. She writes in the morning when she first wakes up, and if she's had any dreams from Agnes and Ruby, she writes them down. Sometimes she runs in the morning or takes her cocker spaniel out for a walk. She only answers the phone for a few hours and then shuts it off. In the afternoon she sees people, either socially or for work. She likes to go out to dinner with friends at quiet places, and has a macrobiotic cook who makes lunches for her. She has a wonderful massage therapist who does deep tissue and Shiatsu work. At night she reads and studies before going to bed early. She enjoys spending time with her daughter, Vanessa, who she says "is interested in shamanism but has to make her way in the world first. The foundation for shamanism is making your life in the physical."

When Lynn is in New Mexico, she gets out of bed in the morning and walks, then spends much of her day writing. Her tiny Santa Fe adobe is only five minutes from the Pecos wilderness.

She says she's happy with her life, but that it's not without its ups and downs: "I create a lot of drama in my life because I have things to work out." She says she is never led peacefully to her next story and adventure with the Sisterhood; instead, "there are always these extraordinary events, this melodrama, some incredible conflict, which is part of my own journey and provides a mirror for my life." Somehow this drama leads her to look more deeply at herself: "It's what we choose not to look at that rules our lives."

Her current plans are to follow her dreams, to follow the guidance of her teachers, and to continue to chronicle the lives and teachings of the Sisterhood of the Shields. She has learned from these women how to nourish herself in a deeply meaningful way and wants to pass that wisdom and nourishment on to others.

"What we're really doing this lifetime is giving up this separateness. We're all one. We must walk in balance on the earth—a foot in spirit and a foot in the physical. We wait so long to be born into a physical body, and then so many of us throw it away. It is a temple and needs to be treated with extraordinary respect. Treat yourself with nourishing care."

PERSONAL TRUTHS

1. An act of power is essential. An act of power provides mirrors that nothing else can give you, and those mirrors do not lie. You discover who you really are. Without an act of power you just slide through life.

2. Follow your dreams. People can do whatever they want—it is just a matter of manifesting it. We don't give ourselves permission to follow our dreams.

3. We need to manifest feminine consciousness in the world in order to heal this planet. The medicine that is needed is feminine consciousness in all of its aspects: harmonizing with nature, balancing the ecology with human life, and a conscious use of money and goods. Balance of the physical and spiritual is needed. We have to learn to tend our garden, or we aren't going to have one.

LYNN ANDREWS
Author of

Windhorse Woman. New York: Warner Books, 1989.

Crystal Woman: The Sisters of the Dreamtime. New York: Warner Books, 1987.

Star Woman: We Are Made from Stars and to the Stars We Must Return. New York: Warner Books, 1986.

Jaguar Woman: And the Wisdom of the Butterfly Tree. San Francisco: Harper & Row, 1985.

Flight of the Seventh Moon: The Teaching of the Shields. San Francisco: Harper & Row, 1984.

Medicine Woman. San Francisco: Harper & Row, 1983.

Anne Wilson Schaef

Anne Wilson Schaef, Ph.D., *is an internationally known author, teacher, and organizational consultant. She is the author of* Women's Reality, *in which she first wrote of the white male system and female systems. Her own recovery from codependence motivated her to study and work in the field of addiction. The discoveries she made in this area led to the writing of a number of best-selling books:* When Society Becomes an Addict; Co-Dependence Misunderstood-Mistreated; The Addictive Organization, *coauthored with Diane Fassel; and* Escape from Intimacy: Understanding Addictions to Sex, Love and Romance, Relationships.

She received her graduate training in psychology at Washington University, Columbia University, and Teachers College. She studied theology at Union Theological Seminary in New York City, and in 1986 she received her Ph.D. in clinical psychology with a specialization in treating the addictive process from the Union for Experimenting Colleges and Universities. She founded Wilson-Schaef Associates in the late 1970s. She currently trains people in the Living in Process System, which she developed, and gives workshops and lectures worldwide.

I interviewed Anne Wilson Schaef on a hot, sunny day in Calistoga, California. She met me at her hotel lobby in a bathing suit and sandals. I arrived overdressed and was relieved when she later lent me a bathing suit so I could go for a swim.

Anne was on a publicity tour for her new book, The Addictive Organization. *She had given a series of talks and workshops in the San Francisco Bay Area and was presently taking a few days off to enjoy the mineral waters of Calistoga. It's one of the many beautiful places she retreats to for nourishment.*

I had read When Society Becomes an Addict, *and it seemed to be sending shock waves throughout the country. I was glad to see that someone had written what I was feeling—that we are living in a society that functions like an addict.*

Anne has the unique ability to look at the whole picture without losing sight of an individual's needs. She's close to her friends, family, and students. She went out of her way to offer encouragement to me on this project. She would ask me how I was, and I'd tell her some issue I was in the middle of, and she would tell me some funny story about a similar experience that she had gone through. I'd laugh and feel that I was not alone.

She speaks candidly about her life. She appears comfortable with her humanness. She strikes me as being able to be completely at ease, with not a care in the world; yet if called to action she would be on her feet at a moment's notice, prepared, alive, and willing to get involved. Although it would be a lousy job, I thought she would make a great U.S. president with her qualities of honesty and intelligence and her terrific sense of humor. In fact, I saw her and Barbara Marx Hubbard on a ticket together. Anne likes a challenge but says she is not interested in being president. What she is interested in is writing, teaching, and "living her process."

I made the choice to live, early on," Anne Wilson Schaef says of her life. "One of the things I find when working with people is that they've made the choice not to die, but they've never made the choice to live."

She says she had to make that decision after a difficult birth. "I believe that my birth was significant because my mother, a horsewoman, had a very serious riding accident as a teenager and was told she would never have children. When she became pregnant with me, she was told she would never have a normal delivery. She also had a systemic infection when I was born, and when she nursed me I got the infection and almost died. The first two months of my infancy were really touch and go. An old country doctor prepared potato water and rice water for me, and later lent my mother two goats so I could have goat's milk."

Anne grew up with the love and support of a mother and father who were her mentors in many ways. "Besides being a horsewoman, my mother was a poet, a painter, a mystic, a psychic—open to almost everything. She was black Irish, named Lonnigan. I think she was a natural psychologist. When I was growing up she always said, 'Try to understand why people do what they do. Look behind that and see what's going on with them.' But she also had a terrible temper, and I mean she would just blow up. I laughingly tell people that we scraped many of our meals off the kitchen wall and went through several sets of dishes as I was growing up. I grew up thinking that anger was normal and not being afraid of it. My mother's anger never lingered. She never kept at me or picked away at me. It was out, it was gone, it was done.

"Many people can't deal with anger. I've never had that problem, and my mother always said it was because I'm Irish. Lots of thing were explained to me as being 'because you're Irish.' Neither my mother nor I ever met a stranger. Everybody was a potential friend because we were Irish, and we always believed in the Little People and trusted nature. We were Protestant. It was not until I became an adult that I met Irish Catholics who had gloom and doom and guilt and suffering.

They just look at me when I talk about these wonderful 'because I'm Irish' kinds of things.

"My mother also gave me a gift by being the world's worst housekeeper. I just grieve that she felt bad about that. For me, no matter what I do as an adult about my house, it is better than what my mother did. I've seen so many people with so much guilt because of being raised by perfectionistic mothers. They never can keep their houses clean enough.

"Another thing that I learned from my mother was that everybody is equal and that we're all connected. The older I get, the more I see how deep that is embedded in my soul. Being born in Arkansas in the thirties, I thought everybody was a racist except my mother. She had respect for everyone regardless of who they were. She had a really deep oneness that also extended to nature.

"She was adopted by the Cherokees because she saved the life of an Indian boy, and later he saved her life. He was one of the pallbearers at her funeral and, I felt, was probably the only person there who really knew how to grieve. The white people thought he just cried and carried on something awful, but I said to myself, He knows how to do it. So I grew up partially being raised like an Indian.

"Much of my early childhood was spent in the woods. I marvel at the freedom I was given and realize that couldn't happen today. When I was five years old my mother used to pack my lunch, and my dog and I would disappear into the woods and be gone all day. We'd come back just before suppertime after having a wonderful day. I think because of that I have impeccable directionality and almost never get lost. I have almost a psychic sense. It's a right brain function, and I think I learned it very early from those wanderings. The time alone, the freedom, and the trust that my mother had in me at that age, I think, was very Indian. I still go to the woods to be healed, and I hold a lot of my workshops in places that I think are healing.

"My great-grandmother was a big part of my early years because my grandmother had died in childbirth and my great-grandmother raised my mother. She was the opposite of my mother. She was very staid and very British. The two of them never really understood each other, and I feel I am a bridge between the two of them. My great-grandmother was a tremendous herbal healer. Mother was a kind of fiery, outdoorsy, black Irish who rode wild horses and had the wind in her hair, a poet and a writer. My great-grandmother was so proper, wore white gloves, and tried to corset my mother up, and Mother would always break her corset. Theirs was always a tense relationship. It's also not insignificant that my great-grandmother's only daughter died when my mother was being born.

"I had very strong women in my life who gave me a lot of philosophy and spirituality that never was specifically articulated—it was part of the living. I grew up in the Southern Methodist Church and loved gospel hymns. I still have gospel hymn sings at my house on all holidays. As I'm more sophisticated theologically and listen to the words, they're absolutely ghastly. But the music is terrific. I think what I got out of church was the community, the hymns, and the Golden Rule. Somehow in my child's mind I believed in all of that, and I lived it. 'You will know the truth and the truth shall make you free.' I now see so many people believing it in their minds, but they don't live it.

"One of my most important spiritual experiences in the last three years occurred while I was shopping in the drugstore with a friend. The store had thousands of posters with wise sayings on them, and I realized I believed those sayings. One of my favorites is, All that is necessary for the forces of evil to prosper is for enough good people to do nothing. I think the difference between me and a lot of people I know is that they like them and give lip service to them, but I live those verses I grew up with."

Anne's natural father abandoned her and her mother when Anne was just a baby. He left to find work during the depression and never came back. When Anne was three, her mother married the man whom Anne calls father.

"It seems that this man who raised me was really meant to be my father. He was a mathematician, engineer, and problem solver. When I was growing up we used to play math or grammar games at the table. Since there were only the three of us, it was who could stump whom and I had equal rights in the family. One of the main things I've learned from him is problem solving. Until the time he died, last year, if there was something that needed to be done, he would go sit in his chair for a day or two and pretty soon he'd say, 'That's how it has to be done,' and then he'd go do it.

One of the things I learned from him is that problems can

be solved in many ways, that you generate options. My father stimulated my left brain with mathematics. I took math in college to keep my grade point average up; I took calculus and things like that for fun. I was also real good in science."

Anne says sometimes her father's science and her mother's mystic intuitive sense would be in conflict. Her mother had a deep connection to a horse that she had been forced to sell during the depression. Much of Anne's childhood was spent looking for that horse, and when it was eventually found it died soon after of old age and pneumonia. After that, whenever something was going to happen in the family—a job transfer, a death, or some other major event—her mother would have a Technicolor dream of the horse whinnying on a green hill. The family came to trust that omen.

As a child, Anne explored haunted houses with her mother. She says her mother was not afraid of the paranormal, although she remembers one house where her mother said, " 'We're getting out of here; this one's not good.' I remember backing down this long lane as she held a flashlight on the house.

"My parents taught me to trust my own perceptions and my own opinions, even when they differed from theirs. There were times it was really hard for my parents, politically or religiously, but they always said, 'Trust yourself,' as they dealt with their feelings. I've tried to raise my kids that way too. I believe that a large part of my writing has come about because I trusted my own perceptions, even when people told me I was crazy."

Anne's family moved often because her father did research for the government. Being an only child and moving a lot meant she had to be able to be alone. Nevertheless, her parents took her friends with them on their vacations, and Anne says they were always taking in stray dogs, cats, and people. She always had playmates and is still friends with people from grade school.

When Anne was very young she lived in a small Oklahoma town of one hundred people. She not only experienced the freedom of the woods, but also freedom within the small town. Everyone looked after one another, and the children wandered around in a pack. "We knew what our limits were. We knew we couldn't cross the highway or the railroad tracks, or go near the river, but other than that we had the whole town as our playground. As an adult, because of that experience, I feel safe inside and I feel safe in the world. It's very easy for me to travel to different parts of the world and feel right at home.

"We had very little money when I was a kid. I wore flour sacks and feed-sack dresses which my mother always made very creatively. Still, they were what they were."

During the fifth grade Anne went to three different schools before the family finally settled down in Indiana. She attended a three-room country school from the fifth through eighth grades and had an enlightened teacher who believed everything was a potential for learning.

"We walked through the woods and gathered leaves. We learned about the clustering on the branches. For him everything was a possible focus for our curiosity. My dad and I were using trigonometry to help me with my math problems. My teacher said, 'I don't understand how you're doing this, but you're getting the right answer, so it's okay with me if you're using a form of math that I don't understand.' For me he was a fabulous kind of person. I've had people all my life who have fanned my curiosity."

When it came time for her to attend college, her parents encouraged her to apply to several fine schools. She received five scholarships to five different colleges and chose Washington University in St. Louis.

She had known since the fifth grade what she wanted to do when she grew up, but she didn't have a word for it. When she got to college she leapt on psychiatry. She was involved with the campus Y, was a member of a sorority, and sang opera on the side. "I was also a rebel during the civil rights movement. The NAACP sponsored the first black woman to go through rush, and her name didn't even come up at the first cut in the sorority. I asked the pledge mistress why her name wasn't mentioned, and she said, 'Of course we're not inviting her back.' I said, 'If you don't, I will blackball every possible pledge.' I said, 'We don't have to pledge her, but we have to invite her back at least two times.' I took some stands like that, always doing things I believed were right."

Her parents helped her at every step. If she wanted to take voice or tennis lessons, they found a way to make it happen. "I was active in college and was invited to be a national delegate to the YMCA's International Centennial in Paris. This was in the fifties, and, of course, we didn't have the kind of money to send me, but we brainstormed. Every organization in my small town gave fundraisers which paid my way. When I came back I gave slide shows and talked about my trip. It was during the McCarthy era, so I came back and said, 'Look at what's happening. Countries think we're crazy. They live right next door to communism, and they're not acting like we are.' I was putting it out there."

Anne graduated in 1956 in premed psychology and was offered a Danforth graduate fellowship that she happily accepted. Danforth offered students a year of self-development, and in that year Anne discovered how to do what she knew she wanted to do. "I always tell people who train with me that our most important decisions are discovered; they're never made. That we can afford to make the unimportant decisions but that the real ones we discover. I knew what I was supposed to be doing, but I had to find the vehicle."

During that year of self-development, she became certain that she would not go to medical school. She was accepted into the school of social work and decided she wouldn't do that either. "I think it was too codependent for me." Then she discovered her vehicle, and the doors were almost magically opened. She had applied to the psychology department at Washington University but hadn't heard from them, so she walked over to the department and was interviewed and offered a scholarship.

"I did my doctoral work there. I passed my comprehensives the first year and decided that if I wanted to know who I was as a person, I needed to know what I thought theologically. In the meantime I had gotten involved with a guy who was going to a theological seminary in New York, so I decided to take a year out of my doctoral work and go to seminary. Everyone was horrified because I had been the top graduate student in psychology."

Anne attended the Union Theological Seminary in New York and took psychology courses at Teachers College at Columbia. "It was a play year for me. I could do whatever I wanted, and I didn't have to make good grades for my doctorate work. I just took courses. They gave me a fellowship and an assistantship in the departments of psychology and religion, and then waived all the requirements. I could take anything I wanted.

"Again, my life, in some ways, has been so magical. I went over to Teachers College at Columbia and picked out the biggest names in psychology and asked if I could take their courses. The courses were limited to graduate students at Columbia University, but when I went directly to the professors and talked to them, they agreed to let me take their classes. Joseph Zubin, who was a well-known psychologist at Columbia Presbyterian, asked me to be his special assistant. That's the kind of thing that happened to me. I was just so lucky."

She was also fortunate to have the opportunity to study with great thinkers such as Robert McAfee Brown, Reinhold Niebuhr, Paul Tillich, and Martin Buber. She went to plays, museums, lectures, and concerts. She says she really "did New York" and dated everyone.

"While in seminary I got pregnant and we got married. I went back to my graduate work and he came with me. I had my first child, Beth, on the day of my last exam. My husband was going back to the seminary to finish up, so I decided I could do my doctoral internship in New York City. I applied at four places. Three of them accepted me without any question, and the fourth told me I should stay home with my child and interview after a year. I chose Bellevue Hospital to do my internship."

During the application process it had somehow not registered with Anne that Bellevue was a diagnostic hospital only. This meant that she would not be able to see clients long-term. She expressed her unhappiness at this and sought a way to change it. Her desire and determination were rewarded, and through a series of events it became possible for her to do long-term treatment.

"Then I found that I didn't like the supervision I was getting, so I went around and chose people with different backgrounds. I had about three supervisors on each case, which gave me a hell of a lot more information and training. Then I decided that the psychology interns really got the short end of the stick, so I asked if I could sit in on the medical and psychiatric residents' training. Nobody had ever asked before, and they said, 'Well, we guess so.' I had a tremendous training, and, again, I got to work with some of the real greats and some of the nobodies who were really good.

"We lived in the East Harlem projects while I was at Bellevue. I was taking classes to be certified as a school psychologist, and I used to walk home at night. I really felt that nothing would happen to me although a lot of my friends were scared. I felt I had a protective shield around me. Sometimes, when I did get scared, it was because I felt my shield wasn't working or my guard was down. At Bellevue I worked my final rotation in the male violent ward, and I was the only psychologist on that ward who didn't get beaten up."

After completing her doctoral internship, she took a job as a school psychologist, in Westchester County, for three years. "The thing I'm most proud of is that when I took that job, 90 percent of the caseload was referrals for psychological testing of kids who were having trouble, and 10 percent was self-referral. When I left it was 90 percent self-referral.

"What interested me were the kids who were hurting and needed someone to talk to. There were two boys who particularly touched my life. One was reportedly the most brilliant kid in the high school, and there were a lot of geniuses there. The whole family was brilliant, but they never left the house. He came in to see me, scared to death, and was shocked at how young I was. I could tell that he was checking me out, and I finally said, 'You're smarter than I am, there's no question about it. So let's not pussyfoot around.' I told him I knew more than he did about some of this stuff, and that I was willing to see if I could help, but that I wouldn't try to compete with him on an intellectual level. He just started crying. I worked with him three times a week. Those kids taught me a lot."

While at that school Anne began to identify what she would later term "the addictive system." She saw how, through political pressure and manipulation, some people were able to force others to do their bidding. She began to realize the school didn't exist for its students or teachers; it existed for its own reputation. "That process was destroying the teachers and the kids, and I was pointing that out when I was in my twenties."

After three years of work as a school psychologist, Anne returned to graduate school to complete her doctorate. She also applied for a part-time position as supervising psychologist for the adolescent treatment program at a state hospital in St. Louis. There she was interviewed by the man who would become her second husband. "My marriage to my first husband was pretty dead at the point that Bob and I got involved with each other. We were both married, and that went on for about three years before we finally left our respective spouses. We married and I had my second child, Roddy. This was during the sixties, during the sexual revolution and human potential movement. Bob introduced me to all that. I had the opportunity to learn from his friends and work with people like Virginia Satir and Carl Rogers.

"Our marriage got crazier, culminating in Bob's threatening to kill me. I was certainly involved in that too. I started having dreams of killing him. I knew that I had to quit and get out, so I did.

"He and I had one of those addictive relationships. We had a real intense loving connection, but we didn't know what to do with the disease part. I still have some anger because just as we were splitting, I went to his psychiatrist and said, 'I think Bob is an alcoholic,' and his psychiatrist told him to quit drinking for a month or two. He said, 'If you can do that, you're not really an alcoholic.' I felt like that was Bob's death. The doctors said he died of cancer, but I really feel that he died of alcoholism.

"The thing I loved about Bob was that he was a seeker, but after a while I learned he never found anything. He could be standing on a hill of diamonds, and he'd be looking out there at the next thing that might work. We had a fairly stormy, painful love. He didn't know how to relate other than sexually, so he was always seductive and always seducing. When he looked at me I felt like I was loved, and if you're codependent you feel loved through other people's eyes. When he shifted to someone else, it was as if I didn't exist. It was like being in the sunshine, or total darkness. It was so painful to see that and to experience that. I learned later that's typical of the disease of codependency. I saw myself becoming competitive with all these people, and I told myself I had to stop it. I was becoming a very bitter, angry, destroyed woman. He once told me that one of the reasons he married me was he knew he couldn't destroy me, and he couldn't. I was his fourth wife. I know now I would not have learned what I've learned about addiction without that relationship."

During her years with Bob, Anne studied sensitivity training and became involved in the civil rights and women's movements. Her life expanded professionally. After completing her doctoral work, she became clinical director of the Youth Center at Alton State Hospital in Illinois. In 1968 she went into private practice and became a consultant to a multitude of state, community, and private organizations. It was then that she began gathering the information that would reach fruition fifteen years later in her first book, *Women's Reality*.

"In the years when I was getting ready to write *Women's Reality*, I didn't read anything," she says. "I thought I had to filter out all other perceptions in order to find my own."

She spent years listening to her individual clients, her friends, and groups of women.

"It didn't matter who the group was, whether it was Presbyterians or executives or a group of hippies. I began developing concepts that captured what I was hearing. Then I began to shape them into a theory.

"I shared with women that although we've done all the right things, we still don't feel right. We think there's something wrong with us, not that the system could be wrong. I tested out what I was learning by talking about it. The response was terrific. People kept telling me I had to write a book.

"I can't even express the terror I felt at the thought of writing a book. In college I had had trouble writing. My English composition professor tried to convince me I was a nonwriter. He used to read my papers in class as examples of how not to write. It was very traumatic. Even with that background I became convinced that I had to write. I took a boat to Hawaii, all by myself, and told the people seated at my table that I was there to work on a book.

"It was a five-day trip. I got everything else done first. I caught up on all the undone things in my life, including writing to my ex-husband trying to make amends, and then finally I sat down and outlined the book. Soon after that trip I took myself up to my mountain cabin and locked myself in for two weeks and wrote *Women's Reality*."

Women's Reality, published in 1981, delineates major systems in our society. The *white male system* holds the power and influence in this nation. It makes the laws, runs the economy, and establishes the roles that people will play within the system. The *reactive female system* is a way to cope with those roles and expectations. The *emerging female system* does not cope or react to the establishment; it is a system born out of women trusting their perceptions.

Shortly after she started writing, an unsolicited call came from Winston Press. The publisher had seen a transcript of a speech she had given and was interested in having her write a book. She told him the book was almost completed.

"I really believe my books just come through me. I feel I get out of the way and they just come. I also do a lot of listening to people, and I'm a good synthesizer. People say you have to think of your audience. I don't write books for a certain audience. I write what I think I need to write. I write to speak my truth and because I think it needs to be said. I've been lucky in that it seems to strike a chord in other people.

"That first book came when my kids were growing. I spent a lot of time with them, but I've always had this thing that even though I had relationships, even though I had kids, I also had to do my work. At times it's been real hard on my kids. In fact, my daughter once said, 'Mom, sometimes when you go out, I don't miss you.' In my codependence I thought that was terrible. I wanted her to miss me. But I also realized that it was really great that she had her own life and was not dependent on me."

After leaving Bob, Anne got involved with a man who was totally monogamous. "That was the thing I liked most about him. My kids and I moved into a big house he bought for all of us. Later, when we split, one of his daughters stayed with me, and I moved into a house we called 'All Women and Our Children.' It was a group of us who moved in together for emotional and financial support."

While Anne was gathering information for *Women's Reality*, increasing numbers of people asked to study with her. In response she and some associates opened the Women's Institute of Alternative Psychotherapy in Colorado, where she had moved.

"We tried to start an alternative graduate school that would be accredited. I didn't have my doctorate then, but we were told we could get a grant if I would be the director. I was still trying to spend time with my children and start writing. I think it was my codependence that got me into that one. My idea was to get the institute set up and work myself out of a job as soon as possible. But it became an albatross. It has been one of the most painful things in my life.

"What we wanted to do was set up a grassroots institute. I invited anybody who was interested to come—not just

Ph.D.'s in psychology. There were also clients and people who just came to help. I wanted to generate ideas on how it should be done, from the care-givers to the care-receivers, but a group of feminist therapists were upset because they didn't have control.

"We were criticized because we didn't have enough professionals and because I didn't have my degree, even though I had all these Ph.D. people coming in. I didn't need a degree—I was just the director. When I went out of town, I hated to come home because there would be a certified letter or a new attack or a phone call. It was just awful. At one point I thought, my God, what is this preparing me for? I think what it has prepared me for is to deal with what I'm dealing with now. It's what my next book is about. I'm really calling all the helping professions into question. I know now that when I get this kind of reaction, I am getting near somebody's stash.

"It felt as if they were out to kill me. They accused me of sleeping with my clients and all kinds of things. They circulated a list of accusations. They had me investigated by the Colorado Psychological Association and Board of Psychological Examiners. I was completely exonerated; still, I didn't know what hit me. I wasn't prepared for it."

She then discovered that one of the women in her household was an alcoholic. She says the codependent feelings she had at work and home had nearly fatal results.

"I was so stressed out my heart stopped. I was out to dinner one night with a group of people and things just got too intense. It was like my final dinner, the last supper, and my heart stopped. I had an out-of-body experience. I entered another realm of consciousness. The only way I can describe it is like the opening scenes of the musical *Brigadoon*. I was out there, and then I said, Look around and see who you know here. At that point this person screamed at me, 'Come back! Anne, are you all right?' I heard it, yet I was clinically dead—I can remember the whole thing so clearly. My whole being said, I guess I'd better go back, I'm not finished; then I felt myself climbing through levels of consciousness to get back, and I immediately started saying to people, 'I went somewhere else.' I knew if I was going to come back and stay, I had to be totally honest. That was my commitment and the beginning of this work I'm doing now. People have said that it's difficult to be in my aura and not be honest. It's almost like my being demands it."

Anne's near-death experience and the trials of living with an alcoholic led her into codependent recovery. Her alcoholic housemate went into alcoholism treatment, and Anne gathered thirteen family members for codependent treatment—her children, her secretary, her ex-husband, and some of her clients who asked to come. There were too many of them to go into a facility, so the group hired a treatment staff and went to a motel.

In treatment she was told that she was probably one of the 4 percent of Americans who did not grow up in dysfunctional families.

"My response to that was instant fury. The counselor thought she was telling me something wonderful about myself, and she was, but what I realized was that I had *become* codependent even if I hadn't grown up that way. The place in my life where I have seen this most is in my intimate relationships with men. It just hasn't been that satisfactory. Bob and I really loved each other, but both of his parents were alcoholics and he was an alcoholic, so in that process I certainly became codependent. I learned it well. I now feel codependence is like diabetes; it's a disease I have that I'll be recovering from all my life. I'm constantly invited back into it by everything around me. I've had to work my program."

Following treatment she did what she says is very typical of her: she learned everything she could about the disease of addiction. She read, talked to people, and went to meetings. She was a full-time therapist at the time and discovered that five of her long-term clients were alcoholic. She also received a Ph.D. in clinical psychology in 1986 (with a specialization in treating the addictive process) from the Union for Experimenting Colleges and Universities in Cincinnati. She began to realize that the characteristics of the "white male system" were similar to the characteristics of alcoholism or any other addiction.

"I was speaking at a wellness conference in Minnesota, and I heard the words come out of my mouth that the white male system and the addictive system were the same thing. There was this moment of silence, and then everybody was on their feet applauding, and I was in a daze. I realized then that I hadn't wanted to take that next step because I had seen how

hard it was for an individual addict to recover, and the thought
of what it would take for a whole society to recover was
overwhelming to me. But now I look at it differently. I know
that individuals do recover, and that without naming the disease society doesn't have a chance to recover. It means society
malfunctions as an addict does and is deteriorating in the
same way as an addict does, so the majority of the power in
the world possesses a fatal disease."

She then wrote about her discovery. In *When Society Becomes an Addict* (1987) Anne describes the addictive system as
one that "calls for addictive behaviors where the individual begins to operate out of an addictive process. An addictive system is a closed system in that it presents few choices to individuals in terms of roles they may take and directions they
may pursue."[1] Writing that our society functions as an addict
and is in need of recovery, she explains that the addictive system encourages people to numb their feelings and deny what is
really happening to them.

In *Co-Dependence Misunderstood-Mistreated* (1986) she
says that codependence is a primary disease with its own
symptoms and outcome, not just a term to describe people in a
relationship with an alcoholic or chemically dependent person.
She says codependents are addicted to relationships, finding
little meaning within themselves. They suffer low self-esteem;
have trouble identifying or dealing with their feelings; and suffer from depression, dishonesty, fear, and negativity. Codependence is a disease within the addictive system. She goes
on to discuss the impact of her theory on the fields of mental
health, chemical dependency, family therapy, and the women's
movement.

As her books gained in popularity, she found she was
traveling more and seeing fewer private clients. For years her
identity had been that of a psychotherapist, so it was a difficult but timely decision to let go of her private practice. Anne
continues to train individuals and to do organizational consulting. In the late seventies when the Women's Institute of Alternative Psychotherapy closed, she opened Wilson-Schaef Associates.

Anne trains people in what she calls the "Living Process

---

1. Anne W. Schaef, *When Society Becomes an Addict* (San Francisco: Harper
& Row, 1987), 25.

System," whose purpose is to embrace and honor a person's feelings, her history, and what she is currently working through. She believes:

> To be a living process facilitator is to embrace a whole new way of being in the world. As we make a systems shift ourselves, we work differently with people. I have been training people (mostly other therapists) in the living process system for several years, and the major focus of that training is helping them come to terms with the addictive system and co-dependence by working with their own process to make a systems shift.
>
> I believe that living process work bypasses the cognitive and works with other parts of the brain and the being and then brings it back to cognitive for closure. I also believe this is where real healing (not just adjustment) occurs.[2]

"When I live my process, I am in touch with all the processes of the universe. My process is God, and God is more than my process. God is the *whole* process. Living my process means living a life of faith. It means I go ahead when I don't know. It doesn't mean that I'm impulsive or irresponsible or any of that stuff. It means I trust the process of the universe of which I am a part.

"My workshops are hard to describe because they're experiential. What happens is a group of people, most of whom have never met, come together. There are about twenty-five attending the workshop, and fifteen staff members, about one staff member for every two attendees. First we go around and introduce ourselves and tell why we're there. Usually I say a little bit about 'Living in Process.' I don't say a lot. I encourage them to know when to go to the bathroom or when they need to take a break. I tell them, 'There's not necessarily a direct relationship between the amount of time you spend in this group and what you will learn. Everything you do is an opportunity to learn about the process—for example, kitchen work, when forty people are trying to cook at once.'

2. Anne W. Schaef, *Co-Dependence: Misunderstood-Mistreated* (San Francisco: Harper & Row, 1986), 96.

"People start to share their stories. We try to facilitate whatever feelings come up, but we don't use any techniques or exercises. We're modeling what we're talking about. Most people find it to be the most profound experience in their lives. I always come away feeling rested, relaxed, and happy. I don't get drained with the intensives. I think it's because I'm in recovery with my codependence and the work that I do is nondraining. I facilitate their work. I don't have to do it, so I don't burn out.

"People train with me because they know they're going to get honesty. I don't let anything pass, and I call them on whatever I see. I feel like that's what they're paying me to do, and that's the honesty. Honesty is one of our most precious gifts, and to be ruthlessly honest about everything we can is the way to freedom, health, and spirituality. As Jesus said, 'Ye shall know the truth, and the truth shall make you free.'

"I believe working with people keeps me grounded. Many people become leaders and then move gradually away from the grassroots. They become more ethereal; they write books and move farther away from what they're writing about. In doing that, I think we do ourselves a great disservice. For instance, one of the things I really enjoy doing is cleaning the stove, because I think it keeps me grounded. When we become important, people do our cleaning. We lose contact with working with the car, or cleaning the garage, or cooking, or cleaning out the closet."

Anne says that for her to be a teacher it is important that people not "guruize" her. "My work is to help them find their own strength. I don't want followers, and I don't think that's what this work is all about. On the other hand, it looks so seductive. I feel that guruitis is a progressive, fatal disease. I have seen a lot of good people develop what I would call a severe case of guruitis and really lose touch with themselves and lose their effectiveness. I basically believe that Westerners have absolutely no ability to be gurus. If I don't participate in my own work, there's always the danger of getting guruitis."

Reflecting on the people she's studied with, she says, "I knew and learned from them all, but they didn't feel like mentors to me. I haven't allowed myself mentors. I have felt I had to find my own way, that I knew the truth, and that each of us has access to that. We can't contaminate it with others' perceptions of the truth.

"I had mentors when I was younger. I would say that Jesus is one of my big ones. I was sort of surprised when I realized that. I've really learned a lot from what I consider to be true Christianity. That doesn't have much to do with the way it's practiced, but certainly the teaching I received as a child was very important.

"When I was younger, two of my most important mentors were my parents. Both of them told me to follow my own path. The combination of my father being an engineer and my mother being a poet really encouraged me to follow every kind of path I wanted to, whether it was math or science or horseback riding. Their philosophy was to open every possible door and do what you need to do. They modeled that in their parenting.

"In some ways, my mentor has been the universe, and my mentors have been nobodies. My mentors have been the common people I have seen and worked with. They have been my teachers.

"I was in Florida a couple of years ago and stopped at a small gas station out in the country. When I went in to pay, the guy who filled my tank picked up his guitar and started playing it. He started singing gospel songs. I sat down and harmonized with him. We sang for about a half hour together. He shared about having had lung surgery and knowing he had to save his life, so he found Jesus. We just had a wonderful time together. Then I left. He was one of my teachers."

Anne says it is always a temptation while on a book tour to work too much, but she makes a point of taking good care of herself. The first thing she does before scheduling her workshops and seminars is to plan her vacation and private time. She usually takes a vacation every four to six months. She also enjoys spending money on herself and visiting beautiful natural environments.

"I get a massage almost every week, no matter where I am. I eat a healthy diet, I schedule time alone, and if I get to a point where I feel I need a block of time and I don't have it, I'll cancel. In general, I really listen to my body and pay attention to my needs. Now I feel like I may be needing more private time, just fooling-around time, writing time. To me, writing is really not work at this point of my life. Editing is work, rewriting with the publisher is work, but writing isn't work and so I need more time with that."

After *When Society Becomes an Addict* she and coauthor Diane Fassel wrote *The Addictive Organization* (1988). It addresses the dysfunctional addictive systems in organizations. The authors show how to identify and recognize addictive systems and how to begin the recovery process.

For both Anne and her coauthor, the writing of this book was the culmination of years of work they began separately in the sixties as organizational consultants. Fassel, a Sister of Loretto, is an organizational consultant and mediator. She works with national and international corporations, civic organizations, schools, and religious communities. She and Anne met in the early eighties when Anne was doing organizational consulting for the Sisters of Loretto order. They had been hearing about each other for years, and people often told them that they should meet. They had just met when they were both invited to a convention on women's theology.

"We got to the conference, and it was one of the ones that are so ghastly we couldn't stand it. The conference planners said, 'If you don't like it, do something,' and so we did. We had only just met, but we put our heads together and planned something for the next session. It was fantastic. It broke things open, and we spent a lot of time getting to know each other while we congratulated ourselves.

"I think that was a time in Diane's life when she knew she needed to break through to a new level of awareness and come to terms with herself. We have a household that does that. That's how we live. At that time there were just a few of us living together, so she suggested that she move in. She's been part of the household ever since. We work together some, but mostly we work separately. This book was very easy—we collaborated and wrote it in three weeks.

"We organized the whole addictive organization material the same way that I did with *Women's Reality*. We were working with organizations, and then we began to put the ideas together. In general, the response from organizations has been relief: 'Thank God there's a way to name this.' I think that on some level organizational consultants are stuck in trying to find the fix. We said the fix is a lifelong process of recovery. Some people still want the quick fix, and we say, 'That's your disease talking.'

"We've also found key people in the corporations who are recovering themselves saying, 'I know this is true. My own recovery is even being threatened by the corporation,' or 'I see the corporation as an addict and I want to change it. What can I do?' This response has been a surprise because we thought we were going to have to convince and to challenge." Talking about their organizational work, Anne says they only go where they are invited, and they follow the same philosophy as Twelve Step Programs—attraction, not promotion.

"We are finding a way to get through to those who are ready. The book has received a tremendous response. I think, like all my books, it's not one that's going to come out and sell a million the first month. My books seem to build over time and sell more and more. I really do believe that until the organization comes to terms with itself, society is not going to. It's really the organizations that are holding the addictive society together. As the organizations start to change, I think that's going to start to impact society."

Now that Anne has started writing, she has no intention of stopping or even slowing down. In 1989 she wrote *Escape from Intimacy: Understanding Addictions to Sex, Love and Romance, Relationships.*

"I think one of the problems we're seeing is that writers in these areas have combined sex, romance, and relationship addiction as if they're the same thing, and they're not. Any one of those three, or a combination, results in an addictive relationship. As long as we keep the three confused, people aren't going to get the help they need. Relationship addicts can say, 'I'm not a sex addict, so I don't have to deal with this.' Romance addicts can say the same thing, and they're hurting just as bad. All are destructive diseases. And I think all of them are escapes from intimacy."

She has been working on *Beyond Science, Beyond Therapy* for several years. "Basically, I think the helping professions have been a systemized practice of codependence. They are to the addictive society as the enabler is to the alcoholic. And the very way we have been trained to practice our art assists people in the disease.

"I just gave a speech at the California Marriage and Family Therapists Convention. I expected to be drawn and quartered, but I thought it would be a good place to test these ideas out. It's real interesting that about 90 percent of the evaluations were rave reviews, and the rest really hated me. I was astounded. Again, I think I'm onto something here. My basic belief is that people in the helping professions want to be helpful. I think if we can see what's going on we'll be open to change, but I think we have to see that what we're doing isn't working.

"I check myself out just as I check others out. I'm going to share my own mistakes, and yet I believe I was a good therapist. I made some huge mistakes, though, because I didn't know any better. It's not that I'm criticizing from outside; I've been there myself.

"I think psychotherapy and everything that we've done with therapy is going to have to change totally. The participatory nature of the Twelve Step work, and its influence, is tremendous. I think the limitation with the Twelve Steps is that they really don't know what to do with feelings, how to work with them."

Taking her time to prepare her new book is giving Anne time to prepare herself for the response—both positive and negative—to it. In some ways the therapeutic community that she loves is the last group she wants to take on.

"One of my heroes is Martin Luther. One of the things he said was, 'Here I stand, I can do no other.' I mean, there's nothing in the world that Martin Luther wanted to do less than to take on the Catholic Church. He loved the Catholic Church.

"Growing up Irish, I learned that there's nothing as fun as a good brawl. I used to start these brawls just to have a good time. Sometimes I got the shit beaten out of me. What I've learned is not the dualism of fighting or not fighting; it's doing what I must."

Anne sometimes sees herself as an Auntie Mame character and as filled with life and adventure. She says she's curious about everything, and that she probably got that trait from her father.

"I think I'm really funny. I'm really profound, and I put the two together well. I think I'm very courageous. I believe I'm here to speak my truth and that's all I have to do. I don't have to make people understand it; I don't have to make them agree. I just have to speak the truth. I'm real easy with life.

"My personal integrity has always been of utmost importance. Sometimes I alienate people. Some people think I'm harsh, like when I call my trainees on stuff. People who know me know that that's loving. I don't let things pass. Especially with the people I care about.

"I'm also an interesting combination of an extrovert and an introvert. I really am very outgoing, very comfortable with large crowds. I love having the stage, playing with my audience. I have a lot of fun.

"On the other hand, I really have to have my time alone. I'm thinking of building a house in Hawaii with a wing for myself. I'm going to have a room that's totally separated from the rest of the house. That will be my space for hiding and writing and being by myself. That's the first room I've planned, but I'm already planning a writing gazebo down by the stream, which is my retreat from my retreat. I laugh at myself, because where I live in Colorado is miles up a mountain, but I need a retreat from that.

"All my life I've taken alone time. I see my kids that way too. My son, when he was eighteen months old, would go up into his room and close the door and play by himself every day, for just a little while. My housekeeper would say, 'Do you think he's all right?' and I would say, 'I just think he needs alone time.' He's still that way, and so is my daughter. In my family I think we've encouraged one another to tune into what we really need.

"When I have bad days I get into a cloud of despair. I think, What am I doing? My God, I should shut up. People are listening to me. Do I really know what I'm talking about? Sometimes I get into that around my kids. What have I done wrong? What a bad mother I am. Oh God, I'm a failure. It's not often, but I certainly do that.

"Another thing I do is that I begin by saying all the work I'm doing is so important, that I've been chosen for it. Then I'll turn it on myself and say I'm not the best person; I don't have the skills or the awareness. I call that my imperfect vessel routine.

"I really got into that a couple of years ago when I was in Germany. I got into this thing where I felt I wasn't good enough. I should have been a man, more charming, more this, more that. Virginia Satir was there too, at that time, and I saw people just worshipping her. It seemed so easy for her, and for a moment I thought it would be nice to have people falling all over me. Then one of my friends said, 'I don't know why people aren't just falling at your feet, because all you're telling them is to change their whole lives. I can't imagine why they're not just thrilled!' And then I knew that my path and my work were just as they should be, even if sometimes I did not feel up to them. It is my very commonness, my earthiness, my grassrootness that ground me. It is *because* of who I am, and what I came from, that I can see what I see and speak my truth."

Sometimes Anne has what she calls codependent attacks. Once she was on a doctoral committee for a woman who had given her an unsatisfactory dissertation proposal to comment on. Anne found herself getting more and more uncomfortable about having to tell this woman that her proposal had problems.

"I got into this stew. But as I talked with her, I realized that the comments and the input I was making were very valuable to her. It was my disease that was keeping me from doing that, that was telling me to 'be nice.'"

Anne lives in what she calls a "household of recovery." She shares her house with her friend and coauthor, Diane, and John, a man she describes as a backwoods-type man. "The three of us have a really good relationship. Our commitment is to live our own process and to call each other on our disease, and we do that. We have the kind of household where a lot of people come and go."

Anne says they also have a lot of fun together. They have a big screen to watch movies on, which she enjoys. She also loves to dance. "That's been one of the limitations in not being in a couple, but there are more limitations to being in a couple than there are in not being in a couple."

Anne likes to take walks and loves being outdoors. She has a camper she takes into the woods. She likes spending time with her two grown children, who also reside in Boulder. "They're great kids. I really feel gifted that they chose me to be their parent. They're a couple of my most important mentors, especially my son, Roddy. I tell people frequently that he is probably my most important teacher. He's integrated a lot of what I teach and thrown it back at me. When I'm not being consistent and have to deal with my own control issues, he'll say, 'Mom, you're not practicing what you preach.' He's always teaching me something."

At present Anne is not in a sexual relationship with anyone. "I have been celibate for several years now. I decided that if I couldn't be sexual with someone who was clear, and be clear myself, I wouldn't be sexual. That's resulted in celi-

bacy, so I don't identify myself as a heterosexual or a homo-
sexual. I think all that's crazy, to identify ourselves by our
sexuality. I think probably if I ever move into another whole
intimate relationship, it will be with a man. That just seems to
be where my life is moving.

"In my codependency I have felt like I had to be in a relationship in order to be okay. That hasn't been true for years.
I feel complete in myself, and I would never get into another
sick relationship with anybody. I feel open to a relationship if
one happens, but going out and looking for one doesn't appeal
to me. I feel good with my life right now. I have for several
years. I think I've learned a lot in my relationships, and I also
think it's been relationships where I practiced my disease, so
I've needed this abstinence."

Anne is known for poking fun at the new-age movement.
"I think there's a lot of new-age pookie-pookie. I'm really very
positive about the new-age movement, but it's my style to go
right for the jugular if I care about something. I believe the
new-age movement is very important and it gets off track
sometimes, and I feel very free to say so when I think it does.

"It gets addictive by the use of techniques. It's like trying
to control, not trusting people to take the information. All
these creative visualizations are control mechanisms. And
when you're into control, you're in the same old addictive system. It's like changing the content when you're trying to do it
the same old way, like using techniques as a fix.

"One of my best examples is, I know a woman who is an
active alcoholic. She knows it and she admits it. She went to
AA a couple of times, and it didn't help her, so she hangs
herself with crystals. She goes to every channeler on God's
earth, and she reads all this new-age stuff. I believe that
transformation is not possible without recovery. It is not possible until you've faced your recovery from the addictive process. I think that what a lot of people are trying to do is
transform without doing the hard part of working through their
addictions.

"A lot of the new-age people are just looking for some
outside fix that is going to make everything better. It has nothing to do with who you are. I think it acts the same as any
other drug. I think it keeps you from discovering who you are,
what your process is, why you are here, what it's about.

"I think in order to learn to live your process, you have

to simultaneously confront your addictive process. The addictive process is the norm for this society. All of us are infected by it. It's an illusionary system. As one of my friends says, it may be what Jesus called principalities and powers. You have to confront and deal with that while simultaneously learning to live your own process. You can't do one or the other. A lot of the spiritual movements try to help us learn about our spiritual process without confronting the addiction, and a lot of the addiction work tries to just deal with the addictions without really knowing how to facilitate learning your own process. I think the two have to be simultaneous and overlapping. That's what I'm doing. It's by looking into the very pit of our lives that we see what is really going on.

"I think struggling with our truth is spiritual. I'm angry when people say, 'This new guru or that new guru is so spiritual.' What it usually means is that they're not on this plane. I think what that does is deny the reality that we're all spiritual, everything is spiritual. We don't have to hunt for our spirituality. It's a by-product of living our lives."

PERSONAL TRUTHS

1. Life is a process. I am a process. If I honor and trust my process, I am one with the universe. As I honor my process, I find myself honoring the process of others.

2. There is no transformation without recovery, and there is no recovery without transformation.

3. The practical should always be in the service of the important.

4. I wouldn't miss life for anything!

ANNE WILSON SCHAEF
Author of

Escape from Intimacy: Understanding Addictions to Sex, Love and Romance, Relationships. San Francisco: Harper & Row, 1989.

The Addictive Organization. Coauthored with Diane Fassel. San Francisco: Harper & Row, 1988.

When Society Becomes an Addict. San Francisco: Harper & Row, 1987.

Co-Dependence: Misunderstood-Mistreated. San Francisco: Harper & Row, 1986.

Women's Reality: An Emerging Female System in the White Male Society. San Francisco: Harper & Row, 1981, 1985.

Louise Hay

Louise L. Hay, D.D., *author and metaphysical counselor, is a leader in the alternative healing movement. She is the author of* Heal Your Body, You Can Heal Your Life, The AIDS Book: A Positive Approach, I Love My Body, *and* Your Personal Colors and Numbers. *She believes that by changing our beliefs and mental patterns we can change the way we feel about ourselves, thereby increasing wellness of body, mind, and spirit.*

While she is known for her work with cancer and AIDS patients, her primary focus is to teach all people to love themselves. She believes "dis-ease" is caused by self-hatred and self-criticism. When these negative attitudes are changed into positive ones, disease can be healed, she says.

Louise Hay is a graduate of ministerial training at the Church of Religious Science in New York City and holds a Doctor of Divinity degree from the Science of Mind College.

It seemed that everybody I knew was suddenly talking about Louise Hay's book You Can Heal Your Life. *My clients, friends, and parents were all reading her book. Wherever I traveled, people would ask if I'd met Louise Hay and then proceed to tell me of the profound and positive effect her work was having on their lives. Because of this, I thought of her for this book.*

I interviewed Louise in her office on Wilshire Boulevard in Santa Monica. It was a comfortable place, and a picture of teddy bears hung on the wall. I was immediately at ease with her. She has a great sense of humor, and at points I laughed so much that later my typist had trouble transcribing the tapes.

Louise combines the qualities of glamor and graciousness with a down-to-earth simplicity. I sensed the strength of the metaphysician. She knows and uses the principles she teaches.

She told her story easily, having made peace with her past and remaining focused on the demands of her success, which include a multitude of requests for her lectures and workshops.

S he was raped when she was five. She testified in court and can still remember pointing to her vagina as they questioned her.

The rapist was the wino down the street. Even though he was sentenced to sixteen years, she was told it was her fault. For years she waited for him to come back and get her.

That is why today, when asked if she knew as a child what she wanted to do with her life, she says, "I didn't know if I'd be alive when I grew up."

Louise Hay was born in Los Angeles on October 8, 1926. She was raised in Beverly Glen Canyon, which she says was "pretty ticky-tacky" in those days. Her parents were Henry Lunney and Vera Chawla.

"As far as I know, my life was wonderful until about eighteen months. Then, from my point of view, everything went bad." Her parents were divorced and she was boarded out. She was told she cried nonstop for three weeks at one of her temporary homes until finally her mother came back for her.

"My mother was working as a domestic. I thought of them as rich people's houses, but maybe they were just people who could afford help. They might have even hired her for less because she had a little girl with her. I learned to be very quiet, not to make noise, not to be enthusiastic, and not to disturb the family by crying. My mother was grateful that I was allowed to be with her.

"Then, somewhere along the line, she met a middle-European man and decided to marry. There was a three-month period of time before my mother ended her job when I was left with him. It felt like an eternity and was extraordinarily difficult for me. I was around five years old, and my mother only came back on weekends.

"About that same time I was raped by a neighbor. That was a very sticky time. There was a big court case, so I remember bits of that. I remember being examined by the doctor with my feet up in the stirrups. I remember being on the stand and gesturing down there [she points to her vagina]. I remember getting some chocolate that night, which was a big treat.

The guy got sixteen years, but I was still scared and guilty because I was told it was my fault. I thought he'd come out and get me for being so awful as to put him in jail. It was a very difficult time."

Other memories are of physical and emotional abuse from her stepfather. She says her mother, who was also European, was raised in a tradition of male dominance, and whatever her husband did or said was what mattered. "My mother used to stand there and say, 'Please don't,' which didn't do a damn bit of good. I can see now that was as far as she felt she could go."

Louise says that years later, when she began to do some of her own forgiveness work, she started to understand her stepfather, who had come from a badly brutalized family. He didn't know how to treat people in general and had little respect for women. It was also the depression, and he had been reduced from practicing landscape architecture to doing gardening. She says she realizes that life was not easy for him, yet knowing this now does not make the physical and mental abuse she endured as a child any easier.

Looking at the beautiful, elegant woman of today, one needs to stretch the imagination to see her as an impoverished, friendless school kid. But that child is very much a part of Louise Hay. One aspect of her work is to help people reach back into the past and embrace their child within: that child from the past who many would rather forget. Her experience and compassion help others reach that injured child. Knowing where she came from and who she is today gives others courage to seek, express, and forgive.

Her own loneliness as a child was deep. She can remember only one semester at school when she had a friend. "There was a little fat boy. Nobody liked me and nobody liked him and we sort of got together."

Although Louise has a half sister, they have never been close. "It was always my stepfather and my sister against me and my mother.

"When I was about thirteen or fourteen, my stepfather stopped beating me and started going to bed with me. That was, in a way, much harder to take. After a few months I left in the middle of the night and trotted down the road. 'Here I am, World! Let's see what we can do!' " She laughs when she says, "At least it wasn't cold in southern California.

"You know, when it's right, things sort of fall together. I

remember somebody got me a job at a soda fountain. The first day I talked to the owner, he told me all the things I would have to do and said he expected me to work really hard. At the end of the first day I thought, This is work? This is nothing compared to what I've been doing, and I can eat ice cream too!"

Young and vulnerable, alone in a frightening world, Louise was drawn to the only kind of love she knew. "I was a waitress for a while, a very lower-echelon waitress at a diner. Having been so incredibly love-starved as a child, now that I was out of the house, if anybody put their arms around me I was theirs.

"So just around my sixteenth birthday I had a baby. I had it in someone else's name so it was automatically adopted. I lived with them for the last few months and went to the hospital in their name. You know, I can remember the mother's first name now but not her last." Louise says she remembers the baby's big toes, which were unusual, like her own.

Not having the support that single mothers have today, she experienced little of the joy of birth.

"The whole experience was so shameful that I just felt extraordinarily lucky that I was able to find a home for her. There's no way that I could have handled it, and here this wonderful opportunity came along and I knew in my heart that this was the right decision for her and me."

She says she has never regretted the decision. Although it has passed through her mind that it would be interesting to meet her daughter, Louise says she would not initiate this.

Soon after the baby was born, she went back to "save" her mother from her stepfather. "I told her she didn't have to live like that anymore. I told her I'd help her get out of there." Louise says she did not realize that her mother was passionately in love with this man.

"Now I can see that. At the time I couldn't. You see, we were one of those families who didn't talk about anything. How could anybody know what was going on? The only thing I could understand was that this was my mother and she was being beaten. At the very end of her life, the last year we lived together, my mother told me that she left him because she thought I needed her."

After finding her mother a job and a place to live, Louise went to Chicago for a month. She stayed five years.

"That was not a good period, really, because I was very,

very poor. I just struggled to get from week to week, not knowing that I could do much else." No one had ever believed in her, and she did not believe in herself. She criticized herself the way she had been criticized as a child. She attracted men who mistreated her and often beat her.

Then two things happened that changed her life. She had just started working in a department store in Chicago when she heard about a free introductory modeling class. She'd always loved clothes but hadn't had the money for them. "When I was a kid I used to love paper dolls and I made lots of clothes for them. They were very popular and came with little fold-out things that you could put on them. I loved that." So, motivated by her love for clothes, she enrolled in Chicago's Patricia Stevens Modeling School.

She still remembers the first clothing class she went to, in which the instructor criticized each student's attire. "Every single thing I had on was wrong. You see, I only owned two outfits, and if I had worn the other, that wouldn't have been any better." Shortly after, serendipity struck again. She went to an Arthur Murray dance class and was sold five hundred dollars' worth of dancing lessons. "I was making only twenty-five dollars a week, but I signed the contract. I went home that night and suddenly thought, My God, what have I done? What have I done! So I called them up the next day and told them there was no way I could pay. They said, 'You have signed the contract; however, we do need a receptionist.' " She went from working in a department store's handbag shipping room to being the receptionist at Arthur Murray. Besides supervising one hundred women teachers, she made hourly introductions of new clients, scheduled appointments, and answered the phone. It changed the way she felt about herself.

"I found out I had power, that I was capable. I could do things." The pay increase of five dollars a week was a lot of money, and soon the studio gave up trying to give her dancing lessons in exchange for her work. "My whole life changed enormously. I didn't start working until 10 A.M., was given dinner, and worked till ten at night. I had a bunch of new friends. Not only that, but I fell in love with one of the teachers. He was in charge of the music and so he played all love songs. The teachers complained that all they had to dance to were his romantic ballads. It was wonderful!

"Somehow that ended, and I went to New York. I went

for a month and I liked it—liked the energy." Louise started
her modeling career there. "I heard that somebody needed a
model at David Crystal's Seventh Avenue dress house. It was a
big house with ten models. In those days it was a big name. I
remember, while auditioning for them, I was so scared my
knees were shaking. They asked if I had experience, and I
said, 'Oh, yes, I've been modeling for a while.' "

Once hired, she began a rigorous routine. "Every two
weeks they had something that they called the review. Four or
five designers for the house, and the models, stayed all night.
They bought us dinner and we modeled the clothes for the
people in the firm. Everybody discussed everything. They
asked us what we thought about the clothes. Well, I was so
naive I thought they wanted to know. That was the end of that
job." But at the end of those two weeks she had earned a valuable commodity, experience.

Louise then worked in New York's Garment District. It
was fun and paid relatively well for someone who had no formal education, and it allowed her to meet people like Bill
Blass when he was a sketcher and she was a model for Anna
Miller. They became friends, and later she worked for him.

She met her husband through an odd series of events. A
girl she barely knew had asked Louise to take her thirteen-
year-old poodle because her new boyfriend didn't like it, and
Louise adopted it because she loves animals. One day, while
she was walking the dog, it stopped to talk to another poodle.
She looked up, six feet six inches, into the face of a gorgeous
Englishman. He had arrived in America on the Queen Mary
only two days before and was staying with friends. He had offered to walk their dog.

Louise remembers coming home from the long walk and
looking in the mirror. It had been one of those drizzly, misty
days. Her hair had gone flat and her makeup was droopy and
runny. She looked again and thought, Well, either you killed it
completely or you are okay, 'cause you will never look worse.

"I didn't see him for four or five days. Then, when I was
out walking, I saw him a block ahead of me and I picked that
dog up and I ran like a son of a bitch. Once I got near him I
put the dog down, trying desperately not to huff and puff. And
that was how we began.

"The only problem was that he was married, although un-
happily. His wife was still in England and was going to follow

him over later, so we had some time. When she arrived, I
suggested we not see each other for a month, until he knew
what he was feeling about her. He was going to call me at
noon on a certain day a month later. At 12:01, the phone
rang.

"We got a place together, but it took him three years to
get a divorce. She wouldn't give him a divorce until she met
someone, and then she insisted on first-class passage back on
the Queen Mary. Why not?"

They were married for fourteen years. They had a house
in the country and an apartment in the city. She modeled and
entertained for her husband's business, an old East Indian
merchant trading firm based in England. He headed the American branch. "We did a lot of traveling for the firm until he
became the president of the British-American Chamber of
Commerce in New York City. We moved into the fringes of
diplomatic society. I learned so much. It was a marvelous
time." Then, one day, it was over. He had met somebody else.
"I was wife number-two. He is now on wife number-four. It
was a sort of messy divorce because he was well known then.

"With my track record it had seemed like nothing good
ever lasted, but after fourteen years I thought maybe this was
going to last. The breakup was difficult for me. I kept asking
myself why I was so upset, because I had felt much worse
and always bounced back. It took almost a year to come out
of it.

"I look back now and I see that he gave me the freedom
to pursue what I really needed to do. I would never have gone
in the direction I have if I had continued to be a good married
lady."

For a time, after the marriage, she continued to work in
fashion. Feeling it was too late to be a model, she taught
modeling and managed a skincare salon.

Although she had had a good marriage and worked as a
high-fashion model, her self-esteem remained low. "When I
looked at my life, I had gone from one disaster to another
even though I was moving up the scale all the time. I didn't
feel good about myself at all. I'd get mad and slap my own
face.

"You keep going and do the best you can. But your best,
when you don't know any better, can be rather poor."

Then something amazing happened. "A numerologist predicted that in September a very small thing would really change my life. You know, it was so small that I didn't realize it at the time."

September was the month she first went to a Church of Religious Science class taught by metaphysician Raymond Charles Barker. She grabbed onto the principles immediately. These were the first people to tell her that she could change her life by changing the way she thought.

"I had been a high school dropout and had never found any subject that interested me, but when I discovered this, I couldn't stop studying. I not only went to Sunday classes; I went to *all* the classes. I couldn't get enough!"

The only formal religious training Louise had while growing up was three weekends of Christian Science Sunday school. Her mother was a lapsed Catholic, and her father an atheist. This was a plus for her, she says, because when she finally found the things that interested her there was nothing to unlearn.

Her studies took priority, and as her thinking changed, so did her life. She started to feel better about herself. Her friends changed. People left her life, and new people came in.

She studied with Eric Pace, one of three ministers at the Church of Religious Science in New York City. Louise says Pace was a wonderful person who was born only twelve days apart from her, in the same year. They had a lot in common and understood each other.

Also during this time and in the years to follow, she exposed herself to a variety of new-age schools of thought. She attended workshops in mental dynamics, Silva Mind Control, Loving Relationships Training, rebirthing, EST, Insight, the Advocate Experience, SCI, and Gestalt synergy. She also nurtured her interests in numerology and astrology.

In 1972, after three years of study in Science of Mind, she became a licensed practitioner. To become a practitioner, she had to produce documented studies of three persons whom she had healed.

Louise's practice expanded rapidly. Whereas most practitioners work in the evening or on weekends, within three months she was working full time. "I was a natural. People just started to come. I stumbled and bumbled, but I learned and I got better and better. I attracted a lot of gay people too. For some reason they felt very safe with me. They would come in and think that they were going to talk about the car that was always breaking down or something, but within seven or eight minutes they would be telling me their innermost sexual problems and all sorts of stuff. Of course, when that starts to happen, the word gets out. All of a sudden I had a large group of people coming to me.

"I also had the opportunity to speak at the Church's daily noon meetings. It was wonderful training for thinking on your feet." Soon she was taking Pace's place at the noon meetings when he was away. She did that for almost a year.

Ministerial training appealed to her but was not offered that year. Meanwhile, she was drawn to transcendental meditation and had heard about Maharishi's International University (MIU). She decided that if she could sublet her apartment in New York for six months, then she would go to MIU. When a woman offered her forty dollars more than she was asking, she left for Fairfield, Iowa. She lived in a college dorm, and this time Louise was one of the richest kids on campus. She immediately walked to J.C. Penney's and spent a hundred dollars decorating her room.

The students meditated three times a day, and each class started with a short meditation. They started with a subject on Monday morning, were tested on Saturday, had Sunday off, and started a new subject the next day. Louise studied biology, chemistry, and the theory of relativity. "It was marvelous because I would never have been able to study in New York City. There were too many distractions." There was no smoking, drinking, or drugs on campus. They were served a mostly vegetarian diet with lots of homemade bread.

Six months later and ten pounds heavier, Louise returned to Manhattan and began her ministerial training. During this time, in the process of working with clients, many of them terminally ill, she started writing what came to be her first book, *Heal Your Body*.

She eventually showed her work to a couple of people and one of them suggested that she write a booklet. Louise had never taken a writing course, nor did she think of herself as a writer: "I bought a book once on how to write, but that was after I'd written the book." She had gathered valuable information she felt others needed to know and, with the encouragement of friends, put a small book together. In it she wrote:

The mental thought patterns that cause the most disease in the body are criticism, anger, resentment and guilt. For instance, criticism indulged in long enough will often lead to diseases such as arthritis. Anger turns into things that boil and burn and infect the body. Resentment, long held, eats and festers away and ultimately can lead to tumors and cancer. Guilt always seeks punishment and leads to pain.[1]

The original edition had twelve pages and included an alphabetical list of diseases, their probable causes, and the new thought patterns that would promote change. "I remember very proudly showing it to Dr. Barker and him saying, 'Oh, this is nice, Louise. How many did you have made? Two hundred?' I said, 'No, five thousand!' and he said, 'You've got to be crazy.' " (At this writing, over three hundred thousand copies have been sold in nine languages.)

Louise completed her ministerial training after a year and was offered her own church in Dayton, Ohio. But Ohio did not appeal to her. If she had to leave New York, she wanted to move somewhere exciting and warm. So she turned down the position, stayed in New York, and continued to work as a metaphysical counselor. It was during this time that she had her own bout with terminal illness.

Cancer. "It scared the hell out of me," she recalls. "Like anyone else who has just been told they have cancer, I went into total panic. Yet, because of all my work with clients, I knew that mental healing worked, and here I was being given a chance to prove it to myself. After all, I had written the book on mental patterns, and I knew cancer was a disease of long-held deep resentment that literally eats away at the body. I had been refusing to dissolve all the anger and resentment at 'them' over my childhood. There was no time to waste. I had a lot of work to do."

Louise describes her feelings about her disease in *You Can Heal Your Life*: "The word *incurable*, which is so frightening to so many people, means to me that this particular condition cannot be cured by outer means and that we must go

---

1. Louise Hay, *Heal Your Body* (Santa Monica, Calif.: Hay House, 1976), 5.

within to find the cure. If I had an operation to get rid of the cancer and did not clear the mental pattern that created it, then the doctors would just cut Louise until there was no more Louise to cut."[2]

It was not a mystery to her why she developed vaginal cancer. She still had resentment and self-hatred to heal from the emotional and physical abuse she had endured as a child. She chose to take absolute responsibility for her disease and for its cure. Instead of being operated on immediately, she asked the doctors for time. They gave her three months.

She immediately contacted her practitioner, Eric Pace, who told her she couldn't have come so far in her life just to die. With his help she began working to dissolve the mental patterns that had caused the disease. She was willing to use what she knew and do what she was told.

Louise worked with a therapist who helped her release deep resentment and anger. As part of the physical release, she beat pillows and howled with rage. Her nutritionist put her on an "extreme" program to cleanse and detoxify her body. She lived on sprouts and asparagus, douched with goldenseal, and put a blue light on her vagina. She also worked with a re-flexologist and a colon therapist.

"Then I began to piece together the scraps of stories my parents had told me of their own childhoods. I started to see a larger picture of their lives. With my growing understanding from an adult viewpoint, I began to have compassion for their pain; and the blame slowly began to dissolve."[3]

Six months later she was absolutely free of cancer.

Out of her own experience and her metaphysical knowledge has come the basis for most of her work. Her workshops, books, and tapes teach wellness of the body, mind, and spirit. She believes that the key to wellness is self-love and that stored resentment and negative thoughts cause disease. Using affirmations, visualizations, guided imagery, mirror work,[4] and forgiveness exercises, she teaches people to change their beliefs and thoughts about themselves and others.

---

2. Louise Hay, *You Can Heal Your Life* (Santa Monica, Calif.: Hay House, 1984), 199–200.
3. Ibid, 201.
4. Louise asks people to stand in front of a mirror, look into their eyes, and say their affirmations. She says mirrors reflect our feelings about ourselves.

It is her belief that people learn how they feel about themselves, and life, by the time they are three to five years old. As a result, people continue to react to things with a three- to five-year-old's decisions and mindset. Although many of these beliefs may have been useful then, they are outdated in adulthood.

To help heal the deep beliefs that people learned so early, Louise believes in reaching the child within. Through visualization and guided imagery they can make contact with their childhoods and are able to express their painful feelings. People can change these thoughts and beliefs. As Louise writes in the beginning of *You Can Heal Your Life*,

> We are each 100 percent responsible for all of our experiences. Every thought we think is creating our future. We create every so-called "illness" in our body. The point of power is always in the present moment. Everyone suffers from self-hatred and guilt. It's only a thought, and a thought can be changed. Self-approval and self-acceptance in the now are the key to positive changes.

After her experience with cancer, Louise began to think more seriously about what mattered to her. She began to think about leaving New York. "I got fed up with the winters and the summers there. I wanted flowers and sunshine, so I came out to California." At fifty-four she was willing to leave her city of thirty years, as well as her close friends, associates, mentors, and clients, to make a change in her life. This was just the first risk of many that would expand her career.

When asked where she got the courage to take each risk, she says, "I never think of things as courageous when I'm doing them. Even when I was little I was doing the best I could to handle all that stuff. I don't question whether I can do something or not, and I've learned over the years that if someone comes and asks me to do something, I'm ready for that step. I never push anything, but when the opportunity presents itself, I take it."

She took the train to Los Angeles in the fall of 1980. "I hopped on the train and came out, thinking I might never have time to take another train ride again. I brought some books and my typewriter, blender, juicer, and hair dryer. That was important, you know, a few books and a few clothes. I had three days in a little roomette, and I spent most of it sort of lying down watching the countryside go by. It was really nice, three days of nothing."

After she arrived in Santa Monica, she stayed with a friend for a month and then got her own apartment. She intuitively realized that not much would happen for the first six months. She went to the beach a lot and took steps to open her counseling practice in town.

"I remember getting a copy of the *Whole Life Catalogue*. I went to every single meeting that was listed and, if it seemed appropriate, I handed somebody a copy of my little book, *Heal Your Body*, and said, 'I am Louise Hay and I am new here. I'm just in from New York.' It was my way of saying to the universe, 'I'm here!' "

She began her practice with the client who had encouraged her to come out to California. Gradually things opened up. She got several more clients, then there was a speaking engagement, and her business started to grow.

The next turning point was moving to an apartment on Berkeley Street, which doubled her rent. "No matter what your rent is, if you double it, it feels big! Then I remember getting a letter in the mail from an ex-client whom I had hardly seen. She wrote thanking me profusely for all the help I had been and saying how much I had helped her change her life around. She wanted to share this with me, and she enclosed a check for two thousand dollars. I said to God, It's okay. I believe. I trust."

Other changes would soon take place for Louise. "When I came out here, I discovered that my mother had been blind for five years and nobody had told me. It was that kind of family. We communicated like crazy," she jokes. "She was an independent Taurus. She wanted to live by herself and did very well. My sister, who lived nearby, did her shopping once a week and sort of recleaned her apartment. Then one day I got a call from my sister: my mother had fallen in the shower and broken her back. When she came out of the hospital, there really wasn't any other place for her to go except to my house.

"I said, God, I will not run from this. I will accept the lesson, whatever it is, but you have got to give me the help and the money. I can't do it by myself.

"I brought her home on a Saturday, almost blind, almost

deaf, with a broken back, throwing up all the way. The following Friday I was due in San Francisco for a workshop. I couldn't leave her alone and I had to go, so I said, God, you've got to take care of her. On Thursday a woman named Julie Webster turned up. She was wonderful. She slept on the living-room floor in her sleeping bag, by choice. Tuesday and Thursday mornings she cleaned houses. She did what you call 'castle cleaning'—nothing too dirty. She stayed for a year and helped me with my mother and with my work."

Louise loved having her mother with her. "The last year and a half of her life was probably the most exciting time she had had in ages. Here was a woman who hadn't had a man in her life in thirty-five years, who hadn't been to a party in something like thirty years. Now, when I periodically had parties, she was the belle of the ball. I got this velvet outfit for her and put pearls and stuff on her, and it was wonderful. There were people in and out of her life all the time, and I conned her into having a cataract removed so she could see. Then she could read again, and her whole life opened up."

Meanwhile, Louise's business was flourishing. She was seeing private clients, lecturing, and had developed a variety of workshops, among them Love Your Self, Heal Your Body, The Power of Loving Yourself, Increasing Your Prosperity, Heal Your Relationships, and AIDS and Herpes: A Positive Approach. She also started a small mail-order business to sell her books and tapes.

In 1984 she decided to write *You Can Heal Your Life*. She had been thinking about the book for some time and wanted to share her work with people who weren't in her workshops. But in order to write a book, she had to take another big risk. It would take two months, during which she couldn't see clients and would have to let the mail-order business support her. She wondered if she could make it financially but decided to try. "I took the time off to finish the book, and, you know, the money came in. It came in and we could pay the bills."

You Can Heal Your Life was published in October 1984. Four years later it made the *New York Times* self-help paperback best-seller list. Originally published by Coleman Publishing, it was later redesigned and published by Louise's own publishing company, Hay House.

About the time that book came out, she did her first

weekend workshop at the Russian River, north of San Francisco in Sonoma County.

"Elisabeth Kubler-Ross had given a workshop the week before, and now I was up there. It was beautiful. There was a man there who just fell in love with me. He was a middle-aged gay carpenter named Charlie. He cooked, he did everything. He said, 'Louise, I want to sit at your feet. I want to work for you.' I told him that was all very nice, but I didn't have anything open. I already had a secretary. When I got home, Julie told me it was time for her to leave. So I called Charlie, and the next thing I knew, he arrived.

"The first thing he asked me was, 'Where do I put my things?' And I didn't know, because I had no idea where Julie put hers. Charlie wasn't going to sleep on the floor, so he got the couch in the dining room. He was also with me for a year."

Things just seemed to work out for her. She'd just bought a computer and Charlie had been a computer programmer.

"Vera, my mother, fell in love with Charlie—the first man in her life in thirty-five years. She was always coming into the office saying, 'Charlie, can I help? Charlie, what can I do?' Charlie would do the dishes at night, and she would come in and ask to dry. It was wonderful. She loved it. Then one day she got very, very sick and we rushed her to the hospital. She was in a lot of pain and they wanted to do a monumental operation and I said, 'No way! The woman is ninety-one years old and her body is giving out. You keep her out of pain.' Her system just shut down. She died on a Monday. I had a class on Thursday night, so I turned it into a class on death and dying, and I invited the people who needed to come, like my sister and her niece. We sang her favorite song, which was 'Let Me Call You Sweetheart,' and we all had those hard, round peppermint candies that were her favorite. It was a wonderful, wonderful thing. Her ashes are now under my apricot tree."

Business continued to grow, and Louise ended up renting the apartment next door. For a while she ran a residency program, but that became too much work. "You don't realize what these projects are till you get into them. You take three people who want you to save their lives, and you nurse them from morning till night for a whole week."

She also began to expand her staff. "Charlie had a friend

who came through town who worked for a while. First I had two employees, and then the next thing you know, there were three. When it got too much for us, we brought in another person, and then another, until we had eighteen.

"People come when I need them to take me to the next level. I attract really wonderful people, people who are willing to work their asses off and give far beyond the call of duty. You know, when you are working with an issue like AIDS, you have to give from a very deep space in your heart."

Louise has been working with clients who have AIDS for years. Her experience tells her that people can heal themselves of disease, and some people who have been working with her are in remission. To her, the mental patterns that create AIDS are similar to those that create cancer (deep hurt, resentment, and self-hatred), although it has the added factor of sexual guilt.

We didn't learn to call our genitals by their proper names when we were growing up, she says. Our genitals were referred to as "down there" or something even more derogatory. There was a feeling that something wasn't "quite right" between our legs.

Even though the sexual revolution came along, people still did not deal with what she calls "Mama's God." From her point of view, people continued to carry sexual beliefs of their mothers and their mother's Gods into the revolution, which produced guilt. She believes guilt breeds punishment and therefore creates sexual diseases.

Louise says the gay community has all the guilt and problems that everyone else has, with the added problem of parents and society judging them. This self-hatred from within and without creates a climate in which disease can grow.

In her work with people who have AIDS, Louise focuses on self-love and self-acceptance. She believes that if people can learn to love themselves and forgive others, they can contribute to their own healing process. She strongly encourages people to seek the aid of a good nutritionist so they can rebuild the body's immune systems as they are rebuilding their mental immune systems.

Her Wednesday-night healing group, which has received publicity for its large gathering of PWAs (Persons with AIDS), began with six clients in January 1985 in the Berkeley Street apartment. Charlie made dinner for everyone. The group grew from six to three hundred in less than a year and was moved to a nearby park.

The response to her work with AIDS has been almost overwhelmingly positive, but she has also received criticism from both the straight and gay populations. She says it's an unpopular area. "Some of the gays are angry at me because they believe I'm saying they created AIDS. They must have taken that out of context."

Occasionally she receives death threats at her office. When this happens, she and her staff stop and form a healing circle, sending love to the person who made the threat.

While the majority of her publicity has been through her work with cancer and AIDS patients, Louise says the main focus of her work is in teaching people to love themselves. "People who are into self-hatred are attracted to me because that's what I work on. I work on loving yourself."

Judging from the kind of response Louise has had, a lot of people want that message, so many that it is becoming less and less possible for her to work with individual clients and personally conduct workshops. "Last year I spent a great deal of time on the road. I did workshop after workshop. It was wonderful, but my desk was piled with mail, and just as I got through it I had to hit the road again. I never got beyond on-the-road and doing my mail. I didn't get a chance to do anything else."

Recently, Louise decided to turn the duties of running Hay House over to her staff, which has allowed her more time to develop her books and tapes. Linda Tomchin became president, and Louise is chairman of the board of Hay House.

"Basically, I am not here [in the office]. I check things out, but the day-to-day running is left up to Linda because I don't want to put my energies into running a business. That is a full-time job which I don't want to take the time to learn. I want to be creative." She knows her voice can soothe the terrified. She has gifts she wants to share. She has plans for more books, and has just completed *The AIDS Book: A Positive Approach.*

She also decided to plant a garden. "Up to now, everything that happened just went right back into the business. I didn't take a salary. But this year I decided I really wanted a garden and you don't get a garden without a house, so I bought a house—my very first house, and I love it. It's in Pacific Palisades. The thing that gives me the most joy in my life is to go out into the garden with plenty of time and just grub in the dirt. That is my renewal."

She works up to six and a half days a week, but likes to take two hours in the morning "to do my own little thing," the meditation and exercises that precede all creative work at the computer.

Since *You Can Heal Your Life* reached the *New York Times* best-seller list, increasing numbers of people are learning of her work and the demands on her are extraordinary. Although she is generally in the best of health, she has recently found that colds and sore throats are a message for her to slow down. "We don't always do what we teach," she laughs.

She says that when she first heard her book had made the best-seller list, she started to cry. She was excited and overwhelmed. The little girl inside of her was scared. She thought, Ma, look at me.

Her support system consists mainly of the people at work because that is where she spends most of her time. She has a few women friends in her neighborhood and close friends in London and New York. Success has affected those close friendships because it has limited her availability. The other day she had to cut short a visit with a close friend although she wanted to spend the whole day with her.

About men and romance, Louise says, "It's interesting. Ever since metaphysics came into my life, romance has more or less left it. You know, the higher you go, the more rarefied the atmosphere. I won't settle for the things I used to settle for. I have much more specific things I'm looking for. I spent my whole life going from one man to another. Now there are fewer men and further spaces between."

She says she has considered remarrying but hasn't met the right person yet. "I don't think there has been anyone for about three years. However, I am extraordinarily busy, and I can't say that I sit around being miserable. This is where I am meant to be right now, and this is what I am supposed to be doing."

Louise continues to work on herself. She is continually healing self-doubt and self-criticism, and is continually increasing her self-love. "I think it's a lifetime thing. You don't ever get it all. There is always more. Always." At the moment, she is not in counseling, "but I no doubt will be very soon because that's the way my life works."

She is not completely fearless: "I fear earthquakes. I know that I have always been and will always be divinely protected, but I still fear lack of control and falling. It brings up a lot of terror. I guess I haven't worked that one through." She does not fear old age, "because I know that will be perfect. I will always have whatever I need at any age."

When asked where she sees the human potential movement going, she says, "Speaking for myself, I think the goal is to try to create a world where it is safe for us to love each other. We can't expect it from other people until we are willing to give it to ourselves. When we can love and accept ourselves, then we can love and accept each other. I think the ultimate goal for everybody is unconditional love.

"They say we only use 10 percent of our brain, so my question is, What is the other 90 percent doing? What is it waiting for? I think that we all have tremendous potential and capability that we can't even dream of at this point. But until we can get beyond prejudice, until we can get beyond all this judgment nonsense and cruelty, we aren't going to get love. We will just find more ways to torture and kill each other. If we can add the knowledge of how the mind works with an ability to love, we will have it made."

Louise Hay is living her life teaching people to expand their capacity to love and is a major figure in the alternative healing movement, but she does not think of herself as a leader. What she does know about herself is, "I am a very simple lady with a simple message: Love yourself."

PERSONAL TRUTHS

1. The subconscious mind does not have a sense of humor. It takes everything you say at face value, so don't belittle yourself, don't criticize, and don't talk about what you don't want to happen.

2. It is vital that we forgive. This has nothing to do with condoning bad behavior, but we need to be willing to forgive so we do not destroy ourselves and so we can be free.

3. If there is one thing we all can drop, it is criticism. Criticism of ourselves or another person keeps us stuck where we are. If we can come to a place of acceptance and self-love, it is easier to make changes. You are not making the change because you are a bad person and you are doing it wrong. You make changes because you love yourself and you want to improve the quality of your life.

LOUISE HAY
Author of

The AIDS Book: A Positive Approach. Santa Monica, Calif.: Hay House, 1988.

Your Personal Colors and Numbers. Santa Monica, Calif.: Hay House, 1987, 1988. Updated yearly.

I Love My Body. Santa Monica, Calif.: Hay House, 1985.

You Can Heal Your Life. Santa Monica, Calif.: Hay House, 1984.

Heal Your Body. Santa Monica, Calif.: Hay House, 1976, 1984.

Laura Davis

Laura Davis *is a nationally known author, workshop leader, and educator in the field of incest and child sexual abuse. She and coauthor Ellen Bass wrote* The Courage to Heal: A Guide for Women Survivors of Child Sexual Abuse. *Their ground-breaking work not only identified the damage caused by sexual abuse, but it also let survivors know that healing is possible.*

The combination of Laura's expertise in the field and her own recovery from incest serves as a source of strength and inspiration to others. She is a leader in the adult survivor movement.

Laura is a former radio talk-show host and media professional. She has also written The Courage to Heal Workbook.

My friend Joni called me from Seattle late one night, and the first sentence out of her mouth was, "You have to go out right now and get The Courage to Heal." *She went on to say that this was the book that would explain everything about incest. She only wished she'd had this guidance six years ago when she began the healing process.*

Joni, a therapist for incest survivors, knew that many of my clients had recently broken denial about their experiences. I'd spent hours and days with Joni talking about incest. Now she was telling me there was a book that would explain the healing process.

I found a copy the next day. I opened it, read a paragraph, and cried. I ran home, read some more, called all my friends and all the therapists I knew and told them to buy this book.

A few months later I attended one of Laura Davis's "Courage to Heal" workshops. I was moved by her. She is a warm and charismatic teacher. She's extremely articulate, funny, and knowledgeable. I felt that the women in the room were receiving hope from her presence, her experience as a survivor, and her own healing. It was the kind of hope and courage only one who had been through it could offer.

Laura lives in a large loft apartment above a grocery store in the Mission District of San Francisco. When I arrived for the interview she was making borscht, and later she invited me to lunch. In the living room where I interviewed her were comfortable couches, a hammock hung across the bay-window alcove, and artwork on the walls. Sun streamed through the windows. She shares her home with a couple and their child, and it felt like a relaxed and happy place.

After years of healing from sexual abuse, Laura Davis feels she can finally start to live like a regular person. Her first twenty-seven years were spent in the nameless pain that survivors of sexual abuse feel, and only in the last six years has she been able to identify what happened to her—give it a name—and begin the recovery process.

During what she calls the "lost years" her favorite book was Ursula Le Guin's *The Wizard of Earthsea*. Le Guin writes of a man pursued by a shadow, and at the end of the book he wrestles with the shadow and finds himself. "I read that book eighteen times because I really identified with it. I had the feeling that something was chasing me. I moved every six months. I was always running away. I didn't know what I was running away from, but I felt this terror that if I ever stopped moving, if I ever stopped doing, if I ever stopped pushing myself, something would get me. Now it's clear that something was incest."

Part of her healing has been through the process of writing *The Courage to Heal*, in which she and her coauthor, Ellen Bass, outline the steps to recovery from sexual abuse. Another part has been her willingness to share her story and inspire others with her experience and knowledge. She tells survivors at her "Courage to Heal" workshops that if they stop and face the incest, healing is possible.

"Today there is no shadow chasing me. It is an incredibly liberated feeling. When people ask me why it is worth it to heal, one of the main things I say is that I don't have that feeling of dread anymore. I just feel I am who I am, and now all I want to do is be a regular person. I don't need that negative 'specialness' that I carried for so many years."

Laura was born in Long Branch, New Jersey, in 1956. She was a survivor from the start. Now five foot ten inches, Laura was born two months premature, weighing two pounds twelve ounces. "I had an uphill battle at birth. I have an older brother, but my mother had had two miscarriages before I was born. She was rushed to the hospital early and was convinced that she was going to lose yet another baby. After I was born, the doctor said, 'Hold on, Mrs. Davis, there's another one coming,' and then she gave birth to my identical twin sister, Vicky, who died twenty-four hours later. I was in isolation for six weeks, fed through a tube in my nose, and never touched except by the rubber-gloved hands of the nurses. The doctors said if I lived, it would mean I was a real survivor. Afterward, there was this message that I was the strong one. 'You're strong, you can survive anything, and you can get through anything.' Also, being Jewish, I was raised on stories about the Holocaust. I was told, 'We are survivors and we are strong.' This message was imprinted on me from the beginning."

Being born a twin has greatly affected her, Laura says. "It has to do with the way I am intimate with people and the way I bond with people. It has to do with my friendships. I have formed very close friendships with women my whole life, and I've always been drawn to people who are very similar to me. In recent years I've started to say to people that I *am* a twin instead of I *had* a twin, because when I talk to twins I identify so strongly with their way of being in the world.

"My family was interesting. It was a middle-class family with working-class values. My parents saved money. They never bought anything on credit. My mother was very frugal. I rarely had new clothes. I was always being dragged to discount houses and factory stores.

"The best thing about my childhood was that I had tremendous creative stimulation. My father was a music teacher. My mother was an actress. There was a piano in our living room, and under the piano was every musical instrument that you could possibly play.

"I hung out backstage at the community theater. My father built sets and my mother acted. I got to climb on the ladders, paint the sets, and play in the costume closets. My father also did a lot of artwork. He would wake me up at two o'clock in the morning and we would go downstairs and silkscreen in the basement, listening to news about the Vietnam War on WBAI, the Pacifica station in New York.

"I wrote my first short story when I was seven years old. I was always encouraged to write. My creativity was encouraged in many, many ways. I think today that is my greatest asset. I feel very lucky that I have an easy creativity and am very disciplined, which I think is an unusual combination. I have wild, crazy, funny, off-the-wall ideas, a well-developed sense of intuition, and I know how to use them.

"My intellect was stimulated at home. Education is very important in Jewish families. We got together for family court to discuss certain issues, like when I should be allowed to get my ears pierced. I think my ability to articulate and to assert myself came from that.

"My family was very political. I remember when John Kennedy was killed. I was in second grade. My whole family dropped everything and we went to the funeral in Washington, D.C. While Martin Luther King was alive, my parents took me to all the marches on Washington.

"I think the Jewish religion is oriented toward social action, political change, and work in the community. My father, particularly, was a real radical. He used to subscribe to *Ramparts* magazine, and I was reading it at ages nine and ten.

"We did a lot of camping as a family and took summer-long trips together. My father was a schoolteacher then and had summers off. So, on one hand, there actually was this very idyllic family life, which is all I remembered until my late twenties. But at the same time that this 'idyllic life' was going on, I would visit my mother's father in New York. We would go there once a month, and my grandfather would put me to bed and tell me stories. His stories soon turned to fondling. He started sexually abusing me when I was three years old. They were Orthodox Jews so the lights were always on during Shabbat. While he touched me, I would pretend to disappear into the light on the wall. When he was done with me, he would pay me off with Lifesavers. I never told anyone about it. As time went on his assaults got more violent. The last incident I remember was when I was ten and he raped me.

"My family, for the most part, believes I made this up. Yet my grandfather had a tradition where he would inspect the breasts of every pubescent girl. I had a big family. This started with my mother and all her sisters and all my girl cousins. When a girl hit puberty, he would ask her to undress so he could see and touch her breasts. This was seen as 'just Papa's thing, ha ha, isn't it funny,' and everyone joked about it. Twenty years later, the same people turned to me and said, 'He *couldn't* have molested you. How dare you make such a heinous accusation?' They didn't want his image tarnished. He had the reputation of being this incredible immigrant patriarch of the family, but I remember him as a frightening and brutal man."

Part of the way Laura coped with the abuse was by becoming a superachiever. "Growing up, I felt that just being a person wasn't enough. I was loved for what I did, for my achievements and accomplishments. I excelled at school. I always got *A*'s, and from the time I was a young child I was an overachiever. I was a swimmer. I used to race and I had a room full of trophies. I always felt that I had to be the best. Now, knowing what I know, I think I was trying to make up for the bad feeling that I had about what was happening with my grandfather."

Dramatic changes took place when Laura was fourteen. Her brother left for the University of Colorado, and her father went to a month-long seminar at Esalen Institute in Big Sur, California. When Laura returned from a summer canoeing trip for teenagers, there was a letter waiting for her from her father. It said, "I am not coming back."

"I handed the letter to my best friend, Mindy, and she started to cry. Here my father was abandoning me and I never shed a tear. He said he loved me; that was all I cared about. I must have already cut off my feelings, because I decided never to show anyone that this hurt me. I was the total stoic. I bragged about the fact that I had this hip, groovy father who lived in California, this hippie dad who I could visit.

"Of course, I vented all my rage on my mother. I blamed her for everything, even though he was the one who walked out. She was the one who was disciplining me and making the rules. When I visited him, we would have all kinds of fun adventures. I was there when my father took acid for the first time. We smoked pot together. He took me to see gurus. We did all these things that for a fifteen-year-old girl were just fantastic.

"Meanwhile, my adolescence with my mother was horrible. I hated her because she was crying all the time and falling apart. I felt that she was weak. She began drinking when my father left. Now when I think about it, I realize what she was trying to cope with. She was the only woman of her generation, in her crowd, to get divorced, and my father left all his affairs in total disarray for her to deal with. But at the

Ruldolf Steiner. After living in the ashram, she wanted nothing to do with a spiritual philosophy.

She returned to Denver to discover that Nona had fallen in love with a man from California and had moved to Mendocino. Disappointed but not knowing what else to do, she moved into Nona's old house and started working at a restaurant down the street.

"I remember at that point I had my first panic attack. I called Nona and told her I was going to realize God, die, or commit suicide. She told me to breathe. It was the best advice I ever received. Nona was worried about me. She invited me to California to live with her, and I went. She was living with the man she is married to today. Things between us got really bad. I was so jealous because I was really in love with her, although I was so oblivious.

"I consider those my lost years. I mean I had no sense of any of my inner feelings or motives. I wouldn't have known a feeling if I had fallen over one. I was always a victim, in every circumstance, and I felt like life was horrible to me. Yet I had some spirit that kept me going. I guess I always had a feeling there was something I was meant to do.

"Nona and I started battling. When she and Lee got married I couldn't handle it. I decided that I had to make the break with her, so I moved to Santa Cruz. Very soon after that she and I got together for breakfast. Over waffles at a cafe in Mendocino, she just looked at me and said, 'Laura, why don't you come out as a lesbian? You have always been in love with me, and I think you should just face it and come out.' I had tears streaming down my face. It was an incredible moment of recognizing who I was. It made everything in my whole life make sense, all the terrible relationships I had had with men, all of it. Those were the first tears I had shed since I was a little girl. I went back to Santa Cruz and went through a coming-out process.

"I was twenty-three. My life started to come together because I was no longer suppressing something so vital about who I was. I got involved in meaningful work for the first time. I worked as a counselor's aide at a counseling center. I started writing for the women's newspaper in Santa Cruz. I got on the radio. I had my own radio show in Santa Cruz and I really blossomed. Nona and I remained friends during this period.

We got trained by Hogie Wyckoff, one of the founders of Radical Therapy, which was a form of people's therapy. We were trained to run groups, and I began running groups for women. I did that for a couple of years and found I had a knack for it. I was very good in groups. I was funny. I was always very intuitive and very sharp and able to cut through to the core of whatever the issue was. I always came up with creative solutions for people. From the time I was quite young, I have always been a catalyst for change in others.

"Santa Cruz was my haven. My closest friends now are friends from that period of time. I started to have relationships that meant something, where I wasn't being abused and I wasn't being victimized, where I really loved someone and they really loved me."

Laura also had a reconciliation with her father at this time. She'd spent several years furious at him for abandoning her. But during a heart-to-heart talk he apologized, saying, "I never realized how much it would affect your life." She forgave him, and they began to build a relationship as adults. "He has always been accepting of me and my choices. When I told my father I was a lesbian, he said, 'Well, I think in some ways it will make your life harder, but whatever you want to do, I love you and I will support you.'

"As I started feeling better about myself, I naturally stopped using drugs. Now I have a glass of wine or beer sometimes, but I stopped abusing alcohol. I stopped wanting to be wasted. I wanted to be *in* my life, not *out* of it. There is something in me that has always had a drive toward health and being whole. I think it's the part of me that got me out of the ashram and a lot of other bad situations. I think it is the result of the love and the good parts of my childhood."

After living in Santa Cruz for a few years, hustling to make ends meet in an area where that can be difficult, Laura decided it was time to have a *real* career. She chose to build on her experience in Santa Cruz and pursue a career in radio. She went to a community radio conference in Colorado and met some people from Alaska who had an opening for a reporter. Because radio communication plays a crucial role in Alaska, the company had plush stations with plush salaries. She was offered a job in Ketchikan, an island in southeast Alaska.

"There were twelve miles of road in one direction, fourteen miles of road in the other. It rained thirteen feet a year and it was a real redneck, working-class town. Life was on the waterfront. And here I was, this kind of sophisticated dyke from Santa Cruz who was used to living in a wonderful, idealized lesbian community. At first I thought I couldn't do it, but I loved the work and I could see that being a reporter there meant something. I would have responsibility. I'd get paid a grown-up salary. I would be able to do things that were meaningful.

"I lived there for two years, and it was the best job I'd ever had. I loved being a reporter, and at the end of the first year I stayed on and became the public affairs director. I had my own interview show every day for an hour. Whatever I wanted to do I could do. I gave out recipes, invited an astrologer on, had the mayor or a city councilman on to debate issues. I did a whole series on death and dying and a series on incest. This was years before I knew I was an incest survivor. I had free creative reign. I fell in love with a woman there and lived with her for two years. We had a positive relationship, but at the end of a couple years I knew I had to leave and return to California. Alaska was beautiful, and if I moved there today I probably would love it, but at twenty-five I was not ready to be that far away from my support system. I was still very dependent on people mirroring back to me who I was. There were very few Jews and very few lesbians, and let's face it, it was an island where it rained thirteen feet a year. There was very little outside stimulation. We got television programs a week late, the Christmas shows on New Year's Day. Now that's depressing. There were ten thousand people in this town, and it was like the fourth-largest city in Alaska! I'm a real culture junkie—I love popular culture. I subscribe to *People* magazine and I read it every week, and I love living in San Francisco because I feel I am at the edge of popular culture. It's something that really feeds me.

"Also, when I lived in Santa Cruz I had made a home for the first time in my life, and it was important to me to be with people I loved. I am a strongly family-oriented person. If I don't have that as a base, I really can't do anything else."

With the money she saved in Alaska, Laura returned to Santa Cruz. A short time later, wanting more diversity and better economic opportunities, she moved to San Francisco. She struggled with unemployment, wrote television news, and had

various short-term media jobs, eventually landing a job at
Youth News. For three years she trained teenagers in radio
production and produced a show called "Youth on the Air." It
was a fun job and she enjoyed being a teacher. Again she
found herself producing shows on incest and abuse for young
people.

"I worked at that job, lived in the city, and got involved
in a relationship with a woman named Wendy. It was my first
serious relationship. Although I had been in love with this
woman in Alaska, I knew that she was going to stay there and
I was going to leave. When I fell in love with Wendy, I really
felt like this was it. We were planning a family and we were
going to live together.

"After about a year in that relationship, I found that the
closer we got emotionally the harder it was for me to make
love. I started to get more and more shut down. I had always
been spaced out when I made love, but I didn't know that that
was unusual. Wendy got really freaked out by this.

"One Sunday morning we were in my bed and started
making love. Suddenly I found myself thinking about breakfast. I was going to make waffles, and yes, there were these
leftover baked potatoes, and they would make wonderful home
fries. I was no longer there. We hadn't made love in a long
time, and it was a big deal that we were going to do it. Suddenly I wasn't able to be there. She had been very patient for
many months, but at that point she just lost it and started to
yell and scream at me: 'What happens to you? Where do you
go? What's the matter with you anyway?' I got very quiet and I
started sobbing. This bubble of knowledge was coming up from
deep inside. At that point she was holding me, stroking my
head and kissing me and asking, 'What's the matter?' I said in
a tiny child's voice, 'I was molested.' I didn't know it was true
until I said it, but as soon as I said it, I knew it was true.
That was the beginning, six years ago.

"When I realized what had happened to me, I was thrown
into a total crisis. I had wanted to make love before, and now
I couldn't stand to be touched. My body felt like foam rubber.
I couldn't concentrate on anything else. I couldn't concentrate
on work. Wendy and I started fighting all the time, and after
six months she broke up with me. I was just desperate. I felt
suicidal. I was obsessed. I thought about incest twenty-four
hours a day. It was horrible. I was having flashbacks all the

time. At first I didn't know who it was that had abused me, but then I started to fill in the pieces and realized it was my grandfather.

"I naively called my mother to tell her about this, thinking that now I would finally get the support I had never had when the abuse took place. I told her what her father had done to me. Her initial response was very sympathetic, but within twenty-four hours she called up, at four in the morning, screaming on the phone, 'How could you do this to me?' She said I was destroying her life, that I couldn't have hurt her more if I had shot her, and that it was just because I was a lesbian. I just hated men and wanted revenge. She turned on me completely. That was the beginning of a very painful period of estrangement from everyone on her side of the family.

"I wrote letters to most of the people in my family. I wrote to a lot of my cousins. I wanted to find out if it had happened to them. I got back incredibly hostile responses. There are many people I have never spoken to since. I am no longer invited to family gatherings. I wasn't prepared for the denial and rejection. I wouldn't advise people to do what I did without preparing ahead of time. I was not prepared to handle it. I had always felt that I was close to my family, and I expected their support. I was tarnishing the image of the family patriarch."

Laura had wonderful memories of her idyllic childhood— the camping, the creativity, the political marches; and yet there had also been the forgotten childhood—the fear and victimization of the incest survivor.

"It was horrible trying to integrate the two. I couldn't for a long time. I thought, If this could have happened and I could have forgotten it so completely, how could anything else in my life be real?" Laura got herself into therapy. She went to an incest writing workshop and joined a survivor's group.

"I have always been oriented toward books, so I went to my local women's bookstore and started reading everything I could about incest and sexual abuse. There were books like Ellen Bass's *I Never Told Anyone* and first-person accounts of survivors. There were books like Sandra Butler's *Conspiracy of Silence: The Trauma of Incest* which talked about this as a political problem. The message I got from reading those books was twofold. First, that I wasn't alone, and second, that yes, my life was ruined. But I wanted to know what I could do

about it. I was twenty-seven years old. I needed more help
than those books offered me.

"Also, at that time, I was trying to decide what to do ca-
reerwise. I called a meeting of twelve friends. I wanted to
have a brainstorming session on what to do about Laura's career. I made lunch for everyone; then I got up and talked
about my skills, the kind of environment I wanted to work in,
and how much money I wanted to make. I had a questionnaire
that they filled out about me, how long they had known me,
what they thought were my greatest skills and my weaknesses,
and what kind of fantasy job they could imagine me doing.
Some people thought I should run for President; someone else
said I should write a book.

"Ellen Bass was one of the people I invited to that meeting. I met Ellen ten years ago. She had been my writing
teacher years before she started doing incest work. She knew I
was a good writer. At the end of the meeting I went up to her
and said, 'Would you like to collaborate on a book about healing from child sexual abuse?' She said, 'No, absolutely not.'
She had written five books and knew how much work was involved. I persisted and asked her to reconsider. We sat down
and finally worked out a deal, and she said yes. In fact, in my
office, I have the card she sent me. It has balloons on the
front, and when it opens up, all it says on the inside is a single word: *Yes.* That is still on my wall because it was a real
turning point for me.

"The two of us started to collaborate. My job the first
year was to do all the interviews. During the first year of
working on the book I was still in the "emergency stage" of
healing myself. It was fabulous because during the interviews,
I could ask any personal question I wanted an answer to. I
would be struggling with sex and the woman I was interviewing
would tell me what she did with her partner in bed, and then
I would ask, 'Then what did you do? And what did your partner do? And then what happened?' I cried through many of
those interviews. I chose people who had had five or ten years
of healing under their belts, who felt good about themselves.
They had really gone through the process, so the interviews
were very cathartic and healing for me. That is where I got my
role models and inspiration. That is where I started to have
hope that I could heal myself.

"After about the first year and a half, I started to feel

more resolved about my own abuse. I started to feel more like a journalist on a project than a survivor desperate for answers. After my experience in the ashram, I am cynical about a lot of new-age thinking, but I do believe that I was meant to write *The Courage to Heal*. I was driven to do it. I felt compelled. This book had to be out in the world, and I was meant to write it.

"Ellen and I worked very closely for three and a half years and actually wrote the book together. We brainstormed about what should be in a particular chapter. One of us would write the first draft and then we would switch, and the other person would write the second draft. I mean, I can't tell who wrote what sentences. It is a true collaboration.

"Writing the book was a key part of my healing. Doing it was a real act of fighting back and not being a victim. It was a totally empowering experience. Ellen was a mentor to me in many ways. She knew how to get a book published. She had that experience under her belt.

"Our book was the first to show that it is possible to heal. Instead of just speaking out about the problem, we talked about how survivors can heal and reclaim their power. We wrote about how to take anger and channel it into changing the world. We described the recovery process without using any psychobabble, psychological jargon. We wrote the book for the layperson, in a warm, friendly voice. We wanted to say to our readers, 'We are going to take you by the hand and walk you through this process. You are going to meet hundreds of other people who have gone through it, and you'll hear their words of encouragement. We are not going to minimize the pain. We are going to present realistically what it takes to heal.'

"I think it is radical to tell the truth. The other thing about the book is that we treated lesbian relationships as if they were just like any others. We wanted to broaden society's acceptance of gay people. Ellen and I had a long discussion about whether we were going to come out as lesbians in the book. We decided that, politically, it was *something we wanted to do*. Lesbians are at the forefront of so many of the movements against violence in this country, yet they are usually invisible. We wanted to be visible."

More difficult for Laura was admitting publicly that she is an incest survivor. "I knew that I was going to use my name

and my picture, that this was going to be my thing in the
world, but I had to deal with the fact that I was potentially
going to be disowned. I didn't care about how the world reacted to the book; I cared about my family. I had to get to the
point where I could live with their reaction, whatever it was. If
they never talked to me again, if they wrote me furious letters,
if I was disinherited, or if they felt I had ruined their lives, I
would have to live with that. Using a pseudonym was ridiculous because the whole point of healing from incest is breaking
the secrecy."

What Laura is dealing with now is the huge impact her
book has had on the public. *The Courage to Heal*, published
in 1988, sold over one hundred thousand copies in its first
eight months. She suddenly became a best-selling author and
was deluged with requests for media interviews, workshops,
and lectures. "It has been hard adjusting to people treating me
as though I have all the answers and am somehow better than
they are. I had a guru, and I don't want to be anyone's guru. I
think it is very seductive having people idolize you. We get
letters all the time from people saying 'You saved my life. I
was going to kill myself. I read your book and I didn't kill
myself. Your book has totally transformed my life. It's my bible.'

"I have also experienced people unleashing their painful
feelings on me because they feel safe with me. If I absorbed
the pain from every person I talked to and every story I read,
I would not be able to get up in the morning. I not only want
to get up in the morning, but I want to get up joyously. I want
to be able to leave a workshop and go out to dinner, not just
go home and collapse.

"It is too easy for me to absorb people's feelings. I have
had to get very good at creating boundaries while doing this
work. Otherwise, I would never make it. One of my favorite
words now is *no*, which is something that I certainly never had
a chance to say as a child.

"I am still trying to learn techniques to release other people's energy and to stop absorbing other people's stories. The
more I work on my own healing, the less my own memories
are restimulated by other people. I meditate sometimes, I nurture myself, and I don't expect much of myself after I do a
workshop. I know that it takes a lot out of me, and I give myself a few days to recover. I am learning to take a lot of

breaks. I can't do this work all the time—I have to pace myself."

Laura is leading nationwide trainings and workshops for professionals, survivors, and partners of survivors. "I hear a lot of horror stories about therapists who have sexually abused survivors, who have told them not to have any feelings, who have told them to hurry up and forgive and get over it. When I do a training for professionals and I ask, 'How many people here have ever had a class on dealing with child sexual abuse?' very few people raise their hands. Psychologists, psychiatrists, and social workers need this training. I would like to see *The Courage to Heal* used as a textbook across the country. I would like to see it used at the training level.

"I do small workshops with survivors, and I have started to do larger educational programs, like a one-day workshop for eighty people. I do a lot of lecturing, and I have also done work with partners. I am not a therapist but an educator. As an educator I can come out and tell my own story. It's valuable for people to be able to talk to someone who is farther along in the process of healing, and to get straight answers.

"Right now I am finishing *The Courage to Heal Workbook*, which I wrote on my own. The next thing I would like to work on is a book that looks at the connection between pregnancy, childbirth, and child sexual abuse. I am collecting articles and stories for that. Having put something like *The Courage to Heal* out into the world at such a young age, I feel like I did what I was supposed to do. Besides the workbook I've considered other projects, but they no longer have the urgency that the first book had."

The Courage to Heal Workbook reflects Laura's continual evolution and change. There are divergences in some of the ways she sees things and new material and new stories that are exciting to her.

"I am learning all the time. One of the things I have thought a lot more about is the value of coping mechanisms. When I first started to heal, my attitude was that I wouldn't deny anything. I wanted to eradicate any shred of these coping mechanisms, and as a result, I left myself totally defenseless. What I have learned since is that sometimes those coping mechanisms are pretty good. They have their helpful side. It is okay to use them sometimes. I don't have to be totally vigilant about everything at every moment. Another thing has changed:

now when people ask me how far along they are in the healing process, I ask them how well they are taking care of themselves. I don't say, 'Have you confronted your abuser?' or 'Have you gotten enraged?' I don't say, 'Are you in touch with your memories?' I ask, 'How well do you take care of yourself?' To me, how people nurture themselves and pace themselves is a real indicator of how far along they are in the healing process.

"I call my workshop 'Courage to Heal,' and what I am trying to do is teach people skills for the lifetime process of healing. I am trying to teach people to be more gentle about it, that you have to persist and work hard, but you also have to find ways to enjoy life. The two go hand in hand. It is not like you heal so that then you can live. You heal and you live; they go together. In the beginning you are often in a period of real crisis, where healing is all you are doing and you can't think about anything else, but after that initial period, survivors can strive to have some balance.

"I think I'm always going to be a working person. A lot of my self-esteem derives from the work I do. In a lot of ways I feel that this work is just beginning for me. Everything I do opens up to something else. It is not that I have a plan. I have certain values that I work with and things I really value that I won't compromise. I have a strong sense of personal ethics, but I am not sure where it will take me or what is going to be next.

"But while I love the work I do, by itself it is not enough. I have no aspirations to spend my life as a workaholic. There are other very valuable parts of life, and there is healing I need to do through having a family of my own. I would like to have a child, maybe two. I would like to be in a long-term partnership with a woman. I'd like my own home.

"Now I can start to live like a regular person. I feel other people had that privilege from childhood. I am thirty-two years old and just starting to feel like I can have the same things that other people can have. I can have happiness, love, and a home. I can have some stability. Now the challenge in my life is going to be how I can have my own ordinary life while I am doing extraordinary things. The more ordinary moments I can experience now, the better.

"I am single right now. I live with a couple and their

daughter who are my family. We have holidays together and we eat dinner together. As I said, I am a communally oriented person, and I much prefer living with people to living alone."

"My friends have been great. I couldn't do what I'm doing if I didn't come home to people who were telling me, 'Laura, wash your damn dishes.' They treat me the same and at the same time are very proud of me. They are encouraging and have provided a safe, secure grounding for me. Coming from an incest family and being a lesbian make friends more than just friends. They *are* my family. They take care of me when I am down. They support me when I am feeling shaky or when I am feeling I can't possibly do this thing that just got offered to me. They calm me down and tell me I can do it. They are the ones who have really helped me through the changes.

"I have my own sense of spirituality. After living in the ashram for four years, I have such a reaction against anything spiritual. I hate New Age everything. I have become very much an individual after that experience of being part of a religious group. Culturally, I have a strong identity as a Jew, and I celebrate Jewish holidays.

"I really live in the moment. I take a lot of pleasure in very simple things, like playing with the little girl I live with, cooking a beautiful meal, having an intimate conversation with a friend, or eating an ice cream cone. To me, spirituality is taking a bath while reading *People* magazine.

"If I don't get a certain amount of time alone, I start to feel hungry for it. I need solitude. I try to foster the attitude of enjoying the simple pleasures in my life. That is what I would say my spirituality is. I do have a sense my spirituality is growing. I used to feel that nothing would work out for me. I used to feel that I was never going to fall in love. I was sure that something bad was going to happen to me. This was connected to being a survivor. Over time I feel that I am developing a sense that things can work out for me. I am gaining patience, which is something I have been sorely lacking in my life. It is more a sense of just letting things unfold; I don't have to force things as much as I used to. I think part of having a major accomplishment is that I can relax. Writing, to me, is a spiritual thing. A way of getting in touch with myself."

When Laura is at home, she wakes up when she wakes up. She makes herself a cup of tea and, still dressed in her pajamas, heads for the computer. She writes till noon, then makes herself something to eat. She works another few hours, showers, dresses, and goes out.

"I'm disciplined. I do tend to work Monday through Friday. If I want to go to a matinee one afternoon, I do that too, because I know that I am a disciplined person. I always come back to my work, and when I take a few days off I miss working. I miss that feeling of thinking and developing things."

Laura says working at home has the disadvantage of isolation, and she sometimes misses working with someone. "When Ellen and I did the first book, we both really cared about it. I miss having a coworker, and I miss having someone who really cares as much as I do. It's like being a single parent. No one cares as much when the baby's first tooth comes in. I am also traveling a lot, which I find hard to adjust to because I am a real homebody. I have been developing skills for coping with the isolation, but it is not really my preferred lifestyle.

"I love to play. I am an avid Scrabble player. I play anything—Yahtzee, poker, pinochle, Scrabble. I see a lot of movies. I like the outdoors, so I go camping and to the country. Because I travel so often, I don't seem to want to go on vacations. I just want to be at home. I like simple things. I have a lot of friends with kids, so I spend a lot of time with children and reading. This week I was working with my friend, Nancy, making a book for the little girl I live with who is having her fourth birthday. It's called 'Travels with Ruby.' I went through all the photographs that were taken of Ruby over the last couple of years and picked out my favorites. Nancy and I made a storyboard to go with it. We copied the photos; I wrote the story and Nancy did the design. It's Ruby's first reader. It reads, 'See Ruby run,' 'See Ruby swim,' 'Ruby goes to sleep.' To me, making that book meant just as much as writing this workbook which may reach a hundred thousand people. To me they are equally valid ways to use my creativity and my energy."

Because of her own healing, Laura experiences a considerable amount of satisfaction today. Living in the moment and her times of simplicity and doing ordinary things are important to her. She says she has bad moments, and anyone who says they don't is a liar. She tends toward depression rather than anxiety.

"I think the most difficult things are when I feel my life

isn't balanced enough, when there is too much work and not enough personal satisfaction. For instance, I've had bad moments over breakups and my father's recent illness. He has had two heart attacks and a mini-stroke within the last six months.

"The main way the incest still affects me is that I have a very hard time dealing with loss. If a relationship ends or I think of my father dying, I have a hard time dealing with that and I can get depressed. I get cranky sometimes, but I think I am really a pretty good person to be around. After living around people so much of my life, I am pretty attuned to other people's needs.

"I don't think I'll ever be through healing. I will always be an incest survivor, and I will always have an Achilles heel. When people ask me, 'Are you healed?' I say, 'Now I'm a normal neurotic just like everyone else.' I don't feel like a damaged person anymore. I have gone through a radical metamorphosis. I mean, I am not just teaching something—I have lived it. My life, to me, shows radical change. I am still the same person I was, but I have healed a lot of the damage. I spent many years feeling it was hopeless, that I couldn't change the sense of despair or the self-destructive patterns, but I have changed. I really feel like a different person.

"Although tremendous opportunity has come to me from doing this work, I would trade all the opportunity and recognition I've gotten for my grandfather not to have spoiled me. I feel good about where I am, but it has been an incredible battle. It was a violent crime, and I lost years of my life because of it. It certainly made me a more compassionate person, but I would never say it was a good experience; I don't care what has come from it. What it tells me is I am the kind of person who makes the best of things. I get really furious with people who say we choose things because we need to grow. That's bullshit! I did not choose to be sexually abused. I did not choose to be raped. I did not choose to have someone put a knife at my throat and threaten to kill me. If I had a choice, none of those things would have happened to me. I would have found a way to be happy and to get to the place where I am by doing something else—without having to be traumatized and work through all that pain. I would rather have made an opportunity out of a good thing than out of a devastation.

"Sexual abuse underscores so many of the problems in

this society. People have eating disorders and there is alcoholism and drug addiction and violence. When you scratch beneath the surface, you often find a history of child sexual abuse. It is a core problem in this society. Until it is addressed openly, until it is considered a violent crime unilaterally throughout the court system, things are not going to change. This has to change at the root of society. Things are not going to change until everybody starts healing.

"Doing this work has changed my political perspective as well. *The Courage to Heal* was written for women, and yet I've chosen to write the workbook for women and men because I see myself as a bridge builder. When I do workshops, I have women of all sexual preferences. Sometimes the heterosexual women are horrified when they find out there are lesbians there, but by the end of the weekend, the common ground of what we are dealing with is so strong that there are alliances built that weren't there before. I am interested now in building those same alliances with male survivors, because I have had so many men at my workshops or my lectures or who've read the book say, 'I don't feel I belong here because it's for women.' There are many men out there who are also suffering from sexual abuse who are not offenders, who are going through the same thing.

"I don't think the goal of healing is just to have a personal solution. For me the work I have done in therapy and the work I have done to heal myself have gone totally hand in hand with the activism I practice in the world. I encourage survivors to go out in the world and do something about it. I don't encourage them to do that at the beginning of the process because your attention needs to be on yourself then. If you go out before you are ready and try to tilt at windmills and save the world, you are repeating a pattern of caretaking others, instead of taking care of yourself. But once you have a certain solidity in healing behind you, I think the only way the world is going to change is if survivors turn things around. They are the ones who have the compassion and the understanding of suffering. They can make changes in the world, fight to change the laws, and do all the things necessary to help bring this to an end.

"I think that survivors rising up together can be an incredibly powerful force to change things. If people who have healed just go back into their little lives, we are not going to have an impact. I encourage people to do something with their healing. If it is not on this issue, pick some other issue that you feel particularly strong about, but take action in the world. Give something back."

PERSONAL TRUTHS

1. Don't run away from remembering and dealing with the abuse. Until you face the abuse and deal with it, it will underlie all other problems in your life. It is possible to get to the root of it and heal. Take the risk.

2. It is worth taking the leap for something you have always wanted to do because until you try you'll never know. Through the experiences I have had and the risks I have taken, I have gained courage and confidence. I didn't start with the courage and confidence. I started with the risk.

3. Every moment is really precious. I want to enjoy my life in the present as much as I can. I spent most of my life living for the future, thinking that someday things would change, someday things would be better. Now I want today to be a good day and this moment to be a good moment.

LAURA DAVIS
Author of

The Courage to Heal Workbook. New York: Harper & Row. To be released in 1990.

The Courage to Heal: A Guide for Women Survivors of Child Sexual Abuse. Coauthored with Ellen Bass. New York: Harper & Row, 1988.

Terry Cole-Whittaker

Terry Cole-Whittaker *is a nationally acclaimed speaker and spiritual counselor. She is the author of* How to Have More in a Have-Not World, What You Think of Me Is None of My Business, The Inner Path from Where You Are to Where You Want to Be, *and* Love and Power in a World without Limits: A Woman's Guide to the Goddess Within.

As an ordained minister in the Church of Religious Science since 1973, she is widely known for her eight-year television ministry based in southern California and her message that people can be beautiful, prosperous, and happy while advancing spiritually.

Since leaving the ministry in 1985, Terry has undergone a personal transformation that has caused her to let go of worldly ideals of success, money, and prestige to find what is important for her. She founded "Adventures in Enlightenment" in 1985 and has become increasingly in touch with the feminine within herself. She teaches that the resurgence of feminine energy is vital to restoring balance within individuals and to the planet.

The first time I met Terry Cole-Whittaker was on the island of Maui. She was giving "Adventures in Enlightenment" workshops while I was assisting Shakti Gawain at a six-week intensive course, and cowriting Living in the Light.

I was already familiar with her work. Several of my friends had read Terry's books, and my friend Constance had studied with her in California. She used to quote Terry so often ("Terry Cole says you can have what you want. . . . Terry Cole says imagine the best for yourself. . . .") that I nicknamed her "Cole-Constance." I had also read What You Think of Me Is None of My Business *and had seen Terry on television several times. Her vibrancy and willingness to say what she thought inspired me. I also knew that she had recently given up her ministry and was living on Maui.*

Shakti was renting the place next to Terry's, and throughout the summer I could hear laughter and music coming from her hacienda. One rainy night several of us were invited over. I still remember the warm welcoming hug she gave me and the relaxed conversation we had sitting on her floor eating popcorn. Since then I've always had the feeling that she is someone interested in experiencing the joy of life. She has also stood out as a leader to me, an example of someone who said what she felt, even when I thought she was being too vulnerable and taking too great a risk. I'd always been afraid of offending people. She wasn't. When it came time to do this book, I naturally thought of her.

It wasn't until I told people that she was going to be in the book that I realized how negative the press had been at the end of her ministry. One of my closest friends, critical of the financial reversals that ended the ministry, couldn't believe that I would include her, someone whom the San Diego Tribune *called "the High Priestess of Yuppiedom." I quickly rose to her defense, saying that I liked her and would prefer to go on my gut feeling rather than on press coverage. Besides, he and I didn't have to approve of Terry's actions for her to be a leader. She took risks while a lot of us were afraid to be noticed.*

I spoke to her staff in Washington State and arranged to interview her at a hotel in Oakland. She had just come from a one-day workshop on balancing male and female energies. She looked much the same as the woman I had met three years before in Maui but younger (is that possible?) and happier. She told her story willingly and as if she had told it many times before.

Terry Cole-Whittaker was a leader right from the start. "I always thought my sisters were my staff members," she says. Those early management abilities thrived as she directed plays in the garage, circuses, talent shows, the construction of sand forts, and all manner of other projects. "I remember once we made bacon and eggs, burned them, and then charged our folks and the neighbors."

Terry Cole-Whittaker was born Terry Nam Reich on December 3, 1939, in Los Angeles General Hospital. She believes she "probably was a welfare baby."

She spent her first few years between woodsy Bishop, California, and urban Los Angeles. Then when her parents, Nam and Ted, were divorced, she remained in Bishop. It was a time of struggle for her mother, who had four girls to support and little money with which to do it. It was decided that Terry would live with her great-grandmother, Bertha Hall, at her resort in the Sierra Nevada.

"The Sierra Nevada was my playground, so I really lived in a mountain paradise. I was like a little princess. I had my own fishing pond. I rode horses. I had lots of love and attention, and my great-grandmother made all my clothes. I spent a lot of time in the mountains watching the deer, sitting by the stream fishing, climbing mountains, watching the sunrise and sunset."

Her world was expanded by the guests who came to stay at Bertha's resort. Life was a kaleidoscope of varying lifestyles and backgrounds lived through the people she met there. But at the center of this sampler of influence was her great-grandmother.

Bertha Hall was a metaphysician (which Terry would later become), but she never imposed her beliefs on Terry; in fact, she never talked much about them. "It wasn't so much what she said but how she lived her life. She had faith in herself, in an age when women really did not have a lot of power. She had been divorced when she was only seventeen or eighteen and supported herself and two children, which, at that time, was largely unheard of.

"Bertha was a liberated woman in her own time and an amazing human being. She earned her own living, took care of other family members, and ultimately married five times. After her arrival in California by covered wagon, she worked to integrate Piute Indian children with white children in the schools. She was a nurse, helped heal people during the big flu epidemic in the 1920s, and delivered babies. She was involved in Indian welfare work and was a member of the Federated Women's Club.

"She taught me how to work. Even as a kid I did my share. She expected that kind of thing."

When Terry was seven, her parents were remarried and the family was reunited in Newport Beach, California.

Terry recalls that they always had a lot of fun as a family, and that living near the beach was a joyous experience for her and a cherished time with her sisters.

"We did our chores, helped out, and really knew that we could contribute to our parents' lives. But at the same time we had a lot of freedom."

Terry's parents told her she could do whatever she wanted as long as she didn't get into trouble sexually. But for years she suffered from the guilt of the "good girl" stigma, she says.

"In high school I loved sports: swimming, diving, modern dance, and softball. One of my favorites was softball, where I played catcher. My least favorite was field hockey. Tennis interested me, and one time after a tennis game the boys were running by on the track. I wanted to impress them, so I went to jump over the net and caught my foot, fell down, and totally skinned up my knees. I was a real tomboy." She says that being a tomboy enticed her and helped her career because "it looked like it was the boys who had life by the tail." She longed to do, and be, more like them.

One of her first memories of her mother is of a hard-working woman overburdened by the stress of work and supporting four children. After the family was reunited, Terry always feared that if things got to be too much for her mother she would be sent away again. As a result, she always wanted to make life easier for her mother. This pattern of easing other people's burdens has continued throughout her life; in fact, the habit of rescuing others is one of the reasons she became a "savior." "If I save you, you will want to be with me. If I help you, you won't send me away."

While her parents were divorced, her mother waitressed to support them; then, when Terry's parents got back together, her mother was able to work less. Her father was a television repairman and a vacuum-cleaner salesman. "He had a wonderful salesman-type personality, really charming, and all my high school friends wanted to have my parents. They always said, 'God, your folks are so great.' We could curl Dad's hair; we could paint his toenails—he was just a good sport."

Terry also knew her father had wanderlust. "He didn't enjoy staying in one place. He didn't enjoy being a husband, but he enjoyed being a father. We always knew he loved us. He was pretty strict, in a sense, but open. After the last spanking I got at age nine, I decided never to get one again, so I didn't push my dad or my mom to the brink of frustration. But I think in some ways this kept me from expressing myself, because I didn't want to get hurt. One of my key issues in life for a long time was being afraid of expressing myself in the presence of authority figures. I would break out in a cold sweat with heart palpitations. I was afraid of being put down, judged, or hurt. It was very difficult for me as a new minister to stand up and speak in front of the other ministers. I finally got the freedom to express myself at the pulpit on Sunday because when I shared ideas, thoughts, and beliefs, it was okay. No one stood up and told me that it wasn't so."

Even though Terry affirms that her childhood was, for the most part, happy—that she had fun and felt loved—she says she can still relate to people with troubles because of certain things she felt and experienced while growing up.

Her father was prejudiced against almost anyone who was not German Anglo-Saxon Protestant, and she grew up imitating him. One of her trials in life has been to overcome prejudice of many kinds. Before leaving the ministry, she used to concern herself with the way people dressed, what they did for a living, what they looked like, and whether they believed as she did. Her own life experience has taught her to let go of such beliefs.

Witnessing the pain of her parents' relationship has also influenced her life. "For example, in my early years, I had the feeling that all men were going to be like my dad and that I was going to have a relationship like my mother and father's, or that my mom was a martyr in some ways and had to work really hard to support us. I began healing my relationship with my mother and father by really loving both of them and knowing that their life was their choice.

"I wish they had had a little more happiness with each other. They never fought, which is an interesting thing, but I knew that as years went on they weren't really happy. I was glad when they decided to divorce again so that my Mom could have a different life, and so my dad could be free to do what he wanted."

The summer after high school and before college was especially significant for Terry, for it was then, while staying with her great-grandmother, that she received her introduction to the concepts of metaphysics. As a rule Bertha spoke little about her beliefs, but this summer was different. Bertha's friend Violet, a Church of Religious Science practitioner[1] was visiting.

When Terry came home from her dates, she would find Bertha and Violet discussing metaphysics and would join in. "We talked religion all summer long. I finally found a way to think and believe that freed me, made sense to me, and answered my questions. It was something my intellect could relate to." She learned that what a person sees and believes for herself will come true: not only do you create your thoughts; you create your whole universe. It is done unto you as you believe.

One night the three of them, hearing that one of their neighbors was in distress, prayed for his health. Terry said she was filled with a wonderful feeling as she did this. When she awoke the next morning, the man was healed and she knew their prayers had worked.

Terry had not received any religious training before this. Her father was a German Lutheran who had felt imprisoned in church. "He didn't want to do that to us."

Terry quickly grasped the metaphysical principles that were being presented to her and began to apply them to her life. When she arrived at Orange Coast College in the fall, she began to affirm and believe that she could have what she wanted. She became freshman class president and homecoming queen.

At Orange Coast College she studied liberal arts—sports,

---

1. A practitioner is one who attempts to heal herself or others through affirmation of positive thought, beliefs, and the awareness of God in the person.

music, and theater—and met her first husband, John. "He was cute. He was a Korean War veteran who'd been stationed in Germany. He was adorable, dressed well, had a sweet smile, plus he really wanted to go out with me. He was very romantic. He left notes in my car and would find me out on a date and would sneak little messages to me. We started going out and then got married about three months later."

Within a year Terry had given birth to their daughter, Suzanne, the baby she had always wanted. "From the time I was three years old all I wanted was a child, so I just loved her. Being a mother was the most important thing to me." Besides enjoying motherhood, Terry continued her studies. She and her husband moved to Los Angeles, and she enrolled in the theater arts department at the University of Southern California. Terry performed in a couple of university musicals; she also auditioned for the Los Angeles Civic Light Opera workshop, conducted in conjunction with the University of Southern California's School of Performing Arts, and was one of twenty selected from throughout the United States. This was an important time for her. She enjoyed three months of daily acting, singing, and dancing with some of the best coaches in Los Angeles.

Following college Terry and John moved to La Canada, California, where Terry continued performing by joining the Skylarks, a women's theater group. She also joined the Burbank Civic Light Opera and played the lead in some of their musicals. But while she loved theater and her time with her daughter, she began to feel there was something missing in her marriage.

"Little by little I began to be more interested in my spiritual life because I was unhappy in my marriage. I loved John but felt very frustrated in our inability to communicate and to understand each other. He was not unkind, and yet, when I asked him what it was like being married to me, he said that I was very self-centered and righteous. We both had our own points of view.

"I was really looking for help and I was unhappy and depressed, so I began to seek help in the church. I went to a Religious Science church in La Cresenta, near Pasadena. The way the sermon made me feel was maybe the best I would feel all week." She began to rehear what she had learned from her great-grandmother: You create your own thoughts and therefore

your life. . . . You can have what you believe you can
have. . . . All things are possible.

"I started taking classes and reading books. Reverend
Guy Lorraine was a wonderful teacher and really made religious science exciting and interesting. I felt these wonderful
feelings, and I would go home and try to practice it. But it
was like the beginning of anything—it sounds good, but the
application is another thing. Yet little by little I started awakening myself."

Terry's teaching career was launched in 1964 when she
began teaching Sunday school. She had wanted to attend
church more often with her daughter, Suzanne, so she decided
the easiest way to do this was to teach the class herself. She
quickly realized that to keep her students interested she had to
keep things simple. To teach it she had to understand it.

It was this commitment to Sunday school that gave her
the opportunity for growth. Teaching required that she read,
study, prepare, and draw on her own experience. So that's
what she did. Since then her journey and her spiritual path
have provided one opportunity after another: "I don't think I've
had one big revelation, yet in ways I have had many big revelations." She says each step prepared her for the next.

Part of what she was preparing herself for was to leave
her first husband. Up to this point she had felt that her husband was her caretaker, so she had not equipped herself to
enter the job market.

"I loved being a mother. I loved babies and children. I
thought being a wife was what you did, so when my marriage
wasn't happy and when it looked like I had to start taking care
of myself and my daughter, it was a shock. It was a real
shock, just as I know a lot of women have experienced." Even
though she grew up in a matriarchal world where the women
worked, Terry says, she still had learned that her goal was to
be married.

To prepare herself for the changes ahead of her, Terry began using the metaphysical principles she was learning to raise
her self-esteem. As her self-esteem rose, her courage to express herself developed. She decided to start singing again, so
she and a girlfriend who played the piano started doing shows
for women's groups and churches.

Then one day Terry heard about the Mrs. America contest
and sent away for an application. She forged her husband's

signature on the application form and entered the contest. She became a finalist and was flown to what seemed like a faraway city—Concord, California. Applying the principles of Science of Mind to the goal in front of her, she saw herself winning, felt it, and believed in herself. She affirmed to herself, "I am a winner. I am somebody." She was named Mrs. California and went on to be third runner-up in the Mrs. America contest.

For the cooking event she had invented a pancake recipe that interested the Aunt Jemima people and as a result was chosen to be Mrs. Pancake of America. In the course of traveling for nine weeks in twenty-six major cities, she discovered that she loved television, interviews, glamour, and excitement.

"It was fun because I got what I wanted, and I was using visualizations, affirmations, and emotional creation. I wanted to travel; I wanted to do something to help my career, whatever it was. It was one of the first times I actually was conscious that I created something for myself. That infuriated my husband because he was losing control. I was breaking away from the old standard." With these changes Terry and her husband decided to separate.

Terry says that the week they separated was the same week she met her second husband. "The object was that I move from one relationship into another. The relationship that I moved into was basically to have someone take care of me, support me financially, and take care of my children. I am really glad that happened because I got to stay home with my kids and continue going to school." She had her second daughter, Rebecca, in this marriage.

Terry continued her Church of Religious Science studies and became a practitioner. Then, recognizing her natural ability to communicate, she knew her next step was to become a minister.

She felt happy and satisfied in this work. Upon completing her ministerial training, she was offered an assistant ministry in Guy Lorraine's La Cresenta church. She loved ministering and learned that when you offer the world your best gift, the world will always want more.

She worked as assistant minister from 1973 to 1975 but knew the position could not last forever. "He fired me and said, 'This fish pond is too small for the both of us, so one of us has got to leave and it's not going to be me.' And that was good, because at different times in my life when I lacked the courage to move on, I have either been fired or created a condition where it really looked like change was the only choice I had."

At that point Terry was offered her own Church of Religious Science in La Jolla, California. The church was on the brink of closing. There were fifty people in the congregation, and a lot of them slept through the sermons. The church decided to take a chance on Terry.

"The whole thing blew wide open the first Sunday I was there. It took me by surprise—every Sunday more people came."

Even though success was drawn to her, Terry found it difficult to accept. At first she did not trust that she could continue to express her feelings and beliefs and that people would continue to come. "I had a total fear of loss of love."

The more successful she became, the more frightened she became of losing love and acceptance. Her insecurities drove her to seek alternative ways to heal herself. She attended Werner Erhard's EST program, which, she says, helped her feel her feelings. "I pretended I was happy when, in a lot of ways, I was miserable. I realized I wasn't real in many ways and that I wasn't feeling what I was feeling. So that led me on a new journey." She learned through EST that feelings are not good or bad or right or wrong; they just are. She began to feel more, opening a floodgate of repressed emotions.

She brought what she was learning back to her church services. "I was growing in the presence of everyone."

She taught the principles of Ernest Holmes and Religious Science but also expanded her services based on the new information she was learning. "Not only had I been open to the EST training; I had begun structural integration of body change through Rolfing and was interested in nutrition, meditation, and exercise. I was open to other philosophies. In some sense I was a rebel, and my teaching techniques went beyond lecturing. I used more experiential kinds of teaching techniques than were standard." But her basic message that people can have and deserve to have what they want remained constant.

As she and her congregation grew, independence started to seem possible. She left her second husband and moved in with a roommate in La Jolla. Her older daughter stayed in La

Canada to finish her senior year in high school, and her younger daughter, Rebecca, stayed with her father for a few months before following Terry to La Jolla.

"Basically, I stopped being a mother and a wife, to a large extent, and became a career person. I was in this beautiful place, La Jolla. All of a sudden I was living a life of a much freer woman, with a girlfriend as a roommate, her daughter, and then later my daughter. I was the spiritual leader of a church. I was creating this growing organization. I was into a whole new life which was very exciting and very rewarding and satisfying, but at the same time dealing with my own fears, my own guilts, and my own judgments."

Her personal and sexual beliefs were being challenged. Male/female issues and sexual issues began to block other areas in her life.

"Here I was, this very conservative, almost-member of the John Birch Society by the time I was twenty or twenty-one, white Anglo-Saxon Protestant with a lot of sex hang-ups and with a lot of fear of authority and a desire to please. I was caught up in the male/female roles of wanting and needing to be loved." Her fears, judgments, guilt, and misunderstanding kept her from realizing the sexual joy and freedom available to her.

"I didn't have an orgasm till I was thirty-six years old. I didn't even know what it was. I had been giving my power away to men for years, so I just decided to take the problem by the horns, so to speak, and ventured into the area of sexuality. Now I feel I've processed everything, and it has become just a natural part of my life. When my partner Reuben and I feel our energy move in that direction, it just becomes a natural expression. I think it's also a great way to blow off steam or energy, but it has taken me years and years of processing to see it this way.

"Half the time I think sex is totally not important at all, and then, sometimes, it's very important. When it's not important at all is when you have no judgments, you have no hangups, you love your body, and you love to share intimately and equally with your partner. When it's a natural part of your life, it is no more important than any other aspect—it is just a part of the way you express your love and sharing. When I feel that all-importance, that's when I judge myself, I judge my body, I judge sex, I use sex to achieve validation from men or others, and I'm left feeling guilty and resentful. That's giving your power away. If you let people abuse your body, you are not expressing yourself and not asking for what you want. When that happens with sex, it can block every other aspect of your life."

When Terry found something in herself that she needed to confront, she sought it out and went after it. Whatever she learned was reflected in her teachings. People responded to her openness.

Within three years her church had grown from fifty to five hundred. After her television debut in the late seventies, her ministry grew to what some believe was over two million. People responded to Terry's less orthodox approach to religion. People prospered, grew, and benefited from her teachings. She not only reached people on Sunday but also taught classes, created a video series, recorded tapes, and wrote three books.

During this time her books *What You Think of Me Is None of My Business* (1979) and *How to Have More in a Have-Not World* (1983) were published. In these books she writes of her metaphysical beliefs in a practical way. She asserts that each person is already perfect and that we need only remember this. People are exposed to a barrage of false beliefs; recognizing and changing these beliefs is the key to achieving a happy, successful life. People can choose to believe and think differently.

To aid the reader in identifying these beliefs, Terry's books point out limitations in individual and societal belief systems, and provide inspiring alternatives to them. *What You Think of Me* challenges people's thoughts on such topics as death, relationships, money, sexuality, and children. Terry identifies what the majority of us have been taught and then offers the reader an alternative: "So, death is not an end, but a beginning and sex is God's way of giving you an opportunity to love and be loved." The book encourages people to risk doing what they want rather than do what others think is right for them. The God within us allows us to be loving, healthy, abundant, and fully self-expressed as we learn to trust ourselves, she says.

How to Have More expresses her belief that you can trust yourself, that it is possible to give up self-pity, guilt, and fear and put intimacy, passion, and power in your life. The reader is offered a way to give up false beliefs and develop a new way of living. She believes practice and commitment are catalysts to change.

Both books contain self-awareness exercises that include thought-provoking questions, visualization activities, and affirmations. These give the reader a chance to examine old beliefs and a way to change them.

As Terry wrote, taught, and led others toward self-acceptance and love, she was also experiencing them for herself. As she evolved, so did her values. She began to question what she was doing, seeing herself enslaved by success, fame, fortune, and power, and wanted out. In her book *The Inner Path from Where You Are to Where You Want to Be* (1986) she chronicles the changes she went through from 1981 to 1985 that led to her leaving the ministry.

Reflecting on that time, she says it was important for her to make it in a man's world and she did. Once she knew she could support herself financially, that was enough. Her values and desires changed, and, eventually, the organization began to reflect those changes.

"Basically, what was happening was that I wasn't creating executives who could responsibly handle the organization. I wasn't getting financial reports or budgets. I wasn't getting accurate information. There were a lot of new-age people with no real business expertise. I was creating an empire, in a sense. I demanded that the people around me be "yes" people, because I didn't want anybody to say anything I didn't want to hear. I began to wonder who my friends were and whether I was even a friend, because the whole process of building this empire didn't support great friendships. A lot of it was based on fear."

Her work began to have less meaning for her. Religion had become routine.

"I remember my last baptism. I baptized a hundred people, and as I was doing it I thought, This is the last time I am going to do this. I've done it. If my life means that I have to keep baptizing people and I have to keep giving a sermon every Sunday, or that I have to think of a new product to sell or a new direct-mail letter to raise funds, then that's all I'm about."

By then she had met Reuben Ziegler and traveled to Israel and India with him. "Reuben was such a joyful man-child and free spirit, and that matched my true nature. I had found a real pal, playmate, lover, and friend; and I wanted more freedom and happiness in my life."

These trips had a dramatic effect. "When we went to India and Nepal, I saw that there is such a different lifestyle in Asia. The values I held before, concerning lifestyle, designer clothes, big houses, fancy cars, and fame, began to crumble. I realized there was another way to be. I could no longer believe that I had the only way, that I had the truth for all people, or that I wanted everyone to believe as I did—so how could I do religion anymore?

"Religion was over for me. I talk about a God or Goddess, but it is important, I think, for people to recognize that they are the source and yet not the *all* of it. There is much more, and it is greater probably than we have any idea of. Part of what we need to do here is to be responsible for ourselves. But again, I am not even really attached to that."

Terry also began to realize that her joy in life would not come from business meetings. "I'm not happy doing that. Plus, to keep this machine going and to stay on television, I had to keep raising from $500,000 to $700,000 a month, and the price was rising. Things were getting out of control, and I didn't know who to trust anymore. Everybody told me only what they wanted me to know and basically were taking it for their own ride. That's just human nature. I was also getting a lot of heat from the press and a lot of judgment because of the money I made. There was no hanky-panky. There was no hiding of money. I wasn't like Jim Bakker, not even close to that. There was no misappropriation of funds or any of that sort of thing; it was just—what would you call it?—bureaucratic mismanagement."

Knowing she was the one who was ultimately responsible and who would have to pull the multimillion-dollar business out of its financial crisis or re-create it from scratch, she decided to bring it to an end. She let go of the ministry, the organization, and everything that went with it.

The following excerpts are from her last sermon, on Easter Sunday of 1985:

> When I awoke this morning it was very clear to
> me. When you know what is right for you, when
> you know how you really feel about something,

when you know what you really want, the only thing left to do is step out and do that or have that or be that. Your mind will say, But what will I do? How will I survive? How will I live? And it will go on and on. And what you do is say, Thank you for sharing, and go right ahead and do what you want to do. . . .

When you hear the call to come home, go home. . . .

Within each of us is the seed of our Creator. No matter how far away we go from the Source, when we choose to go Home, the way Home has already been mapped out and planned. In fact, you mapped it out before you left. So the script was already written. Even the day of your awakening. . . .

I am not your ideal, and I am not your hero— you are! And when you lose yourself in well-known people or gurus or masters, which all of us have done at some time or other, you lose your Self, because then you do not own your Self. Others can inspire you. Let them be fully who they are and enjoy their dreams. But when you lose your Self by making others more beautiful, more powerful, more anything, and you sit there and worship, you have lost yourself. . . .

Worship yourself. You are the Light.[2]

Upon leaving her ministry, she says, "I felt free and was sure this was the thing to do; yet it was a crash. The organization fell like a house of cards. People were angry and crazed.

"I stayed at home, trying to remain peaceful, while some people on the staff handled the falling pieces. There were a lot of things to take care of: moving out of the building, selling things, trying to create as much money to pay as much of it as we could. And then, dealing with people's anger, lawsuits, disgruntled employees, and ex-husbands [by then she had been married four times].

2. Terry Cole-Whittaker, *The Inner Path from Where You Are to Where You Want to Be: A Spiritual Odyssey* (Riverside, N.J.: Rawson Assocs., 1986), 79– 81.

"The hardest thing to let go of was being famous, being a celebrity, and I think the money, too."

She compares leaving the ministry to withdrawing from a drug—"a heavy drug of lifestyle. Sometimes I thought, my God, what have I done to myself? I worked so hard for this, and now I've just let it go. Sometimes I think if I had to do it over, I would have done it more gradually; but then I realize the lessons I gained from departing so quickly and the shock of it, the cold turkey, basically, were so immense that I wouldn't be who I am if I had done it any differently."

Needing to restructure her life, she moved to Maui for five months.

"I knew it was a healing process," she says, "so I gained weight; I learned to wear old clothes and not wear make-up. I learned that I was beautiful even if I didn't have the trappings." At times she felt embarrassment and shame, "as if I had done something wrong and was rejected."

Out of these feelings came many changes, beginning with her relationship to God. "My awareness had shifted [before and after the end of the ministry] so much that my basic motivations were no longer the same. It was as though life had no meaning for me, and I had to create meaning from a whole different point of view. No longer was I certain about God's will or putting that power outside of myself. I thought, wait a minute, there may or may not be some divine plan, but this is my life and it is my world. So instead of giving that power to some God figure or Holy Spirit or Allah or whatever, I owned the responsibility for myself. For myself in my world. I couldn't stand behind God or a religious figure and pretend I was doing their will anymore because I could see through all that stuff."

Her relationships with other people changed as well. "I choose my relationships now simply by choosing people I enjoy being around. My friends come from all walks of life now and all lifestyles, including people I judged before. If they are important and they happen to be a friend, that's great. But what's important? I don't have importances anymore. I think people just do what they do. But I don't think anyone is more important than another, and I don't think any job is more important than another, and I don't feel that anyone makes a greater contribution than anybody else."

Out of her many changes came a different way of teaching. She knew she liked teaching, but she did not want to have all the burdens that the ministry had brought with it. While she was in Maui, she started "Adventures in Enlightenment." It was founded as a spiritual educational organization dedicated to discovering ways and means to promote harmony and wellness for people.

"The 'divine experiment' is what we call our commitment to discover and experience what happens when two or more align and agree on an idea, a thought, a desire, an objective, a dream, or a vision. The underlying purpose of the 'divine experiment' is for all life forms to live in harmony.

"It is our feeling and created belief that all people are perfect. They have everything they need, for whatever, into forever. Our job is to support people in discovering and loving who they are."

Her time away from the public eye gave her a chance to reflect more deeply on her own feminine nature and that of the world's. In her workshop "The Unfolding Female Master—the Return of the Goddess," Terry teaches that it is time for women to break the last strings of attachment to the old way and become the masters they are. The primary goal of the workshop is to bring Goddess consciousness into the body, to release self-pity (which Terry says is a disease of women), victim energies, and centuries of old beliefs that have kept women from seeing themselves as whole and worthy. She encourages women not to give their power to male dieties and to be fully actualized, owning their own power and love. Ways in which the feminine can reemerge and women can learn to honor their bodies and one another are the subject of *Love and Power in a World without Limits: A Woman's Guide to the Goddess Within*. Published in 1989, the book tells how the world turned away from the female goddess and urges us now to reclaim that feminine energy within ourselves. It provides exercises to help release the centuries-old negative beliefs around women.

People come from all over to enjoy workshops with Terry, Reuben, and other staff members. The retreats are held at their farm in Washington State, at a center they rent in Maui, and occasionally in other locations, such as Palm Springs, California, and Sedona, Arizona. They also set up events for an evening, a day, or a weekend in major cities like Los Angeles, San Francisco, Seattle, Portland, or New York. People also hire Terry to speak or lead a workshop for their particular group.

Participating in one of Terry's workshops today, one gets the feeling that she really has let go. As always, she is blond and beautiful, yet she is not the TV personality of several years ago. It's not just that she wears fewer suits and can be found leading a workshop barefooted; it's that she has evolved and changed. She sees herself as being less interested in what the world sees as acceptable and more interested in self-acceptance. She trusts herself and appears to enjoy life immensely. Her teaching, that the moment is the only thing that matters, is obviously true for her. She may have a set topic for the workshop, but she spontaneously says whatever she feels at the moment. When she speaks, she radiates joy.

If her teachings have changed, it's not so much in her basic beliefs—that people can have what they want and that beliefs need to be healed and changed—it's more in her acceptance of the individual, her acceptance that each one of us knows what he or she wants. She affirms that God is in each of us.

When she is not conducting workshops, Terry lives on the farm with her partner and fellow teacher, Reuben. Her office, with two staff members, is also there. She keeps her business and financial affairs much simpler since her experiences with the ministry. She does not let other people handle her money, even if they're experts; she writes her own checks and makes all her own financial decisions.

"I do things differently now. I run my organization on a cash basis, no credit. Personally, I have some credit cards, but I like the ones I have to pay off each month, because if I can't pay it must mean that I don't have the money."

She says the ministry never declared bankruptcy and the creditors have been understanding in accepting gradual payments.

For relaxation Terry enjoys spending time alone with nature, just as she did at her great-grandmother's resort. "My greatest pleasure is to hike around in nature, to walk through our woods or any other setting of natural beauty, with my family and friends."

Her farm is an important part of her life: "We bought an old farm with a new loghouse, so it's been a lot of work and there is always more work to do. We like the thought of being out and away from people and just being quiet. We grow our own food. It's a good place to keep your values more earth-bound. When people come to the retreat center they can play on the farm.

"I like hanging out with people who I love to share with, who are stimulating, exciting, alive, creative, nice, loving people. I love playing with my granddaughters. They're fun." She says one day she became aware that Austin, the older of her two granddaughters, was her great-grandmother Bertha Hall in her prior life. "It was an awareness that came over me one day. I wasn't looking for it or asking for it, and then this knowingness that 'this is Nanny' came over me. I just cried and got shivers. It's one of those things you can't prove in a body. It was totally through feelings." She's given up constant self-analysis and doesn't question these occurrences. When she was in the public eye, Terry was constantly working on herself, but that's no longer the case. Her "therapy" is mainly sharing with close friends—her daughter Suzanne and Reuben.

"A lot came forward during the ministry, because I have a feeling that the bigger the game you play, the more stuff is going to hit the fan. Where normally there's a few people to deal with—the person next door whose dog is barking—when you're on TV you have a lot of people who reflect off of you, your likes and dislikes."

Even though Terry gives the appearance that everything could be play to her, she says, "We were working all the time for a while. Then we decided, well, let's not work so much. Let's relax more. So for a while we just enjoyed the farm, but now we realize that we haven't been doing enough, just loaf-ing. I think I have come out of a period of hibernation. I've shifted my values, in a sense, and now it is becoming very clear to me what I feel, what I believe, and what I want to share. So right now I am stepping back into the world."

She explains that she is developing a new television show with the producers of "D.C. Follies," Sid and Marty Krofft. It will focus on the latest new-age happenings around the world in ecology, science, medicine, self-help, lifestyles, and feeding the hungry. "It will be a program of exciting information and people who are working to make the world a more beautiful, loving, safe place.

"I'm deciding to get back out there and be a voice to be heard because I feel I have things to say, and there are people who need and want to hear it. Those who don't, don't have to listen. I don't think I have *the* truth anymore, but I have *a* truth that I think is real valuable.

"I am not interested in being a celebrity. I am not going to share much about my private life. I used to share everything about myself because I thought it would help people, but I realized that a lot of people just found ammunition to use against me rather than inspiration."

Sharing her views on the New Age and her part in it, she says, "I think what people call the New Age has been categorized and limited by people who think it is only crystals, past-life regression, and channeling. I have been doing this since I was born, and to me it is self-love and love of humanity. It is moving into levels of love, happiness, bliss, and joy while leaving behind fear, guilt, and judgment. I think it is a time of physical and spiritual immortality. I think it is a time when incredible technology can help humanity to rise above starvation, disease, and poverty. It is, I hope, an end of materialism and a beginning of compassion, love, understanding, and sufficiency.

"The New Age is a time of cosmic consciousness, not just consciousness of one's self. Possibly it will include the exploration of other galaxies and other solar systems. It is an awareness of our bodies, ourselves, and our relationships.

"I think what we call the New Age will be a time of learning how to be together and of one world where we don't live with borders. It will be the end of war, the end of crime. It will be an understanding and an awareness that we cannot imagine yet.

"All I can say is that my part in it is to be myself and to live my own dream. I care about people, so I will be out there sharing my vision and my truth and doing my thing, whatever it is. I'm a visionary and a mystic, and one of the players."

PERSONAL TRUTHS

1. Love yourself with all of your heart, soul, and mind. Love others as you love yourself.

2. Live your dream, your vision, in a way that supports the well-being of all life forces.

3. Be responsible for creating your own life to be the paradise it can be right here on earth. Create your life to be as beautiful and loving as you desire it to be. Know it is up to you.

TERRY COLE-WHITTAKER
Author of

Love and Power in a World without Limits: A Woman's Guide to the Goddess Within. San Francisco: Harper & Row, 1989.

The Inner Path from Where You Are to Where You Want to Be: A Spiritual Odyssey. Riverside, N.J.: Rawson Associates, 1986.

How to Have More in a Have-Not World. Riverside, N.J.: Rawson Associates, 1983.

What You Think of Me Is None of My Business. San Diego: Oak Tree Publications, 1979.

Sondra Ray

Sondra Ray, *founder of the Loving Relationships Training and the more recent Evolution Training, is a leading authority on rebirthing and how birth affects our relationships. She is the author of ten books including* Loving Relationships, Celebration of Breath, *and* How to Be Chic, Fabulous and Live Forever.

She received her masters degree in family sociology and public health from the University of Arizona, and is a former nurse practitioner and sex therapist. Dedicated to the promotion of health and immortality, she left more traditional forms of medicine and discovered the healing practice of rebirthing, and later uncovered the connection between our births and our relationships. She is world-known as a teacher devoted to the health and peace of people and our planet.

I first heard of Sondra Ray in the early 1980s. I knew she was the originator of the Loving Relationships Training and a rebirther.

My personal experience with her began with reading The Only Diet There Is. *In this book she writes of a spiritual diet: having the body you want, not by watching what you eat, but by changing the way you think and feel about food, yourself, and others. I was thirty pounds overweight. I had tried everything else, so I thought, Why not? Over the next weeks a friend and I read the book and did the exercises. What we experienced was a profound sense of emotional clearing and a large weight loss. Neither of us changed what we were eating; we changed how we felt about ourselves.*

I remember being impressed with how Sondra shared her feelings and journey in her book. I also remember thinking that she was "too far out" because of her emphasis on breathing, the expression of her feelings, and her talk about living forever. It was all too much for me. After all, back then I was working a nine-to-five job I didn't like and was just trying to survive.

So when it was time to do this book, she was one of the first women I thought of. I wanted to know if her life was still an adventure. She didn't disappoint me.

I interviewed her twice in person and once on the phone. Each time we talked, she had just returned from another journey to Yugoslavia, New Zealand, or the Soviet Union. She is a woman with a mission, devoted to her own spiritual growth and that of the planet. She trusts her inner voice and goes where she is guided.

I met Sondra at the home of two San Rafael, California, friends who had organized an evening talk for her. Although she had just gotten off a plane before the talk and said she was tired, she embraced the interview as I assume she embraces life—with energy and excitement. Sondra remarked on the importance of doing this interview on the day after the signing of the Soviet-American Arms Treaty. One of her great concerns is planetary peace.

Sondra, being an authority on how birth affects our lives, began her story with her birth.

S ondra Ray was born on the kitchen table. "My mother always says I came straight from the kitchen, like I'm a dessert or something," she says. While still in the womb she communicated to her mother that she wanted to be born at home, and she was. It was a highly social event, just as her life has been. Relatives dropped by and her mother was whistling and talking with people during labor.

Sondra grew up in a little Iowa town of three hundred people with her parents and a sister who was four years older. "Everyone knew me and I knew everyone, so I had the idea of extended family right there. That's what I later created in the LRT [Loving Relationships Training]. There were no cops; we had no crime. Everyone left their doors open; everybody trusted everybody. I could go anywhere and I had many 'parents.' The whole community knew each other and everybody agreed that they would parent each others' children, so my mother didn't worry. I could roam everywhere. Even as a very little child, I could go out at night, walk around, play, and it was completely safe. People were extremely religious. There were farmers in the area, so I still think farmers are very holy, working with the earth and growing things. Everyone went to the same church—it was Lutheran—so it was all homogenous. That was pretty fantastic for a kid. Of course, I had certain problems with the religious restrictions later, like why my father died.

"I always wanted to be a missionary. The desire to be a missionary was very strong, and since I grew up in this little town I was very curious about the world outside. But I feel very grateful that I grew up there because I became used to being known. I was known by a very small number of people, but at that time it seemed like a big town to me.

"I was very social and, no kidding, I went to visit the poor and the old people. I built little caves to play in and I had a playhouse. My grandmother gave me her her woodshed and it held all my mother's clothes that she had saved from the Roaring Twenties. All my girlfriends and I would dress up and parade around town. I still dress up and parade around town. It's fun. Almost childlike."

Sondra's high school years were dominated by basketball. It's easy to see that the five foot eleven inch slender reddish-blond was a player, not a watcher.

"I was a basketball star, so most of my high school days were about being that. We won thirty-four straight games! I was playing guard, and from the time I was in the ninth grade we were winning. My team averaged five feet eleven inches in height. My cousin was six two. It's hard to believe in a small town that they were all as tall as I was or taller. We were giants, just Amazons. And so we won—until we missed the state tournament by one point.

"I learned a lot about good preparation and teamwork. It was very valuable to me to be on that team, a winning team."

Sondra's father was sick most of her life, which she believes was the reason she became passionate about studying disease and health. "I used to come home from school and the ambulance would be there with no notice; and he would be taken away to the hospital for absolutely months at a time. I would long to see him, yet I wasn't old enough to visit at the Catholic hospital, so I'd sneak up the fire escape into his hospital room. I'd sit on his bed just for a few seconds.

"Then, when he finally came home from the hospital, he would have months of recovery. He'd get well and go back to work, until one day I'd come home and the ambulance would be there again, and the whole thing would start over. My life was really hard that way because I took care of him from the time I was three years old. I was his nurse.

"My mother was a very wise person, very positive. I never heard her complain, even though the man she loved was dying in front of her eyes. She just worked really hard. She was a teacher. Not only did she teach home economics and English, she was able to repair and fix anything; she could remodel the whole house overnight. Even to this day she restores and repairs old houses. Because my father was sick, she held the family together.

"People said my father was the smartest man in town. He was trained as an engineer, but he didn't finish college. He worked for my grandfather's hardware store and was kind of the town electrician."

Sondra's father died the night before her high school

graduation. "I was sixteen when I graduated from high school. As salutatorian of the class I had to give a speech, a message to the parents, which is the traditional speech the salutatorian gives. Everyone knew that my father had just died and the whole town was there and I just froze. I was like ice. Everyone I saw was crying at my graduation."

Her father's death and the effects of living with his disease would have a dramatic effect on Sondra. A desire to understand his death led her into nursing. "I wanted to know why he died, why they couldn't save him. I wanted to know what the cause of his disease was, and why people were getting these diseases, and why we couldn't have permanent healing.

"The first year I had a scholarship to go to a church college in Sioux Falls, South Dakota. I studied premed and nursing. I was really having a hard time about my father's death so I had long periods of insomnia, severe insomnia, but I still made straight *A*'s. I was so obsessed with perfection, being a Virgo."

In an effort to leave the Midwest and the memories of her father's death behind, she left South Dakota and attended the progressive University of Florida College of Nursing. "I saw a whole different life. It wasn't what I was used to. People wore shorts and thongs to class and went braless."

She met her husband there. "I had asked myself, How come my father died when I was sixteen? Does that mean God kills people? And I never could handle that. I went into extreme rebellion and married an atheist because I was so upset God killed people. How can I be a Christian and believe that? No one could ever answer the unresolvable conflict." Still wanting to be a missionary but unable to reconcile her religious beliefs, Sondra joined the Peace Corps along with her husband.

It was the early sixties, when Kennedy was still alive. "We were really excited in those days. I was in Group 10, so I was in one of the first groups the Peace Corps sent out. I've always been a pioneer. I certainly didn't consciously plan it, but I must have been guided because I would always end up at the beginning of new things."

The Peace Corps first sent Sondra and her husband to the University of Denver, where they underwent six weeks of intensive training in cultural knowledge and Spanish, and then to Puerto Rico for further language and physical training. "In those days the Peace Corps gave you very rigorous training, and you had excruciatingly difficult tests to pass: psychiatric, FBI clearances, physical endurance tests—we had to swim a mile a day, run a mile a day. We had to rappel down mountains, go on jungle hikes, survival hikes by ourselves, know contour maps and compasses. It was very challenging, but I loved it and I was a very spirited person, so I liked that kind of excitement." They were then assigned to Peru.

"I was stationed first in a desert camp called Chimbote where they had no bathrooms, no running water, no electricity, and no roof on our straw house because it never rained there. It was very, very primitive, and I learned as much as I could. Conditions were very poor and there was a plague and smallpox epidemic the first week we arrived, so we had to vaccinate the kids right away. I was a very new nurse."

Later, because her husband knew how to fix jeeps, they were sent into the Andes. "At least we had running water. We bought horses in the market and traveled around to little villages and taught the children very basic good health in Spanish."

It was near the end of this two-year period in South America that Sondra's husband got amoebic dysentery and nearly went bald. "We came back to the States. He went back to college, and I got a job at the University of Florida. I worked as a nurse in an eye, ear, nose, and throat clinic, which was important to me because my father had donated his eyes when he died and I'd been wondering who'd gotten them. I worked with the greatest cornea transplant surgeon at the time. Before that I'd read to the blind as a volunteer in college. I was into serving, being a waitress or a nurse or something. I had worked my way through college as a waitress."

They remained in Florida long enough for Sondra's husband to finish college, and then it was time for more travel. "We decided to go abroad again because I had this global mentality coming out and I wanted to learn, so my husband joined the Smithsonian Astrophysical Observatory. Because he had some engineering background, they trained him to track satellites. He was a genius."

Sondra believed she could live anywhere and do anything after surviving the Peace Corps. She got a chance to prove that when the Smithsonian sent them to what Sondra calls the "ends of the earth." Comodoro Rivadavia is in the cold desert regions of southern Argentina, near Tierra del Fuego about five hundred miles above the Falklands. The area's ninety-mile-per-hour winds have been known to lift Volkswagens off the ground.

Their social life consisted of people who were either oil-company employees or sheep ranchers. Being from a small town, Sondra decided the first thing to do was to make friends. She found out quickly that people weren't talking to one another. "The Europeans had unlimited amounts of money because their oil companies paid such huge sums as hardship pay. They would throw parties to entertain major dignitaries, yet they didn't talk to one another. The women were walking on eggs, feeling they might have to seek therapy, and the dignitaries were under the pressure of million-dollar contracts. I walked in, a small-town girl, and I met all of them and I liked all of them. I tried to heal all their relationships with each other. I became friends with them and they found me refreshing. I would have them all over to my tiny apartment for a party. By the time I left there, they all kind of related to one another. I didn't think about it until later, but I was doing a kind of Loving Relationships Training without even knowing it." Sondra also taught Spanish to members of the U.S. Air Force. It was the only year she did not have a "regular" job.

After a year in Argentina they were transferred to Hawaii, where they lived on the island of Maui. Sondra worked as a nurse at the Maui Medical Center. Adjusting happily to the cultural change, they lived on the beach. Sondra loved the islands.

Two years later they were transferred to Arizona, and Sondra attended the University of Arizona for graduate studies in family sociology and public health.

"That's the year my marriage broke up. There were several problems. One was I married an atheist. I was very spiritual, but I was angry at God because my father died.

"I created the end of my marriage on the day of my graduate school graduation, which was like re-creating my father's death on that earlier graduation. The minute graduation came up, that whole circuit of death was triggered into the death of the marriage.

"My hair fell out and I was really low. I was so upset, I just wanted to die. I wanted someone to come and take care of me so I could recover." She sought help from everyone she knew in the medical field. No one could help her. She joined the air force, hoping to be sent to Europe. Instead, she became an air force nurse during the Vietnam war, stationed in Arizona.

"I was very privileged because they thought I was good, and they trained me free of charge as a nurse practitioner. I was in charge of prenatal care, which led later to rebirthing. I told the base commander he must train me in sex therapy and gynecology, because everyone was telling me all their sexual problems." She was delighted to be in the field of prevention. As she came to see how the women's emotional problems were causing their pain, she took every course available to become a sex therapist and began to discover how people could free themselves of sexual fears.

But healing others was not healing herself, and she did not want to be in Arizona; it was a continual reminder of her divorce and, by association, her father's death. She went to a base psychologist and asked for a hardship transfer. He told her to quit running and go to therapy, which she did for a year. "I was really desperate and didn't want to be bald and a woman. I felt suicidal.

"I hadn't recovered from my divorce, let alone my father." Her hair continued to fall out as she continued to seek help. One of her quests for help led her to a dermatologist who confirmed that she had a serious problem. He prescribed the book *Peace of Mind* by Rabi Joshua Liebman. That was the first metaphysical book she had ever read, and it explained the power of the mind over the body.

Sondra says very simply, "So I read this book and I felt better. My hair stopped falling out, even though I still had this bald section.

"The next thing, my ex-husband called me up and wanted me to come back. So I said yes, because I felt maybe I should try again. I packed my bags and sent everything to Florida, where he was living. I was to leave the next day. That night I was sitting on the floor talking to a friend in the air force, and I had one of those major mystical experiences. I felt something in the back of my head, and I was suddenly filled with white light. It was like laser beams hitting my body. It was very profound. Then I heard this voice actually out in the air (I was not the kind of person who heard voices) which said, 'NEVER

GO BACK.' Then it said, 'NEVER GO BACK' louder. Finally it said, 'GO TO CALIFORNIA NOW.' "

Sondra was mystified by the message. She'd already written to the California Nurses Association and was told there were absolutely no jobs for nurses in California. "I literally knew no one in California. But after I had this experience, my friend looked at me and I looked at him and he said, 'You'd better go to California,' and I agreed.

"It was a total religious experience. It was the kind you read about in the Bible that you cannot ignore. So I got in the car and I drove to California on pure faith, which I always had a lot of."

When she got to California, she turned the car north. She had read an article about two medical researchers whose work interested her, and she planned to call them when she got to San Francisco.

"The minute I crossed the California line I felt different. I felt my life was totally changed. What can I tell you? Miracles began occurring to me right and left, every second, because I followed the voice. I wasn't resisting. I went on total faith. So I was driving the car in San Francisco, up and down those hills, not knowing my way around; then my car quit on Scott Street. My name is Sondra Ray Scott. I looked up and saw 'Furnished Apartment for Rent.' And I needed a furnished apartment.

"I went to the door and I told this guy, 'I need to live here.' And he said, 'Ma'am, you need the first month's rent and the last month's rent and a deposit.' The California prices were pretty outrageous and I didn't have any money. So I said, 'I don't have it, but I need to live here.' He said, 'Ma'am, I told you you need the first month's rent. . . .' And I just stood there and he kept going over and over it. Again I said, 'I really need to live here.' I did not move.

"So, anyway, finally he said, 'I don't know what it is about you, lady, but I'll let you move in. I haven't done this in twenty-five years.' I couldn't believe it, so I moved in." The next day she looked up the people she had read about, and although they did not have work for her, they made a phone call to Kaiser Hospital. Overnight Sondra had a well-paying job. She was in charge of the prenatal, GYN, and family-planning clinics and had additional work counseling in the abortion clinic. She later founded the hospital's sex therapy clinic.

During this time Sondra continued to look for answers to her own health problems. She was still wearing wigs and continued to have pain in her body that she had had since her father's death. She started meeting people in her neighborhood and asking questions. Through a local beautician she heard about EST (Erhard Seminar Training). She took the training when its originator, Werner Erhard, was still teaching it and says that it was a very profound experience for her. Shortly afterward, however, she started having other problems. Her Fiat was rear-ended repeatedly. As soon as she'd get it fixed, someone would bang into it again. She didn't know if she could keep driving. She felt frantic.

"One night I went to the EST graduate seminar and I was crying about the accidents. They said, 'Oh, don't worry, we'll take you to this new guru in town, Leonard Orr. Just trust us.' I was willing to try anything at that point. I was desperate." On Sunday morning she was taken to Portola Valley, where she heard Leonard speak on what he called the "Five Biggies," which included the birth trauma, the death urge, the parental disapproval syndrome, specific negatives, and *A Personal Law*, your most negative thought about yourself.

Sondra knew that she fit into one or more of these categories, so she asked for an immediate private consultation. During their session, Orr introduced her to the use of affirmations (positive thoughts or statements) that she was to write or tell herself in order to change her consciousness and thereby transform her outside circumstances. Being skeptical, she decided to test the affirmation theory by seeing if she could get men to call her while she was at home. She had always managed to be out when men she cared about called her. She began writing, "I now receive an abundant inflow of calls from men when I am at home." The phone began ringing, all her old lovers called her, and she even began receiving calls from men she didn't know—wrong numbers in the middle of the night. There were so many wrong numbers, in fact, that she went back to Leonard for more advice. He revised her affirmation to read, "I, Sondra, now receive telephone calls only from men I want to hear from." That affirmation got the desired result, so she began writing the affirmations Leonard gave her to heal her car accidents: "I, Sondra, now have a safe driving consciousness. My life urges are stronger than my death urges. As long as I weaken my death urges and strengthen my life urges, I will go on living in increasing health, happiness, usefulness, and youthfulness." She hasn't wrecked her car since.

Shortly after that, Leonard led her in her first rebirth. Rebirthing is a pattern of breathing that connects the inhale with the exhale in a relaxed, connected rhythm. This gentle, continuous breathing releases negative thoughts and emotions that have accumulated through the years back to birth. In *Celebration of Breath* Sondra writes:

> Rebirthing originally started, it was thought, to heal the birth trauma. This is a major part of it. However, we have learned that it is really a spiritual purification process and letting go of the birth trauma is only one part of that much greater, all encompassing process of going for God. . . .
>
> I want everyone to know how it can heal the body, how it brings joy and happiness out, how it increases aliveness and has a youthing effect on the body, how it increases psychic ability and develops intuitive power, how it releases old hurt, pain and misery and how it increases love and prosperity.[1]

Leonard had just begun leading people through this process, so Sondra was the third or fourth person to experience it. At the time, they used a snorkel in a hot tub. Later, Leonard Orr developed dry rebirthing—breathing lying down, out of water. Sondra found the effects of rebirthing to be miraculous.

"I began changing totally. A pain I had had for fifteen years left my body. I had all this energy. I started remembering who I was. I started feeling fantastic. My naturally curly hair grew back. I healed my own baldness. I have witnesses. So I have proved that you can heal anything.

"That was it! The miracle I had been looking for. I became Leonard's chauffeur, and he taught me to do rebirthing. I would work at the hospital during the day and come home and rebirth my friends all night."

Her passions became self-awareness and rebirthing. Growing increasingly frustrated by the medical profession's lack of

---

1. Sondra Ray, *Celebration of Breath* (Berkeley, Calif.: Celestial Arts, 1983), ix.

solutions for illness, she gave up nursing and became a full-time rebirther.

"I just couldn't stand the idea that I gave these people pills and they were not permanently healed. I gave them perfect nursing care, they went home, went off the pills, and got the diseases right back. I was completely frustrated with Western medicine.

"I went from being probably one of the highest-paid nurses in the country to making twenty dollars an hour as a rebirther. Again, it was like this great leap of faith to follow the voice.

"My intuition was getting stronger, and I knew it was right, so I began rebirthing people night and day. I lived with Leonard Orr and several others in the basement of the Theta House on Lyon Street, in the Haight-Ashbury. We put people in this hot tub, and miracles happened with that snorkel. That was the great thing about California and San Francisco at that time. We could be outrageous, experiment, and still be accepted.

"Then I began to notice something. One of the things rebirthing did was to make me more and more creative, and everyday I became clearer and clearer. You get your birth trauma out, and the Holy Spirit comes through. I became more conscious in every area and started to experience some of my talents that I hadn't remembered—they just came through."

Sondra began writing during that period. Her first book, *I Deserve Love* (1976), begins with affirmations that she had written for clients at the hospital's sex therapy clinic. Some of the affirmations helped them so much that she decided to put these, and the discoveries she had made around sexual fulfillment, in the book. *I Deserve Love* teaches that the power to get what you want is within you and that you can release that power through simple affirmation techniques. One technique Sondra introduces is the response column. The reader divides a paper in half and writes positive affirmations on one side and any negative or limiting responses to that affirmation on the other side. The negative thoughts can then be released.

This book was just the beginning, and Sondra's growing creativity continued to amaze her. Then one day she had what she calls a "lightbulb experience": she made a discovery that would change her life and the lives of those she reached.

"I had a rebirthing client whom I'd seen several times.

She was sharing her problems with sex and her relationship because she knew I had been a sex therapist. Then, when I rebirthed her, all of a sudden I realized that her birth was related to her relationships.

"I began to see it with everyone. It was a moment of discovery, but I just kept it in my head because I wanted to study it. I naturally did research on my hospital patients. I asked them when their illnesses began, and they often said it was right after a relationship broke up. I was starting to see connections between relationship traumas on the body and birth trauma on relationships. Everything was connecting and making sense to me."

With time Sondra would begin to see how her own birth affected her life and relationships. Sondra attributes her self-esteem to not being separated from her mother in the first weeks of her life. She also wrote in *Birth and Relationships* that as a baby she was kept in a basket normally used for freshly washed clothes. She says this carries over into a current compulsiveness about clean clothes.

Although she wanted to be born at home, being born on the kitchen table had its repercussions. Every time she'd sit down to eat, her birth trauma became activated and she wouldn't be able to eat or relax without leaving the table. The negative side was that it made her neurotic about food and tried the patience of her friends. On the positive side, she fell in love with several restaurant owners.

A miracle happened at her birth. Her grandfather, who had been in a mental institution for severe depression, was instantly healed when he saw her. She heard about this only much later; it was kept quiet at the time. Her family thought it was weird. She internalized some of this, she says, and had ambivalent feelings about being a healer. She also says that she felt disappointment in the room when she was born because her sister wanted a baby brother. For years she believed she was not perfect because she was a girl—"I should have been a boy to please everyone."

Sondra began to share her discoveries about birth and relationships with groups. She gave her first workshop in 1976.

"One day when I came home, Leonard said, 'They want you in Hawaii and I told them you were coming. Just give them a seminar.'

"When I arrived, thirty people were sitting there. I had

never taught a seminar. I had been a nurse, and I was just becoming a rebirther. I said to them, 'Let me share with you everything I've learned about how your birth affects your relationships.' They said, 'Great.' "

The knowledge she gave them moved them profoundly. "They said, 'This explains everything.'

"I was flabbergasted at their response. All I did was share. Then they told me I couldn't leave until their friends got to hear this."

She stayed and gave another seminar the next day. There were more people with the same reactions. They agreed that this was too much information to assimilate in one day, so they suggested that she outline a two-day seminar. She agreed to do this and return. "I wrote the whole outline in two days, and that became the first Loving Relationships Training. I tried it out on twenty friends in my living room, and it worked perfectly except for the jealousy section, which I had to rewrite fourteen times." Sondra gave the first LRT in San Francisco in 1976 and the second in Hawaii, the beginning of many throughout the United States and the world. Her organization grew until she had, at last count, thirteen centers worldwide. In the United States there are centers in New York, Philadelphia, Atlanta, Indianapolis, Fort Lauderdale, Los Angeles, and Seattle. The foreign countries with centers are England, Spain, Sweden, Israel, New Zealand, and Australia. Longtime associate Bob Mandel is the national director of the LRT.

"Now I have twelve trainers. The LRT weekend training is taught by two trainers, which makes it unique. They demonstrate a good relationship. Some of them are married to each other and some of them are best friends, but we are all able to interchange. It takes many years to become a trainer, because first you've got to crack your own rebirthing phase, your own birth trauma. Then you've got to learn to be a rebirther and then learn to be a trainer for LRT. It used to take about four years to produce a trainer." As in her childhood basketball days she thinks in terms of teamwork. "I could have taught it myself and made millions of dollars, but who cares? I want everyone to learn how to work with other people.

"This is the age of group action, as far as I am concerned—the New Age." The trainers work together in teams, with assistant teams under them.

"Trainers have to have their relationships perfected with

each other. They can't sit up in front of the room together and teach relationship training if they don't have a clear relationship with the co-trainer. It is unique that you get to watch the two trainers living the training. This is the way I designed it. The trainers and I practiced the training itself to get to the point where we could all work together in peace. It has been quite a challenge to try to get twelve powerful leaders together. This is our mission—to teach people how to do this—so we had to practice it ourselves. Ultimately, I want to have twelve groups of twelve trainers. That would be manageable to me. The original twelve would supervise the other groups of twelve."

Describing the training itself, she says, "On Friday night we ask people to write down their goals for the relationships in their lives. We cover logistics, and then everyone stands up and meets everyone. They state their names, their careers, the current state of their relationships, and if they are available they can put it out!

"Saturday is about clearing the past, learning what prevents you from having good relationships. Anything unresolved with your parents will affect your relationships. In the morning we go over metaphysics, how the mind works, and how we create patterns in our relationships that prevent us from having good ones. Relationship patterns are repetitive behavior that repeats without our being conscious of it. We study examples of nine or ten patterns. For example, one pattern is that you tend to attract a mate who is like the parent you had the most trouble with. You may not see this until you move in with them. We go over all these patterns and study them. We study them and let go of them.

"On Saturday night we actually go deeper and deeper into childhood, and finally we get to birth. This is the most exciting part. We discuss the birth trauma, prenatal trauma, and conception trauma. We discuss all of those and how they affect you. Then we do a rebirthing. Everyone lies down and breathes together. We breathe it all out.

"Then the next day we can really go for it. It is about restructuring your life and creating new-age relationships. We talk about how to attract a mate and what to do when one shows up. What is a loving relationship? How do you set it up? How do you keep it going, and how do you keep it from falling apart? We talk about sex and jealousy; then we set up a self-support system to maintain relationships. At the end we have a celebration. We cover a lot in two days. We even teach physical immortality.

"Although the trainings are structured, no training is exactly alike. Each trainer adds a personal touch and does it a little differently."

Besides founding this growing business, Sondra is a prolific writer. She is the author of ten books and has several more planned.

After *I Deserve Love*, Sondra wrote several books on rebirthing and how birth affects our lives. She coauthored *Rebirthing in the New Age* with Leonard Orr (1977) and *Birth and Relationships* with Bob Mandel (1987), and wrote *Celebration of Breath* (1983) and *Ideal Birth* (1985).

Loving Relationships (1980) contains many of the concepts from the LRT and guides readers in healing themselves of negative thoughts and patterns that prevent them from having what they want in their relationships. Sondra expounds on self-love and believes people can have love and joy in their relationships at all times. *The Only Diet There Is* (1981) describes how we can transform our bodies and choose the weight we want by changing our thoughts about food and ourselves. *Drinking the Divine* (1984) is a workbook based on Sondra's experiences and use of "A Course in Miracles."

The underlying message in all her books is of spiritual healing and evolution, self-love, and self-esteem. Achieving physical immortality has been a part of her teaching for years, and increasingly she writes and lectures on the subject. *Rebirthing in the New Age* (1977) and *Pure Joy* (1988) have sections on physical immortality, but her latest book—*How to Be Chic, Fabulous and Live Forever* (1989)—is devoted to understanding it.

Because Sondra is the originator of the Loving Relationships Training, it is natural for people to wonder what her relationships are like. "I have a very unusual lifestyle, so I have very unusual relationships," she says. "I am pretty married to my business. I have been married to my associates and my staff, or it has felt like a marriage. It's been wonderful. I treat the trainers with as much love as I would a husband. I like that intimate feeling. I call it a spiritual family, and so I feel intimate involvement. Because I want to feel that way with everyone, I work very hard to get my relationships closer and deeper every year, instead of the opposite.

"I don't think relationships are ever ending, just going forward, so I don't teach people about ending or breaking up.

"I also have many friends who are not in this business. I just basically like people. It is very easy for me to meet people, and I have been able to handle great friendships because I work at it, I really do. I write people letters and I call them. I don't waste time waiting to make a person my friend. When do they stop being strangers and become friends? Instantly. I can do this because in the small town I was raised in we didn't have strangers. Everybody knew everybody, so it is normal for me to treat people as my friends. I think that is the way we should all think. We are all in this together.

"I have been very blessed to be mated with a wonderful man who was a yogi in India for nine years. We have come together to serve the world and our Master Babaji [Sri Bhagwan Herakhan Wale Baba]. The story of how we came together in the Himalayas is very touching and very beautiful. Surely I should write a separate book about it. We are just beginning to come out together. We'll need to become more and more visible. It's blossoming. The actual flower of it will be a surprise later on, I feel."

About two years after rebirthing had begun, a letter addressed in pencil arrived at the house on Lyon Street. The stamp was unreadable, and there was no return address. When the letter was opened it said simply, "Come to India." Sondra looked at Leonard and said, "We'd better go."

Eleven of the household members jumped on a plane, and landing in India, spread out to look for a teacher. That year Sondra studied with two teachers she met there. When she returned to the States, she found that one of their group had met the true Babaji in Paramahansa Yogananda's *Autobiography of a Yogi*. They all immediately returned to India and met him.

Sondra hesitates before talking about this important relationship. "I don't want anyone to think that I am dependent on a guru. That isn't the point. I don't feel that I am dependent. I feel that my teacher has pushed me to become all that I am as fast as I can take it, and I don't see the guru as someone you give your power away to. He empowers me. I think that a guru does purify your body and mind on every level. There is nothing as fantastic in my mind as to hang out with a totally God-related person. To me this is wondrous.

"Somewhere it was said that of all the things a person can do, association with The God-Realized Saint is the best.

"To me this divine privilege of association with Babaji is ecstasy. It purifies the body at every level. Being connected with that supreme power is not only glorious, it is total satisfaction. It is the best road I know of to spiritual enlightenment, salvation, peace, happiness, and total liberation. The potential for pure joy and creativity is unlimited. Naturally I feel that the practice of devotion to a spiritual master is the true and perfect way of life.

"Babaji said God and the guru are the same. The true guru knows everything. In Babaji's case, he descended straight from God and was not born from a woman. We are talking about a true avatar. In the gospel of St. Thomas it says, 'If you see him who has not been born of a woman/throw your face to the ground, and worship him. He is your father.' "

Sondra now takes graduates of the Loving Relationships Training to India every year for the Divine Mother Festival to experience what has brought her so much joy.

Sondra has a beautiful home in Seattle, Washington, but she is seldom there. Her work has made her a worldwide traveler. She remains committed to that inner voice that grows stronger every day. What some would call courage, she calls following intuition. Last year, while in meditation, she was called to Yugoslavia to see the Virgin Mary.

"I went the day after the Harmonic Convergence. I left from Glastonbury, England, where I had been speaking. I did a speech on physical immortality in the town hall on August 17, 1987, which was a real thrill. I got on the plane and went to Yugoslavia immediately after that. I went by myself and basically knew nothing about how to get there. I landed where no one spoke English, so I got in a taxi and $250 later I ended up in Medjugorje, which is a little village in a farming area. There's a big Catholic church right in the middle of farmland, no hotels or anything. I arrived there and the taxi driver said, 'No hotel!' and I had all my world-tour luggage. I had no idea what I should do or where I would stay. A little boy took me to his family farm, and I lived with this Yugoslavian family who didn't speak one word of English. The second day I was there, I was called in by the priest to go into the apparition room, which was quite astonishing to me. I didn't have any idea before I got there whether they'd let me enter.

The Virgin Mary decides who goes in and tells this priest. So I was quite surprised to be called in with twenty-five male Catholic priests from all over the world. It was very difficult to get in because thousands of people were shoving and pushing outside, wanting to be in the area when the Virgin came. She comes everyday around 6:30 P.M., and when she does, the energy changes and the sun starts spinning and changing colors, which I was able to witness.

"The priests and the children were crammed into a very hot, small room. They started some prayers and chanting and the man in front of me nearly fainted. I was shoved out on the floor, up front next to the children, when the Virgin appeared. Then the priest said, 'Now she is coming, no cameras.' It was very profound. I feel it was completely authentic, which I already knew or I wouldn't have gone there. Of course, no one sees her except the children, but their eyes go up instantly and they go into a trance of ecstasy which is pretty amazing to watch, and then all of us burst into tears. After that I don't remember much—I was very spaced out. But I actually felt the energy of the Virgin Mary enter me. The energy I seem to be integrating this year is the energy of the Divine Mother. It was an incredible gift! It is now my obligation to share it."

A few months following this experience Sondra was in New Zealand. "On New Year's Day I was out on a boat and I really let myself let go. I imagined putting everything behind me, not thinking about the past at all, and entertained the idea that I might be doing something totally different. I laid down in the back of the boat and breathed, and this training called 'Evolution' came through me.

"I was extremely thrilled to receive it. The Evolution Training is dedicated to the Divine Mother, so the energy was quite different. The feminine aspect of God, I think, has to do with being on the other side of Harmonic Convergence. It's how to evolve yourself and take responsibility for your own evolution. It's about service and being aligned with the Divine Mother." (The first Evolution Training took place in Palm Springs, California, in January 1989.)

Sondra was invited to the Soviet Union in 1988 as a diplomat with the Center for Soviet-American Dialogue. While there she was asked to appear on Soviet national television, where she spoke on rebirthing and physical immortality.

Sondra is on a spiritual path. She cares most about her

relationship to God and does whatever she needs to do to stay "spiritually pure." In *Pure Joy* she examines ways she has discovered for achieving spiritual purification, some of which are affirmations, rebirthing, chanting, prayers, meditation, fasting, and bodywork. She consistently works a spiritual program. For her there is no distinction between what is fun and what is spiritual—it is all the same.

"Everything I do is pleasurable, every moment is fun, so it doesn't matter what I am doing. I don't have to get away from my work in order to have fun. I love strolling and going shopping. I love beautiful things, and I meet people that way. When I go away by myself, I like to write. Recently I went to Barbados because I like to write near the water. People kept asking me, at this resort, 'Are you really here by yourself?' and I said, 'Yes, I am,' and they were always shocked. They couldn't understand the pleasure I got out of solitude. I like solitude a lot, and then when I am not alone, I have a very, very, very social life with people around me all the time. But I can be extremely happy either way. Not too much bothers me. Because I have learned to live with myself, it now enhances my relationship with Martin.

"I am very happy to be a woman now, at this time, because I think it is an extremely exciting and powerful time since the Harmonic Convergence. It is a time for women to be out there and exposed and become leaders. I do have self-respect as a woman and as a leader. Self-esteem is a must. I have always known how to achieve what I needed to do in my life as a woman, and I feel happy about that.

"As far as the world goes, I am optimistic. I don't feel it does anyone any good to be pessimistic. I always look at the bright side of everything, and I always have. I feel that everything is going to improve; even if the stock market goes through changes or if the Earth goes through changes, I feel it is all favorable. I know there is a divine plan.

"I am excited. I think it's good that corruption is being exposed in the media. That is one of my roles too, to help people wake up. By waking up I mean becoming spiritually enlightened and aware that we are responsible for what we create. Blame is off the track. I feel that people are going to continue to have to face that, and eventually will. By the year 2000 it is quite possible that everything will be much, much better through all this purification we are going through. I don't know what it is going to look like, but I am very optimistic about it and about my role. I trust people's innate goodness."

PERSONAL TRUTHS

1. It is possible to be happy all the time, and it is possible for your relationships to work.

2. It is possible to be healthy and live forever through purification and spiritual enlightenment.

SONDRA RAY
Author of

How to Be Chic, Fabulous and Live Forever. Berkeley, Calif.: Celestial Arts, 1989.

Pure Joy: My Spiritual Journey Through India. Berkeley, Calif.: Celestial Arts, 1988.

Birth and Relationships. Coauthored with Bob Mandel. Berkeley, Calif.: Celestial Arts, 1987.

Ideal Birth. Berkeley, Calif.: Celestial Arts, 1985.

Drinking the Divine. Berkeley, Calif.: Celestial Arts, 1984.

Celebration of Breath. Berkeley, Calif.: Celestial Arts, 1983.

The Only Diet There Is. Berkeley, Calif.: Celestial Arts, 1981.

Loving Relationships. Berkeley, Calif.: Celestial Arts, 1980.

Rebirthing in the New Age. Coauthored with Leonard Orr. Berkeley, Calif.: Celestial Arts, 1977, 1983.

I Deserve Love. Berkeley, Calif.: Celestial Arts, 1976, 1987.

Elisabeth Kubler-Ross

Elisabeth Kubler-Ross *is a world-renowned author, scientist, and humanitarian. In her best-selling book* On Death and Dying *she was the first to identify the five emotional stages of dying. Since the mid seventies she has also become known for her studies and lectures on life after death. She has authored fourteen books, her most recent being* AIDS: The Ultimate Challenge, *which describes her work with AIDS patients.*

Elisabeth Kubler-Ross has been instrumental in bringing the hospice movement to the United States and in founding Children's Hospice International, Inc. She founded Shanti Nilaya (The Final Place of Peace) above the hills of Escondido, California, in 1977. People retreated there to heal from emotional pain and learn to live until they die. Her organization, now called the Elisabeth Kubler-Ross Center, moved to Virginia in 1984. Elisabeth and her staff give seminars around the world.

Elisabeth received her M.D. from the University of Zurich in 1957 and completed her psychiatric internship and residency in New York State. She has been awarded more than twenty honorary degrees, including Doctor of Science from both Albany Medical College (1974) and Smith College (1975), and a Doctor of Laws from the University of Notre Dame (1974).

As much as I wanted to interview Elisabeth Kubler-Ross, it looked like it was not going to happen. I had planned to interview her months earlier but then was informed that she had suffered a minor stroke. When the time was right for her, I was in the final stages of completing the book and was hesitant to add another woman. I called her center in Virginia and said I would probably not be coming.

A few days later I checked my answering machine, and a woman with a heavy Swiss accent said, "This is Elisabeth Kubler-Ross. Call me." When I called her back she asked, "When are you

223

coming?" I rattled on about why I wouldn't be coming and that maybe we could do a phone interview, but she, a master of the broken-record technique, kept asking, "When are you coming?" Before I could end the conversation, I heard myself setting up the interview. I hung up and wondered what had happened. I was both excited and scared. On the one hand I felt that this interview was going to be an important meeting for me, and on the other I couldn't imagine dragging my then-weary body to a farm in Virginia. But I did.

I arrived late Friday evening. Elisabeth immediately came down from her home to her guest house, where I would be staying. It was love at first sight. She has one of those beautifully lined faces that promises a story from each line. She has brown eyes, glasses, curly short hair that rarely sees a salon, weathered hands from farming, and a beautiful smile. When I first saw her I almost said to her, "I've missed you," but since that made no sense I said, "Hello."

As I sat at the farmhouse table eating Elisabeth's home-cooked food, she looked at me with that scientific curiosity and said, "Why did you choose these women for your book? I wouldn't have chosen some of these women." I have to admit I felt slightly intimidated at that point. Then I explained that certain names had come to me almost spontaneously. I'd accepted that and put those women in the book. She said, "Oh, coincidence." I replied, "More like intuition." Although that was not a scientific response, the mystic in her seemed satisfied.

That first night she took me up to her home, a Swiss chalet of cedar, for a visit. She said it was her teepee. It is built with a high ceiling that peaks in the middle. The living room has a fireplace and a large wood stove that she keeps burning through the winter. She loves to do her canning and cooking in her large kitchen. She says feeding people is her favorite thing, and she had just made a lemon cake and a rhubarb pie for my visit. I became obsessed with what I am sure was the best lemon cake I have ever eaten and nearly finished it in the course of the next two days.

I was surprised that I felt so comfortable with her. Even when she talked about spirit guides I felt safe. I shared with her that it wasn't that I didn't believe in spirit guides, past lives, and astral travel; it was just that I didn't want to have anything to do with them. When I was a child my father had talked so much about that stuff. We would buy a house and move in; then my father would start to tell us who had lived and died there and what spirits were still hanging about. I wanted my father to be like other people's fathers. I was embarrassed when he was on television for spotting UFOs.

Elisabeth asked if my father saw *spirits. After thinking about it I said, "He must have because he described to us what they looked like." Elisabeth then said, "If you could see spirits, you would see this room filled with them." I looked up and around the large, peaked ceiling and didn't see anything. I remember being a little girl and wanting the spirits to go away, but that night it felt fine that they were there. Then I asked if she was talking to them, and she said, "No, because I am talking to you now."*

The next day I sat and listened to her life story for hours. We took a break for lunch, worked in the greenhouse a few hours, fed the lambs, and then did more interviewing. As I listened to her story and we spent so much time together, I realized something was happening that I couldn't explain. Somehow I knew that our time together was changing the course of my life, but I didn't know what that meant. It is weeks later now and I still feel the same way. What I do know is that it took every event in my life before that weekend to bring me to the place where I could listen to this amazing woman's life story and know right then and there my life was changing.

I would have liked to have put every bit of the 150-page transcript I have from her interview in this book, but as with the other women I needed to limit the length of the chapters. Her biographer, Derek Gill, wrote a beautiful and moving book, Quest: The Life of Elisabeth Kubler-Ross, *in which he details her life from birth to 1969. Because of this I chose highlights of her early life and then focused on her experiences, many of them mystical, after 1969.*

Being with Elisabeth was a very nurturing experience for me. I felt loved and cared for. The tiredness I had felt for days preceding the trip left me. It is remarkable to be with a woman who has given, and given, and then given some more. Beginning with her relief work during and after World War II and continuing through her life as a physician, she has never charged for any private consultations. People pay to attend lectures and seminars, but not for the hours and hours of time she spends with people after the workshops and into the early morning hours. Just as she loved her time as a Swiss country doctor, she continues to see local residents of Virginia who are in need of her services. A pumpkin pie or some other gift might arrive as payment for her time.

On Sunday morning she again invited me up to her home to visit and have another piece of lemon cake. For some reason I felt as if I had known her forever and that I would miss her deeply when I left. For what felt like a long time we sat silently in our chairs, looking at the blazing fire she had built. Finally I got up the nerve to say, "When I first saw you, I wanted to say I have missed you." She looked at me intently and said, "Oh, yes, you have been with me before," and I knew that that was true.

Fighting for her life was Elisabeth Kubler-Ross's first battle. Her second was fighting for an individual identity among the Kubler triplets. She would weather other trials throughout her life, but winning these two was essential to the journey that followed.

Elisabeth was born in Zurich, Switzerland, on July 8, 1926. She and her sister, Erika, weighed two pounds each, while the third triplet, Eva, weighed six and a half pounds. Her mother, fearing for her babies' lives, took them from the hospital and nurtured them day and night for the next nine months.

"Being born a triplet, I had a group identity, not an individual identity," Elisabeth explains. People could not distinguish Elisabeth from Erika, although they pretended to know the difference. "The first lesson I learned is that grownups are not honest. My parents didn't want to admit they couldn't tell us apart."

Elisabeth hated her identical identity. "We had identical dolls, identical bedspreads, identical shoes, identical dresses, identical everything. We had to pee at the same time and weren't allowed to get up until we had all finished. My father was a regimented disciplinarian who didn't tolerate any acting out. Naturally I became a rebel.

"We had to cut the sausage in three pieces when we went out to dinner, and my father picked which sausage we could have. He demanded we have the same initials because it was cheaper to make a dowry that way. The whole family had the initials E.K, so not even our initials were our own. It was to that extent that I did not know who I was."

Her father expected things to be done the way he wanted, when he wanted. Elisabeth said the positive side of this was that they all learned discipline. For example, he drilled them on the names of trees, flowers, rivers, mountains, and capitals of countries to strengthen their memories.

"As a buyer for a large company of stationery supplies, he trained people in his field and was good at his work. He was a most beloved teacher, though a tough, tough employer, a tough teacher, and a tough father. He was stern but very good, meticulous, and very reliable. The outstanding thing about my father was that he had a lot of fun. For instance, he and my big sister had terrific voices which they made the most of."

After dinner the family would sit around the piano singing. Elisabeth was relegated to the kitchen to do the dishes because she could not sing. "Though my father was tough, there was a certain degree of fairness in him. Since I had to wash the dishes, he said I could tell them what to sing. I'd hurry up and finish the dishes, then receive my own private concert. I literally felt like a queen, a little girl sitting on a big counter, and my big-shot father had to follow *my* orders. 'I'll Be Loving You Always' was my favorite song, and they sang it with schmaltz.

"We had a huge house and garden and an area of lawn with a swimming pool in the yard from which you could view the twelve-thousand-foot mountains. Everything was covered with the most gorgeous flowers you can imagine. My mother and I were the ones who worked in the garden.

"My mom was all love. She was a workaholic and was always worn out, but she was the best cook and the best baker. She walked miles to get the right piece of roast from the right butcher shop, or the right little rolls for Sunday breakfast. She was an expert housewife—I mean super. She loved to have fun but was sometimes too pooped.

"Every Saturday people came from all around to visit because my mother was such a damn good baker. The people came and indulged, but she was left with the work. She taught us how to be housewives. The big dream of her life was to be a teacher. She never knew that she was our teacher."

Elisabeth's individual identity began to surface when she was a small girl. She couldn't stand white dolls because, as she explains, "Everything in Switzerland was white." She became very excited by a picture book of an African village, and from that time on she wanted a black doll and refused to play with the others. She also remembers making herself a beautiful native shield and spear.

At age five she contracted pneumonia and was kept in a hospital isolation unit for weeks. She remembers acutely the sterility of hospital procedures and the pain of being kept from her family. To soften her pain, her father promised that when she got well he would bring her a black doll. She was "in heaven," she says, the day her father brought her that doll. From then on her individuality was established.

Elisabeth started earning her living at seven or eight by doing the daily grocery shopping. During morning recess at school, instead of playing with the other children, she went grocery shopping. At lunch she'd carry the heavy cart home. "For this I got ten cents, the price of a caramel candy cluster. It was the only thing I had which was mine, which my two sisters didn't have. It was my little piece of heaven."

Elisabeth says she never learned to play. After school she'd go home, study, and work in the garden until dark. She feels it was her workaholic nature that caused her father to announce that she would come to work for him at his office. When he simply announced this as fact she told him, " 'No, it's not what I am supposed to do.' That was the first time I said no loud and clear. My sisters almost passed out, and my father was stunned. He raised his voice and made a big fist and said, 'If you don't become my office assistant, you can leave the house and become a maid if you prefer that.'

"I knew that if I started in an office it would ruin my chances. My dream was to be either a doctor or a farmer, and I thought that when you are old your brain doesn't work as well, so you better become a doctor first and then add farming later. Exactly what I am doing now. The ultimate dream was to be a researcher of nature, nature of humankind or anything else that is alive."

Elisabeth refused her father's request and was given a few weeks to find a job and get out of the house. She quickly found a job as a maid working for a prestigious family in the French part of Switzerland. "I worked there from six in the morning until midnight—nonstop—I mean, literally nonstop. This woman had a huge, old, fancy house and three little children. She was a widow and had guests like you wouldn't believe."

Enduring overwork and receiving no appreciation, Elisabeth worked there a year. The breaking point was on Christmas, when her employer refused to let her join the children around the Christmas tree. She decided to leave and wrote Madame a note saying, "I'm leaving because I was not allowed to see the Christmas tree. I will plant myself a Christmas tree I am welcome to see."

She returned to Zurich. When she arrived home, her

father again told her she must work in his office. She refused, and he gave her two weeks to find another job. Near the end of the two-week period she found a lab job in a biochemical research laboratory, which was followed by an apprenticeship in a hospital laboratory.

"Then something really important happened that changed my life. It was 1941 and the refugees started arriving from France. I mean hundreds and hundreds of children. Some came with fur coats; some came with rags. They could barely walk. Their parents had sent them on the road to save their lives. They walked all the way from France to Zurich with a few grownups leading them. The hospital needed volunteers who would help bathe the children and delouse them. They were malnourished and covered with itchy, painful scabies. Suddenly the whole hospital basement—they called it the bathhouse—was filled with hundreds of children and no staff. I volunteered and I loved it. Everyday I gave baths to hundreds of children."

Switzerland was not prepared for the arrival of hundreds of thousands of refugees. Food was being rationed, and there was no food for the children. Elisabeth plotted with a coworker to organize a food line. The children were fed, but Elisabeth was told that unless she supplied ration cards for each and every meal, she would lose her job, which would have meant a loss of her science diploma. "It was two weeks before graduation, and in Switzerland, if somebody kicks you out, you have to start over from scratch. I couldn't have made it. I couldn't have found a job. I would have been totally devastated."

Her boss at the lab, a doctor from Poland, heard of her possible dismissal. He told her that within three days he would have the needed ration cards. "Apparently he went to the synagogue in Zurich and to the Jewish community—I don't know where he went—but he found enough money and enough coupons to save my life. Right then I made a commitment that I would go to Poland and help his people."

The day after World War II ended Elisabeth, penniless and with only a knapsack on her shoulders, left for Poland. Once she left Switzerland she quickly saw the physical devastation the war had had in Europe. One of her first jobs was to help rebuild a French village that had been flattened by bombs. People were literally living in the ruins. She did relief work for the International Voluntary Service of Peace, which involved cooking and physical labor.

She continued to work her way around Europe doing relief work, and finally, after a series of adventures, made her way to Poland. She ended up in a camp organized by the Quakers to rebuild the village of Lucima, Poland. There she set up a makeshift medical clinic with two other women. "One day I was alone, and this pregnant woman who had walked three days and two nights came in with a huge tumor," Elisabeth recalls. "It had to be removed before she had the baby. I took the knife and opened it. We had no tools, no anesthetics, no nothing. After it was opened and removed, she said she was going to walk home. I said, 'You'll never make it,' and she said, 'Yes, I will. I am going to have my child at home.'

"I slept outdoors in my blanket, and one night I heard whimpering and crying. It sounded like a child. I thought, If I don't get any sleep, I am going to drop dead. I tried to pretend I was asleep but I could still hear that whimpering. At about two in the morning I finally got up and asked, 'What is it?' and this woman said, 'You have to help my child. He is very, very sick.' She had a three-year-old child who had all the signs of typhoid. I couldn't cure typhoid—I had no medicine. I told her all I could do was brew a cup of tea for her and for him, and that there was nothing I could do for him. She said one thing: 'You have to save him. He is the last of thirteen children; all the others died in the concentration camp.' She had brought him out of the camp and was determined that he would not die.

"So, in the middle of the night, I made a cup of tea. Then I receive this incredible message. I didn't know anything about my guides then, but the message I got was, 'The only way you can save this child is to walk to the hospital in Lublin.' That was a whole night's walk. I questioned how this woman, this sick child, and me, exhausted, could walk an entire night, but we did."

They finally arrived at the hospital in Lublin but were told to go away. The hospital already had too many patients, and they refused to admit a dying child. Elisabeth explained the situation, to no avail. Angry, she was finally driven to nationalistic bullying to get the child admitted. "I told the doctor I would go back to Switzerland and tell them how this Polish

doctor would not save the life of one child." He succumbed.
"It takes a nationalist to get to a nationalist," she says. The
child was admitted, but the doctor told Elisabeth and the
mother they could not stay. He told them to return in three
weeks, when the child would be either well or buried.

Both women returned to Elisabeth's clinic. They worked
together during the day and at night shared Elisabeth's blanket
and slept under the stars. One morning, three weeks later,
Elisabeth arose to find that the woman had left. About a week
later, Elisabeth found a handkerchief filled with dirt by her
bed. At the bottom of the dirt bundle was a note that read:
"From Mrs. W., whose last child of thirteen you have saved, a
gift of blessed Polish soil." Elisabeth's friend had walked all
night to find her son well, then walked back again to Lublin to
take him home. In gratitude, she took some Polish soil to a
priest and had it blessed, and walked two days and two nights
more to bring Elisabeth the precious gift. Elisabeth says it was
the finest present she had ever been given.

It was shortly after that experience that Elisabeth knew it
was time to journey home. But before she left Poland, she
asked to be taken to Madainek concentration camp. She felt
that if she went there, she might gain some understanding of
the horror that took place.

When she arrived at Madainek, she walked through the
barbed-wire fences into the camp. She saw the crematorium
and two railroad cars filled with shoes and human hair. In the
barracks that the prisoners had been inhumanly crammed into
before their deaths she saw initials carved in the wood—messages of the dying—and figures of butterflies carved everywhere. It was then that she grasped that the last messages of
these men, women, and children were not of despair, but of
hope and freedom. She would carry the image of the camp,
the barracks, and the butterflies with her forever.

Leaving Madainek, Elisabeth began her long and dangerous journey home. When she finally arrived in Switzerland,
she was shocked to find herself in such a prosperous country
again. Her family welcomed her back with joy and warmth.
She gained twelve pounds in one week and was rehired at the
hospital lab. But adjusting to the wealth and luxury around her
was difficult, and listening to conversations about what she saw
as meaningless things bothered her as well. There seemed to
be a lack of purpose in what people did, so Elisabeth was

glad when the volunteer work force contacted her and asked her to work on a construction project in Italy. Her parents said they had no objection as long as she did not go into eastern Europe. She agreed, but shortly after arriving at the site she was asked to take two children into Warsaw to meet their parents. She decided to do so. It was an uneventful trip but had dramatic results.

When she returned home her father banned her from the house. He would not let her in to collect her clothing. Angry and lost, she wandered downtown. She did not know where she would live or what would happen to her. She ran into a school friend who offered to share her apartment. The next day Elisabeth's tearful mother brought her clothing to her.

Elisabeth again began work at the lab and studied day and night that next year in order to pass the most difficult of Swiss exams. After passing the Matur she entered medical school at the University of Zurich. Although she and her family had reconciled, she still did not expect financial assistance, so she continued to work at the clinic.

It was in a medical anatomy class that she met Emmanuel (Manny) Ross, a Jewish student from New York City whom she would marry. As Elisabeth attended medical school, her dream to work as a country doctor in Africa or India solidified. Meanwhile, she and Manny had fallen in love, and at graduation he asked her to accompany him to the United States. She told him she had no intention of living in such a materialistic society. She invited him to come to Africa or India and he refused. Shortly after, an Indian medical group offered her a job and promised to send her a ticket to Bombay. She was thrilled. "I was going to be the Albert Schweitzer of India," she says. Then, when she did not hear from them, she discovered that the project had fallen through, and with it her dreams of going to India.

It was then that she decided to accompany Manny to the United States. Since he was six months behind her in taking his exams, she worked as a Swiss country doctor until he passed. She loved her eighteen-hour workdays.

Elisabeth and Manny were married and left for New York in 1958. In order to avoid staying longer than necessary with relatives, they quickly found a $100-a-month apartment. They worked as interns for one year at the community hospital in Glen Cove, New York, and then Elisabeth decided she would specialize in pediatrics and eagerly applied to New York's Columbia Presbyterian Medical Center. She was told during the application process that because of the grueling schedule, pregnant students were not allowed. She understood.

"The letter of official acceptance finally came. I was so nauseated I thought I was just excited," she says, but soon discovered she was pregnant. She immediately went to tell Columbia Presbyterian of her pregnancy. They refused to make an exception for her. She lost the residency and three months later lost the baby.

July was an almost impossible time to find a residency. "I was shopping around, trying to see if any place in the world would hire me. I was at the bottom of the list, a woman and a foreigner. Then somebody told me there was a Swiss psychiatrist at the state hospital who needed people all the time because nobody lasted more than a few months with him. He was unpredictable and impossible to work with, but, if I needed a job, I could certainly get one.

"I went for an interview at Ward's Island Manhattan State Hospital, and in ten minutes I had the job. My boss appeared charming, but I knew that under the charm was a monster. I worked there two years as a psychiatric resident. He was cruel, insensitive, and very ambitious. He experimented with all his patients, forcing them to take mescaline and LSD. The experiments continued day and night. Patients screamed and pleaded and begged.

"I was assigned to the ward with forty-nine schizophrenics. I think I brought a human touch into the place. I talked with the people. I listened to them. I touched them and I just knew that with a little love they could get well. Some of them had been locked up there for twenty years without visitors, without anything, and half of them were not even schizophrenics. I used my own brand of psychiatry, and after two years I was able to discharge 94 percent of the patients."

The next year she was invited back for a pediatric internship at Columbia Presbyterian, but by then she did not want to leave her patients at Ward's Island. She believes now that she was divinely guided to complete her psychiatric training and to her eventual work with death and dying.

In the summer of 1960 she and Manny moved to a three-room apartment in the Bronx, and shortly after Elisabeth gave birth to her son, Kenneth. A year later Elisabeth began her third year of psychiatric residency at Montefiore Hospital, where she received more all-around training. Manny was completing his residency there in neuropathology.

After their residencies, Elisabeth again hoped that they could become doctors if not in a third-world country, then at least in a rural area of the United States. But because Manny had specialized in a rare field of medicine, he would need to work in a large city hospital. They both received appointments at the University of Denver.

"The university was very competitive, and everything had to be analyzed on paper," Elisabeth recalls. "You had to follow a school of thinking. I needed something different, so I found Dr. Sydney Margolin, a researcher in psychophysiology, a psychiatrist, and the best lecturer at the university. He was European and a bundle of wisdom like a walking computer. The students loved him. You could talk to him about anything. I worked in his lab assembling machinery for his study of physiology.

"Then one day, while I was putting together a polygraph machine, he came in and said he had to go somewhere and I would have to take over his lectures. This was like replacing God! I died a thousand deaths. I was very shy in those days and couldn't talk in front of five people. He said it had to be about psychiatry, but I could pick any subject. I went to the library to see if there was anything written on death and dying because I thought the students really needed to know about it.

"I created a lecture of everything I could find from anywhere. It was a lecture on the ritual of mourning and death and the origin of funerals. It took a lot of work but it had nothing to do with patients, so after the break I brought in a girl who was dying and I said, 'Now that you have the theory, here is the practical. I want you to interview this girl about her eminent death.' The students couldn't open their mouths. They were so struck with this sixteen-year-old gorgeous girl. I said, 'Well, since you don't have any questions, I will interview her.' I started to talk to her very openly and bluntly. She was angry because her mother had put an ad in the newspaper saying her daughter was turning sixteen and was dying, and would people send cards. A mailman came in with bags of cards from strangers and dumped them in her room. She was relieved to be able to talk about what it is like to be sixteen and instead of going out to a prom or dance or a graduation party, you get only Happy Sixteenth Birthday cards from strangers. At the end I said, 'I need three or four students to volunteer to ask her a few more questions just to get the feeling that people, even if they are dying, are human beings who can talk to you.' They asked about her chemotherapy. They asked about her blood count, all stupid clinical stuff. They couldn't ask one human question. The lecture was tape recorded and transcribed. I didn't know that it went all over the country.

"About that time I began to feel that there was something missing for me in Colorado. I worked one-half day in child psychiatry and one-half day on an adult psychiatric unit, but I was not gratified. I needed to find what was missing. I went to the three best people at the University of Colorado. One was Dr. Rene Spitz, a very famous Swiss psychoanalyst in his eighties who studied babies who died from lack of touch and love. I trusted him 100 percent. Another was a very well-known man, Dr. John D. Benjamin; and the third was Dr. Margolin, my boss. I didn't tell them what the others had said, but I presented them with the same problem. I said, 'There is something missing in my life, and I need to find out what it is.' All three, independent of each other, told me I had to go through psychoanalytic training. I hated the idea. I hate to sit and talk while somebody sits behind me and takes notes for years and years."

Even so, Elisabeth applied to and was accepted by the prestigious Chicago Psychoanalytic Institute. Although it was inconvenient, Elisabeth planned to fly twice a week from Denver to Chicago for her appointments. Then she discovered that she was pregnant with her second child, Barbara, so she chose to postpone this additional training. After she gave birth to Barbara, she and Manny both received appointments in Chicago, Manny to Northwestern University and Elisabeth to the University of Chicago. She began her analysis training.

Elisabeth worked as an assistant professor of psychiatry at the University of Chicago Medical School. It was there she began a series of lectures on death and dying. "When we moved to Chicago, the theology students told me they'd read a lecture of mine and asked me to lecture to them. They said, 'We are not going to be physicians, but we are going to be pastors and ministers. We need to know how to work with dying patients.' " She agreed. The first half of her seminar would be lecture, and the second part would be an interview with a terminally ill patient.

Her colleagues were critical of her work, calling her a vulture preying on the pain of others, but the patients themselves were grateful for the opportunity to talk. The patients were not the only receptive people. Her classrooms were standing room only, and she earned the favorite teacher award at the University of Chicago Medical School for five consecutive years. Elisabeth says, "I learned to listen to my own gut reaction, not to do what somebody tells me to do. I learned to follow through when I believe in something and to trust, no matter how hard it is."

Despite criticism from colleagues her work was receiving academic recognition. During this time she was invited to teach at the Lutheran Theological Seminary, and from 1965 to 1971 she was a consulting psychiatrist for Chicago Lighthouse for the Blind and the Peace Corps.

In 1969, Elisabeth experienced two important events that would open her work to even larger audiences. The Macmillan Publishing Company asked her to write a book on her work. Every night after work at the medical school and after her family was in bed she would write until early morning. It took Elisabeth only three months to write *On Death and Dying*.

On Death and Dying defines what the world has come to know as the five emotional stages of dying: the first stage is denial and isolation; the second, anger; the third, bargaining; the fourth, depression; and the fifth, acceptance. The emotion that usually persists through all these stages is hope. *On Death and Dying*, read by millions over the next twenty years, was to become the textbook for courses on death, grief, and care for the dying.

"Then, in November 1969, a *Life* magazine article came out about my work, including an interview with a twenty-one-year-old girl. The article made my work world-known overnight. *Life* magazine sold hundreds of thousands of copies. I got letters from India, Australia, Africa, all over the world, from people who wanted to help this girl live. My house was cluttered with thousands and thousands of letters. Suddenly I moved from being an inconspicuous professor of psychiatry at the University of Chicago to being a well-known person. The telephone rang nonstop. It was crazy—overnight. November 21, 1969 changed my life.

"The hospital was very upset about it. They said, 'Now we are going to be famous for our dying patients instead of for cancer research and cancer cures.' I was blamed. The clergy, rabbis, Catholic priests, and ministers who packed my classes didn't dare to come back. They would stop me in the hallway and say, 'We can't come anymore because we don't want to lose our jobs.' They all deserted the ship. I said, 'If you are afraid that the establishment does not like you and you'll lose your job, then you are not a minister or doctor in the first place, so make up your mind whether you are going to help dying patients or whether your job and your security are more important.' Still, none of them came back except one superb black minister. He and I continued the seminars by ourselves. Then the establishment forbade my bringing patients from the university, so I had to import them from suburbia."

While she was receiving little support from her medical community, demand for Elisabeth's workshops and lectures was growing worldwide. She began traveling nearly a quarter of a million miles a year in response to requests for her seminars. "I naturally did more and more lectures and was gone all the time, but my children didn't suffer. All kids need to know is that they are loved, and mine were loved. Barbara and Kenneth were home one day when I came back from a trip, and I had brought them some junk from an airport. They both said, 'Mom, you don't have to bring us this junk all the time. We don't need it.' I said, 'Why don't both of you start collecting something small, and whenever I go overseas I can bring it home with me, and by the time you are twenty-one you will have a nice collection.'

"Barbara chose thimbles, which you can put in your pants pocket and cross the border and nobody knows. Typically, Kenneth said he wanted to collect gold coins. He had good taste. He had been a coin collector since he was tiny. I told him he could have a coin on Christmas and his birthday. The first time I went to Texas I took Kenneth. For him Texas was 'a super country.' He was maybe nine years old. That's when I bought him his first gold coin. It was ninety dollars, and for me that was a fortune. There was a time when my husband and I were somewhat broke, and my son was worth more than both of us put together."

She jokes when she says, "It is almost pathological that I had so few problems with my kids. I never had to take them to the emergency room. They never had a broken bone or needed a suture. No drugs, booze, or promiscuity. They were just wonderful kids."

As her children were growing, Elisabeth's fame was expanding. People wanted to attend Elisabeth's seminars. Ministers, counselors, psychologists, social workers, and terminally ill people and their families were all eager to come. Elisabeth's goal was to help people live each moment fully until their deaths.

Her five-day workshops are profound experiences, in which people heal and release negativity they have held within for years. People let go of any unfinished business whether they have one day or eighty years left to live. By releasing the negativity, Elisabeth believes, people can live each day more fully. As she writes in *To Live until We Say Good-Bye*:

> The purpose of these workshops is to share with
> a group of people everything we have learned from
> the dying patient. Participants share their own
> griefs, search for their own unfinished business,
> for their own fears and guilts, and we help them
> to . . . do away with the drain of energy required
> to repress all these negative feelings. We help
> them to free themselves of guilt and fear, and we
> try to teach them unconditional love and ser-
> vice, . . . things that regrettably no one helped
> them accomplish earlier so that they would have
> been able to say, "I have truly lived."[1]

In the following years Elisabeth wrote many more books to further people's understanding of life and death. *Questions and Answers on Death and Dying* (1974) seeks to answer questions often asked through her work. It also provides new information on suicide, terminal illness, euthanasia, home care for the dying, and family concerns. *Death: The Final Stage of Growth* (1975) is an anthology, edited by Elisabeth, that includes poems, essays, and letters written by former patients, colleagues, and students. It addresses the difficulties of patients dying in institutions, talks about the taboo of death, and

1. Elisabeth Kubler-Ross and Mal Warshaw, *To Live until We Say Good-Bye* (Englewood Cliffs, N.J.: Prentice Hall, 1978), 149, 150.

the sources of our own fears. Her books for children and about children's deaths, *Living with Death and Dying* (1982) and *On Children and Death* (1983), describe how children regard death and how bereaved parents handle this crisis. Her beautiful children's book *Remember the Secret* (1981), illustrated by Heather Preston, is a story of love, caring, and loss. *The Dougy Letter* is a booklet written and illustrated by Elisabeth in response to a young child's questions about life and death. About working with children she writes:

> I love to work with dying children. They're just so beautiful. Nobody knows what pearls they are. They have all the wisdom in the world. They know that they are dying. They know how and when they are dying. They teach you all about life if you can hear, if you can listen to them. They use an incredible symbolic language to convey to you how much they know. If people would only understand their symbolic language.[2]

Two exquisitely photographed books are *To Live until We Say Good-Bye* (1978) and *Working It Through* (1982). Mal Warshaw, who spent several years working with Elisabeth, is the photographer and Elisabeth wrote the text. In *To Live until We Say Good-Bye* Warshaw photographed Elisabeth's counseling work with the terminally ill. *Working It Through* depicts Elisabeth's workshops for people whose lives are touched by death or who are terminally ill themselves.

Sometime after she had completed her psychoanalytic training and her lectures were well under way, Elisabeth says, "I started to feel more and more that I was on a spiritual path. I had all sorts of experiences that I couldn't explain."

She also began to ask some interesting questions, like what is death really? "Medicine deteriorated at the end of the sixties. Suddenly everybody had to be worried about lawsuits. We had to become specialists in moral, ethical, and financial issues. It left no time for what the patient wanted to feel and ask. But if we could come up with a definition of death that

---

2. Lynn Gilbert and Gaylen Moore, *Particular Passions: Talks with Women Who Have Shaped Our Times* (New York: Clarkson N. Potter/Crown Publishers, 1981), 266.

was valid and all inclusive, not just a flat EEG, then we could not only save the hospital millions of dollars, we could go back to being practicing physicians, not worrying about money and liability insurance. I said to my minister friend, 'You are up on the pulpit every Sunday. You believe if you ask, if you knock, the door will be opened.' I said, 'I am going to ask now. I am going to look long enough until I come up with a definition of death. Then we can go back to being physicians and ministers.' I pointed my finger up to the sky and asked, 'What is death all about?'

"Five days later I received a request from a woman who wanted to come to my death and dying seminar. She had been in the intensive-care unit fifteen times, always on the brink of death. She always died and came back. The nurses regarded her as odd. It was too spooky for them. I said, 'She probably can't die because she has some unfinished business. Let's find out what that is.' She shared that her husband went into psychotic episodes and tried to kill her youngest son. She couldn't die because she knew that her husband would fall apart and would kill her son. I said, 'We'll make arrangements that in the case of your critical illness or impending death, the custody of your son will be transferred to another family member. This way, if your husband has a psychotic episode, the son is safe.' She was very grateful. We made the arrangements and she left, thanking me a million times.

"Then maybe ten months later, I got another request from her to come to another seminar. Normally I wouldn't interview her again for my class, but she said she had something very important to tell me. She told me that after our first seminar she went back to Indiana, where everything went well for a while, but suddenly she again became critically ill. They put her in a local hospital in Indiana, and in that bed she suddenly knew that she had to make an all-important decision: Should she hang onto life until her son was sixteen, or should she just let go and be at peace? Just as she made the decision to let go, a nurse walked in, took one look at her, and ran out. Then the resuscitation team burst in. In the meantime she was out of her body, floating about three feet above, watching the resuscitation team and hearing every word they said. She listened in great amazement and tried desperately to tell them to relax, take it easy. She said she even went down there and shook them, but because she had no body she went right through their arms. The more she tried to tell them she was all right, the more frantic they worked on her. After forty-five minutes one of the young doctors got very uptight and told a peculiar joke. She registered the joke, began to realize that she could not get through to them, and gave up and 'lost consciousness.' They declared her dead and started the preparation of her body. Then she decided to come back to life, because she realized that before she died she needed to tell me what had happened to her. Nobody wanted to listen to her in Indiana. She even tried to tell the joke that the resident shared when she was supposedly dead. They were shocked that she knew that joke and couldn't figure out how she knew, but that was it. She told me what happened and asked if she was going crazy. I told her I could vouch that as long as I had known her, she had not been crazy. She hugged and kissed me with tears streaming down her cheeks.

"When I went back to my students to discuss what I had heard, I was attacked: 'Why didn't you call it a hallucination or a psychotic episode?' I said, 'Maybe this is a lesson in humility. If I blow a dog whistle in this room none of you can hear it, but that doesn't mean that sound doesn't exist; it just means that we are not tuned into it. Maybe this is what that woman experienced at the moment of her death, that she was able to do things that we cannot do yet when we are in a dense physical body.'

"They could not understand how a physician and a psychiatrist could believe this woman. When the class was over, my minister friend and I were very excited. We said, 'Listen, if she could observe that, then there must be thousands of other people who can do that. Now the only problem is we have to find at least twenty cases before we publish it.' Everybody whispered, 'I'll tell you my experience if you promise me you'll never tell this to anybody.' We realized that lots and lots of people had these experiences but were too afraid to share them because they would be called psychotic or given other labels. It was like sharing a beautiful psychic experience and then someone making something vulgar out of it.

"We now have twenty thousand cases we have never published. Years later, Raymond Moody wrote *Life after Life* and they refused to publish it because he was not yet a physician and it was 'not scientific enough.' The publisher sent it to me and said, 'Would you please endorse his work because it should be published so people can at least have an inkling of this.' I read it in one night and I wrote the foreword to it and it has become a million-dollar best-seller.

"I began to have more experiences I couldn't explain. When I was in Santa Barbara, California, for a lecture, a woman picked me up at the airport and told me I had to come to her house for an urgent message. I didn't know her, but I had a few hours before the lecture, so I went. The moment I walked in, a man, talking in a normal voice, said, 'I have a message for you now. Just sit still for a minute and it will come through (meaning through him).' I had never seen or heard of channeling, was not a Californian, and wasn't into that stuff at all. Then this gorgeous voice came through the man and said, 'You have passed your first assignment. You have brought death and dying into the light, and there are millions of people now who can listen to dying patients and hear them. You have completed this task. Your next assignment is to tell the world that death does not exist.' I said, 'What?! I am supposed to be the death and dying lady. Forget about it!' He said, 'No, you made this commitment, and you will fulfill this commitment just as you did with the first commitment. You have three commitments to keep.' I said, 'Why don't you get a minister? Tell him that death does not exist.' 'No, it cannot be a clergy. It has to be a woman, somebody from science and medicine, somebody with credibility. It has to be somebody who is not afraid of sticking their neck out.' He gave me a long list explaining why me, and finally I said, 'Okay, okay, okay—I'll do it, but you are going to help me.' He said, 'Haven't we always helped you?' and I said yes. That was my first channeling experience. It blew my mind.

"Then I went to my lecture. I thought I would begin telling them what death is like, but I was tired of talking about it. I wished somebody would walk in with their own experience so they could do the talking. I did my normal routine during the first part of the lecture. Then during the break I talked to my guides and said, 'You promised to help. I really need someone who has had a life-after-death experience to come on stage and share it with the group.' Then I went back, and the woman who organized the lecture said, 'A man called up. He said he is what we would call a Bowery bum. He is in town and would love to share his death experience with this group but he doesn't have bus fare. He asked to be picked up.' I told the woman to pick him up and to bring him up on the stage when he got there. She was worried that he might be a kook. I said, 'No, he is an answer to my prayer,' and she just looked at me as though she thought I was crazy.

"About half an hour later this good-looking man, not the Bowery bum I expected, walked in. Without saying a word to this stranger, I told the audience that here is a man who wants to share his own experience with us. I said, 'I have not heard it, so I have no idea what is coming. If it is inappropriate, I will take the liberty to stop it, but I have the feeling that this is something all of us really need to hear.' And the man sent me the most grateful look in the world and shared the most incredible experience I have ever heard in my lifetime.

"He had been a happily married man. He had five children and they were planning a family outing. His parents, wife, and the five children were on their way to pick him up at work. Their car got hit by a gasoline tank and the gasoline poured over all of them and everybody was burnt to a crisp— his five children, the wife, the parents, everyone. He could not cope with it. He started to drink, and then he found drugs. He wanted desperately to die. He tried every kind of drug and couldn't die. The last memory he had was of lying on a road too drunk to move when he saw a big dirt truck coming toward him. He couldn't get up. The truck drove over him, and he saw himself moving out of his smashed body. He tried to tell the truck driver not to be so upset. The truck driver was just out of his mind. He called for help and they brought an ambulance.

"During the ambulance drive he apparently went out of his body and his whole family came to him. He saw all his children again, his parents, and his wife as one happy, healthy family together. He realized he hadn't lost them; they were just in a different place.

"Somehow they conveyed to him that if he came to them by killing himself, he would be separated from them. He had a mission to fulfill. He was to share his life-after-death experience with people on the Earth plane.

"When the ambulance arrived at the hospital entrance, he walked away. He had no DT's or aftereffects of the drugs. He started to work very mediocre jobs, just to feed himself, while he waited. He asked, 'How can I tell the world?' They said, 'When you are ready, the opportunity will come.' Anyway, he waited in Santa Barbara and one day after praying, 'Please, give me a sign,' he saw a big announcement—'Kubler-Ross Talks about Death and Life After Death.' He knew it was his answer. When people heard his story they were in tears. I mean everybody. It was the most moving lecture ever.

"After that I started to talk about life after death in public, except I was forewarned that in certain places like North Carolina, in Bible-belt country, you don't talk about stuff like that.

"Then, about two years ago, I was in a fundamentalist church. I did my regular routine—regular conservative, acceptable stuff—but I felt unhappy that I couldn't talk about everything.

"At the end of my lecture I said, 'I'll take one more question.' A woman jumped onto the stage and grabbed the mike and said, 'I came here for one thing. I have to know what children experience at the moment of death.' She sounded pleading and very desperate so I said, 'Well, we have five minutes, so I'll be brief.' I told them that as they float out of their bodies they will see somebody who is either their guardian angel or guide, or a loved one who has preceded them in death, so they're not alone. They know that this is not the end. It is just a transformation into another form.

"I ran through the steps that people experience and then she said, 'I have to share something with you.' She told me she had a young boy—I think two years old—who reacted to penicillin and died. The doctor was out of his mind with grief and regret, and the mother was totally devastated with the dead child lying there. They stayed with this child, praying and crying and pleading and not knowing what to do. Suddenly the boy moved, opened his eyes, and talked like a wise old man. He said, 'Mommy, I was dead.' She wanted to shut him up but he said, 'No, I have to tell it. It was the most beautiful experience anybody can have. Jesus and Mary were waiting for me and it was all love. I didn't want to come back, but Mary kept saying in a very firm but loving voice, 'Peter, you can't stay—you have to go back.' Then, because I didn't want to, she simply took me gently by the wrist and pulled me away (meaning from Jesus) and said, 'Peter, you have to go back. You have to save your mommy from the fire.' This woman was devastated because it was her understanding that she was destined for hell and it was up to her son to save her.

Upon hearing this she went into a horrible depression. This was the first time in thirteen years she'd talked about it. I asked her why she was depressed and she said, 'Well, because I never thought I would end up in hell or that my son would have to save me.' I said, 'No, no, no—you don't understand the symbolic language. You are not able to hear what Mary tried to tell you; otherwise, you would dance and celebrate. She gave you the biggest gift.' I said, 'Tell me very spontaneously what it would have been like thirteen years ago if Mary had not sent Peter back to you.' She grabbed her hair and she said, 'Oh my God, I would have gone through hell and fire!' Mary saved her from the fire. Everyone in the church was crying, and my beliefs were out in the open.

"One night, two or three days later, I came back home and Manny said, 'Now you are really going too far.' There was a headline in the *Chicago Tribune*: 'Psychiatrist Discovers Life After Death.' To my Jewish husband, it was just too much."

Some people began to call her a kook, and her colleagues in the medical profession, who had softened somewhat, were now outraged again.

She needed a retreat and when traveling began to search for a farm. Every time she found one she liked, Manny would balk at the last minute. It was on such an outing, in Virginia, that she had one of her first psychic experiences. She'd been to the Monroe Institute to study out-of-body experiences.

"We were driving a jeep on this farm, heading to the Monroe Institute—Manny, Mr. Monroe, my children, and I. We drove by a very strange house. One that didn't fit the place. A middle-aged woman came out, waved to me, and said, 'Dr. Ross, could you come in quick like?' My husband was impatient to get going, so I said, 'I will come in for two minutes.' She said, 'That's fine, that's all I need.' As soon as we were in the house she showed me a picture with a fairy on it. She said, 'What do you think of it?' I said, 'I'm not into fairies, but thank you anyway for showing it to me.' She said, 'Do me a favor. Take my Polaroid and go to any bush outside and take a picture and you will see a fairy.' Just to appease her I took the picture, and to my surprise there was a fairy in that picture. That was one of my first special experiences, and I knew it was real.

"My husband had to return to work but asked me to bring this fancy, expensive camera that he used for work home with me on the plane. He and the kids were traveling by car. The last thing he said was, 'Don't touch it because it does not belong to us. It is hospital equipment.' I told him not to worry.

"The minute he left, I had that fairy in my mind. I found a typical Virginia hill with a forest and a meadow at the end of it. I said to myself, I am not interested in fairies, but I am interested in guides. If there is such a thing as a guide, perhaps I could photograph that, so I took one picture of the meadow with the trees in the back. Then I did not move from that place and I said to myself, If I do have a guide, make yourself visible on this next picture. I took the same picture a second and a third time.

"About a month later I came back from a trip to New York and had put a nice meal on the table when my husband called from work. He was very unhappy. I asked him, 'What's bugging you?' 'You know what's bugging me,' he said. 'You did it again. You broke the camera. I told you it was very expensive hospital equipment. It is obvious that you broke my camera, because now it superimposes pictures and it never did that.' " Elisabeth was so excited she exclaimed, "Manny, hurry home!"

What she saw on the photograph was a beautiful Indian man who appeared to be almost superimposed against the forest. She knew this was her guide. "My biggest problem was that my husband wasn't ready for it. Later on, in California, when I started to have my guides materialize, he couldn't cope with it. He didn't know what it was all about. For a while I thought he was ready to experience some of these things, but it didn't work. We grew further and further apart."

Elisabeth had already left the University of Chicago and was much in demand as an international consultant. She founded Shanti Nilaya, which means "The Final Place of Peace," in 1977, located in the hills above Escondido, California. It was a peaceful place of retreat where terminally ill children and adults could come to find answers to their questions. It was for people who had the courage to live each moment until their deaths, putting aside their unfinished business, and to experience all their fears, pain, and joy.

She also was influential in bringing the British-founded hospice movement to the United States. There are now thousands of hospices throughout the United States. In 1986, she cofounded Children's Hospice International, Inc., an umbrella organization to facilitate the entrance of children into regular hospices and establish children's hospices.

Elisabeth has trained many people in her work, and even though she is not always present at workshops, the spirit of her work is always there. Her own organization, which moved to Virginia five years ago, is now called the Elisabeth Kubler-Ross Center.

It was in the late seventies and early eighties that Elisabeth experienced some personally painful events that led her to question her future. She had become involved in the work of a psychic and his wife whose work was later discredited. At gatherings on the couple's California ranch followers witnessed spirit guides being materialized into human form. Elisabeth says it takes a certain kind of body chemistry to be able to do that, and this man had that.

"I was living in Chicago, but to have my spirits materialized, I had to link up with this couple in California. He was a good healer, but unbeknownst to me, he started to alter things and to misuse his gift. My husband wanted to protect me, but I had to have these experiences myself. I had to go all the way. If it was true that this guy was turning into a crook, then I had to find out.

"For a long time I learned a lot of things from the entities this man could materialize. I had many days of intensive training, and hours of fantastic teachings. I mean, no human being would know all these answers, so I know the man was not a fake.

"I got books full of knowledge and recorded everything that I could. I have a whole safe full of tapes from that teaching. But I knew that the time had come when I had to call it quits, because by then there were too many bad rumors going around. He was doing a lot behind my back and I tried to catch him. I must say that I have never found any proof of wrongdoing, but I knew I had to sever contact, which I did."

Elisabeth began receiving death threats, was bitten by black widow spiders, and nearly died. Her Escondido home was burned down. "In the meantime my husband had left me and I was without my children, my husband, or anything. I had lost everything I had collected in fifty years and brought from Europe. I was living in a trailer. To move totally alone without my family was not easy."

The next two years were lonely. She continued to give

workshops and lectures and to rebuild the Escondido house, but she felt empty. "My husband married another woman and they had a lovely baby. I thought maybe this was the time to start farming."

She found her Virginia farm of 250 beautiful acres in 1984. It was completely dilapidated. She restored the original farmhouse and barn, and built a large greenhouse, her beautiful cedar home that she calls her teepee, and a log cabin completely decorated with original antiques for sister Eva's visits.

In the beginning, though, she was still suffering from the experience on the West Coast and having doubts in general. Then, she says, "I was sitting here in the living room on the first Thanksgiving night and Jesus materialized. He came under the door totally recognizable—not full body but chest and head. He told me to call this place Healing Waters Farm. He said that someday he would be here and everybody present would see him heal people. He told me other things that would happen here.

"He said, 'Make time your friend.' I hung onto what he said. Then I started to fix up this dilapidated old garden. There was nothing here that was not falling apart or needing repair or painting, and the land hadn't been used for fifteen years. It wasn't fertilized or plowed. It was the most neglected farm you could ever see, and I paid an arm and a leg for it. My big dream was to have Noah's Ark with two animals of each, but they multiplied and I ended up with more than sixty sheep and lots of cattle, many ducks and chickens, bunnies, donkeys, St. Bernard dogs, cats, and llamas—two of each animal! They are all my babies. I am also growing vegetables for the workshops."

Elisabeth began building her center several years ago and has hopes of holding her workshops there. Since she began working with AIDS patients in the early 1980s she has had plans to open part of the center as an AIDS hospice for babies.

In her book *AIDS: The Ultimate Challenge* (1987) she chronicles her work with men, women, and children with AIDS. It was in early 1981 that a man with AIDS called and asked to attend her five-day workshop and she said, "Of course." She wondered if the others would mind, wondered whether he would need special bedding and utensils. He attended, and it was the beginning of her work with AIDS patients. He was able to share his pain. Two women who had sons with AIDS were able to share theirs. Instead of judgment and guilt, people experienced great understanding and compassion.

Elisabeth later initiated a scholarship fund for people with AIDS. She spends many nights knitting warm neck scarves, then at the end of each of her workshops, they are auctioned off. These auctions supply scholarships for people with AIDS. Elisabeth says they have never had to turn down a needy person.

In *AIDS: The Ultimate Challenge* Elisabeth writes:

> Since we can no longer deny that AIDS is a life-threatening illness that will eventually involve millions of people and decimate large portions of our human population, it is our choice to grow and learn from it. We either help the people with this dread disease or abandon them. It is our choice to live up to this ultimate challenge or to perish.[3]

Elisabeth became increasingly concerned about babies with AIDS when she learned that parents could not find agencies that would care for them. She writes:

> I was soon haunted by the images of babies dying of AIDS, uncared for, in alien, institutionalized care centers instead of in a home full of love and compassion. Instead of generous offers of help, many a family is forced to go into hiding. The most vulnerable and threatened were single mothers who were former drug addicts and often terminally ill themselves. These women had previously been able to care for their children, but because of their own illness and the child's constant needs, were unable to do so any longer. They had no support system, no church to fall back on, no husband to support them, and few if any friends left.[4]

3. Elisabeth Kubler-Ross, *AIDS: The Ultimate Challenge* (New York: Macmillan Publishing Co., 1987), 13.
4. Ibid., 57.

She also learned that in some instances the hospitals that were caring for the babies kept them in order to receive the $1,000-per-day fee, and that they received additional grant funding for their research on these babies. Some hospitals referred to them as "pincushion babies."

Concerned for the welfare of these children, she decided to open an AIDS hospice on her land. She planned to build a simple home for fifteen to twenty toddlers and their caregivers. She also began to collect dolls, clothes, and washable stuffed animals.

As plans for the hospice progressed, Highland County residents became frightened, fearing that AIDS would be brought in from outside. A public meeting was called for October 9, 1985. Elisabeth published the transcript from that meeting as well as letters to the editor of the local paper in *AIDS: The Ultimate Challenge*. Both state the residents' fears for their families and for their security. In response, Elisabeth and other experts in the field addressed and answered questions, offering information showing that families and children would not be endangered and that, if anything, business would increase, not decrease, in the county.

Elisabeth's request for a hospice permit was nevertheless denied. In 1989 she had more than 150 families who were willing to adopt an AIDS baby, but she was having trouble getting the hospitals to release the children.

Undeniably, the lack of support from county residents hurt, and their actions toward her center cost her time and money. The county approved a permit for workshops of up to thirty-six people at Elisabeth's forty-acre center, but to make a workshop pay for itself there must be nearly eighty people.

"All my dreams were shattered, and every time I said, 'Now, I can move,' the county put up another block. They think I am going to import AIDS into the county.

"Then I had my stroke, and I couldn't speak for a time."

She says her "spooks" have given her the most difficult assignment of all, resting. "They told me if I don't rest and I don't stop smoking, I'll have another stroke." She knows she has to slow down and rest more. Elisabeth says her mother couldn't stop working, so she had a stroke that paralyzed her and she had to let others take care of her for four years.

What she calls resting would still wear out most people. She cooks and gardens daily, looks after the farm, answers some of the 250,000 pieces of mail after eight secretaries have handled most of it. She still likes to be present at her workshops.

"Often I have to give a lecture just to pay the bills for the milk and the coffee and basics and to support my two children, who are still in college. In another two years they'll be on their own feet.

"I am very self-sufficient here. I don't need anything. I have more than I need. We eat all our own vegetables and beef, and make our own breads. The only thing we bring in is milk and butter. It has been a long, hard road, but I hope it has been worthwhile."

Elisabeth has great friends around the world and is close to her family, including her ex-husband and his new family. Her eighty-year-old Quaker friend from her relief days in Poland and her sister Eva are yearly visitors. Even so, Elisabeth says it can be lonely.

"I will keep active until I fulfill one more task. I finished telling people about death and dying, and I finished telling millions of people that death does not exist, and the third assignment is coming soon. It is the in-between times that are very difficult. It is the waiting, and answering a quarter million pieces of mail, working your butt off, and having no income at all. Here I have enough food to eat, and I have enough for the day-to-day, but every nickel I make goes back into running the worldwide office. It costs us a minimum of $55,000 a month! Since my stroke I don't give workshops anymore. My staff gives the workshops and we have half the attendance. Every month we are from $5,000 to $20,000 in the red and we can't continue this way, so I know something has to give. The day before I went to the AIDS conference in Washington I prayed about it. I knew as of Monday I would not be able to pay people. When I got back we had a check for $170,000 from a patient of mine from years ago. She'd wanted to leave her money to somebody who was doing something for the world."

If you believe "what goes around comes around," you know that Elisabeth Kubler-Ross will always be taken care of. She has spent her life giving to others: her relief work during and after the war; the hours and hours she spent with blind, mentally ill, and terminally ill patients; the years she has spent supporting the beginnings and continued growth of the hospice movement; and her work finding people a Final Place of Peace—Shanti Nilaya. She continues to follow her heart and wait for her next assignment.

It says in the first Shanti Nilaya calendar, "To love means not to impose your own powers on your fellow man but offer him your help. And if he refuses it, to be proud that he can do it on his own strength. To love means to live without fear and anxieties about tomorrow. To love means never to be afraid of the windstorms of life: Should you shield the canyons from the windstorms you would never see the true beauty of their carvings."

Elisabeth says, "I hope people choose to expose themselves to these windstorms so that at the end of their own days they will be proud to look in the mirror and be pleased with the carvings of their own canyon."[5]

---

5. Elisabeth Kubler-Ross and Mal Warshaw, *To Live until We Say Good-Bye* (Englewood Cliffs, N.J.: Prentice Hall, 1978), 155.

PERSONAL TRUTHS

1. Listen to your own truth, not to what others say is right or wrong. Follow your heart and listen to your own drummer.

2. We need to know and not just believe that we are responsible for every thought, word, and deed of our entire lives.

3. We have to learn not only why we are in the world, but also what the timing of things is. "Thy time, not my time."

ELISABETH KUBLER-ROSS
Author of

AIDS: The Ultimate Challenge. New York: Macmillan Publishing Co., 1987.

On Children and Death. New York: Macmillan Publishing Co., 1983.

Working It Through. Photographs by Mal Warshaw. New York: Macmillan Publishing Co., 1982.

Living with Death and Dying. New York: Macmillan Publishing Co., 1982.

Remember the Secret. Illustrated by Heather Preston. Berkeley, Calif.: Celestial Arts, 1981.

The Dougy Letter. Letter to a child with cancer, in booklet form. Headwaters, Va.: Elisabeth Kubler-Ross, 1979.

To Live until We Say Good-Bye. Coauthored with Mal Warshaw. Englewood Cliffs, N.J.: Prentice Hall, 1978.

Death: The Final Stage of Growth. Englewood Cliffs, N.J.: Prentice Hall, 1975.

Questions and Answers on Death and Dying. New York: Macmillan Publishing Co., 1974.

On Death and Dying. New York: Macmillan Publishing Co., 1969.

Barbara Marx Hubbard

Barbara Marx Hubbard is an internationally known speaker, writer, and activist who has worked more than twenty-five years for the peaceful transformation of this planet. She is an active citizen-diplomat with the Center for Soviet-American Dialogue. In February 1988 she served as the program director of the first Soviet-American Citizens Summit in Washington, D.C. Barbara is a founding director of Global Family, a nonprofit organization committed to positive social change, and of EC2000, a program to involve people throughout the world in unified action on behalf of the Earth. She is also on the board of directors of EARTH BEAT, a television campaign promoting environmental issues.

In 1984, her name was placed in nomination for vice president of the United States at the Democratic National Convention. Her Campaign for a Positive Future called for an Office for the Future and a Peace Room in the White House. She cofounded the Committee for the Future in 1970, and initiated Harvest Moon, a plan for the first citizen-sponsored mission to the moon.

She is author of The Hunger of Eve: A Woman's Odyssey toward the Future *(her autobiography)*, Evolutionary Journey: A Personal Guide to a Positive Future, Happy Birthday Planet Earth: The Instant of Co-Operation, *and* Manual for Co-Creators of the Quantum Leap.

Barbara graduated from Bryn Mawr College with a cum laude degree in political science. She is the mother of five and grandmother of three.

People kept suggesting that I interview Barbara Marx Hubbard. They said she is a woman of vision and action. After interviewing her, listening to her tapes, and reading her books, I can easily see why people say that about her. She is dedicated to planetary peace and the spiritual evolution of all people.

The late R. Buckminster Fuller said, "She is the best-informed human now alive regarding futurism." Barbara says she has been a futurist, but now she is a "presentist," because the time for planetary peace and cooperation is now.

At the "Dreaming the New Dream 1988: Choices for a Positive Future" conference in San Francisco, where she spoke on building a new Soviet-American relationship, I was impressed that she'd spent days attending the workshops of the other speakers so her own talk could evolve and incorporate their ideas. She is interested in people grasping the whole picture. She believes in synergy, separate elements coming together to create something greater than the sum of their parts.

After the conference, I interviewed her at her Global Family residence in San Anselmo, California. She has shiny platinum hair. Her skin and eyes glow, and her body is slim and relaxed. She is fifty-nine but has an ageless quality about her. She says she has no sense of age. "It's not that I feel young. I don't feel related to chronology."

As I spent time with her, I gained some insight into how she could show up at the 1984 Democratic Convention in San Francisco, without any political support or money, and find herself with over two hundred electoral votes. Her enthusiasm and her faith in humanity are catching. She believes that the process of evolution is moving us toward a cooperative world in which humanity will learn to be co-creative with nature.

Being a presentist, she began her story with what she is currently doing and worked back to her beginnings.

Barbara Marx Hubbard says, "When a woman falls in love with a purpose, she is as powerfully driven as when she is pregnant." She calls this drive for vocation "supra-sex," and it is that energy which fuels her nonstop participation in life-giving projects.

"Supra-sexuality is the joining of genius and vocation to create works in the world. While sexuality is the combination of genes, male and female, to create a new baby, supra-sexuality joins genius, not genes, through creativity and attraction, to a vocation. The result is gifts, projects, and activities. These acts fulfill people and serve the world. People experiencing supra-sexual co-creation feel attraction, joy, spontaneity, and service. It activates the same passion that falling in love, sexual intercourse, gestation, birth, nursing, and nurturing activate.

"Being in love with a purpose is not professionalism. It is not careerism. It is not self-expression alone. It has the quality of self-transcendence and is comparable to loving an unknown child. When women become passionately attracted to creating something in the world, they don't have to know what the reward is. They are like mothers, and their energy is the pure energy of creativity."

Barbara says the reason supra-sexuality is happening now is that masses of women are having fewer children, thereby creating a "hormonal reserve." This reserve is a new, untapped maternal energy not going into pregnancy. Men experience it secondarily; they too have more creative energy available because they no longer have to support large families.

"A signal has gone out to the human race that we are to have fewer children. Many women will now have one child or no children, unlike my generation. I had five children without thinking. It never occurred to me not to have children. This newly available force is the most profound energy there is in life."

Barbara also points out that our extended life spans mean even more untapped energy. Whereas people used to live to their mid-fifties, they are now living to their mid-seventies. Having more time and more energy, people are looking for new meaning in their lives. Barbara calls this desire for self-expression "vocational arousal." An indicator that one is being aroused is the frustration of feeling there is something more in life to be and do.

"A woman can love her children, her husband, and her house; then vocational arousal strikes and suddenly she is discontented. We have been through this with the women's movement. The women's movement was the first push to say, 'We are to be equal with men.' But this is more than being equal. It is a desire to be fully human, a co-creative human, an heir of God. The feminine energy of reproduction is being transmuted to the feminine energy of co-creation."

Barbara believes that when a woman becomes co-creative she is motivated to fulfill her own potential within the whole human community. She experiences the sacredness of her own life and of all life.

"When I first got pregnant I was twenty-one years old, and I didn't want to be pregnant. I wanted to get a job in Paris. Then, in the seventh month of pregnancy, when the milk started to come, I noticed that I was dreaming of the child. I was falling in love with the child. I wanted it. My hormonal system was programming me to love the unknown child. The shift in me was not a conscious choice; it was a profound unconscious change in my whole attitude. Women are now feeling that way about their vocations."

Barbara also attributes this desire for vocation to increased education. As women have become more educated, they have become increasingly interested in entrepreneurial businesses. She is currently working on a project called "Curriculum for the Genius of Women," through which women who are moving into their co-creative phase can receive support. "Instead of looking for a job that is defined by existing systems, women are finding ways to do what they love to do. I think this is one of the most positive trends there is.

"Also, supra-sex usually involves joining with others to do what you love to do. These relationships can be even deeper and more profound than sexual relationships. They don't have the old requirements of possessiveness, domination, and submissiveness."

Supra-sexual relationships are beyond gender and beyond

age. They have to do with people seeking more meaning in their lives and fulfilling their needs for growth.

"I had a twenty-year marriage that dissolved when my vocational arousal occurred. I experienced myself as being creative in this world. I did not know how to transform my marriage into a co-creative marriage. My husband experienced my expression of creativity as a rejection of him. In our marriage, he had been the artist and I was the appreciator, the editor, and the helper. When I became the creator, it was a terrible blow to the marriage.

"I had another relationship for twelve years, a magnificent relationship in that John was attracted to the passion I had and the vision of a new world. For six or seven years we had a genuinely co-creative relationship, but he began to see my spiritual growth as a threat.

"I tried to get John to go with me on a spiritual search to northern California and to Findhorn, Scotland, but he didn't want to go. He was becoming jealous, possessive, alcoholic, and abusive. He said he loved me so much that he couldn't stand for me to do anything other than work with him. I couldn't stand to work *only* with him. I did everything in my power to make it work. But gradually he became ill and discovered he had cancer. He died of a brain tumor. Just after he died I stood beside his body, in deep shock, and asked him from within, 'Why did you die?' and he said, 'I died to set you free. I loved you too much and I couldn't allow you to grow beyond me. I didn't want to change myself, so I didn't want to stay here,' and he left.

"Since he left in 1982, I have had no intimate relationships with men. I found that if I even got slightly attracted to a man, I would begin to think he could do it better.

"There does seem to be, for many women, a requirement to spend some time without a man, because we are so patterned to be in a relationship. In a relationship with a man, it is exceedingly difficult, if you have the kind of pattern I do, to integrate your own masculinity. In the last six years, when I felt I should send out a rescue signal, I went within and activated the masculine aspect of my own being. The result is that for the first time in my life I feel whole.

"In my wholeness, new relationships have emerged which are co-created with peers on the same path. We are creating a new family unit, joined together by our passion to create."

Barbara describes core groups as a resonating core in which members practice meditation, unconditional love, shared insights, and co-coaching. Then, when it is time for action, people commit to one another to bring their ideas to fruition.

Core groups are the natural evolution of those formed when Barbara was running for vice president in 1984. Out of them she cofounded Global Family with Carolyn Anderson, Marion Culhane, and Jeff Daly, who had managed her Campaign for a Positive Future. In a Global Family unit, people usually choose to live in the same home. There can be couples within the family unit, "but there seems to be a natural tendency to separate from the dyad," Barbara says, "to become a whole being and a co-creator." Global Family units are spiritually based households in which people practice meditation and work to love one another as they love themselves. "In a co-creative core, the higher self of each individual is brought forth and nurtured by the group.

"At Global Family in San Anselmo we are joined together out of shared vocation. Our purpose is to shift consciousness from fear and separation to unity and love. We start with ourselves, and we are guided to serve others to do the same. We model the change we would like to see in the world. By changing ourselves we have more to give.

"In the co-creative cores we are overcoming the illusion of separateness. It is a work unit. The very force that draws atom to atom and molecule to molecule draws us together. That fusion of creative vocation fulfills the uniqueness of the individuals involved. It is a phenomenon that is as powerful as the sexual drive to reproduce the species. For some people supra-sexual co-creation is even more exciting than sexuality.

"These core groups are often formed and led by women. Men are encouraged to release their feminine and balance their masculine within their feminine, so a core group is an area in which both men and women become whole."

Barbara says the core groups often work in their communities or for societal causes. Two projects that Barbara and Global Family members have worked on together are the 1988 Soviet-American Citizens Summit and EC2000, an ongoing program to involve people worldwide in actively supporting the planet.

Barbara was program director of the Soviet-American Citizens Summit, in which one hundred leading Soviets and four hundred and fifty Americans, including author Virginia Satir and economist Hazel Henderson, met in Washington, D.C., for three days. Their goal was to create joint projects furthering peace between the two nations.

"In order to do that event, we created a committed core group. We sat together for a half hour every morning, experienced our love for one another, and voiced our highest aspirations for that day.

"We asked who needed help from whom, and what the top priorities were. In the first half hour, the experience of bonding was cultivated so that the office staff experienced loving relationship all day long. People who came into that office did not want to leave.

"Just as hostility is catching, so is love. Because most of the volunteers experienced this vibration of love, it permeated the event itself. Many veteran conference-goers said it was the highest experience they had ever had. Given the nature of the conflict that the Soviets and Americans have endured, the conference was historic."

Barbara has also had a fifteen-year vision of a global television system that would scan the world for new ideas and creative solutions to promote peace. Plans are being made to broadcast EARTH BEAT on Turner Broadcasting System sometime in the future.

"In a war room you scan for every possible enemy. In EARTH BEAT our situation room is a "peace room" where we scan for every breakthrough that leads the world toward greater cooperation and caring, for innovations in energy, health, education, and so forth. If people want to support and get involved in the projects they see, there will be a 900 number for them to call."

Barbara Marx Hubbard's life, and her journey toward personal and planetary transformation, began with her birth in 1929 in New York City. "My father was Louis Marx, a self-made toy tycoon. He was known as the Henry Ford of the toy business. He had been a poor Jewish boy in Brooklyn, and his parents had emigrated at the ages of sixteen and seventeen. My father was thirty and had made a fortune by the time I was born. He represented the American success story, so I was born into a feeling of tremendous hope and power.

"Whenever I asked my father, 'What is our religion? Who are we?' he said, 'We are Americans. Do your best.' I had the feeling that anything was possible. I was the oldest of four children, growing up in a triplex apartment on Fifth Avenue directly opposite the Metropolitan Museum. We spent summers on Lazy Day Farm, which was in Cornwall Bridge, Connecticut. My father used to invite people like Hank Greenberg, the baseball player, and actors and actresses to visit us there. It was a blessed childhood.

"When I was about twelve, my mother became ill with breast cancer. She died a year later. The divine childhood that I had had was abruptly and shockingly brought to a close. When my father came back from the hospital, I remember the surging anger that went through me. I said, 'It's not acceptable. I refuse to accept this.' It was so outrageous, I was refusing to accept death."

While she was growing up, Barbara's father gave her little support for her feelings and beliefs.

"I adored my father, but I was slightly frightened of him because he was bombastic and loud. I always challenged him. For example, when he said, 'You are all going to be spoiled brats, I have given you too much money,' I would say, 'Okay, take it away.' I loved him deeply, and I feel I incorporated his energy, but his success was in the material world. When I asked him what he thought the purpose of life was, he said, 'To marry somebody with money or make money'; and when I said, 'What do you think I should do in terms of service or society, he said, 'Nothing—just get more money.' He exaggerated because he liked to be shocking. He didn't fully mean that, but we got absolutely no direction about doing anything good other than making money. He often said, 'You don't understand the world. You don't know how tough it is out there or how fortunate you are. All your problems are made up. The only problems that are worth anything are poverty and illness, and you are wealthy. You have got it all.' I thought, If I've got it all, it's a pretty sorry story for the human race. I remember saying, 'I know there is more, and I am going to find out what more there is.'

"I really craved my father's understanding. Later on in my life when I did something, he would occasionally get what my life was about. But he never held it for more than five minutes, because it required him to have an entirely different belief system. My search was for something more, but I respected the material success because I knew it was a launching pad for the new.

"My memories of my mother are much less strong than my memories of my father. She was gentle. She was beautiful, and in my memory she was passive, quiet, and seemed never to fully express herself. I think she was of a generation that had no skills for full self-expression, especially in relationship to a man like my father. I can remember feeling I never wanted to be like that. I never wanted to put up with that. So I didn't have a model of a woman that attracted me, and my model of a man attracted and, at the same time, repelled me. I loved my father's energy, power, and charisma, and I loved my mother very much."

Barbara was the oldest of four children. She felt protective of her brother and sisters, and they grew closer after her mother's death. When her father challenged them by saying one was better than the other, they would tell him they were all equal. Barbara says they've supported one another throughout their lives, even though they are very different.

Barbara received her first years of schooling at the progressive Dalton School in New York City. Students were given a month-long assignment, after which they were rewarded with an opportunity to be creative. They could take Greek dance, paint, or do what they chose. Barbara always finished early, and her creativity flourished.

"I had a marvelous relationship with the boys at Dalton, and I became like a den mother to the whole eighth grade when I was still in the seventh grade. Every day they would walk home from school with me and sit and talk about life. I was always helping them with their homework, guiding and counseling them. I developed a wonderful relationship with males that was more like a partnership, but I was definitely the leader. It worked fairly well. Evidently I gave something in return that they liked. Everybody loved me, and I never thought it could be any different."

It was when her mother was dying and the family moved out of New York City, to Scarsdale, that Barbara found things could be very different. She attended Rye Country Day School, an excellent but more traditional school. Suddenly she was exposed to anti-Semitism and was not invited to country-club dances and other events.

"It was really shocking to me after New York and the somewhat blessed life that I had led. I think because those first twelve years were so happy, so filled with creativity, love, and joy, that when things didn't work well for me, I felt it was abnormal. The norm was joy! I knew that something great was coming."

When she was a senior in high school, she decided to become president of her class and got herself elected. She remembers being immediately disillusioned with power for power's sake. She stood in front of the school giving her acceptance speech and thought, But why are you president? This is meaningless. You don't have anything to do! Since that experience, she has never aimed at power or position.

She was an *A* student, interested in academics and philosophy. Although her sisters and brother were good at sports, she was not—she scored goals for the opposite team. She did like to walk and swim. She also played the piano, but says she had no rhythm and could not carry a tune.

Her mother's death and her refusal to accept it led Barbara to ask questions about life and its meaning. "It started me on a search. It awoke the metaphysical need for something more. I lived in this secular Jewish, slightly anti-Semitic environment. We were never told that we were Jewish, and in a sense we weren't because my father had no religion—he was an agnostic. He made fun of religion. He had friends who were priests and clerics, but he always teased them about their beliefs.

"In 1945, when I was about sixteen years old, the atomic bomb was dropped on Japan. That, for me, was the next unacceptable step after my mother's death. The shock was not just that humans died, but that the planet could be destroyed. I saw that progress was not inevitable, that the very power to create was the power to destroy. Some very deep questions arose in my mind which have motivated my entire life. The questions were, What is the purpose of this power that is good? What is the purpose of science, technology, industry, and Western civilization itself that is commensurate with our deepest aspiration? Where are we going as the human race?

"With these questions in mind I started to read, thinking that I would somewhere find answers. What I found was that it is not even dealt with philosophically. The Greeks looked back to a golden age. The Stoics said everything is cyclical and there is no meaning. The Eastern philosophies look toward the transcendence of this life altogether, and the existentialists look toward the running down of the Universe to a death. I started to read through the religions, searching for answers. When I read the Old and New Testaments I was very struck by the words 'Behold, I show you a mystery. You shall not all sleep. You shall all be changed. In the twinkling of an eye at the last trumpet, and the trumpet shall sound, this corruptible flesh will become incorruptible. Death shall have no dominion.' The new Jerusalem is beyond death, beyond sorrow. . . . The former things shall be passed away. I thought, Now that is exciting! That corresponds to the sense of hope. It *feels* true.

"I had been given, through my background and my innate nature, a sense of something great coming. I didn't want to accept the inevitability of the death of the individual or of the death of the human race through misuse of power. I felt that if I joined a church, maybe I would understand what the Bible meant by 'You shall all be changed.'

"I joined the Episcopal church in Scarsdale. I remember asking the minister, 'How shall we all be changed? What are we changed into, and how do we do it?' He was unable to respond to my question. I asked him, 'What does the Resurrection really mean? Are we to have a new body? I mean, literally?' I wanted to know, and he didn't know. He made it all into a metaphor. The church was just becoming more liberal and getting into civil rights, whereas I was going into transformation and evolution. I went to church and prayed for guidance, but I heard nothing."

Not finding answers through her religious studies, Barbara turned to academics. She attended Bryn Mawr College and, to her disappointment, discovered that there were no courses on the purpose and direction of the human race.

"We study things as separate disciplines that do not have connectedness. That is why our educational system is irrelevant now, and why so many students are dropping out. That is why it doesn't satisfy the human heart. I hated it at Bryn Mawr. I just stayed in my room and read all day long, trying to find the answer."

Barbara decided to spend her junior year in Paris. It was 1947, and she was seventeen years old. She found a French family to live with and attended the Sorbonne in political science. She was disappointed again when she saw that with all

their knowledge, the instructors had no purpose—they were
repeating lectures they had been giving for generations. In her
frustration, she became an existentialist, attempting to give up
her quest for life's purpose by reading Jean-Paul Sartre, drinking wine, smoking cigarettes, and accepting a meaningless life.

"One day I was lunching alone in a little restaurant on
the Left Bank, Chez Rosalie. It was the first time I had separated from my friends. It was a November day, and one place
was open in the restaurant, opposite me. A very handsome
man walked in—an American—and sat down. I had ordered a
half bottle of red wine and a beefsteak. (Now the thought of
that food makes me ill.) I asked him what I asked just about
everybody else: 'What is the purpose of our power? What is
the meaning of life? What is *your* purpose?' He said, 'I am an
artist and my purpose is to discover a new image of man commensurate with our power to shape the future.' With that sentence, it flashed in my mind: I will marry him. Just like that.

"Earl Hubbard told me that from the time of Michelangelo
and his beautiful *David*, you could look at modern art as the
breakup of the image of man. You could see the human self-
image disintegrate from Michelangelo through Monet, Manet,
Pissarro, Picasso, and Jackson Pollock. 'Who are we?' he
asked, 'and what is the purpose of our power?' Now *that* was
the question!

"I went back and told Madame Mercier, at the home
where I was living, that I had met the man I was going to
marry. She was appalled at the idea of meeting the man you
were going to marry in a little French restaurant, so she called
my father. My father flew to France with General Rosie O'Don-
nell to bail me out. He took me and the rest of the family to
the Riviera. I reentered my father's glamorous life. We even
met Elizabeth Taylor, gambled at the casino, and sunbathed on
the rocks. I went back to the United States with my family.
But I met Earl again.

"Earl came from a much less dynamic background than I
did, but it was still a successful background. I told him my
father made toys, and he thought I meant in the attic, by
hand. He was upset when he found out my father was wealthy,
because that meant he could not support me.

"We got married and I remember walking down the aisle
and feeling, Oh my God, I don't want to be a wife—it doesn't

feel right. But I did get married. There was no notion at that time of any other type of relationship.

"Earl wanted to live in the country. He said, 'The art world is a funeral for the image of man, and I am going to create the new image. We have to get out of here.' I followed him to Lime Rock, Connecticut. Then I became pregnant and thought, Oh my God, I am stuck! I was literally like a caged lion. I thought I was marrying to fulfill *my* life's purpose, but Earl was the only one doing it. Every day he went to the studio and I was left to take care of the baby, play the piano badly, and do the housework. I had never done housework, and I didn't like it. Actually, the only thing I liked was having babies. In the moment of pregnancy, birth, and nurturance, I had a purpose that fulfilled that 'hunger of Eve.'

"I didn't make many friends in Connecticut because my goals and purposes were so different from the average suburban couple's. I read more, and I wrote in my journal. I think my journal saved my life because it was the place where I could honor the quest.

"Seeking answers to my frustration, I talked to a Freudian analyst, who was a friend. His analysis was so far from the truth. He said there was something wrong with my sex life and something wrong with my relationship. He never suspected that it was unexpressed growth potential, unactualized vocation, that it was supra-sexual energy. I was told that I was sick because I was not satisfied with having children and being in the country, going to local parties, and being part of the League of Women Voters. I had no model for something else."

Barbara tried to accept her life but continued to feel unfulfilled. At one point she thought she would die of meaninglessness. It was at this time she occasionally began to hear an inner voice. It told her, I won't let you die, and guided her back to New York City.

"But when I got to New York, there was no answer there. It was very much what my husband had said: 'People in the art world are talking about the failure of humanity.' A sense of despair engulfed me."

But Barbara's search continued. In the early sixties she came across three books that began to turn things around for her. She read Abraham Maslow's *Toward a Psychology of Being* and realized that her desire for self-expression was not sick; it was normal—it was a growth need for self-actualization. "That was an enormously important revelation to me. It affirmed my search, and it started the whole human potential movement. I now realize that what was driving me was co-creative energy."

Her second discovery came when she read Pierre Teilhard De Chardin's *Phenomenon of Man*. "He wrote that evolution leads to a higher degree of consciousness. The entire planet is becoming a living system integrating into a whole, evolving to a higher state of being. Maslow affirmed my desire for personal growth. Teilhard De Chardin affirmed my evolutionary passion and intuition that collectively the human race was to do something new and great.

"Those intuitions were right. The existing culture was not affirming personal or planetary potential. The current intellectual and art world said that growth potential in women was neurotic and that the desire for a higher state of being for the whole human race was a false, unscientific superstition. Then I read Buckminster Fuller's *Utopia or Oblivion*. He said we have the resources, the technology, and the know-how to make this world a 100 percent physical success. I thought, if the human being has untapped potential and all our frustration is growth wanting to be expressed creatively, and if the planet is moving naturally toward a higher state through interaction and union, and if we have the technologies and resources to feed, house, and educate every human being on earth, then the situation is great!

"One day while taking my afternoon walk, I found myself saying, 'Thank you, thank you, thank you.' It was a spontaneous prayer of thanksgiving. Then, from the depth of the universe, I heard a response, 'Thank you, Barbara.' That was my first experience of a relationship between the individual and the creator. I loved Teilhard De Chardin because he saw the universe as evolving toward personhood rather than toward impersonality. Christ was, for him, the God-realized person, the model for us all. From that moment on I felt personal about my relationship to the creative intelligence of the universe, which encouraged me as I advanced.

"I began to *know* that I was part of the pattern. When I was on the right path I was being moved, and yet I was also doing the moving. The relationship was not passive. It was cooperative. I became ecstatic, filled with an ever-present inner joy that warmed my heart and transformed my life.

"At that time I realized I would have to express myself. I began some very interesting dialogues with my husband. I questioned him about the nature of our power and who we were. We had breakfast dialogues that would last three and four hours. We taped them and I edited them.

"Through those beautiful dialogues we developed a positive philosophy of hope. We saw this period of life as the birth of humanity as one body. Everything began to make sense. Even our high technologies like the space technologies, biotechnology, and cybernetics made sense. We saw them as serving the human species. They were an extension of our consciousness and capabilities. At the very time when people in the environmental movement were saying technologies were bad because they were destructive, we said, 'We don't want nuclear power, but if the human race is to become a universal species, we need those high technologies. We need extended life and intelligence if we are to become *physically* universal.'

"On the inner plane, humanity was becoming more sensitive to the patterns of evolution, or the will of God. On the external plane, our technologies could empower us to meet our basic needs, to begin the exploration of the immeasurable universe beyond our home planet. Everyone could be emancipated from the drudgery of unchosen work and subhuman activities.

"Jesus was right when he said, 'Look at the lilies of the field how they grow and yet they toil not.' Buckminster Fuller was actually saying that there was enough for everybody if we could understand how to do 'more with less.' We were moving toward a whole new cooperative economic era which would foster human community and creativity. To preserve our environment, we would learn to reconnect with one another, nature, and God. We would experience the next stage of evolution— which is to become co-creative with nature."

In 1964, Barbara heard that Jonas Salk, creator of the Salk polio vaccine, was opening an institute to study the whole person from cell to self-image. By learning how nature works scientifically he planned to learn more about how human society works. Barbara wrote to him, and they met for lunch. She told Salk there was a need to develop a new image of humanity through the arts and described her love of the future. He told her that the characteristics she possessed were precisely the ones needed by evolution now, what she had looked at as faults were really virtues. At that moment Barbara went from frustration and despair to become a person the world needed for evolution. Salk introduced her to several men he had found over a quarter of a century who also believed, through their scientific knowledge, that the human race was in the process of transforming itself.

"Then, in 1966, I had the fundamental experience of my life. I pieced together the evolutionary path and received my vocation. I had just been reading Reinhold Niebuhr on community. He was quoting Saint Paul: 'All men are members of one body.' On my afternoon walk I felt frustrated. In the Gospels there was a simple story—a child was born, and all the rest followed. Then I asked, What in our age is comparable to the birth of Christ? What is our story?

"I went into a slight daydream. Suddenly I was pulled into a Technicolor movie. My mind went into the blackness of outer space. I witnessed myself as a cell in the living body of Earth. The whole planet was struggling to coordinate, was heaving for breath with the pollution, and was feeling the pain of starvation. I felt all the pain of the world at once. It was horrifying. Then there was a little flash of light in space, a moment of shared attention. Suddenly I could see empathy and waves of love running through all of us. The joy became greater than the pain. Everyone was experiencing some kind of light from within, and we became one body. We opened our eyes and the entire planet smiled. The whole human race awoke and saw the light. There was intelligent light surrounding and bathing us, communicating with us. I heard the words 'Our story is a birth, we are one body, we are being born.' What Christ and all the others came to tell us was true: 'You are one body born into this universe. Go tell the story.' Then I suddenly went back in time. I tumbled through a spiral—the creation of the universe, life, multicellular life, human life, the present, the future. I lived through a fifteen-billion-year story in a minute—a second. I knew that the process of creation does not stop with us. We are co-creative with it now. I saw that my vocation was to go tell the story. I ran back home and told my husband, 'We are going to tell the story of the birth of humankind as one body.' I thought it would be he who would tell it, but I was the one who felt it.

"I had received the answer to my question, 'What is the purpose of our power?' The purpose of our power is to become one planetary body capable of caring for all members. We can restore this environment. We can overcome hunger on this earth. We can educate everyone to the awareness that they are co-evolutionary, co-creative with nature itself, that the human race is at the threshold of the next phase of evolution—a restored Earth and a regenerating humanity. I saw that when the cold war is over, the resources and technologies locked up by the military will be emancipated for the restoration of the Earth, the meeting of basic human needs, and the evolution of our species. High technology will be transformed from weaponry to livingry."

Fulfilled by the vision she had experienced, Barbara continued writing in her journal and began to edit the conversations she and her husband were having, which later became the book *The Birth of Humankind* (1969). She wrote to Abraham Maslow, telling him that his book *Toward a Psychology of Being* had saved her life, and that she wanted to meet others who felt this way. Maslow encouraged her to bring people together who believed in the growth potential of humanity and gave her a list of hundreds of people who were self-actualizing, what he called the "eupsychian network." Carl Rogers, Viktor Frankl, and Michael Murphy of Esalen were a few of these names, and she added the others she had gotten from Jonas Salk and other friends.

In August 1967, Barbara sent out a mimeographed letter to everyone on her mailing list, asking those who believed, as she did, in the future good and positive evolution of humanity to correspond with her. She received hundreds of letters from around the world, and she published many excerpts from them in her letter, which she called "The Center Letter." Through it she met many people who shared her beliefs. Encouraged by the success of this project, she sought avenues for more direct action.

The opportunity came through a meeting with Lieutenant Colonel John Whiteside, who was officer of information for the air force in New York City. They met in September 1969.

"I was organizing a conference on the meaning of space when I met John, who had been involved in the live coverage of the space program. He told me he had been intuitively driven to insist that the coverage be *live*. I said, 'John, you were covering the birth—it was essential that it be live so we could all feel our oneness at once.' Suddenly he understood his own motivation. He saw that the space program had a much greater purpose than a technological achievement—it was a planetary event. He was so thrilled he fell in love with me. I thought our purpose was to get my husband out in the world so he could tell everyone, but one day John said to me, 'Barbara, you are the one who is going to be doing the speaking, and as long as you stand behind your husband, it won't happen.' It was quite a shift in my life, from feeling I was supporting a man to having a man tell me, 'You're the one who can do this.'

"Gradually, with deep regret, I separated from my husband and finally divorced him. The drive for co-creation superseded all others. It was very painful for me and my children. They accepted it and have always been supportive of me, yet it caused us all pain.

"Earl and I had not failed. We had loved each other and produced five wonderful children and the seed of a philosophy for the future. This was success. We were actually moving forward to a new relationship."

Barbara and John Whiteside founded the Committee for the Future in 1970. They met with international and national groups, inventing a new conferencing process called SYNCON to show people how all parts of society could work together for the good of everyone. The first SYNCON conferences took place at Southern Illinois University at Carbondale in 1972. They gathered groups of people from the environmental sphere, technological sciences, social needs, business, and government, and placed each group in a sector of a wheel-shaped environment. The groups were asked to state their own goals, needs, and resources. Television cameras and monitors were placed in all sectors. At the center of the wheel was a SYN-CONSOLE, a "social mission control" consisting of TV screens showing the work being done in the various groups.

Gradually groups merged to compare goals and resources. People became aware of the needs of the whole and the possibility of meeting those needs without abandoning their own. "At the end, in an all-walls-down ceremony, the whole group met in a planning session to see how to function as a whole. There was an experience of 'social synergy,' great excitement, a bonding of former adversaries like nuclear physicists and en-

vironmentalists, black-power leaders and conservative econo-
mists. It was an early demonstration of 'cooperative democracy'
in embryo."

Barbara and John produced twenty-five conferences over
the next five years. They also initiated Harvest Moon, which
was a plan for the first citizen-sponsored moon flight. During
this time, Barbara continued to write. Her fascinating autobiographical story, *The Hunger of Eve*, was published in 1977
and reprinted in an updated version in 1989.

*Evolutionary Journey: A Personal Guide to a Positive Fu-
ture*, published in 1982, was a book based on a ninety-minute
multimedia dramatization of the story of creation called *The
Theatre For the Future—Previews of Coming Attractions*. The
book explores the scientific, social, and spiritual aspects of the
evolutionary process; in addition, it provides exercises and
ideas for people who want to participate in the positive evolution of the planet. Both the media event and the book were
born out of what Barbara calls the "planetary birth experience"
that she had in 1966. They map the process of creation from
the origin of the universe to the potential of humanity's future.

It was around the time of their last SYNCON, in 1975,
that Barbara again began to feel that something was missing in
her life. She knew that she was exhausted, and John was
drinking a lot.

"I had a spiritual longing. I went to northern California
with my sister Patricia Ellsberg [wife of Daniel Ellsberg]. I
told her I wanted to meet everybody she loved. She introduced
me to women who are now leaders in the transpersonal psychology and human potential movement. For the first time I
met the New Woman. I had had no female models until that
time. The people I admired were Pericles, Lincoln, Churchill,
and John F. Kennedy. When I met those women, I found the
model of this co-creative woman who was not antagonistic to
men or feministic in the sense of separate—women moving toward wholeness and co-creation."

Pursuing her spiritual quest, Barbara visited Findhorn,
Scotland, where she saw that government by attunement was
possible. Then she met and grew close to the inspirational
teacher Jean Houston and global economist Hazel Henderson,
spending several weekends with them discussing feminine consciousness. A book, *The Power of Yin*, based on those discus-
sions, is to be published.

"After these encounters I realized that I was still a dependent feminine person even though I was a visionary. John was managing everything. He was producing the events and running the house. He was marvelous, but when I had a different idea or wanted to do something like meditate with women, he felt I was deserting him. He told me I was losing my mind. He became abusive. I went through another really difficult period. It seemed as though the same pattern I had experienced with my first husband was repeating itself. My growth was breaking up my relationship.

"In 1980, when I had just turned fifty, I went to Santa Barbara, took a house by myself, and planned to write a book on the next stage of evolution. Day after day I experienced writer's block. One day I just gave up. I surrendered. I called my sister Jacqueline and decided to go have some fun. I was driving around, looking for the botanical gardens, when I saw a little wooden sign to 'Mount Calvary Monastery.' The same field of light I'd felt in the cosmic birth experience suddenly surrounded me. It felt like a living presence. I swerved off the road and headed up toward the monastery. When I got to the top of the mountain, this light presence was surrounding me. I heard the words 'My Resurrection was real. It is a forecast of what the human race will do collectively when you love God above all else, and your neighbor as yourself, combined with science. What I did as the Resurrection, you will do collectively as the transformation. Will you accept this for yourself, Barbara? I want demonstrations now.'

"I felt a Christ presence, and I suddenly realized that Jesus Christ is the next stage of human evolution. He is a living presence who can manifest at any time, on request, to anyone. This presence, in essence, said, 'I want demonstrations that you can do the work that I did.' I said, 'I choose it, but I don't know how to do it.' The presence said, '*You* choose it, and *I'll* do it. Your choice is essential, but you don't have to know how. Did you know how to be born? The universe will produce this result with you if you choose it.'

"The presence guided me to look again at certain passages in the New Testament. I read, 'Behold, I show you a mystery. You shall not all sleep. You shall all be changed.' I began to see the New Testament as coded evolution. I started to write, and the words came pouring out. I wrote that we shall all be changed as we were changed from animal to hu-

man; we will be changed from human to co-creator, joint heir
with Christ.

"Evolution selects. If you choose to be separate, you will
be. If you choose to be part of this whole, you will be transformed, not by human will *alone* but by human will *combined*
with the process of evolution, the will of God."

Barbara worked for six months on these ideas, but has
not published them because, she says, they tend to polarize
many Christians and non-Christians. She then received, from
her higher self, deep meditations and exercises for co-creators
that she recorded on tape and eventually included in her 1986
book *Manual for Co-Creators of the Quantum Leap*, written
with Ken Carey.

"The basic concept of co-creation is to identify yourself as
your higher self, which means to be one with God, and to shift
your identity from the separated self to the God-self until you
experience yourself as the 'I am' presence."

With the experience Barbara had at Mount Calvary Monastery present in her heart and mind, she was about to become
an evangelist for the Planetary Pentecost. Then a close friend
from Seattle came to visit and asked her why she didn't do the
one thing that could make a major difference. Why didn't she
conduct a presidential campaign?

"I had these two choices, both of which were somewhat
extreme. After a lot of agonizing thought, I made a decision to
run for the vice-presidential half of the Democratic ticket in
1984. I campaigned for a positive future based on the ideas of
Buckminster Fuller, Maslow, and Teilhard. My platform was
that the human race is at an evolutionary crossroads. We have
the power to destroy or create, and if we commit our powers to
be utilized in a positive direction, the human race has an unlimited future. If we cooperate with other nations to do this,
our destiny is infinite.

"I crossed the country campaigning for a Peace Room in
the White House. I chose political action over spiritual evan-
gelism. Yet I believe a new synthesized form is needed
wherein our spiritual motivation and social action are joined—
so means and ends become *one*.

"Wherever I went, groups formed which we called 'Positive Future Centers.' I discovered people were actually combining spiritual and political motivation. Thousands of people in
those centers were self-organizing in core groups, connecting at

the heart, loving and coaching one another. I realized then that political transformation will be accelerated by us modeling the change we'd like to see in the world, rather than simply changing something outside ourselves.

"Our mission was to get me nominated so I could give a speech called 'To Fulfill the Dream.' Its message was that the purpose of the United States of America is to awaken human potential to fulfill our destiny as universal humanity.

"Twelve of us went to San Francisco with no money, no media, and no passes to the convention. We practiced the core-group processes together—meditating together, loving one another, praying, and visualizing our goal. There was *no* pragmatic possibility of my name being placed in nomination for the vice presidency. I was told I would be lucky to get one delegate. Nonetheless, acting on pure faith, we went out and met delegates in the halls, in the lobbies, and in the bars. We asked them to sign a petition to place my name in nomination for vice president. I got up and made speeches at early-morning caucuses. I mastered the thirty-second speech: 'My name is Barbara Hubbard. I ask you to place my name in nomination for the vice presidency to create a new Office for the Future and a Peace Room to identify innovations and creative solutions and plan for the victories over hunger, disease, illiteracy, and war.'

"A political miracle happened. The first day a hundred delegates signed the petition, the second day, another hundred. We were heading toward three hundred signatures by the third day. Some very powerful people were campaigning, and they did not get nominated. None of them made it except Geraldine Ferraro and I.

"My campaign manager took the petitions to the Democratic National Committee. They said it was impossible, yet they verified the signatures. I feel I was destined to give that speech. It was like placing a seed in the political ether so it is there when it is time for it to manifest in the 'real world.'

"I am now proposing the organization of a presidential team and cabinet members who understand and can successfully activate our new potentials for interdependence, global sustainability, and the sacredness of all life.

"Now that the Soviet Union is attempting to free itself from the cold war, we can activate a new relationship with the Soviets that will make us literally co-creators of new worlds, in cooperation with China, Japan, Europe, and all other countries. The resources now locked in our military-industrial-technological establishments are what is needed to restructure the world. I think the presidency, vice presidency, and cabinet should be balanced male and female."

Up until 1984 Barbara had done much of her spiritual and political work in Washington, D.C. In 1984 she left Greystone, the family mansion, and lived with different Global Family units.

"I think the reason I have not gotten into a single relationship in the last six years is that I am more attracted to modeling a co-creative relationship and becoming whole than I am to the security, comfort, and joy of a dyad. For me the dyad is a lesser option. Now that I have experienced personal wholeness as an individual and deep co-creative relationships with so many others, I believe I could have an individual relationship with a man. He would need to have undergone the same process in his own life and have come to a balance of masculine and feminine. He would need to have given up possessiveness and domination, just as I am no longer submissive and dependent.

"Just in the last year I've decided I want a home again. I will move to San Anselmo, California, to make a home near the Global Family community."

Barbara's spiritual practice is to rise early, meditate, write in her journal, and take a walk. "I am very deeply engaged in self-development and self-evolution all the time, and I handle my own feelings by going within and truly asking them to let me know what I am feeling. Then I move into my higher self and heal and treat myself with compassion as I would someone else. When I feel discouraged, I take a long walk and let my inner voice speak to me. I remember that I am part of the planet, and the planet itself is integrating into one body. Then I tune into God. I have a very deep relationship with Christ.

"I find that when I am depressed, it's usually that inner critic, self-judgment. It can crop up again and tell me I am a failure or I am no good. I've finally got hold of the critic. I acknowledged that it had good intentions, and then I really told it that it was obstructing me from fulfilling the very things that it was activating me to do. Only if I could experience unconditional love of myself could I fulfill my purpose in the world. I convinced the inner critic of its destructiveness, and it released me. It still crops up every now and then, but as I move deeper into my relationships with others, self-judgment tends to come up less frequently. It is really a matter of designing our lives to 'follow our bliss,' as Joseph Campbell says."

The most nurturing things Barbara does for herself are walking, meditating, and spending time with close friends. She also takes silent retreats. She finds herself moving toward a semi-vegetarian, noncaffeine, nonalcohol diet.

"I don't have an ordinary social life, and I find that type of life uncomfortable for me because it is so superficial. The only friends I have, other than my direct family, are people whom I am in relationship with to create. I do have some very deep friends, and they tend to be people I am working with or whose work is connected to my work. I feel very close to my children. My sister Patricia is one of my dearest, closest friends, as is my sister Jacqueline."

Barbara says her whole life is a synthesis of work and play—co-creation. She enjoys movies but doesn't see many of them. She loves being close to nature and traveling, which she does for work.

"My work seems to be the way I enjoy myself. I'm a little single-minded, I have to admit. I could branch out more. If someone holds my hand and takes me sailing or to the theater, I'll go. I won't do it on my own, simply because I am too interested in my work."

She describes herself as intense. "I can be light-hearted if I am in a creative mode. I am humorous, creative, and loving, but I also experience this almost uncanny sense of a deep mission. Some people see me as distant because of this, but I can also be a wonderful listener and coach for people. I love to do that. I attract people's potential, and I can help them see it and fulfill it. I am a very good speaker. I can really lift audiences to see what they haven't seen before. I think my deepest vocation is telling the story of humanity's collective potential.

"I believe that the co-creative feminine energy must rise to leadership now, to peership, to partnership, taking the initiative to transform our political and social dialogue. When our technological, industrial capability is transformed to humane purposes, we are at the tree of life, we are Godlings, we're at the threshold of being a co-creative species, co-evolutionary.

This is a jump as great as the jump from Neanderthal to *Homo sapiens*. It is the jump from *Homo sapiens* to *Homo co-creator*. We in this generation are living at the moment of the species-wide shift from the separated human to the whole human, just when Mother Earth absolutely requires it for our collective survival. This is not just a cultural change. This is an evolutionary change.

"The biological revolution, the study of human aging, and the healing revolution are identifying the fact that our attitudes cause illness or induce health, wellness, and wholeness. As we become conscious that we are affecting our bodies by everything we think, say, do, and eat, then we can choose to regenerate.

"I think, eventually, we will have bodies that are sensitive to thought. The concept of materialization, dematerialization, and teleportation will be possible. As we fulfill ourselves as co-creators, the next level of evolution undoubtedly will be beyond the 'animal human' into the 'co-creative human.' I think ultimately the human race will go beyond reproduction and unscheduled, unchosen death. We will live by choice, die by choice, and be born by choice.

"I believe we are born at a time as great as that during the step from animal to early humanity. It is the jump from the separated human to the human connected to all beings, the human co-creative with Nature and, as Thomas Jefferson would have said, Nature's God.

"My life's work is developing new social forms into which creativity can flow. I think of myself as a social architect. I really feel that I am a volunteer on this earth. I came for a purpose. I choose it. I love it. I want to fulfill it."

PERSONAL TRUTHS

1. Follow your compass of joy.

2. Discover your vocation of destiny.

3. Find your life partners and do the work together in resonance with the evolution of our planet as a whole.

BARBARA MARX HUBBARD
Author of

Manual for Co-Creators of the Quantum Leap. Coauthored with Ken Carey. Gaithersburg, Md.: New Visions Press, 1986.

Happy Birthday Planet Earth: The Instant of Co-Operation. Santa Fe, N. Mex.: Ocean Tree Books, 1986.

Evolutionary Journey: A Personal Guide to a Positive Future. San Francisco: Evolutionary Press, 1982.

The Hunger of Eve: A Woman's Odyssey toward the Future, rev. ed. Eastsound, Wash.: Island Pacific Northwest and Sweet Forever Publishing, 1977, 1989.

AFTERWORD
Lessons from Women of Power

My life has been enriched by writing this book. By telling these stories filled with experience and wisdom, I have learned more about trusting my intuition and following my own path—the theme that runs throughout this book.

What I have realized is that self-trust can be a learned thing. It takes practice. As we take risks of the heart, and as they work out, confidence grows. Like most of these women, many of us grew up in dysfunctional environments. We were not taught to trust our feelings, our perceptions, and our intuition. Through these interviews I have realized that the healing of each of these women provided the courage for her to move forward.

Their experience showed me that one could doubt and not know, yet still plunge ahead. So when I doubted and felt afraid, I reflected on their lives, thinking, They did it; so can I. They took risks and didn't always know what the results were going to be, and it worked out. On a particularly low day when I wondered what I was doing, I reflected on my interview with Louise Hay. I saw an image of her as a little girl, afraid and alone. As I leafed through her interview I saw an image of this beautiful, compassionate woman emerging and, then looking at me and saying, "If I can do it, so can you."

I took the images and the supportive words of these women with me. Each one gave me different gifts and enriched my life in different ways. Anne Wilson Schaef's brilliance and fiery Irish spirit were inspiring to me, and I found her love of a good fight particularly reassuring. Shortly after our interview, I found myself in a confrontive situation where I felt hesitant to speak my mind. I could hear Anne saying to me, "I just love a good fight. It's fun. Come on, tell the truth." She became an inner cheerleader urging me on.

Although some of the facts were different, Laura Davis's life story felt like my own. When she said, "I am no longer afraid that somebody or something is going to get me," I knew what she meant. I too had felt lost for years, and through healing had come home to myself.

Often when I think of these women I see their spirits, their energy, and their essence. I see the joy and laughter of Terry Cole-Whittaker and the dedication, commitment, and God-sourced enthusiasm of Barbara Marx Hubbard. I see Sondra Ray's warmth and aliveness. I can visualize them making their first discoveries. I see Virginia Satir and Claudia Black inviting the families and adult children of their clients into their offices. They must have wondered, What next? Then, by following their instincts they discovered what came next.

Many of these women's findings have become integrated into society. Before Virginia Satir and a few colleagues began inviting the families of clients into the therapist's office, nobody knew what a family therapist was. Today, many thousands of professionals have marriage and family counseling licenses and work with entire families. Elisabeth Kubler-Ross actually thought to ask dying patients how they felt, and out of her work came the five stages of death and dying. Courses are now offered on death and dying in colleges, seminaries, and medical schools. Anne Wilson Schaef helped to popularize society's awareness of addiction and to identify the symptoms of codependence. In the late seventies, Claudia Black was one of the first to begin working with adult children of alcoholics. The inspired knowledge she and others gathered would be the foundation for a worldwide grassroots recovery movement.

The affirmation and rebirthing science of Sondra Ray, the prosperity influence of Terry Cole-Whittaker, and the healing work of Louise Hay are now parts of my life. Affirmations, I have learned from these women and others, come naturally to me. I no longer have to sit down, at a structured time, and write positive thoughts for myself. More and more they are part of my inner dialogue. It was in writing this book that I would combine what I already possessed with what I learned from these women.

I believe that by taking our own visions from start to finish we can be our own teachers. We can learn to trust that inner voice that can guide us each step of the way. It is by taking my vision for this book from beginning to completion that I learned more about my own power.

When I saw Lynn Andrews, she talked about her "act of power." She says she was literally forced to take action when her teacher Agnes Whistling Elk told her to write what she had learned or never come back. She described the pain she went through in writing *Medicine Woman*. When she sat down to chronicle her journey her worst mirrors appeared. It took her two years to finish that first book, but when she was done she knew she had completed an "act of power."

I too confronted some very uncomfortable mirrors. At one point I became aware of a louder-than-usual inner critic. Perhaps the stress of such a large project caught my critical attention and brought it to mega-volume status. When I was talking to myself, I would say, You idiot. Who are you to do a project like this? You are spending too much money. What if it doesn't work? I would literally wake up to this screaming voice. Then, if I listened long enough, I would become frightened, anxious, and eventually depressed. For months it felt like a major battle, and I thought the only way to quiet the critical voice was to give up the book. I thought of other times I was about to do something very important and had given it up, because I couldn't take the self-abuse. Fortunately, many other forces were already in motion.

I had learned how to nurture myself, so besides hearing a critical voice, I had another voice inside me that said, I believe in you. Whatever you do is fine. Who cares how much money you are spending? What you learn will be worth it. I am also surrounded by friends who talk to me that way. My husband consistently says, "I believe in you, baby. Whatever you want to do is fine. I am behind you 100 percent." My friends say, "You can do it. It will all work out. We love you. Give it a shot." Over and over, I would hear the same supportive words: "It will all work out." As the book and my interviews with these women progressed, my faith in myself grew and the voice of self-doubt diminished.

My last interview was with Elisabeth Kubler-Ross. She, like the others, knows so much about following her heart. Many times in her life her actions have been both loved and criticized, but she moves forward. She is a good example of someone who throws herself into life. She doesn't simply get out of bed and say, "I am here." She takes a running start, leaps off a cliff into a pool of water, makes a big splash, and in that way announces her arrival. Many times in her life she has been a guide to others into uncharted waters. I am deeply moved by her spirit and the spirits of all these women. I have come to know that we all have that same spirit within us, and if we are willing to honor our own spirits, we too can be guided to new possibilities within ourselves, each other, and the universe in which we live.

More than thirty-five years after Aerosmith played their first gig in Boston, the band remains one of the few from the 1970s (or '80s for that matter) to retain their original lineup. That perceived stability, though, has come with its fair share of turmoil. The rampant drug and alcohol abuse has been well documented by the band's members in several books over the years (so there's really no need to rehash it here). But what hasn't been well reported is the amazing fact that outside of a brief few years Aerosmith has always consisted of the same five founding members. Together, they remain one of the biggest concert draws in the United States.

Early on, Aerosmith took heat for being a Rolling Stones rip-off. From the way they approached the stage and wrote songs together to the way they looked, Steven Tyler and Joe Perry were clearly influenced by Mick Jagger and Keith Richards. But they quickly evolved beyond those comparisons, and with their harder, heavier, louder edge, they became one of the defining arena-rock acts of the 1970s.

CLASSIC LINEUP:

TOM HAMILTON (BASS)

JOEY KRAMER (DRUMS)

JOE PERRY (GUITAR)

STEVEN TYLER (VOCALS)

BRAD WHITFORD (GUITAR)

KEY ADDITIONAL MEMBERS:

JIMMY CRESPO (GUITAR)

RICK DUFAY (GUITAR)

OPPOSITE: Brad Whitford, Steven Tyler, Joe Perry, and Tom Hamilton at Jones Beach, Long Island, August 30, 1994

DISCOGRAPHY

ABOVE: Steven Tyler, Joe Perry, and Joey Kramer at Borgata Hotel, Casino & Spa, Atlantic City, September 22, 2007
OPPOSITE: Eddie and Joe Perry at the XM studio, New York City, June 26, 2008

Aerosmith had the horrible misfortune of releasing their self-titled debut on the same label and the same day in 1973 that a new singer-songwriter from New Jersey named Bruce Springsteen released his first album. Not only was there more hype and buzz at Columbia Records over Springsteen at the time, but the majority of the label's marketing efforts were directed toward his new record as well. And *Aerosmith* is far from their greatest moment. It features Steven Tyler singing in a slightly different style (alternating between a raspier, bluesy growl and the high-pitched signature sound he would refine on later albums), subpar production, and songs written almost exclusively by Tyler. Prior to forming Aerosmith, Tyler had achieved the most local success, so the band deferred to him for direction from the beginning. Only one track showcases the now-legendary writing partnership between Steven Tyler and Joe Perry, which would later come to define the band: "Movin' Out" is the first song the "Toxic Twins" penned together, and a primitive sign of great things to come. The album also contains one of the biggest rock ballads of all time—and according to some, the first ever *power* ballad—"Dream On," which wouldn't become a hit until two years later, when it was rereleased following the success of the band's breakthrough album, *Toys in the Attic*.

Over the years, the band grew and crafted a sound that became a blueprint for so many '80s bands of the MTV generation. Their music bridged the genres of pop and metal without compromising their credibility or edge. It fused hard, gritty guitars with melody in a way that many bands had yet to accomplish, attracted a huge range of fans—from screaming females to guys who love guitars—and inspired imitators from Guns N' Roses to Cinderella.

For me, Aerosmith's definitive album is 1976's *Rocks*. Many would cite *Toys in the Attic* (an album the band played live from start to finish in 2009) as the most revered, with its massive commercial success and monster hits like "Walk This Way" and "Sweet Emotion," but to me, *Rocks* was and still is the essential Aerosmith album. Starting with the dramatic opening build of "Back in the Saddle," which explodes into that unbelievable riff while Steven Tyler screams the first line—"I'm back in the saddle again"—there's nothing tentative about this record. It's the sound of a band who knows they're not kids trying to figure it out anymore but instead stars who've sold a million records and made a sonic statement. They might have finally broken through on their previous album, but with *Rocks*, they discovered their swagger.

I recently spoke with Joe Perry, who said he also considers *Rocks* a fave because it was where everything came together for the band. Like *Toys*, he said, *Rocks* is another candidate to play live onstage. Perry acknowledged that *Rocks* represents Aerosmith at the peak of their sonic powers, before things started to unravel and their drug use became detrimental to the music.

The early 1980s found Aerosmith at an all-time low commercially. Group infighting, management issues, drug abuse, and the brief departure of guitarists Joe Perry and Brad Whitford took a heavy toll—at one point reducing them to a club act. I recall seeing the band around this time in half-full places like Stabler Arena in Bethlehem, Pennsylvania, and even, unfathomably, at a small nightclub in central New Jersey. It was hard to believe that the mighty could have fallen so hard and so quick. But Aerosmith was reborn, thanks to the return of the classic lineup, the groundbreaking fusion of hip-hop and rock on their collaboration with Run-DMC for a remake of "Walk This Way," and the release of solid, fully formed albums like *Permanent Vacation* and *Pump*. Suddenly, after being on the bottom, Aerosmith was cool again, appearing all over MTV, gaining a new generation of fans, and cranking out more hits than they had in the '70s.

Aerosmith's sound evolved in the '80s and early '90s to be much more polished and commercial. They began to use outside songwriters for the first time in their history, bringing in people like Desmond Child and Diane Warren. Some of the danger and dirtiness of the group was gone—replaced by a highly produced pop polish. The band's low point came with albums like 1997's *Nine Lives* and 2001's *Just Push Play*. It was hard to find that filthy garage band from Boston in all the layers of production and slick, stylized songs.

I've been lucky enough to share some great moments with Aerosmith over the years. In 2006, the band embarked on a tour with Mötley Crüe billed as "The Route of All Evil." Aerosmith wanted to do a national live radio special to announce the tour but wanted an interviewer they were comfortable with and who really knew their music. The band and their management sent a list to the producers of the radio special with the names of about five media people they would consider for the gig. I

DID YOU KNOW

In 1976, Aerosmith was looking to purchase their own plane to use on tour and had settled on a pre-owned jet that they'd found advertised. But the pilot they'd hired said he didn't feel good about the safety of the aircraft after checking it out, and he talked them out of buying it. A few weeks later, that same plane was purchased by Lynyrd Skynyrd and crashed, tragically killing several of the band's members and crew.

EDDIE'S PLAYLIST
AEROSMITH

1. ONE WAY STREET
2. LORD OF THE THIGHS
3. SEASONS OF WITHER
4. ADAM'S APPLE
5. NO MORE NO MORE
6. NO SURPRIZE
7. KINGS AND QUEENS
8. BITCH'S BREW
9. CHIQUITA
10. LIGHTNING STRIKES
11. DRAW THE LINE
12. MAJOR BARBARA
13. MY FIST YOUR FACE
14. LICK AND A PROMISE
15. NOBODY'S FAULT
16. SICK AS A DOG
17. TASTE OF INDIA
18. HOME TONIGHT
19. F.I.N.E.

ABOVE: Joe Perry and Steven Tyler at Madison Square Garden, New York City, December 3, 1975

was floored to find out I made the list! In addition to having done TV for a few years as a VH1 Classic host and interviewer, I had also made the news a few weeks earlier when Axl Rose walked into my radio studio for a sit-down interview (something he hadn't done for thirteen years and hasn't done since). In order to land the Aerosmith gig, I, and every other interviewer on the list, had to send the band samples of previous interviews—like a demo that would serve as an audition to host the special. (Only Aerosmith could get away with this.) I sent in my Axl interview because at that time it was both the biggest and most recent one I had done, and I landed the job.

The event took place at the home studio of Joe Perry in Boston. The entire band was present, and we fielded live calls from all around America. To talk to Steven Tyler about obscure songs from the band's catalog during the special's breaks and to watch as he recalled them and sang them back to me was completely amazing! I also recall that Tyler asked me about my encounter with Axl Rose. Tyler told me that he'd been invited to jam with Guns N' Roses but had refused because of the late hour that Axl decides to take the stage. I remember laughing as Tyler told me he would kick Axl's ass if he didn't start to show more respect for his audience. Then Joe offered me a tour of his home studio and gave me a rundown of his vintage gear. Now, I couldn't have told you a thing about guitars from

a technical standpoint beforehand, but if Joe Perry is showing you his guitars in his house, you learn quickly!

The radio special went well and the band was pleased. I would later do a couple of very lengthy interviews with Joe Perry; the most recent was in August 2009, while he was prepping for a solo tour. In 2008, the band staged a massive press conference to announce their own Guitar Hero game and once again called on my services to stand onstage with them and moderate the discussion with the press. I've always found the guys to be really nice people and, needless to say, a no-brainer in anyone's book of essential hard-rock bands.

It's important to point out the unsung heroes of Aerosmith. While Perry and Tyler are no doubt the stars of the band, the contributions of guitarist Brad Whitford, bassist Tom Hamilton, and drummer Joey Kramer are no less important. Many have told me that, from a technical standpoint, Whitford is a far more accomplished player, yet Perry gets the attention because he's the "rock star." Whitford is responsible for writing some of the band's heaviest riffs, such as those on "Nobody's Fault" from *Rocks* and "Round and Round" from *Toys*. The rhythm section of Kramer and Hamilton is also vital to that all-important groove.

It's interesting to note that Steven Tyler is actually a drummer first (an excellent one, by all accounts) and only became the frontman when Aerosmith first formed. Drummer Joey Kramer recently wrote in his own book, *Hit Hard: A Story of Hitting Rock Bottom at the Top*, that because of this, he always felt the need to go the extra mile to please Steven, knowing he never would have had the good fortune of being in the band if Tyler had stayed behind the kit.

In late 2009, the wheels really came off for Aerosmith when Steven Tyler started behaving strangely (e.g., falling off a stage in Sturgis, South Dakota). The rest of the band talked about continuing with a replacement singer. Replace Tyler? Insane! I recall sitting backstage at Mohegan Sun in Connecticut, where I'd been hired to host a Q&A for Joey Kramer's book. Joey asked me what I thought about the band going forward without Steven, and I told him it would be crazy if they did it and still called it Aerosmith. Even when I was asked who I thought would make a good replacement for Steven, I always gave the same answer: NOBODY! I know some of the biggest bands of all time have survived the changes of key members, but there is no Aerosmith without Tyler—one of the greatest rock stars of all time.

I was relieved to hear in early 2010 that Steven admitted that he was battling an addiction, was seeking help, and would return to the band when he was healthy. That summer the band scheduled a massive homecoming show at Boston's Fenway Park. So they continue on as one of the only acts from the '70s to survive with its celebrated lineup intact. Aerosmith is indestructible.

UNDERGROUND CLASSIC

Rock in a Hard Place, released in 1982, is the only Aerosmith album that doesn't feature the classic lineup. Guitarists Joe Perry and Brad Whitford had left (even though Brad plays on some of the tracks) and were replaced by Jimmy Crespo and Rick Dufay. Often written off because of this, the album actually features some blazing hard-rock gems like "Lightning Strikes" and "Bitch's Brew." Joe Perry even admitted to me that he liked some of the songs on the record and was pissed that it was so good when he had nothing to do with it! He didn't mind playing a few songs from it live when he eventually returned to the band.

I also recommend the album prior, 1979's *Night in the Ruts*. Again, it has great, heavy tunes like "No Surprize," "Chiquita," and "Three Mile Smile." Two good albums from the Joe Perry Project (Joe's solo band) came out at this time as well: *Let the Music Do the Talking* (whose title track was rerecorded by Aerosmith, with new lyrics from Tyler when Joe rejoined the band a few years later) and *I've Got the Rock 'n' Rolls Again*. Both feature Joe's bluesy, live-feeling hard rock and are worth owning.

ANTHRAX

knew the guys in Anthrax long before I knew they were putting a band together. I was from Jersey, they were from the Bronx, and we were all close to the same age and into the same type of music, so we grew up going to the same shows and record stores. I first became aware of their own music through Johnny Z of Megaforce Records, who would eventually give me my first job at a record label.

Johnny gave me a copy of Anthrax's first album, *Fistful of Metal*, around the same time he gave me the first Metallica record. I liked *Fistful of Metal*, but I didn't love it. Thrash metal was still very new, and most people—myself included—didn't know what to make of it. I was pretty shocked that these enormous Kiss fans (which was what we'd first bonded over) played extreme speed metal and sounded nothing like that kind of hard rock. But I was truly rooting for my friends to make it.

JOEY BELLADONNA (VOCALS)

FRANK BELLO (BASS)

CHARLIE BENANTE (DRUMS)

SCOTT IAN (GUITAR)

DAN SPITZ (GUITAR)

JOHN BUSH (VOCALS)

ROB CAGGIANO (GUITAR)

PAUL CROOK (GUITAR)

DAN LILKER (GUITAR/BASS)

NEIL TURBIN (VOCALS)

OPPOSITE: Joey Belladonna, Dan Spitz, Scott Ian, and Frank Bello at Park Theater, Union City, New Jersey, May, 1987

DISCOGRAPHY

ABOVE: Frank Bello, Charlie Benante, Joey Belladonna, and Dan Spitz at the Ritz, New York City, September 27, 1991

OPPOSITE: Scott Ian at Starland Ballroom, Sayreville, New Jersey, June 3, 2005

Early on, I told Johnny Z that what I didn't like about Anthrax was singer Neil Turbin's vocals. It wasn't just *his* voice, though; I simply didn' like thrash metal vocals across the board. So when Johnny told me tha Turbin had left the band and that they were bringing in Joey Belladonna— who, he thought, would be right up my alley—I paid attention.

The first EP released with Joey was 1985's *Armed and Dangerous* When I heard it, I was immediately more interested in the band. For the first time, I was listening to heavy thrash with vocals from a guy who sounded like he could have been in Journey. He was incredibly melodi without sacrificing anger or emotion, and he made Anthrax sound totall unique from other bands of the genre.

Around that time, I started to have the guys on my radio show regularl Unfortunately, I was (and still am) the only person to play their music on local radio around New York. They'd come to my parents' house for din ner, and then we'd go to the radio station to do an interview. They became very much like family to me. (My mom still remembers making pizza fo Scott Ian.)

My favorite album is Anthrax's first with Joey on vocals, 1985's *Spread ing the Disease*. The combination of Joey's vocal range and the extremel heavy music gave Anthrax dynamics that other thrash bands didn't have And as the East Coast answer to West Coast thrash, they brought a Ne York attitude fused with elements of the local punk and hardcore scene to what they did.

When *Spreading the Disease* came out, Johnny Z called and asked m to work for Megaforce. The label was not only releasing Anthrax record but also managing the band. Still, it was a small operation run out o Johnny Z's house. At that point, Megaforce's staff consisted of Johnn and his wife, Marsha, and one employee, Metal Maria, who did publicit and watched their kids. I'll never forget heading to their house on my firs day of work to find that my "office" was a phone extension next to one o their babies' cribs. It wasn't exactly glamour-time, but something specia was happening.

Metallica had just left Megaforce to go to a major label, Elektra, so my first assignment was to spread the word about Anthrax. Johnny was bitter over Metallica's departure and was driven to make Anthrax a big enough band to rival them. The guys in Anthrax were already my friends, but I truly believed that their mix of melody and heaviness was the formula that would make thrash metal appeal to a larger audience.

One of my favorite memories of working with the band was the video shoot for one of their best-known songs, "Indians," from the 1987 album *Among the Living*. The guys thought they should put Joey in an American Indian headdress, but no one knew where to find one. I remembered that there was a store called Cherokee Trading Post not far from where I lived in New Jersey, so I was dispatched with a company credit card to get one. The one headdress for sale had been hanging on the wall at this store for years and was very expensive. (Anyone who has seen that video knows how big it was.) I had to struggle to get the headdress in my car without damaging it and ended up driving through upstate New York with

UNDERGROUND CLASSIC

By far, the biggest Anthrax spin-off band was Stormtroopers of Death, better known as S.O.D. The band included former Anthrax bassist Dan Lilker, singer Billy Milano, and Anthrax members Charlie Benante and Scott Ian. S.O.D. was a crossover of hardcore and metal and became so big that they broke up when they became a threat to the growth of Anthrax. Their 1985 debut, *Speak English or Die*, is a classic.

EDDIE'S PLAYLIST
ANTHRAX

1. ARMED AND DANGEROUS
2. ROOM FOR ONE MORE
3. NOW IT'S DARK
4. I AM THE LAW
5. STRAP IT ON
6. INSIDE OUT
7. THE ENEMY
8. NOTHING
9. FUELED
10. METAL THRASHING MAD
11. WHAT DOESN'T DIE
12. LONE JUSTICE
13. IN MY WORLD
14. MADHOUSE
15. SAFE HOME
16. MEDUSA
17. INDIANS
18. ONLY
19. A.I.R.

OPPOSITE TOP LEFT: Frank Bello and Joey Belladonna at Starland Ballroom, Sayreville, New Jersey, June 3, 2005
OPPOSITE TOP RIGHT: Dan Spitz and Joey Belladonna at Park Theater, Union City, New Jersey, May, 1987
OPPOSITE MIDDLE: Dan Spitz and Joey Belladonna at L'amour, Brooklyn, December, 1986
OPPOSITE BOTTOM: Frank Bello, Joey Belladonna, and Scott Ian at Park Theater, Union City, New Jersey, May, 1987

part of it hanging out the window! The headdress became a trademark of that song, and for several years Joey wore it onstage when they toured. Though I'm pretty sure it had its own road case, it fell apart after years of wear.

Later in 1987, I took my first trip to England with Anthrax. They were going to play the Donington Monsters of Rock Festival. I vividly remember getting to England completely jet-lagged. When I arrived at my hotel, I was told that my room wasn't ready yet. So Scott Ian and Charlie Benante told me to sit with them at the bar until it was. Eventually, someone from the hotel came and brought me a key. By this time, I'd gone well over twenty-four hours without sleep and was beyond exhausted.

I went to my room, dropped my bag, and crawled straight into bed. When I got under the sheets, I knew something was wrong. The bed was soaked with water and shaving cream and God knows what else. I looked around the room, and there was shaving cream everywhere. Someone had also taken a huge dump in the toilet without flushing. I'm still not sure which one of them did it (though I think it was one of the biggest ballbusters in the world, my good friend bassist Frank Bello), but Anthrax had stalled me in my tired state so they could get to my room first and destroy it. Back then, the pranks never ended with them.

When we got to the festival, Scott asked me to record the first songs of

their set on his own video camera. The camera was the size of a cinder block, and it weighed just as much, but this was a big moment for them. After the first two songs, every time I tried to put the camera down, Scott would yell at me from the stage to keep shooting. I watched that whole show through a tiny viewfinder, and I still have the video. Even now, it's amazing to watch the reaction of the audience in England at that early show. Anthrax inspired one of the biggest mosh pits I've ever seen in my life.

Around this time in their career, the guys decided to perform wearing a wardrobe of sorts, like Bermuda shorts and tank tops. In the heavy metal '80s, that was a very big deal. Heavy metal musicians looked hard and serious, and they weren't supposed to be good-looking. Anthrax deviated from that. They wore colorful clothes, and some of them played up their looks, often mugging for the camera. It created a backlash that hurt their credibility at the time, so they quickly reverted to more of a street look. But they still had the "Not Man"—the smiley face mascot that had become a trademark on most of their merchandise. Given what was going on with the newer speed metal acts of the day, this just seemed corny after a couple of years.

Their love of rap also became polarizing to many metal fans. Perhaps the one thing they don't get nearly enough credit (or blame, depending on your preference) for was their merging of heavy metal and rap.

Anthrax did it before Aerosmith and Run-DMC and had an unexpected hit in 1987 with "I'm the Man," a total goof that went gold. They also teamed with Public Enemy in 1991 for a cover of "Bring the Noise" and eventually toured with them. Anthrax broadened metal horizons and broke ground for the Limp Bizkits of the world, but they alienated purists.

Many in the metal world also complained that Joey wasn't metal enough and that his voice didn't fit with thrash. The truth was that Joey was never really a fan of heavy music, which made him somewhat of an outcast from the beginning. He was a great frontman but wasn't fully immersed in the band. Before shows, he always seemed to be on the other side of the room listening to Foreigner or Journey. Because of this, the Belladonna-fronted lineup just couldn't last forever. They recorded some incredible records and made huge strides for a band with virtually no airplay, but they soon looked for an edgier vocalist.

In 1992 Joey was replaced by John Bush of Armored Saint. John's voice was grittier and tougher, and unlike Joey, he was a songwriter, so he put his musical stamp on the band in more ways than one. Fans often debate who was the better frontman. I like both singers, but I lean toward the Joey period simply because his voice made Anthrax unique. Without him, the band wouldn't have appealed to the same wide range of fans.

Frequent lineup changes have been the biggest detriment to Anthrax's growth as a band. Even now, there's confusion over who is their real singer. From 2008 to 2010, Anthrax had three different vocalists: Bush, Belladonna, and the short-tenured Dan Nelson, who sang on an album that was scrapped because of a falling-out. That kind of upheaval can break any band, but somehow Anthrax survives and still crushes live.

People often ask why Anthrax isn't a more commercially successful band, since they're considered one of the Big Four of thrash, along with Metallica, Megadeth, and Slayer. It's definitely in part because of the risks they've taken with their sound and image and in their collaborations. Some have paid off, and some have backfired, but they deserve much credit for breaking down barriers and pioneering thrash metal. They were driven by a desire to be faster, louder, and heavier than any of the bands they'd grown up with, taking influences from Aerosmith, Kiss, and Judas Priest and injecting them with a huge shot of adrenaline and speed. For this, Anthrax has always been one of my all-time favorites in thrash/speed metal.

DID YOU KNOW

Anthrax bassist Frank Bello is the nephew of drummer Charlie Benante. And Scott Ian is married to Pearl Aday, daughter of Meatloaf! Ian plays on her 2009 solo debut, titled *Little Immaculate White Fox*.

LEFT: Joey Belladonna and Eddie on the set of the video for "Indians," 1987
OPPOSITE: Dan Spitz, Joey Belladonna, and Scott Ian at Starland Ballroom, Sayreville, New Jersey, June 3, 2005

BLACK SABBATH

Black Sabbath is, simply put, the most important band in the history of heavy metal—they created it! From Iron Maiden to Metallica to Slayer to Slipknot, bands playing just about any style of metal you can think of owe a debt to Sabbath, whose influence is often obviously heard.

Black Sabbath's self-titled debut remains—some forty years after its release—one of the heaviest albums ever created. It's still as haunting and jarring as it was when it came out. The sludgy title track is the epitome of classic Sabbath: the eerie sounds of rainfall and a church bell followed by a heavy, crashing riff, pummeling drums, lurking bass lines, and the chilling vocals of John "Ozzy" Osbourne. It became the blueprint for all things metal. Recorded on a shoestring budget, this powerful, mammoth record is proof that you don't need a ton of money or effects to create music that stands the test of time.

GEEZER BUTLER (BASS)

TONY IOMMI (GUITAR)

OZZY OSBOURNE (VOCALS)

BILL WARD (DRUMS)

VINNY APPICE (DRUMS)

RONNIE JAMES DIO (VOCALS)

IAN GILLAN (VOCALS)

GLENN HUGHES (VOCALS)

TONY MARTIN (VOCALS)

OPPOSITE: Ozzy Osbourne at Madison Square Garden, New York City, August 4, 1975

The incredibly innovative and brilliant musicians in Sabbath often don't get the credit they should. Geezer Butler is simply one of the greatest bass players of all time. In a one-guitar band, he does a lot to fill the spaces in the songs without ever sounding too busy or over-the-top. He also wrote the great majority of Sabbath's lyrics. If you listen closely to what he plays and how he supports the band, you'll hear how incredible he is.

Bill Ward refers to himself as a "percussionist" rather than a drummer, and when you really listen to Sabbath, you can hear why. His playing is reactive, not driving. He plays *around* the other instruments in the band, not through them, and adds to the sound with a range that's heavy, then subtle, as if to lure you in before hammering you over the head again. Bill grew up a huge fan of jazz great Gene Krupa, so many early Sabbath songs merge this style with heavy metal. Complicated time changes and improvised jamming are a trademark of Ward's innovative playing in the band's early days.

No one has ever written as many brilliantly dark and monstrous guitar riffs as Tony Iommi. And they just keep coming to this day. Although Iommi is often rightfully considered "King of the Riff," it's important not to overlook his talent as a complete player. His solos and rhythm are equally perfect for the signature Sabbath sound. In 1970, no one had ever downtuned their guitar the way he did, and his style predates anything

DISCOGRAPHY

BLACK SABBATH (1970)

PARANOID (1970)

MASTER OF REALITY (1971)

BLACK SABBATH,
VOL. 4 (1972)

SABBATH BLOODY
SABBATH (1973)

SABOTAGE (1975)

TECHNICAL ECSTASY (1976)

WE SOLD OUR SOULS
FOR ROCK 'N' ROLL
(1975/6)

NEVER SAY DIE! (1978)

HEAVEN AND HELL (1980)

LIVE AT LAST (1980)

MOB RULES (1981)

LIVE EVIL (1982)

BORN AGAIN (1983)

SEVENTH STAR (1986)

THE ETERNAL IDOL (1987)

HEADLESS CROSS (1989)

TYR (1990)

DEHUMANIZER (1992)

CROSS PURPOSES (1994)

FORBIDDEN (1995)

REUNION [LIVE] (1998)

PAST LIVES [LIVE] (2002)

THE DIO YEARS (2006)

BLACK SABBATH:
LIVE AT THE
HAMMERSMITH ODEON
(2007)

HEAVEN & HELL:
LIVE AT
RADIO CITY MUSIC HALL
(2007)

HEAVEN & HELL:
THE DEVIL YOU KNOW
(2009)

that people consider metal. He was the architect for all heavy music that came afterward, and more than anyone who has ever been in Sabbath, Iommi embodies the essence of what truly makes the band special in his playing, writing, and tone. Briefly a member of Jethro Tull, Iommi incorporated influences of jazz, blues, and rock to essentially invent a style of music. He is the heart of Sabbath's greatness.

Ozzy Osbourne is, of course, the icing on the all-time metal cake. His voice and madman image are the perfect representation for a band characterized by contrasts—good and evil, noisy and melodic, dark and light. His interpretation of Geezer's lyrics about war and religion add an eerie vibe to the band's music. He can sound angelic, then sinister, or like a lunatic being tortured. Onstage, he has a frantic, psychotic energy—he's made weird faces while banging his head; he's hopped around the stage clapping his hands but hardly speaking to the crowd. Watching him live can be like seeing a maniac who's been let out of a cage to front a heavy metal band for a couple of hours. There is no better personality to front the band, and Sabbath could never have reached their level of fame without him. Behind the scenes, Ozzy also wrote many of the melodies to Sabbath's songs.

Paranoid; Master of Reality; Black Sabbath, Vol. 4; and Sabbath Bloody Sabbath still hold up today as the classics they are, created by this per-

OPPOSITE TOP: Geezer Butler and Ronnie James Dio at Radio City Music Hall, New York City, March 30, 2007
OPPOSITE BOTTOM: Tony Iommi at Radio City Music Hall, New York City, March 30, 2007

EDDIE'S PLAYLIST

BLACK SABBATH

1. CHILDREN OF THE GRAVE
2. THE DEVIL CRIED
3. NEVER SAY DIE
4. NEON KNIGHTS
5. THE SIGN OF THE SOUTHERN CROSS
6. SABBATH BLOODY SABBATH
7. VOODOO
8. N.I.B.
9. FAIRIES WEAR BOOTS
10. CHILDREN OF THE SEA
11. SYMPTOM OF THE UNIVERSE
12. HEAVEN & HELL
13. THE MOB RULES
14. HOLE IN THE SKY
15. BIBLE BLACK
16. SNOWBLIND
17. FEAR

TOP: Vinny Appice, Ronnie James Dio, Tony Iommi, Eddie, and (a very drunk) Geezer Butler at the Q104 studio, New York City, March 30, 2007
MIDDLE: Vinny Appice and Ronnie James Dio at the Q104 studio, New York City, August 1, 2008
BOTTOM: Tony Iommi and Geezer Butler at the Q104 studio, New York City, August 1, 2008

fect union of metal masters. The songs are enormous and timeless; they always sound as fresh, menacing, and exciting as they did the first time I heard them. The true legacy of the band lies with its founding members, but that's just the beginning of the Sabbath story.

Over the years, Sabbath has broken up and reunited with Ozzy several times. As he's aged, and because of years of drug abuse, Osbourne has lost most of his vocal ability and simply can't sing the majority of Sabbath songs or his solo material. I've been at many shows where I've seen Ozzy struggle onstage and actually felt bad for him as he tried to get through a set. In the late 1990s and 2000s, his all-too-obvious vocal issues when singing live led to the band's 2007 reunion with Ronnie James Dio, Sabbath's second singer. The Sabbath guys told me that they'd just grown tired of playing the same ten songs that Ozzy could barely get through in a set. As fairly private and low-key people, they also weren't thrilled with Ozzy's new fame as a reality-TV personality and the demands it made on his schedule. They had tried for a while to make a new Sabbath album with Ozzy, but they just couldn't get it together.

For many, Black Sabbath's most important lineup is the original one, but there are some great recordings with other members, especially the Ronnie James Dio-led version of the band. My introduction to Sabbath was actually Dio's first record with them, 1980's *Heaven & Hell*. I won it

(like so many of the albums mentioned in this book) by playing a game on the Jersey shore boardwalk when I was fifteen. I chose it as my prize because I thought the cover image of angels smoking cigarettes looked cool and would probably irritate my parents, but when I heard it, it blew my mind. From the opening track, "Neon Knights," Dio's phenomenal voice and the power of the music consumed me. Afterward, I bought the Ozzy-era best-of compilation called *We Sold Our Souls for Rock 'n' Roll* and quickly discovered the original Sabbath. I loved it, of course, but to this day, there's a special place in my heart for the Dio lineup. Ronnie saved Sabbath at a time when they were floundering in album and concert ticket sales, and although the transition to a new singer did not sit well with the Sabbath faithful, even they could not deny how great the new material was, along with Dio's voice. It was like the band was reborn.

In fact, the Dio version of the band and the title track to *Heaven & Hell* were so important to me that under my high school yearbook graduation photo, I quoted the lyric "The world is full of kings and queens / Who blind your eyes and steal your dreams." To some it might have seemed like I was an angry, disenfranchised kid back then, but the truth is that I had a great family and was pretty OK—it just looked cool as hell to have that under my photo!

For most of the Dio-fronted version of Sabbath, Vinny Appice replaced Bill Ward on drums. Appice is a monster drummer, and his style was a better fit for that lineup of the band. Dio drifted in and out of Sabbath several times because of creative differences and business issues, and I became friends with him after his first departure, when he formed Dio (more on that in the Dio section of this book).

For years, the only way to hear the Dio-Sabbath material live was to see Ronnie's band play it. Over time, I learned that I wasn't the only one to first discover Sabbath with Dio as their frontman. Guys like Geoff Tate of Queensrÿche and Dave Grohl of Nirvana and Foo Fighters also loved that lineup. So every time Tony Iommi would do my show with whatever project he was working on, I'd ask him whether he'd ever revisit the lineup with Dio and tell him how much it would mean to so many fans. I sensed his frustration at trying to work around Ozzy's solo career and reality-TV stardom, not to mention his vocal limitations. Tony always seemed intrigued when I brought up the idea of a reunion with Dio.

Needless to say, it was with great joy that in 2006 I learned a compilation called *The Dio Years* was going to be released. Even more exciting was the fact that the band would reunite for a third time with Dio to record three new songs for it! It was stressed that this would only be a studio reunion, but I held out hope. At the time, I was a host at VH1 Classic (prior to *That Metal Show*), and word came that the band wanted me to fly to England to conduct a TV interview with them before they started recording.

I set off with a VH1 crew to Birmingham—the birthplace of Sabbath and heavy metal—to do the honors. (Did I mention that I was also interviewing Robert Plant on the same trip? That story is in the Zep chapter!) We arrived jetlagged in the middle of the afternoon and went to an old castle

DID YOU KNOW

Tony Iommi cut the tips off two fingers on his right hand in an accident at a sheet metal factory when he was a kid. His tone and signature guitar sound were created when he downtuned his strings so he could play with prosthetic fingertips. How metal is that? Also, bassist Geezer Butler is a strict vegan and has been since the 1970s. How *not* metal is that?

Judas Priest frontman Rob Halford actually fronted Black Sabbath for a few shows when he filled in for Ronnie James Dio, who refused to sing as an opening act for Ozzy Osbourne's solo show in 1992. Dio eventually left Sabbath because they opened for Ozzy that day. It was nothing personal against Ozzy, but Dio felt that the band Ozzy was once in should not be opening for his solo gig at Ozzfest.

that had been converted into a hotel called Wroxall Abbey, which was actually more like a bed-and-breakfast where everybody knew each other. I checked in and was heading straight for my room to take a nap, when I heard a voice calling me down the hall. It was my old friend Mr. Dio. He said, "No way are you going to sleep, Eddie! The only way to adjust to the jetlag is to stay awake. You're coming to the bar. Drop your bags!" Who was I to argue with Dio? He was right, of course! That was one of the most memorable and special nights for me, sitting in that castle, having pints with Ronnie, and hearing his decades of stories. We also talked about our other mutual love: sports. Ronnie, like me, is a huge New York Giants fan, and that night the Giants were on *Monday Night Football*, which starts at around three AM in the U.K. I was already wiped out, but Ronnie broke my balls all night trying to get me to stay up and watch it with him. I love my Giants, but no way would I make it till six AM. Sure enough, the next day, Ronnie knew every play that happened in the game.

The interview went well the next day, and I was thrilled to learn that the Dio-fronted Sabbath would be sticking around, but operating under the name Heaven & Hell to avoid confusion with the Ozzy-era band. I didn't care what they called it—the Sabbath I loved was back for a third go-around and I could not have been more excited. When I asked Tony about his decision to finally reunite with Dio, he admitted that I'd had an influence by always telling him how important it was to so many people.

They made a remarkable record called *The Devil You Know* in 2009, which was as heavy and Sabbath-sounding as it could possibly get, and they toured to support it. There are very few bands, if any, making music that amazing after forty years. It's a testament to their brilliance and endurance as the founding fathers of metal.

I have had the honor of interviewing Black Sabbath/Heaven & Hell on the radio so many times and even got to introduce them at their first U.S. show after the 2007 reunion at Radio City Music Hall. I still get chills thinking about that night. It wasn't the first time I'd introduced them, but it was my first time on the Radio City stage, as well as Ronnie's first American show with the band in thirteen years. The electricity from the crowd that night was something I've rarely ever felt.

After the show, the band came directly to my radio studio and stayed for a couple of hours, something very few artists will take the time to do after playing a huge marquee performance. Geezer was falling-down drunk that night and someone took a photo of the two of us—in it, we have our arms around each other. We always joke about that photo because he said if I hadn't had my arm around him, he'd have been on the floor.

In August 2008, all the members of Sabbath appeared at a private concert Judas Priest performed for me at the Hard Rock Café in Times Square. They had just completed a day of press and were tired but came to help pay tribute to my twenty-fifth anniversary in radio. The concert was an amazing honor in itself, but those guys making that effort for me was the icing on the cake.

In January 2010, the band flew me to Los Angeles to shoot an inter-

ABOVE: Tony Iommi at Madison Square Garden, New York City, August 4, 1975
OPPOSITE: Bill Ward at Madison Square Garden, New York City, August 4, 1975

view with them for a bonus feature on a live DVD. Little did I know it would be one of the last times I would see my friend Ronnie James Dio. Ronnie had been battling stomach cancer and tragically passed away in May 2010. Everyone who knew him was devastated, including, of course, Tony, Geezer, and Vinny. I flew back to Los Angeles for the services and was honored to be asked to host and speak at Ronnie's memorial. Afterward we all gathered at the Rainbow Bar and Grill and celebrated Ronnie's memory. It was a surreal weekend. Geezer and Tony could not believe what just happened—they had been planning to start a European tour in a few weeks and were confident Ronnie would recover. Tony had planned to be in L.A. for rehearsals, not to bury his singer and friend. It was tough on everyone, and the future plans of Sabbath are uncertain. In the summer of 2010 it was announced that they would do one tribute show to Dio in Europe and raise funds for the Ronnie James Dio "Stand Up and Shout" Cancer Fund. Glenn Hughes was one of the singers enlisted for this special performance.

It is a tremendous honor for me to call any member of Black Sabbath a friend. Let me be clear that I love and respect the Ozzy-led version of Sabbath for being the groundbreaking pioneers they were; those albums and songs remain untouchable in metal history. But I have had a closer connection and much more personal experience with the Dio-led Sabbath over the years. Regardless of what version of Sabbath you favor, they remain to this day the single most important band in metal history.

The 1980s saw a revolving cast of members for Sabbath, featuring only Tony Iommi from the original lineup. Iommi told me that outside of the best-known Ozzy and Dio versions of the band, he feels most strongly about the Tony Martin era, which produced albums like *The Eternal Idol* and *Headless Cross*.

My personal non-Ozzy or non-Dio favorite is the Glenn Hughes–fronted 1986 release called *Seventh Star*. Originally intended to be a Tony Iommi solo album, *Seventh Star* was issued as "Black Sabbath featuring Tony Iommi" because of record label pressure. Hughes's time in the band was short-lived because of his massive drug issues—he was replaced for the tour by the late Ray Gillen—but the album includes some great material, including a bluesy ballad called "No Stranger to Love." Iommi and Hughes reconnected years later for an equally strong album called *Fused*, which is worth checking out. Glenn Hughes was one of many great singers to perform at Dio's funeral and was a favorite of Dio's.

In recent years, there has been a new respect for *Born Again*, which features Deep Purple singer Ian Gillan on vocals. This album was initially panned as a sludgy mess with an awful cover, but it has aged well and some cite it as a sort of blueprint for the grunge sound of the 1990s.

BON JOVI

In the 1980s, there was no bigger band in the world of arena rock than Bon Jovi. It's easy to forget where they came from because over the years they have completely reinvented and distanced themselves from the scene they gave birth to: hair metal! Yes, folks, as much as he has managed to strip himself of all connections to it, Jon Bon Jovi is the founding father of '80s hair metal, and he should be celebrated for it!

As a lifelong New Jersey resident, I saw the emergence of Bon Jovi firsthand. They came on the local radar in 1983, when they won an unsigned-band contest held by a now-defunct New York City radio station called WAPP with the song "Runaway." The incredible hook of the song and the pinup looks of frontman Jon Bon Jovi quickly made them the next big rockers to come from New Jersey. The video for "Runaway" is no doubt one of those skeletons in the closet that Jon hates to have to live with, given his styled and sprayed hair and his tight lavender leather pants! But Jon Bon Jovi set the stage for hundreds of imitators over the next several years. He represents how important a charismatic frontman and strong leader are to the success of any band.

CLASSIC LINEUP

JON BON JOVI (VOCALS)

DAVID BRYAN (KEYBOARD)

RICHIE SAMBORA (GUITAR)

ALEC JOHN SUCH (BASS)

TICO TORRES (DRUMS)

KEY ADDITIONAL MEMBER

HUGH MCDONALD (BASS)

OPPOSITE: Richie Sambora and Jon Bon Jovi at Six Flags Great Adventure, Jackson, New Jersey, June 28, 1985

DISCOGRAPHY

ABOVE: Jon Bon Jovi at Six Flags Great Adventure, Jackson, New Jersey, June 28, 1985

Jon Bon Jovi became the face of the hair metal scene and was so influential that even record labels paid attention to the other bands he liked. He kept the scene alive by giving a start to bands like Cinderella (who featured him in their video for "Somebody Save Me") and Skid Row. Ironically, as the most iconic figure from that scene, Jon Bon Jovi is the only artist who hasn't been victimized by it. Jon Bon Jovi is one of the only hair metal frontmen who's been able to attract a whole new audience. The reasons for that are obvious: Not only was his band bigger than those who copied it, but Bon Jovi was also able to transcend genres and demographics because they wrote better songs.

The massive success that Jon and the boys attained in the '80s is well documented, and albums like their blockbuster breakthrough *Slippery When Wet* and *New Jersey* are now a new generation's classic rock. For me, *New Jersey* is a particular highlight, because it saw the band starting to evolve as better songwriters while holding on to their arena-rock party sound with tracks like "Lay Your Hands on Me." All the stresses and uncertainties of a band trying to make it were gone—they had money in the bank, a huge fan base, and an incredible chemistry that came from nonstop touring and playing together. When the album was released, I remember attending a huge listening party at the Roseland Ballroom in New York City. The whole venue was transformed into a replica of the Jersey boardwalk, a place where I'd spent so much time as a kid. As a guy who's Jersey born and bred, I appreciated that the band was so proud of where they came from that they named their record after it.

During that time, one of the biggest moments for the band was when they played a homecoming show at Giants Stadium with Skid Row and Billy Squier opening. What some people—including Billy himself—might not know is how Squier got on that bill. Snake from Skid Row is a good friend of mine who grew up with Jon Bon Jovi in New Jersey. One night, while he was in the radio studio with me, Snake said that Jon was looking for a third act for the big Giants Stadium show. Jon was a regular listener of my first radio show at WDHA in the mid-'80s and from time to time would call in requests. I remember him calling in once and telling me he was on his way to his mom's for some pasta and wanted to hear Billy Squier's song "She's a Runner."

I'd always been a fan of Billy's and had just been given an advance of his latest album, *Hear & Now*. Billy had been really huge a few years earlier but was starting to sink a bit, even though he was still making great music and had a great catalog. I knew Jon was a fan, so I had Snake call him to suggest Billy for the opening lineup and gave him my copy of *Hear & Now* to pass along to Jon. Jon liked the idea and, after listening to the tape, booked Billy for the middle slot of the gig. I provided remote coverage for WDHA during that show, and Billy came to the booth to spend some time with me after his performance. It was cool to know that he was there in front of more than seventy thousand people because of that night in my radio studio.

As huge as Bon Jovi was in the '80s, they weren't bulletproof from

On Bon Jovi's first single, "Runaway," Jon is backed by session musicians who were brought in to record the song for the WAPP *Homegrown* compilation contest, not by the players who would become known as the original lineup. That same version that was recorded for the contest appears on Bon Jovi's debut album. Even in the band's earliest stages, Jon was always the focus. The band we know today was put together once a record deal was secured.

the early-'90s grunge movement, which killed so many bands. The years of nonstop touring and recording had also taken their toll, and the New Jersey brothers were beginning to disband. With his band in limbo, Jon started to focus on solo music, as did guitarist Richie Sambora. Jon also decided to launch his own record label, called Jambco, with artists like Billy Falcon and Aldo Nova in 1991. At the time, I was just coming off a stint serving as a very young VP for Megaforce Records. I had a solid reputation as a young guy in the business with good ears, no drug issues, and a decent amount of experience. I had just started my own artist management company and was working with a New Jersey band I really believed in called Turi (they never made it, but had some great shots). It was around this time that Jon had taken notice and started calling me. He wanted to take the next step with Jambco and had only one other person working for him at the time—a British guy named Steve Pritchitt, who had a background in international label affairs. Jon wanted me to come on board to do a little of everything.

After a few phone conversations, a lunch was set up at the Paramount Hotel in New York City for Jon, Steve, and me. It was a good meeting, and I walked away feeling like I might get offered the gig. A couple of days later, I got the call from Jon asking if I wanted to join him as part of Jambco. He said that he liked my ideas and feedback and that Steve would call me with the offer. I was thrilled. I'd always believed in what Jon could do and had no doubt that if anyone could make a comeback and survive the '80s stigma, it would be him.

When Steve called the next day, the money I was offered to work for the label was less than stellar. Steve also told me that Jon would want a piece of Turi if I was going to continue managing them. I had invested so much in that band that I truly believed they were going to pop. Turi had recently done a private showcase for the legendary Clive Davis and were offered

ABOVE: Tico Torres, Richie Sambora, Jon Bon Jovi, Alec John Such, and David Bryan, Keansburg, New Jersey, April, 1985

a development deal. After the work I had done, I couldn't let Jon come in and grab half the profits of a band I hoped would be massive.

When I told Steve of my issues, he understood. Then he told me not to sweat it because I probably wouldn't have a decision to make in the end. You see, Jambco was already losing money. Aldo Nova and Billy Falcon weren't selling records, but they were doing expensive radio tours for free. Jon's deal was set up so that any money Jambco lost would come out of his own royalties for Bon Jovi, as both had the same parent company. Steve said he felt that once Jon saw the latest Jambco financial statements, Jon would fold the label. Sure enough, Steve was right.

A few days later, as I was thinking about what to do, I got a call from Jon. He explained that the label was killing him and that he was going to have a major meeting at an island resort with his bandmates to see if he could patch things up and reignite Bon Jovi. I wished him luck, and we agreed to talk when he knew if he still had a band. It was a couple of weeks later that I got a call from Steve saying the band was getting back together and making a new album. Jambco was folding.

The resulting Bon Jovi album was called *Keep the Faith*, and it was their first step toward the reinvention that saved their career. As shallow as it sounds, it was pretty significant that Jon cut his hair at this time. The entire band changed their look and their sound to show that they weren't going to rest on their laurels as kings of the '80s; they were going to become relevant again. In the years following, Bon Jovi has completely distanced themselves from the hair metal scene. They never tour with bands from that era and shy away from the harder rock elements they began with. As a result, Bon Jovi has become a more polished, commercial pop-rock act, a change that has alienated most of their metal fan base but helped them reach a new demographic. (Bon Jovi has also never lost the support of the ladies.) And the dynamic of the band has definitely changed. Where Bon Jovi used to be a group effort, it's now very much Jon's band.

I have always had massive respect for what Jon has been able to accomplish in his career. It's no coincidence that while other bands from his era struggle to get noticed, he has turned Bon Jovi into an empire. He's better than most, smarter than most, and works harder than most. In recent years, the band has moved so far away from the high-energy hard rock they were once known for that I've drifted a bit as a fan, but I'll be the last person to question Jon Bon Jovi. Jon is a leader, and I have faith that he knows what he's doing.

ABOVE: Richie Sambora, Jon Bon Jovi, and Alec John Such at Madison Square Garden, New York City, June, 1984

UNDERGROUND CLASSIC

Jon Bon Jovi's solo album, *Destination Anywhere,* was a total commercial bomb. It had a darker, moodier sound than anything the band had done before, but I really liked it. It was also accompanied by an elaborate mini-film. The Bon Jovi song "Edge of a Broken Heart," originally recorded for *Slippery When Wet* but used instead for the soundtrack to the 1987 film *Disorderlies,* would've easily been another massive hit if it had been on that album. Give it a listen.

Finally, do not look past Richie Sambora's first solo album, *Stranger in This Town*. It features some great bluesy rock, and Richie is a tremendous singer in his own right.

LEFT: Jon Bon Jovi, Keansburg, New Jersey, April, 1985

CHEAP TRICK

E ven though Cheap Trick never came close to metal territory, they had a sizable impact on the genre. Hell, even Anthrax proclaimed their love for Cheap Trick and covered their material! In the band's early years, they were a hard rock group that blended Beatles-style pop hooks and melodies with chainsaw-loud guitars. I've mentioned the term "power pop" elsewhere in this book, but if ever there was a band that defined that genre of strong melodies, big and fast guitar riffs, and a forceful, driving drum style, it's Cheap Trick.

The band's first three albums featured some great tunes, like the now-classic "I Want You to Want Me," but they failed to capture the band's live energy and power, nor did they light up the charts. Thankfully, this was the '70s–a decade when live albums mattered. Today live recordings are pretty much considered throwaways, but in the '70s, they were often major releases. For Cheap Trick, a live record was the reason the band took off. *At Budokan* was the album that

BUN E. CARLOS (DRUMS)

RICK NIELSEN (GUITAR)

TOM PETERSSON (BASS)

ROBIN ZANDER (VOCALS)

JOHN BRANDT (BASS)

PETE COMITA (BASS)

OPPOSITE: Robin Zander and Rick Nielsen at Capitol Theatre, Passaic, New Jersey, May 5, 1979

DISCOGRAPHY

saved the band's career and made them international stars. Yet it was actually never supposed to be released in America. For whatever reason, this band from Rockford, Illinois, made a big connection with Japanese audiences. This resulted in Cheap Trick playing the legendary venue to screaming fans for the first time in 1978. One of the shows was recorded and broadcast on Japanese television at the time, and the band's label, Epic, thought it would be a good idea to release a few of the tracks to U.S. radio stations as a promotional EP. The label thought that showcasing the excitement for the band in Japan might light a fire on their home turf. The experiment worked, and suddenly when U.S. fans learned a live album was available in Japan, they began to order it on import. Because of the large demand, an American release of *At Budokan* was arranged the next year, and it became a monster seller internationally.

Much like *Alive!* had done for Kiss songs a few years earlier, *Budokan* took some of Cheap Trick's best material to that point and gave it a massive kick in the pants in their live version. "I Want You to Want Me" was completely reinvented. Gone was the honky-tonk piano of the studio version, and in its place was a roaring guitar by Rick Nielsen and an overall different attitude and aggression. Songs that had gone nowhere as singles from the studio albums were suddenly all over the radio in their amped-up live *Budokan* versions. Unlike many live albums of the day, *Budokan* is truly live. The energy of that recording makes it special, along with the screams of the young Japanese women in the audience reacting whenever singer Robin Zander or bassist Tom Petersson would look their way. To this day, *Budokan* has the greatest live screams and applause ever recorded on a live album. You can just feel the pandemonium in the shrieks between songs. It was no accident that on *Budokan* and several of their studio albums, Zander and Petersson appeared on the front cover, while the less photogenic Nielsen and drummer Bun E. Carlos were on the back.

Cheap Trick has released many albums since *Budokan*, but without question, it remains their defining recording. So much so that the album has been reissued in several versions, including an expanded edition that captures the full live shows and a more recent thirtieth anniversary edition that includes a DVD of the TV broadcast. The band had no idea at the time that those shows in Japan would break them in America, and maybe that's why there is such a great spirit and a loose, freewheeling energy in the performances which is what makes the album so classic. Robin Zander's voice is simply remarkable; the guy could sing the phone book and make it sound good. Rick Nielsen is such a great songwriter and an underrated guitarist as well. And the rhythm section of bassist Petersson and drummer Carlos is rock solid—never overplaying and always keeping it all together.

Even though Cheap Trick had a relatively short run of major success, they are truly a band of brothers. They, along with ZZ Top and Aerosmith, are one of the few bands that have their classic lineup to this day—though there were some brief lineup changes in the '80s. Their songs were a

major influence on so many '80s bands, proving that hard rock coupled with pop hooks could be a potent formula. In 2009, Cheap Trick toured as the opening act for Poison and Def Leppard. I recall conversations with members of both co-headlining bands who told me how much they loved and were influenced by Cheap Trick (and were almost embarrassed that Cheap Trick was opening for them). In the '90s, Cheap Trick toured with acts like Pearl Jam and Stone Temple Pilots, who also considered them influential. But that's part of the story of Cheap Trick. They had brief periods of massive success with hits like "Surrender" in the '70s and "The Flame" in the '80s, but outside of a few radio favorites, they were very much the underdogs and one of rock's best-kept secrets. Cheap Trick continues to march to their own beat, and their true fans would have it no other way. Throughout the 2000s, they've continued to tour and release albums, even playing a thirtieth-anniversary show at Budokan.

Over the years I have interviewed Rick Nielsen many times, most recently in 2010 on my satellite radio show prior to a Cheap Trick gig in NYC. Rick remembers everything and is a total character and great storyteller. He also respects me because he knows I am one of the few radio guys who knows the band's catalog and plays tracks besides their few key hits. We always have fun, but it was my first-ever meeting with Cheap Trick that stands out for me and for Rick. The year was 1989. I went to Los Angeles

ABOVE: Rick Nielsen, Bun E. Carlos, Robin Zander, and Tom Petersson at the Palladium, New York City, September 28, 1978

EDDIE'S PLAYLIST

CHEAP TRICK

1. SPEAK NOW (OR FOREVER HOLD YOUR PEACE)
2. SICK MAN OF EUROPE
3. GONNA RAISE HELL
4. COME ON, COME ON
5. SOUTHERN GIRLS
6. HELLO THERE
7. SURRENDER
8. ELO KIDDIES
9. BIG EYES
10. AUF WIEDERSEHEN
11. CLOCK STRIKES TEN
12. CALIFORNIA MAN
13. WOKE UP WITH A MONSTER
14. TONIGHT IT'S YOU
15. HE'S A WHORE
16. DREAM POLICE
17. OH CAROLINE
18. DOWNED

to spend some time with my friends in White Lion, who were making a new album and invited me out to listen to it and to stay with them for a week. The band was staying in the Oakwoods, a short-term apartment complex in Burbank; at that time, many bands recording in L.A. would rent condos there. I stayed with Vito Bratta, guitarist for White Lion and also a Cheap Trick fan. On my first day hanging with Vito, he told me he had heard that the guys from Cheap Trick were in the apartments next door at the Oakwoods. Vito is kind of shy, but when we came back from dinner that night, we heard some music outside the door of the apartment next to us. It sounded like Rick and Robin working on songs! We couldn't resist and came up with the courage to knock and say hi. After all, Vito was a pretty major guitar star at the time, and White Lion was coming off a massive album themselves with *Pride*, so maybe the guys would bond over their experiences. Rick answered, recognized Vito right away, and invited us in. I will never forget seeing Rick and Robin huddled around a small tape recorder, working out songs for their new album. In the corner was Rick's son, who just slept through all the noise. The pressure was on because the band had a massive hit the previous year with "The Flame," and they wanted to keep the momentum going (sadly, they would not have another hit). Rick welcomed us to stay and listen under the condition that we drink with them. Vito and I had just had dinner and were not

In 2009, Cheap Trick released an album called *The Latest*. The band issued it on CD, vinyl, cassette, and eight-track. When I asked Rick why they would bother releasing it on cassette and eight-track, two formats nobody had any interest in, he explained that by having the only eight-track release, Cheap Trick could say they had the number-one eight-track on the charts!

in a drinking mood, especially at that late hour. But Rick insisted, and we wanted to stay, so for the next few hours Vito and I nursed beers while we watched Rick and Robin write—and drink more than I had ever seen anyone drink up to that point in my life. Rick even had some cans in his jacket so he wouldn't have to walk to the fridge that often. I could not believe what they could consume and how they seemed totally unaffected by it. We left later and made a plan to do a dinner with both bands, which happened soon after.

White Lion, Cheap Trick, and I went to a Mongolian barbecue joint in L.A. Now, I did not work for White Lion or Cheap Trick. At the time, I worked for Megaforce Records. I had tried to sign White Lion but could not get the company to go for it. I remained friends with the band, and since I was one of their first radio supporters, they would fly me out to hang with them from time to time. I was there essentially on vacation. But when we finished this huge meal and the bill came, Rick handed it to me, the label guy. I explained to Rick that neither band was on my label and I couldn't pay it. I would cover my own costs and that was it. Rick couldn't believe it! He said, "Next time we are looking for a label, Megaforce is out because of this Eddie Trunk!" But I couldn't cave. From there, we all went to some nightclub in the Valley, where Rick continued to bust my balls. Once again, the Cheap Trick guys drank to unreal levels. Tom was so drunk I couldn't understand a word he said. When the end of the night rolled around, Tom was nowhere to be found. The other Cheap Trick guys seemed unconcerned, so we all headed back to the Oakwoods without him. The next day, Vito and I were pulling out of the apartment complex when I noticed the bushes moving around. On cue, out of the hedges stumbled Tom Petersson, wearing the same clothes he'd had on the night before and looking pretty rough! We called out to him, but he ignored us and stumbled up to his apartment. Just like Cheap Trick, it was total rock and roll.

ABOVE: Robin Zander and Rick Nielsen, Morristown, New Jersey, July, 1978
OPPOSITE: Robin Zander and Tom Petersson at the Palladium, New York City, September 28, 1978

ALICE COOPER

As a huge Kiss fan growing up, I saw the name Alice Cooper a lot. Kiss was often compared to Alice—who came from Detroit in the late '60s and set the standard for theatrical rock, creating the stories and images that go with it. Kiss came from New York, took what Alice had started, and turned it to ten! While Alice wore some eyeliner and powder on his face, the four guys in Kiss covered their faces completely with makeup—you didn't even know who they were. The same childhood friend who had turned me onto Kiss introduced me to the album *The Alice Cooper Show*, which features images of a demonic-looking Cooper on the cover—his face is smeared with makeup, he's wearing a green jumpsuit, and he looks like he just escaped from a mental ward. There are images of the various props and torture devices with which he crowded his stage and, of course, live snakes. Before that moment, I didn't think there was anyone who was as outlandish and dark as the members of Kiss, but that album cover made me think twice.

MICHAEL BRUCE (GUITAR)

GLEN BUXTON (GUITAR)

DENNIS DUNAWAY (BASS)

VINCENT FURNIER/
ALICE COOPER (VOCALS)

NEAL SMITH (DRUMS)

STEVE HUNTER (GUITAR)

KANE ROBERTS (GUITAR)

DICK WAGNER (GUITAR)

AND MANY MORE!

OPPOSITE: Alice Cooper at the Ritz, New York City, March 12, 1990

When I listened to Alice Cooper's music, though, it didn't seem very metal. At times it was theatrical and very produced, but some songs sounded distinctively garage rock, and Alice even played the harmonica. Some featured orchestration and lavish production from the legendary producer Bob Ezrin. Judging from the ghoulish cover, I expected the music to be much heavier, so I kind of dismissed him.

Alice Cooper's musical career spans five decades and crosses over many genres. While he is known as the inventor of "shock rock," influences of glam, garage, hard rock, experimental, and even "concept" rock pieces have made their way into his giant catalog. After several name changes, the band decided to call themselves Alice Cooper, reportedly after a seventeenth-century witch. Alice's notorious play with makeup, the macabre, and even androgyny had begun.

In 1969, the group's first album was released by Frank Zappa's record label, as Zappa was looking to promote fellow avant-garde acts. The '70s brought Alice mainstream success with major-label backing and a top 10 single in "School's Out." He also perfected his shock-rock stage act with a live show in which he was "killed" at every performance and surrounded by a gruesome assortment of props—live snakes, fake blood, a bed of nails, a guillotine, an electric chair, etc. (Despite how scary some of his live shows could be, he did perform for viewers of all ages on *The Muppet Show*.)

It wasn't until the 1980s that I started to realize how many metal bands—like Megadeth and Anthrax—were covering Alice Cooper songs. Alice's elaborate shows and the quality of his music influenced many of the young metal bands who grew up in the late '70s. Alice's music may not have been straight metal, but there was a sinister quality to it and enough guitar to make it relatable to that audience. I also started to recognize that a lot of popular songs like "You & Me"—a beautiful ballad I'd heard all the time on the radio as a kid—and "Be My Lover" were his. As I got older and my musical tastes opened up, I had to acknowledge that there was so much depth to this guy's catalog. Even though I wasn't a fan of every record of his, I couldn't overlook what an innovator he'd been. Songs like "Is It My Body," "Only Women Bleed," "Under My Wheels," "I'm Eighteen," and "Billion Dollar Babies" are classics with catchy choruses, cool production, and a sound that captured Alice's over-the-top persona.

During the '80s, heavy metal acts helped to introduce Alice Cooper to a whole new generation of music lovers. Alice appeared in several films, and Megadeth teamed up with him for a cover of "No More Mr. Nice Guy" that got a fair amount of airplay. Suddenly some of the top names in metal were singing the praises of Alice. Instead of resting on his catalog and becoming a nostalgia act, he evolved and got even edgier to match the times. Working with guitarist and Sylvester Stallone look-alike Kane Roberts, he became more metal. A few years later, he took a completely different turn and reinvented himself again by working with Desmond Child, who is known for helping Bon Jovi write some of their biggest hits. Alice became much more polished and commercial and made a huge comeback

ABOVE and OPPOSITE: Alice Cooper at the Ritz, New York City, March 12, 1990

DISCOGRAPHY

PRETTIES
FOR YOU (1969)

EASY ACTION (1970)

LOVE IT TO DEATH (1971)

KILLER (1971)

SCHOOL'S OUT (1972)

BILLION DOLLAR
BABIES (1973)

MUSCLE OF LOVE (1973)

WELCOME TO
MY NIGHTMARE (1975)

ALICE COOPER
GOES TO HELL (1976)

LACE AND WHISKEY (1977)

THE ALICE COOPER
SHOW [LIVE] (1977)

FROM THE INSIDE (1978)

FLUSH THE
FASHION (1980)

SPECIAL FORCES (1981)

ZIPPER
CATCHES SKIN (1982)

DADA (1983)

CONSTRICTOR (1986)

RAISE YOUR
FIST AND YELL
(1987)

TRASH (1989)

HEY STOOPID (1991)

THE LAST
TEMPTATION (1994)

BRUTAL PLANET (2000)

DRAGONTOWN (2001)

THE EYES OF
ALICE COOPER (2003)

DIRTY DIAMONDS (2005)

ALONG CAME
A SPIDER (2008)

with the 1989 single "Poison," from an album called *Trash*. In the '90s and beyond, Alice further changed his sound to more straightforward, less-orchestrated rock that showed he knew how to stay current.

I first met Alice in 2005 at the House of Blues in Atlantic City. I knew several musicians in his touring band and was waiting backstage to say good-bye to them after the show when a road manager came up to me and said, "You're Eddie Trunk. Alice would like to meet you." Alice Cooper wanted to meet *me*? I was walked back to Alice's private dressing room, where he was sitting by himself. We sat on the sofa and ended up talking for at least an hour, like we'd known each other for years. It meant so much to me when he explained that he'd wanted to meet me because he'd watched some of the interviews I'd been doing on VH1 Classic. He said it was refreshing to see someone on TV who actually knew something

1. IS IT MY BODY 2. UNDER MY WHEELS 3. BE MY LOVER
4. BRUTAL PLANET 5. BILLION DOLLAR BABIES 6. YOU & ME
7. SCHOOL'S OUT 8. FREEDOM 9. I'M EIGHTEEN 10. ELECTED
11. ONLY WOMEN BLEED 12. NO MORE MR. NICE GUY

EDDIE'S PLAYLIST ALICE COOPER

about the music. I'll never forget it. Ever since that meeting, we've had a great relationship. He is one of the nicest guys I've ever met, and whenever he comes through town to play, I go to see him.

In 2009, when Alice played in New Jersey, my *That Metal Show* co-host Jim Florentine and I went to interview him at the Bergen Performing Arts Center. We had Alice take us on a tour of his stage set before the doors opened, and he demonstrated how some of his over-the-top props worked. He even stuck a giant fake needle into my stomach and maneuvered his notorious guillotine. It was cool to see all of his signature props, which had been the inspiration for the stage shows of so many of the bands I love.

As he showed us around, he pointed out that while these were all stage show devices, they were also extremely dangerous if not used correctly. Though his live show is all about watching him "die" in gory ways, Alice marveled that he'd survived so many years of performing with these things without actually killing himself. He used to suffer from a serious addiction to alcohol, and being wasted for so many years made his stage antics even more dangerous. In recent years, he's been open about being extremely religious. Having abused his body with drugs and alcohol, he is grateful to be alive and is a man of great faith.

Alice Cooper isn't an artist who can be categorized. When you really look at his diverse history, you realize that he's not given nearly enough credit as a writer, singer, and performer. He's been dismissed by critics as a shock-rock vaudeville guy, but without great music to support his theatricality, the show would mean nothing. You can point to great songs on just about every record he's released throughout the decades. And for a guy who's currently in his sixties, it's amazing that no one ever talks about his age. You never hear anyone asking how old Alice is or talking about him being off his game. Granted, when he was in his twenties, he dressed up and wore makeup to look old and broken-down, but now that he's actu-

ABOVE: Alice Cooper and Eddie backstage at the *That Metal Show* taping in Los Angeles, 2010

Alice's career got a boost in 1986, when he released the album *Constrictor*, made a cameo in the film *Friday the 13th, Part VI: Jason Lives*, and also contributed to the film's soundtrack and accompanying music video for the song "Man Behind the Mask." The success of these played a big role in returning him to stages and giving him new exposure to the video-loving audience of the time. His band in the mid-'80s also included an unknown bassist named Kip Winger, who would leave Alice and have success and hits with his own band, Winger, a few years later.

ally aging, he brilliantly looks the same. And now that he's sober, an avid golfer, and in great physical shape, he's an even better performer.

As the years go by, my appreciation for Alice continues to grow. His records sound better and better, and I continue to discover new ideas and musical touches I'd overlooked as a kid. He currently does a radio show called *Nights with Alice Cooper*, on which he's always talking about the underplayed and underappreciated music he loves. He features a wide variety of rock music both past and present and has some great stories to share. One of my favorite stories that he told on *That Metal Show* is how, back in the '70s, his pet snake got loose in the plumbing of the hotel where he was staying and came up in the toilet of country artist Charlie Pride, who was staying in the room next door!

Alice Cooper is one of the most important entertainers of all time—he combined genres, invented his own style of music and performance, and stayed relevant for more than forty years. He paved the way for all the makeup-and-costume-wearing musicians who followed him, and his influence on rock and roll will continue for many years to come. Rob Zombie (who toured with Alice as the Gruesome Twosome in 2010), Marilyn Manson, Slipknot, and so many others owe a huge debt to this pioneer. It's hard to imagine what theatrical rock would look like without Alice Cooper and even harder to imagine what the Rock and Roll Hall of Fame is thinking by ignoring him.

ABOVE: Alice Cooper at the Ritz, New York City, March 12, 1990

DEEP PURPLE

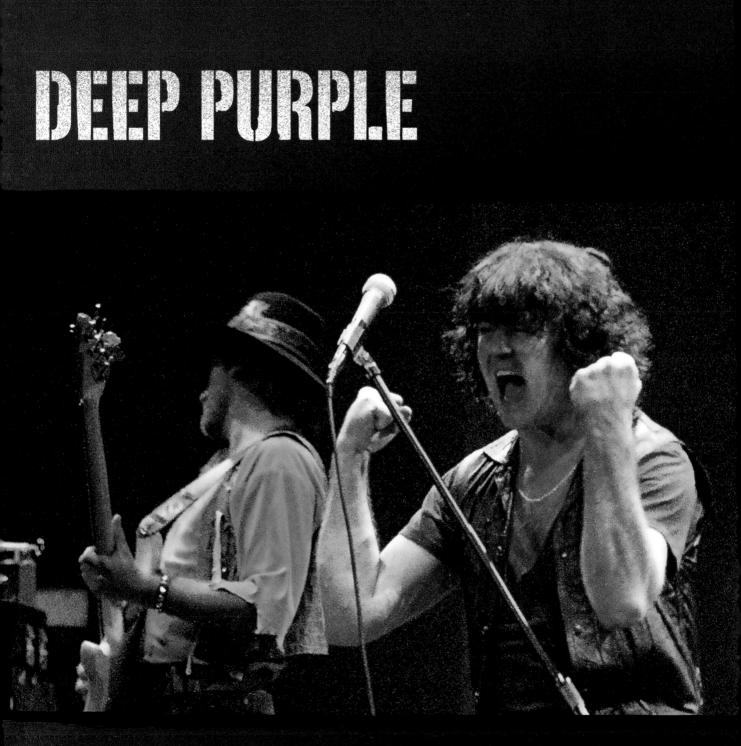

For being one of the true pioneers in the history of hard rock and metal music, Deep Purple is criminally underappreciated in America. Unfortunately, out of the band's entire catalog, most Americans know only two or three songs and don't give Deep Purple anywhere near the level of respect as that the band's contemporaries do. From Lars Ulrich to Yngwie Malmsteen, many musicians who grew up anywhere else in the world cite Deep Purple as their biggest influence and reason for making music. "Smoke on the Water" alone is reason for acknowledging them. It features one of the most iconic guitar riffs of all time. It's not only the first thing that any kid learning the guitar tries to play; it's also become synonymous with rock music.

CLASSIC LINE-UP

RITCHIE BLACKMORE (GUITAR)

IAN GILLAN (VOCALS)

ROGER GLOVER (BASS)

JON LORD (KEYBOARD)

IAN PAICE (DRUMS)

KEY ADDITIONAL MEMBERS

TOMMY BOLIN (GUITAR)

DAVID COVERDALE (VOCALS)

ROD EVANS (VOCALS)

GLENN HUGHES
(BASS/VOCALS)

STEVE MORSE (GUITAR)

NICK SIMPER (BASS)

JOE LYNN TURNER (VOCALS)

OPPOSITE: Roger Glover and Ian Gillan
at Brendan Byrne Arena, East Rutherford,
New Jersey, March 11, 1985

DISCOGRAPHY

SHADES OF DEEP PURPLE
(1968)

THE BOOK OF TALIESYN
(1968)

DEEP PURPLE (1969)

DEEP PURPLE IN ROCK
(1970)

FIREBALL (1971)

MADE IN JAPAN
[LIVE] (1972)

MACHINE HEAD (1972)

WHO DO WE THINK WE ARE
(1973)

BURN (1974)

STORMBRINGER (1974)

COME TASTE THE BAND
(1975)

PERFECT STRANGERS (1984)

THE HOUSE OF BLUE LIGHT
(1987)

SLAVES AND MASTERS
(1990)

*THE BATTLE
RAGES ON . . .* (1992)

PURPENDICULAR
(1996)

ABANDON (1998)

BANANAS (2003)

RAPTURE OF THE DEEP
(2005)

Perhaps one of the biggest detriments to Deep Purple's profile in the States has been their multiple lineup changes and evolutions in sound. There have been so many lineups over the years that they're referred to as Mark I–Mark IV and beyond! The Mark II lineup, featuring Ian Gillan on vocals, Ritchie Blackmore on guitar, Jon Lord on keyboards, Roger Glover on bass, and Ian Paice on drums, is considered by many to be the definitive one. Paice is the only constant in Deep Purple—he's been a fixture of the band in every single lineup.

With the most level of success, the Mark II lineup was easily the most recognizable and realized version of the band. They penned Deep Purple's most popular songs, like "Smoke on the Water," "Highway Star," and "Woman from Tokyo." The albums released during this period, like *Deep Purple in Rock* and *Machine Head*, are their most classic in stature, as well as the bestsellers. Previous versions of the band showed more of an influence of the sounds and images of the 1960s hippie movement, but the Mark II lineup evolved to a more unique sound that laid the blueprint for heavy metal.

Ian Gillan's vocals and Ritchie Blackmore's guitar playing are the signature elements of the Mark II lineup. Ritchie was a dark genius who always wore black onstage while playing this incredible mix of blues and classical guitar. He was such an explosive player that you could literally watch him emoting through his instrument. If he was angry, for instance, you'd see him recklessly throwing his guitar around, taking out his aggression. From one song to the next, it was never the same thing twice with him. His volatility was one of his trademarks.

Many people say that Blackmore is a huge jerk, while others think he's just misunderstood. The legendary video of Deep Purple playing at the California Jam in 1974 is one example of his moodiness. This show was being shot for television, but apparently Ritchie didn't want it to be taped. When the camera came in on him for a close-up, he jammed the neck of his guitar into it and blew it up. Remember, this was the '70s, so the camera was huge! As a showman with an unpredictable streak, Blackmore's behavior fueled the mystique of the band. No one knew what he might do—if he'd leave mid-set or go off on someone—but he was a genius on his instrument and influential in many ways.

When I first discovered Deep Purple as a kid in the late '70s, they'd already been around for about ten years and had released several albums. I had read about this moody and eccentric guitar wizard, Ritchie Blackmore, in music magazines and was fascinated by the whole aura of him. Like most people, I wanted to learn more.

I started with a greatest-hits compilation called *The Very Best of Deep Purple*, which is made up of mostly Mark II material. The cover shows a Fender Strat—Blackmore's signature guitar—with purple sparks coming from it. I liked the music, but I realized I was really more a fan of the artists who constantly cited Deep Purple as an influence. I'd been force-fed "Highway Star," "Smoke on the Water," "Hush," and "Woman from Tokyo," but I knew there must be more to them. People like Bruce Dickinson of

Iron Maiden and my friend Mike Tramp from White Lion would speak to me years later with the greatest reverence for the band and make me curious to know what I'd been missing out on.

At their core, Deep Purple is one of the loudest hard rock bands ever, but they also jam like no one else. Most of the bands I'd listened to before them played three- to four-minute songs, but I knew Deep Purple was about something else when I heard their live album *Made in Japan*. I was shocked to find that this double album had only seven songs! And they improvised and expanded these songs to unbelievable proportions. As a kid, I wasn't particularly a fan of it, but I appreciated that they were doing something different. They opened my eyes to the possibility of musicians

ABOVE: Ritchie Blackmore at Brendan Byrne Arena, East Ruherford, New Jersey, March 11, 1985

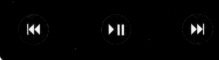

EDDIE'S PLAYLIST
DEEP PURPLE

1. CHILD IN TIME
2. PERFECT STRANGERS
3. KNOCKIN' AT YOUR BACK DOOR
4. SPEED KING
5. BLACK NIGHT
6. WOMAN FROM TOKYO
7. HIGHWAY STAR
8. FIREBALL
9. SPACE TRUCKIN'
10. BURN
11. STORMBRINGER
12. MISTREATED
13. BAD ATTITUDE

playing that way. They played hard rock, but they also touched on jazz and blues while staying heavy. No matter who has come and gone in the band, they've always maintained the quality, diversity, and class inherent in the music of the classic lineup.

While Deep Purple has a signature sound and some truly iconic riffs, their diversity may be one of their biggest contributions to music. They have proved how much musical ground a rock band could cover by adding blues and jazz improvisations and jamming, especially on the live stage. But when you listen to a song like "Black Knight" or "Speed King," you're hearing the roots of heavy metal. "Child in Time"—which features some of the most incredible screams ever recorded—is a dark, epic masterpiece that takes you on a haunting ten-minute journey. It's one of my favorite Deep Purple songs because of vocalist Ian Gillan's performance, but unfortunately, you'll never hear "Child in Time" live. I asked bassist Roger Glover why they don't play it onstage, and he said that Ian simply can't perform it anymore. The band made an agreement to never put him through those vocal acrobatics again.

I've interviewed Ian Gillan multiple times. He's always been great to talk to and has the most unbelievable stories from his time with the band. One of my most memorable experiences with him was in 2007. I was hosting Rock Fest in Cadott, Wisconsin. One of my jobs was to interview bands in their dressing rooms before they took the stage, and the interviews were broadcast to the audience on a screen in front of the stage. When I went to interview Deep Purple, Ian—who almost always performs barefoot—came out with a crazy contraption on his head. Half hat, half helmet, it had all kinds of spikes and needles and barbs coming out of it. From where I was standing next to him, it seemed like he'd take my eye out if he tilted his head.

I asked him to explain his headgear, and he told me that he wore it every time the band played outdoors to keep birds away. I can't think of many instances where birds have been a threat to musicians onstage, but he gave me a demonstration of how it would work. He ran around the room pretending to spear birds with his head. I'm pretty sure he was kidding, which gives you some insight into his sense of humor.

The Mark III lineup, which seems to be a favorite of many, featured the previously unknown singer David Coverdale and bassist and vocalist Glenn Hughes. This version of the band delved into some incredible blues-inspired hard rock with the added dynamic of two powerhouse vocalists trading off. It's rare that two singers of that caliber could exist in the same band.

Most people thought Deep Purple could never exist without Ritchie Blackmore. His antics and musical brilliance were so much a part of why people liked the band. That was until Tommy Bolin joined and brought his funk and jazz background. Deep Purple's first release with Bolin, *Come Taste the Band*, wasn't readily accepted by fans because it was impossible for most to reconcile the new musical elements with the band's sound or the fact that Blackmore was gone. Over time, Bolin gained tremen-

dous respect, especially in Japan, where he'd had some previous success. Sadly, his live performances were often compromised by his massive drug addiction. But when he was on, people widely acknowledged his talent and contributions to the band. In 1976, Tommy died at the age of twenty-five from a drug overdose in Miami.

In 1984, the Mark II lineup reunited for a great album called *Perfect Strangers*, and they toured to support it. Their 1985 show at Meadow-lands Arena (formerly known as Brendan Byrne Arena) was the first time I'd see them live. I was incredibly excited because I never imagined I'd get to see the classic lineup play. And there was always a mystique about seeing Deep Purple when Blackmore was in the band. He was known as a temperamental genius who might leave the stage if something set him off, even if there were twenty thousand people in the crowd, and every fan realized that going in.

I went to the show with my coworkers from the record store I worked at back then. One of them was named Lorenzo. Unbeknownst to us, Lorenzo decided to bring a primitive version of one of those laser-pointer key-chains. Three or four songs into Deep Purple's set, he decided to show his excitement by shining a light at Ritchie Blackmore while jumping on his seat and yelling Ritchie's name. Working in the store, we always got great seats for shows, so we were only about ten rows away and could see Blackmore getting irritated. We kept asking Lorenzo to stop, but he wouldn't. So in the middle of a song, Ritchie Blackmore pointed at Lorenzo, dropped his guitar, and walked offstage. We were furious, but just hoped Blackmore would come back. The rest of the band had dealt with this a lot and knew how to cover for it with a long keyboard jam. Eventually, Blackmore returned to the stage for what was otherwise a great show, but Lorenzo nearly ruined it for twenty thousand fans in New Jersey that night!

In the years since, I've had opportunities to interview Ritchie on my radio shows. I know that he listens to them and has heard his bandmates from Rainbow and Deep Purple on the air. But I've declined having him on my show because interviewing him has always come with a condition: We cannot talk about Deep Purple or Rainbow. He's had very big battles and legal issues with his previous record labels and managers, who he claims have ripped him off. He refuses to discuss anything about those bands. Unfortunately, I cannot in good conscience have him on my shows and not talk about Deep Purple or Rainbow. His current musical project is a band he does with his wife called Blackmore's Night. As a medieval-music act that performs at Renaissance Faires, it's completely removed from hard rock or metal. I'd love to interview him about that stuff if he's open to discussing his history, but so far, he hasn't changed his mind about it. I hope that he will, or that he'll at least plug in his guitar and play heavy music again.

DID YOU KNOW

Joe Satriani was a member of Deep Purple for a brief time. Satriani was asked to join the band in 1993 to fill in for the departed Ritchie Blackmore on a Japanese tour. He stayed on for a bit the following year, perform-ing some European shows with the band, and was of-fered the permanent gig but instead decided to return to his solo career. That opened the door for current guitar-ist Steve Morse, formerly of Dixie Dregs and Kansas.

ABOVE: Roger Glover and Ian Gillan at Brendan Byrne Arena, East Rutherford, New Jersey, March 11, 1985
OPPOSITE: Ritchie Blackmore at Brendan Byrne Arena, East Rutherford, New Jersey, March 11, 1985

DEF LEPPARD

For a band that initially embraced their place in the New Wave of British Heavy Metal, Def Leppard has done a lot to distance themselves from that genre. The new wave of the late '70s and early '80s featured an explosion of all sorts of rock and metal from the U.K. that relied less on blues references and instead took a faster, harder approach. Many of the bands didn't live up to the hype and never made it, but some, like Def Leppard and Iron Maiden, became global stars. Over the years, Def Leppard, which started out as more of a raw metal band, yet one that loved the melodies of '70s rock, evolved into a mass-appealing, superproduced, blockbuster outfit that gave us megahits like "Pour Some Sugar on Me" and "Love Bites." For my money, Def Lep is all about the first three albums—their hardest and most rockin'.

RICK ALLEN (DRUMS)

STEVE CLARK (GUITAR)

JOE ELLIOTT (VOCALS)

RICK SAVAGE (BASS)

PETE WILLIS (GUITAR)

VIVIAN CAMPBELL (GUITAR)

PHIL COLLEN (GUITAR)

OPPOSITE: Phil Collen and Joe Elliott at Brendan Byrne Arena, East Rutherford, New Jersey, March 27, 1983

DISCOGRAPHY

ON THROUGH
THE NIGHT (1980)

HIGH 'N' DRY (1981)

PYROMANIA (1983)

HYSTERIA (1987)

ADRENALIZE (1992)

RETRO ACTIVE (1993)

SLANG (1996)

EUPHORIA (1999)

X (2002)

YEAH! (2006)

SONGS FROM THE
SPARKLE LOUNGE (2008)

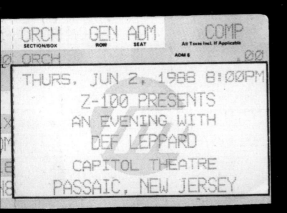

OPPOSITE TOP: Steve Clark and
Phil Collen at Brendan Byrne Arena, East
Rutherford, New Jersey, March 27, 1983
OPPOSITE BOTTOM: Steve Clark at
Brendan Byrne Arena, East Rutherford,
New Jersey, September 23, 1988

On Through the Night, the band's 1980 debut, did fairly well in England, but it is often overlooked because of its lack of hits or airplay in America. The band usually never plays much from it live, but it's a solid album with great riffs, which is especially impressive considering that all the group's members were in their teens when it was recorded. Even with a single called "Hello America"—which shows just how bent these guys were on breaking stateside, something that didn't sit too well with the hometown crowd in Sheffield, England—*On Through the Night* failed to light a spark on U.S. sales charts. But musically, it laid a nice foundation for the hits to come. Songs like "Wasted," "Rock Brigade," and "When the Walls Came Tumbling Down" are early signs of greatness from a still wet-behind-the-ears Def Leppard.

One year later, Def Leppard released *High 'n' Dry*, which remains, in my opinion, the best record in their catalog. Working for the first time with noted producer "Mutt" Lange (who was fresh off of producing an album you might have heard, AC/DC's *Back in Black*), Def Lep had a new sound and approach that's evident right from the start—they'd become a super-charged heavy rock band. Joe Elliott's vocals wail in a much higher pitch than on the first record. Producer Lange is known for whipping singers into shape and adding tons of vocal tracks, and his mark is immediate on *High 'n' Dry*. Joe's powerful, gritty vocal style and higher pitch would become a trademark of the band's sound (and give him fits when trying to duplicate the recordings onstage to this day). The guitars are louder, with more crunch; the drums are huge and clearly more produced. So much more aggressive and in-your-face, the songs on *High 'n' Dry* got a huge boost from Lange's writing and trademark production—those bigger, multitracked backing vocals and the enormous, processed drum sound. Even though it is regarded as their best by metal fans, *High 'n' Dry* failed to have a blockbuster hit, though it came close with "Bringing on the Heartbreak," which would later be covered by several artists, including Mariah Carey! In recent years, Def Leppard has performed the first half of the record from start to finish on the live stage, a true testament to just how well this album holds up.

I first saw Def Leppard on October 10, 1981, at the old Palladium (which is now the site of an NYU dormitory) in New York City. They were opening for Southern rockers Blackfoot. As much as I respect Rick Medlocke and company, I was mainly there to see Def Lep, who did not disappoint. They came out and blew the crowd away—Pete Willis shredding on a white Gibson Explorer guitar that looked bigger than he did; Joe Elliott belting it out over powerful hard rock. When their set ended, I quickly realized I wasn't the only one there just to see Def Leppard, because half the Palladium emptied before Blackfoot hit the stage. It was a strange billing at the time, but I left knowing I had seen something truly special that night. And with the release of their third album, the rest of the world found out just how special they were.

Def Lep's breakthrough and first score of massive hits came with 1983's *Pyromania*. This album also saw the first lineup change, when guitarist

Pete Willis was replaced mid-recording by former Girl guitarist Phil Collen. (Willis's rhythm tracks appear on the album, but the solos are Collen's.) Top 40 mega-singles like "Photograph," "Rock of Ages," and "Foolin'" had MTV play 24-7, and album sales went through the roof. I remember working in a record store when *Pyromania* came out. Girls would come in and buy anything Def Leppard . . . and Duran Duran! What happened to the New Wave of British Heavy Metal band nobody knew a couple of years ago? Suddenly they were pop stars!

Hysteria, their next record, took years to complete. Drummer Rick Allen's car accident, which resulted in the loss of his left arm, was among many issues causing the delay. As an ultimate sign of band unity, Def Leppard stood by Rick and, with the help of some engineers, developed an electronic drum kit that would incorporate more use of his feet to trigger various sounds and samples from the actual albums. The result was a rock band with the first-ever one-armed drummer, and—no pun intended—they didn't miss a beat. A slow seller out of the box, *Hysteria* eventually topped the U.S. charts and became one of the band's classic and biggest-selling albums, thanks to hit singles like "Love Bites," "Pour Some Sugar on Me," and the title track. This success led to Def Leppard's bringing their live show to arenas in the round (I've never been a fan of in-the-round shows, personally). But the band was never quite able to follow the sales and success of their one-two punch with *Pyromania* and *Hysteria*. Mutt Lange would come and go as producer on future albums, and the band seemed irritated by accusations that they might not be able to make a hit without him. Though they were much bigger than most other artists in the 1980s hair metal scene, Def Leppard still struggled in the United States, like most of their contemporaries, when the grunge scene hit. They became frustrated at being called a metal band and did everything they could to distance themselves from the scene they'd helped to create.

Through the 1990s and early 2000s, instead of touring with other bands of their era, they went out with groups like Styx and Journey—anything to avoid the "metal" connotation—in an effort to reinvent themselves in some way. Finally, in 2009, after some mudslinging in the press (which started when Joe Elliott suggested that Poison wasn't a good band), Def Leppard embraced the scene they were originally a part of and actually went on a successful tour with Poison!

I've always had a theory that Def Leppard tried to duplicate the formula masterfully executed by another megaband from their era, Bon Jovi. (While the guys in Def Leppard find this theory interesting, they have told me that there were no calculated plans to follow Bon Jovi as a model.) Jon and the band have reinvented themselves and kept making hit records by changing their look and sound and moving away from all associations with the scene they came from. When Bon Jovi teamed with a country artist, for instance, so did Def Leppard. Though Def Leppard might have followed Bon Jovi's marketing blueprint, it never quite worked as well for them. Don't get me wrong—Def Leppard did make great strides to get back in the game and are still a strong draw on the summer-shed

EDDIE'S PLAYLIST
DEF LEPPARD

1. WASTED
2. ROCK BRIGADE
3. ANOTHER HIT AND RUN
4. YOU GOT ME RUNNIN'
5. LET IT GO
6. TOO LATE FOR LOVE
7. STAGEFRIGHT
8. ROCK! ROCK! (TILL YOU DROP)
9. WORK IT OUT
10. HIGH 'N' DRY (SATURDAY NIGHT)
11. ON THROUGH THE NIGHT
12. DESERT SONG
13. MIRROR, MIRROR (LOOK INTO MY EYES)

circuit, but they never again came close to their 1980s-level stardom like Jon and the boys did. Def Lep, unfortunately, hasn't had a bona fide hit single in the United States in more than twenty-five years. But their old albums are now a new generation's classic rock, and they still put on a good live show.

I give Def Leppard tremendous respect, because even though I've been critical of them for renouncing their roots, they've never held it against me and have always been great to talk to. They are still music fans themselves, so they "get it" when people gravitate to certain eras in a band's history and not others. In my early days at VH1 Classic, I remember being worried about how they would respond when they found out I would be interviewing them. Instead of copping an attitude, those guys could not have been cooler. We had a great conversation, and Joe Elliott, a fellow UFO fan, even went so far as to send me a bootleg live show I'd been looking for. Current guitarists Vivian Campbell and Phil Collen have been frequent guests on my radio and TV shows and have also always been great to deal with. In 2009, I taped a TV special from the Download Festival in England, where Def Leppard was headlining on their home turf. Even though the set list didn't have my favorites, I was very happy for the guys, and most of them came by to say hi at our broadcast booth. Download, which was previously known as Donington Monsters of Rock, was one of the first shows the band did after Rick lost his arm, so it was very emotional for them to be back that day as headliners for the first time in more than two decades.

Def Leppard is one of the few bands from the 1980s that's still relevant. They have a huge fan base that comes out to see them play, and they continue to sell a decent amount of albums by today's standards. Their timeless records like *High 'n' Dry*, *Hysteria*, and *Pyromania* have become classics and even connect with many new fans. Even though they were originally thrown into and marketed as part of the New Wave of British Heavy Metal scene, they were always more interested in classic '70's pop-rock and glam, which has played a big role in the crossover appeal of their sound. To that end, in 2009, guitarist Phil Collen released a raw, punk-inspired album called *Surreal* with Man Raze—a side project featuring Paul Cook of the Sex Pistols and former Girl member Simon Laffy. Man Raze actually opened some Def Leppard shows recently and had Phil doing double duty playing with both acts. In 2010 it was announced that the band was taking a hiatus and Joe Elliott was joining a band called Down 'n' Outz that covers Mott the Hoople and other '70s stuff he loves, while guitarist Vivian Campbell was joining a new lineup of Thin Lizzy. These guys show no signs of slowing down.

UNDERGROUND
CLASSIC

Check out the Def Leppard album *Slang*. It's by far the worst-selling album of the band's career, and one that's rarely talked about, but I think it's actually important to note. *Slang* is a stripped-down, slightly darker sound for Def Lep, who became known, after a point, for huge, slick production. Instead of fifteen vocal tracks and tons of layering, this album is more about the straightforward songs and the playing. It's also the first studio album to feature replacement member Vivian Campbell, whose influence as a songwriter can be heard on a great track called "Work It Out," which was *Slang*'s first single.

WPLJ RADIO WELCOMES
BLACKFOOT
AND
DEF LEPPARD
WPLJ 95.5
THE PALLADIUM ROCKTOBER 10, 1981

Joe Elliott at Brendan Byrne Arena, East Rutherford, New Jersey, March 27, 1983

DIO

Without question, Ronnie James Dio's voice is the one that's heard most on my radio shows. Ronnie was one of the greatest singers of any style of music, and more important, one of the greatest people I have ever met in this business. He had an amazing kindness and respect for his fans and friends. Long before anyone knew him as a metal guy, he was playing and singing in rockabilly bands in the 1950s, before he was even in high school. He also played the trumpet. From those roots, Ronnie somehow turned his voice into one of the most powerful and recognizable in the history of rock and metal. Ronnie actually credited playing trumpet for his enduring voice, claiming it taught him the proper way to breathe. It helped him remain a premier singer until his passing from cancer in May 2010. It often amazed people that such an enormous voice came from such a small man!

CLASSIC LINEUP

VINNY APPICE (DRUMS)

JIMMY BAIN (BASS)

VIVIAN CAMPBELL (GUITAR)

RONNIE JAMES DIO
(VOCALS)

DOUG ALDRICH (GUITAR)

CRAIG GOLDY (GUITAR)

ROWAN ROBERTSON
(GUITAR)

SIMON WRIGHT (DRUMS)

OPPOSITE: Ronnie James Dio at Brendan Byrne Arena, East Rutherford, New Jersey, November 5, 1984

After starting out in hard rock with the band Elf, then singing with two iconic bands, Rainbow and Black Sabbath, Ronnie become known as one of the top singers in the rock world. He'd already established himself as a tremendous talent, so eventually, fronting his own band just made sense. Though it's often viewed as a solo vehicle, Dio the band was always very much a collaboration between its members. That was very evident from the first album they released, *Holy Diver*.

Dio's first guitarist, a kid from Ireland named Vivian Campbell, was a huge part of the band's sound and image. *Holy Diver* brought Campbell to the world's attention, and everyone was talking about him. But Ronnie always told me that Vivian was a reluctant guitar hero. He was painfully shy, and Ronnie usually had to pull performances out of him.

Holy Diver's "Rainbow in the Dark" was a hit out of the box for Ronnie—bigger than anything he'd done previously in America. When that song came out, it was like the stage had finally been set from his years of preparation in Sabbath and Rainbow and the world was ready for Dio's vision.

Known for singing about demons, dragons, and sorcery, Ronnie also wrote lyrics that rallied for the disenfranchised. His imagery and subject matter have always been powerful and sometimes very dark. But to me, it almost doesn't matter what he sings about. There aren't many heavy metal vocalists who can be considered virtuosos. And there aren't many people who can consistently sing the way he did for so many years. He proved that aggressive music could support strong vocals and that the voice is just as important in the overall dynamics of a band as guitars or drums or anything else. People who aren't even metal fans, like my wife, for instance, can listen to Dio's voice and recognize that what he did was remarkable (not to mention head and shoulders above most vocals you hear in the genre, or any genre). Though he was a metal icon, he offered so much more. I remember putting on "Neon Knights" once when my wife was in the car and she said, "Oh, now I can see why you love Dio. That guy can sing."

Ronnie's amazing ability enabled him and whatever band he was in to be more dynamic. He was able to sing a ballad as easily as he was an epic rock song. Whatever music he was writing, he always had a larger palette of styles he could pull from. You just don't hear vocalists like him. One needs only to listen to the softer songs he recorded to get a fuller understanding of his range.

I saw the band often over the years, and it was incredible to hear the quality of music Ronnie was creating, to see how quickly his fame grew, and to experience the magnitude of the stage shows (which included lasers, dragons, and other legendary effects). Some lineups and albums were better than others, but Ronnie always knew exactly what he did well. He pushed boundaries but maintained a remarkable consistency throughout his career.

Holy Diver and *The Last in Line* are landmark records in the history of metal. They are loved and worshipped by hard rock and metal fans as much today as when they were first released. Nearly thirty years later,

heir immediacy still grabs you by the throat. Sonically, they are so great that they don't sound dated in the least, and while they were commercially successful, they haven't been overplayed. I still love listening to them.

Ronnie was a huge sports fan and often wrote some of his most-loved songs while watching sports on TV. He told me it was a way for him to find inspiration. Songs like "The Last in Line" and "We Rock" were composed while he was watching his beloved New York Yankees or New York Giants on TV at his home in Los Angeles.

I will never forget the first time I interviewed Ronnie for VH1. By that time, I knew him well. We'd met in the mid-'80s, and he had been on my radio show often. We had a conversation for about a half hour, and as I ended the interview, thanking him for coming on the show, Ronnie stopped me. He said, "I have to say something else." Looking to the camera, he added, "Everyone watching needs to thank Eddie. This is the guy who keeps this going for all of us. He waves the flag and gives opportunities to all of us who are fans of this music. All of the artists watching owe this man a debt of gratitude. I want to say publicly, thank you for all you do for us." It came out of nowhere. You can actually see my jaw drop on the tape! I reached into my pocket and said, "What do I owe you?" I was new on TV and trying to hold on to my job. His response was, "You owe me nothing but your friendship, and we already have that." That meant the world to me, but it's just one example of the kind of guy he was.

Ronnie was perhaps the most special person I've met in my decades of interviewing musicians. He was one of the most caring, genuine, and kind people I've ever known. Working in the music industry, I often say that there are people you know you're friends with because you work together in the business, and then there are people you're friends with because you have a true connection and love that extends way beyond the business. Ronnie was one of the latter. He was the type of guy who would walk into a room and know everyone's name. Both publicly and privately, he was one of my favorite people to talk to. Ronnie would allow me the honor of introducing him at almost every show he did with any band in the New York area, and then when he would speak to the crowd for the first time from the stage, he would thank me for the intro! I mean, who does that?

Vivian Campbell left the band after the *Sacred Heart* album, so Dio recruited Craig Goldy from the band Giuffria. Craig was down on his luck at the time and literally living in his car when Ronnie rescued him and gave him the gig. He remains a part of the Dio family to this day, along with Doug Aldrich, who replaced Craig on *Killing the Dragon*. Doug, like Vivian Campbell, was lured from Dio into Whitesnake, but he remained a very close friend and collaborator of Ronnie's and worked with him on several recordings, including a track called "Electra," which was the last song Dio recorded. Ask any of the members of Dio (with the lone exception of Vivan, who had a falling-out over business with the Dio camp) and they will tell you that family was Dio's world. Ronnie's wife, Wendy, managed his career for more than thirty years and remains the guardian of the Dio legacy. Drummer Simon Wright moved in with Ronnie to help look after

DISCOGRAPHY

HOLY DIVER (1983)

THE LAST IN LINE (1984)

SACRED HEART (1985)

INTERMISSION [LIVE] (1986)

DREAM EVIL (1987)

LOCK UP THE WOLVES (1990)

STRANGE HIGHWAYS (1994)

ANGRY MACHINES (1996)

INFERNO: LAST IN LIVE (1998)

MAGICA (2000)

THE VERY BEAST OF DIO (2000)

KILLING THE DRAGON (2002)

STAND UP AND SHOUT: THE ANTHOLOGY (2003)

MASTER OF THE MOON (2004)

EVIL OR DIVINE: LIVE IN NEW YORK CITY (2005)

HOLY DIVER LIVE (2006)

OPPOSITE: Ronnie James Dio at Brendan Byrne Arena, East Rutherford, New Jersey, November 5, 1984.

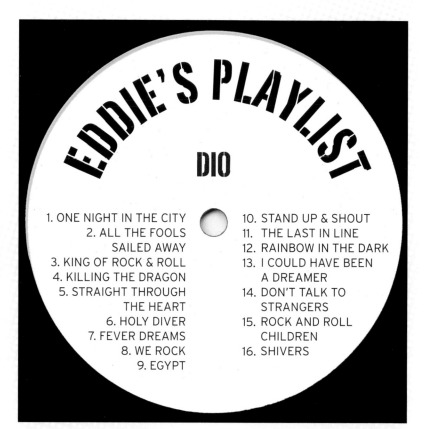

EDDIE'S PLAYLIST

DIO

1. ONE NIGHT IN THE CITY
2. ALL THE FOOLS SAILED AWAY
3. KING OF ROCK & ROLL
4. KILLING THE DRAGON
5. STRAIGHT THROUGH THE HEART
6. HOLY DIVER
7. FEVER DREAMS
8. WE ROCK
9. EGYPT
10. STAND UP & SHOUT
11. THE LAST IN LINE
12. RAINBOW IN THE DARK
13. I COULD HAVE BEEN A DREAMER
14. DON'T TALK TO STRANGERS
15. ROCK AND ROLL CHILDREN
16. SHIVERS

ABOVE: Ronnie James Dio and Eddie at PNC Bank Arts Center, Holmdel Township, New Jersey, August 9, 2008

him when he became ill. Bassist Rudy Sarzo has told me many times that he's never met anyone like Dio.

In late 2009, during some downtime in Heaven & Hell, Ronnie decided to fire up the Dio band for a European tour and to record a new song for the second part of a planned trilogy of concept albums called *Magica*, which he was very proud of. The lineup consisted of Doug Aldrich on guitar, Rudy Sarzo on bass, Simon Wright on drums, and Scott Warren on keys. Rehearsals started in L.A., and a few days in, Ronnie complained of stomach pain. The band knew it was serious because Ronnie, who usually brushed everything off and plowed forward, went to the doctor. A few weeks later, the devastating news that Ronnie had stomach cancer was announced. The tour was canceled, and Ronnie began treatment with specialists in Houston and Minneapolis. I spoke to Ronnie just before he started his first chemo to wish him well and let him know I loved him and was there for him. In typical Dio fashion, Ronnie lifted *my* spirits when he was about to battle for his life. During his months of treatment, the results often seemed to be positive, but it was hard to figure out what was real and what was just Ronnie staying upbeat. He fought so bravely.

On April 8, 2010, I was in Los Angeles to present an award at the Golden Gods show. I had spoken to Ronnie's wife, Wendy, a few days prior, and she told me Ronnie was not doing well. Needless to say, I was thrilled when

I saw him at the awards show walking the red carpet! We spoke and did a brief interview for the pre-show on VH1 Classic. Little did I know that would be my final interview with Dio and his last public appearance. On the morning of May 16, 2010, I woke to many text messages, something unusual on a Sunday. Many friends of Dio's were delivering the news I had been dreading: Ronnie had passed away. It hit me and all of his friends and family very hard. Indications were that Ronnie would make it, and I knew he had even fought Wendy on her decision to cancel upcoming Heaven & Hell European performances. But the cancer had spread, and a new form of chemo had really taken its toll on what had always been a very small, thin man. The music world was shaken, and so many artists released statements about the importance of Dio and the quality of person he was.

The funeral services were set for Memorial Day weekend, a few weeks later. I booked my plane ticket to fly west and pay my respects to a man who I was a huge fan of and who was a close friend. I was then told that Wendy wanted me to speak at one of the three events being held in Ronnie's memory. The weekend started with a private viewing on Friday, followed by a private funeral on Saturday and a public memorial on Sunday. Everything took place at Forest Lawn in Hollywood Hills. At the funeral service on Saturday, I sat in front of my good friend Rob Halford, and as we lined up and approached the casket at the end of the service, Rob joined me on the altar to pay final respects. It was fitting that a legend I regard as highly as Rob was there with me at that very tough moment. I hosted the following day's event—I was honored, to say the least, and a bit nervous. What would I say with my dear friend's casket just a few feet away and with a crowd of six thousand fans, friends, and family members gathered there? I had asked Wendy if we could maybe make it more of a celebration. The day was a roller coaster of emotion that included speeches and performances by Glenn Hughes, Oni Logan, Geoff Tate, Scott Warren, Claude Schnell, Paul Shortino, John Pain, Craig Goldy, and many others, along with video tribute packages and an outpouring from fans. We wanted to send Ronnie out rock-concert style, so we chanted his name and got a little rowdy.

I was told by many close friends that it was one of my finest performances, and if that indeed was the case, I am proud that it was for a man like Ronnie James Dio. The toughest part was finding something to say to wrap up the four-hour memorial. I will end this chapter with the same thing I told the people at Forest Lawn: For as great of a singer as Ronnie was, he was an even better person, and that's really saying something.

DID YOU KNOW

It was actually Sharon Osbourne who recommended Dio for the Black Sabbath job back in 1979. Before Sharon married Ozzy and started to manage his solo career, her father, Don Arden, managed Sabbath. She made the initial introductions that ended up with Ronnie getting the gig as Ozzy's replacement. Even though he was never a member of Deep Purple, Dio had a long history with many of the band's members on various projects besides Rainbow. He scored his first-ever gold record for the concept album *The Butterfly Ball and the Grasshopper's Feast*, a solo outing by Deep Purple's Roger Glover, which also featured that band's Jon Lord, Glenn Hughes, and David Coverdale. Dio's band Elf opened for Deep Purple on many tours and became the first lineup for Rainbow. Dio even sang with Deep Purple for a special live performance with the London Symphony Orchestra at London's Royal Albert Hall in 1999.

GUNS N' ROSES

The first time I heard Guns N' Roses was at a convention held by Warner-Elektra-Atlantic in 1987. I remember it vividly. WEA held weeklong conventions every year, and everyone from the record labels they distributed—including Geffen (GNR's label) and Megaforce (where I worked at the time)—would come together to meet, party, and learn about new releases from other labels in the family. Each label had its own hotel suite where people could eat, drink, meet the members of new bands, and cross-promote.

In 1987 the superproduced, slick sound of glam metal dominated radio and MTV, and most of the bands I heard at the convention were more or less chasing that scene. When I went to the Geffen suite, one of the label's reps asked me to take a second to watch a video by a new band they were promoting called Guns N' Roses.

STEVEN ADLER (DRUMS)

DUFF MCKAGAN (BASS)

W. AXL ROSE (VOCALS)

SLASH (GUITAR)

IZZY STRADLIN (GUITAR)

GILBY CLARKE (GUITAR)

DIZZY REED (KEYBOARD)

MATT SORUM (DRUMS)

OPPOSITE: Axl Rose at L'amour, Brooklyn, October 29, 1987

DISCOGRAPHY

*APPETITE FOR
DESTRUCTION* (1987)

G N' R LIES (1988)

USE YOUR ILLUSION I AND *II*
(1991)

THE SPAGHETTI INCIDENT?
(1993)

LIVE: ERA '87-'93 (1999)

GREATEST HITS (2004)

CHINESE DEMOCRACY
(2008)

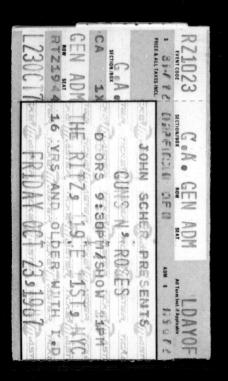

He sat me in a chair in front of a large TV hooked up to a big sound system and blasted "Welcome to the Jungle." What I saw and heard was so dirty and dangerous, so urgent and street, that I knew there was no way these guys were faking it. So much of what I'd been seeing in the mid-'80s was stylized and choreographed. Bands looked the same, and many sounded the same too. They were products of record companies that were just looking for an attractive lead singer, with songs being an afterthought. Guns N' Roses looked like they'd just crawled from the gutter (which they basically had). In the four minutes it took to watch that video, I realized that everything in the music business was going to change because of GNR.

By the time *Appetite for Destruction* came out later that year, I was a fan. I saw them play one of their first New York City shows at the Ritz, which was captured on video by MTV. The place was packed, and everyone was sweaty and cramped. Even though the album had not yet exploded, there was such a buzz about getting in to see GNR. It really felt like everyone in the crowd knew that they were going to see something special. And we did. GNR were young, hungry, and totally authentic. There was a real edge and heaviness to their sound, and true rock-and-roll recklessness, but also a sense of melody that reminded me of early Aerosmith. Axl Rose danced around the stage with a voice as intense as his facial expression. Slash, with his Les Paul down around his knees, played his solos with fire—contrasted by Izzy Stradlin, who was content to just hang back, avoid the spotlight, and fill out the guitar sound. Duff McKagan and Steven Adler were also important to the band's early sound. Duff came from more of a punk rock background, which gave the band an added edge, while Steven, who grew up as a huge Kiss fan, added a straightforward hard rock groove. But even then—as great as they were and as big as they would become—you could sense that they were going to burn out hard and fast. They were volatile, and the rumors of their addictions and antics were already rampant.

By the time they released the sister albums *Use Your Illusion I* and *II* in 1991, their edge was gone, and they had already made changes to the lineup. Guns N' Roses were now overblown and overproduced. Instead of having tight, four-minute songs that hit like a sledgehammer, the new releases had nine-minute piano ballads. Don't get me wrong—there is some great rocking material on the *Illusions*. But the songs aren't nearly as in-your-face as their earlier ones—and none are close to the singular experience of *Appetite*, which stands head and shoulders above anything else in the Guns N' Roses catalog. The band had evolved in different directions pretty quickly. They played stadiums when they toured, and they were still great live, but the circus atmosphere around the band had become too much for me to digest. You never knew if and when they would actually take the stage, and it became clear that the band would soon implode. There were drugs and infighting, but the members were also drawn to different styles: Some wanted to play the punk-edged street rock of their early days, while Axl wanted to be like Elton John.

I've had so many experiences with members from various lineups of GNR, but none that is more talked about or that has put me more squarely into the band's legacy than when Axl Rose walked into my radio show in 2006 for his first public interview in thirteen years.

At the time, VH1 was airing a reality show called *Supergroup*. It featured Scott Ian, Sebastian Bach, Ted Nugent, Jason Bonham, and Evan Seinfeld living together while trying to assemble a band. I hosted a show on VH1 Classic called *Supergroup Post Show*, which was just what it sounds like: interviewing the guys from the show about the episode that had just aired. I was also asked to have some of the guys on my radio show on Q104, which I was happy to do. Scott Ian and Sebastian Bach were in town, so we met at the VH1 offices the day before to discuss the interview.

LEFT: Slash at the Ritz,
New York City, October 23, 1987
RIGHT: Axl Rose at L'amour,
Brooklyn, October 29, 1987

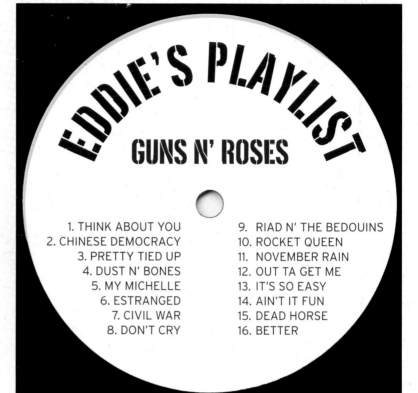

EDDIE'S PLAYLIST

GUNS N' ROSES

1. THINK ABOUT YOU
2. CHINESE DEMOCRACY
3. PRETTY TIED UP
4. DUST N' BONES
5. MY MICHELLE
6. ESTRANGED
7. CIVIL WAR
8. DON'T CRY
9. RIAD N' THE BEDOUINS
10. ROCKET QUEEN
11. NOVEMBER RAIN
12. OUT TA GET ME
13. IT'S SO EASY
14. AIN'T IT FUN
15. DEAD HORSE
16. BETTER

Sebastian told me he was getting text messages from someone he believed to be Axl Rose. They'd toured together years before but hadn't spoken or seen each other in thirteen years. There were rumors that a new lineup of Guns N' Roses was rehearsing in New York for a string of dates at the Hammerstein Ballroom. Sebastian said he was going to get Axl on the phone to try to convince him to come on the air with us. But I didn't think it would happen for a second. Everyone knows that Axl is the ultimate recluse.

The next night, my radio show was packed. I'd scheduled Bas (Sebastian), Scott, my good friend and World Wrestling Entertainment star Chris Jericho, and my future *That Metal Show* cohost Don Jamieson. During the first commercial break, I noticed that Bas was texting someone. He said that it was Axl and that he'd told him to call into the studio. Now, I have known Sebastian for many, many years, and to say he can be "amped up" is a major understatement. He's one enthusiastic guy when it comes to all things rock! When Bas got Axl on his cell, he screamed at me to put Axl on the air but didn't realize, in his frenzy, that I could not do that from his cell phone. I needed Axl to call in on the station hotline. Nobody in the studio believed he would actually call in on the number I handed to Bas. But when Bas hung up his cell, and the hotline flashed minutes later, W. Axl Rose was live on the Eddie Trunk show. I made some introductions, told him who was in the studio with me, and then asked him

ABOVE: Eddie and Slash at Terminal 5,
New York City, September 14, 2010
OPPOSITE: Axl Rose at L'amour,
Brooklyn, October 29, 1987

now his new record, *Chinese Democracy*, was progressing. He confirmed that he was in New York rehearsing, and since GNR are such a revolving door, I tried to find out who the band's newest guitarist was (it was Ron "Bumblefoot" Thal, who has since become a good friend). Axl even held up his phone so we could broadcast a little of the rehearsal! That alone was a newsworthy moment.

Then I invited Axl to come in, hang out, and play some records. Now, I never geek out when dealing with any celebrities. I learned a long time ago that if you do, they will treat you like a fan and you'll have no shot at really getting to know them or gaining their trust. So I played it real casual when I invited him over. He said he would be there soon, but none of us thought he'd really come. A half hour later, the security desk called to let me know a guest had arrived, and minutes later, Axl—whom Bas aptly called "the Howard Hughes of rock and roll"—came into the studio.

Axl had a few people with him, including his assistant and adviser, Beta, and her family, who, I later learned, are like Axl's extended family. I made sure to keep things very low-key—no pictures or autographs for anyone in the room. Knowing how Axl can fly off the handle, I wanted him to feel totally comfortable, like one of the guys. He and Bas hugged—reconnecting after thirteen years—and then we all started discussing obscure bands that we love, while also finding angles to ask GNR-related questions.

It was a tricky interview: I was trying to keep all the other guys involved in the conversation but didn't want them to say anything that would piss off Axl. Every time Chris Jericho (whom I love but who can be very direct) opened his mouth, I yelled at him not to blow it for everyone, right on the air. It was like trying not to cut the wire that makes the bomb go off. Clip the wrong wire, Axl leaves.

Another huge moment in the night came when I had my close friend and Major League Baseball star Mike Piazza call in to talk with Axl. A couple of years earlier, Mike and I had been the first people to ever leak a new GNR song. Piazza had played an early version of "IRS" from *Chinese Democracy* on my show, and it was known that Axl was angry the track had been leaked. It was the first in what became a very long line of leaks leading up to that album's official release. Mike wasn't trying to do any harm. We didn't even know whether the song was legit. But Mike finally had a chance to apologize to Axl on the air that night (though I think Axl still holds a grudge).

Axl discussed where the latest version of GNR was headed, as well as bands he loved and the shows he'd seen as a kid. For all the things that have been said about Axl Rose, I can only say that my experience with him that night was completely positive. That night he wasn't a superstar recluse; he was just another fan of rock music who happened to be on the radio with us. It was a side of him not many people were familiar with. My show was supposed to end at two AM, but word quickly spread to Q104's program director that his station was making history, and he called the hotline to tell me to stay on the air as long as Axl wanted to. We ended up finishing around three thirty AM.

When the show ended, Axl invited us to join him at a trendy hot spot in Manhattan called Bungalow 8. I've never been a club guy, but I knew that this place was a haven for celebrities like Lindsay Lohan and Paris Hilton. (In fact, Lohan was behind me in line while I waited to get in.) Axl gave us all a password to use at the door so we could get in and be taken to his table.

When I arrived, Axl was holding court with Bas. We had a few drinks, and Axl was asking me about bands, saying things like, "What do you think of Nazareth?" I'd name a song I liked and he'd smile. He seemed really happy to talk about music. I rolled out of there around five AM, and I haven't seen Axl since. (Bas, on the other hand, has hardly left his side. He's opened for GNR at almost every show they've played afterward.) Everyone from the guys in Metallica to the guys in Aerosmith has asked me about that night. It was a truly legendary moment, bootlegged and aired on radio stations everywhere since.

After that night, I've had indirect contact with Axl in the form of texts and e-mails from his assistants and managers. The Sunday after he came on the air with me, his then-manager called my cell phone to say that Axl was at the airport, on his way to Europe, but he needed to come on my show immediately to discuss some things. I wasn't on the air at the time—another DJ was—but that didn't seem to matter to Axl, who was intent on going on the air with me right away. I called my program director, and we asked Axl's management if Axl would mind going on with another DJ, but he refused. It had to be me.

After an hour of sorting it out, the plan was for me to interrupt the other DJ's show to interview Axl. This was a rare thing to do, but because it was important to us to have him on the air again, we were ready to do it. By the time we were about to start, Axl had boarded his plane. I still don't know what he wanted to discuss or why it was so urgent. For whatever reason, we've never reconnected, and so it remains a mystery.

In 2008, Axl finally released *Chinese Democracy* and, in typical fashion, did not tour or do any press to support it. There seemed to be a backlash of sorts from people who had grown tired of Axl's antics. The album didn't come close to meeting anyone's expectations for a Guns N' Roses release, nor did it sell anywhere near what people thought it would. It seemed like old news by the time it finally did come out, and everyone already had some version of the songs because of the leaks. *Chinese Democracy* is more like an Axl solo album with different players on every track and massive production that really dilutes the songs. It sounds like an album someone has obsessed over for twenty years instead of one with that raw, immediate energy that everyone loved about the band in the late '80s. Those days and that band were clearly long gone. Over time, *Chinese Democracy* has grown on some fans, but outside of Axl's singing, it has very little to do with what Guns N' Roses were when they first came on the scene and changed the world of hard rock.

In recent years, I've become good friends with Slash. When he had substance issues, you never knew what you were going to get with the guy.

But drunk or sober, he has always been great to me. In 2000, when he was in the band Slash's Snakepit, he came into my studio to promote their latest album, smashed out of his head. As he was leaving, I caught him with my UFO *Strangers in the Night* and Cheap Trick *At Budokan* CDs hidden in his jacket. I demanded them back, but he just took out some money and tried to pay me for them. I told him, "Dude, just go buy them yourself!" He said it would be too much of a hassle and he wanted mine. I'm proud to say I held my ground that night and Slash left empty-handed. Even the great Slash doesn't get between me and my UFO!

In January 2010, Slash invited me to his house in Los Angeles to hear some of his new solo album. He had just moved into this awesome place in Beverly Hills that had an integrated sound system in all the rooms. It wasn't working right, though, so we ended up sitting in his garage listening to it on a boom box.

When he released the self-titled album a few months later, I played a track from it on the radio and talked about how much I liked it. Afterward, I got a text from him, thanking me for playing it and for praising his music. Artists of Slash's status rarely do that. I think it sums up the type of guy he's become. I saw his new solo band in April 2010, and it was one of the best shows I saw all year. He's playing better than ever and remains sober.

I also have great relationships with Steven Adler and Duff McKagan. Duff has reinvented himself as quite the financial guru. Like most of the GNR guys, he's brought balance into his life. Adler was a guest on *That Metal Show* in 2010 when we did shows from L.A., and he talks openly about his desire for a GNR reunion. People often wonder whether Slash and Axl could ever reunite, and I think the situation is far too complex for that to happen. Still, I'll never say never!

There also could never be a reunion without Izzy Stradlin—the unsung hero of Guns N' Roses. Both as a songwriter and a mediator between Slash and Axl, Izzy kept things together. The band members have said, in no uncertain terms, that Stradlin's personality was a calming influence on all of them. Many people have pointed to the fact that when he left the band, the balance of power shifted and everything started to unravel. In the years since, he's been even more reclusive than Axl.

At a time when hard rock was all about manufactured bands and looks, Guns N' Roses completely shook up the scene with *Appetite for Destruction*. That album is so honest and raw that it's become a landmark in the history of rock music. Every day it gains new fans. It's become so ingrained in pop culture that every stadium at every sporting event around the world seems to play "Welcome to the Jungle" at some point. And you can't go a day without hearing it—or one of *Appetite*'s other major hits—on a radio station wherever you are. It's rare that a band would land on anyone's essential list with only one great record, but *Appetite* is iconic.

UNDERGROUND CLASSIC

I really like both Slash's Snakepit albums, especially the debut, *It's Five O'Clock Somewhere*. Eric Dover of Jellyfish fame delivers some cool vocals, and the songs are great. Of all the GNR side projects, I really think Snakepit just might be my favorite. I definitely prefer their releases to the two Velvet Revolver records featuring Slash and Duff. Also, Slash's 2010 self-titled solo album has a wide variety of styles and singers and features some of his best-ever guitar work.

In 2009, Duff released an album called *Duff McKagan's Loaded*. It's his band's second album of killer punk-flavored hard rock. There are moments on this CD that are closer to *Appetite*-era GNR than anything any of the former members have written to date. I saw the band live several times, and they were very good. Sadly, they never caught on, but that album is worth checking out.

OPPOSITE TOP: Axl Rose at Continental Airlines Arena, East Rutherford, New Jersey, January 6, 2006
OPPOSITE BOTTOM: Don Jamieson, Eddie, Jim Florentine, and Duff McKagan on the set of *That Metal Show*, February 11, 2009

SAMMY HAGAR

and in perhaps my ballsiest moment ever, I asked Satriani if he had a son who might grow up to take over on bass for Anthony in Chickenfoot, like Wolfgang Van Halen did in Van Halen. Thankfully, I could get away with that because all the guys in Chickenfoot have a great sense of humor and got the joke.

In addition to his musical success, Hagar has made a huge amount of money in the tequila business over the years and is now opening a chain of Mexican restaurants called Cabo Wabo Cantina. Sammy continues to be the life of any party onstage and off and can often be seen having "*mas* tequila" with his fans and bandmates. He really doesn't need to make music for a living anymore, but he does it because he truly loves playing. That passion comes through in his performances as much today as it did the first time I saw him solo. Now in his sixties, Sammy has been tireless for more than four decades. He's lost nothing vocally and still looks great—a true freak of nature.

In 2005, I was invited to Atlantic City to do a broadcast for my radio show at the Borgata, where Sammy was playing a solo gig and Michael Anthony was a guest in the band. I arrived early in the day and found a spot at a blackjack table. Sammy sat down next to me and we played some hands. I had a really bad streak, losing about eight hands in a row, so I decided I'd had enough. Sammy, being the fun-loving guy he is, made me sit back down and gave me a chip to play with. Then I won.

I firmly believe there will eventually be an outcry for a Hagar-Van Halen reunion. It's easy to get caught up in the Roth-fronted version of Van Halen, but the band was hugely successful with Hagar as the frontman as well. They had lots of hits and garnered a whole new generation of fans. And let's face it, the only way people will hear songs like "Dreams" and "Why Can't This Be Love" will be if Hagar is singing them. Roth just can't. I recently spoke with former Extreme frontman Gary Cherone, who was briefly the singer for Van Halen and had to handle material from both the Roth and the Hagar eras. He said the biggest challenge, every night, was singing the Hagar songs. Sammy Hagar is one of the most powerful voices in rock.

ABOVE: Don Jamieson, Eddie, Chad Smith, Sammy Hagar, Michael Anthony, and Joe Satriani at Irving Plaza, New York City, May 28, 2009

IRON MAIDEN

I was lucky enough to see Iron Maiden for the first time in 1981 on their legendary tour opening for Judas Priest. They played Convention Hall in Asbury Park, New Jersey, in support of their second album, *Killers*. I had bought the record, but I got my ticket because I really wanted to see Priest. Like most people who saw any show on that tour, I still talk about that night to this day. Maiden blew everyone away and made it very hard for Priest to follow them.

After that concert, I immediately became a huge Maiden fan. They'd released two studio albums with singer Paul Di'Anno, who brought a punk sensibility to their sound. But Di'Anno was not a metal fan, and though I loved his style, the writing was on the wall. He was out of place in the way he looked and performed, and despite the amazing albums he made with Maiden, that would be his final tour with the group.

BRUCE DICKINSON (VOCALS)

STEVE HARRIS (BASS)

NICKO MCBRAIN (DRUMS)

DAVE MURRAY (GUITAR)

ADRIAN SMITH (GUITAR)

BLAZE BAYLEY (VOCALS)

CLIVE BURR (DRUMS)

PAUL DI'ANNO (VOCALS)

JANICK GERS (GUITAR)

DENNIS STRATTON (GUITAR)

OPPOSITE: Dave Murray, Bruce Dickinson, and Steve Harris at PNC Bank Arts Center, Holmdel Township, New Jersey, July 27, 2005

When Maiden replaced Di'Anno with Bruce Dickinson for their third album, *The Number of the Beast*, it didn't come as a surprise. Using the stage name "Bruce Bruce," Dickinson had been fronting a band called Samson on the U.K. metal scene for some time. But Maiden had already changed lineups twice by this point—switching guitar players between the first and second albums and now switching singers—so fans were concerned. When they heard Dickinson, though, whose vocal force is like an air raid siren, everyone knew he was perfect for the band.

Released in 1982, *The Number of the Beast* is still considered one of their best and an all-time classic in metal history. Bruce's vocals were melodic yet powerful; he could not only scream but also really sing. His range is what made Maiden's songs more epic and brought greater depth and nuance to their sound—making the album one of the blueprints for all metal to come. *The Number of the Beast* exploded onto the scene, and the rest is heavy metal history.

The Number of the Beast is also an important album because it helped me get my start in radio. I was working at a record store across the street from WDHA in New Jersey. Whenever the program director came in to buy records, I would beg him to play more metal on the station. In 1983, albums like Def Leppard's *Pyromania*, Quiet Riot's *Metal Health*, and Maiden's *Number of the Beast*, as well as the follow up *Piece Of Mind*, were selling tons of copies everywhere in America, with barely any radio play. The number of records sold in the store I worked at alone helped me to convince the program director to give me a shot at playing some music on his station. So he gave me a chance as a new radio show host. The record store agreed to sponsor the show, and I started a program called "Metal Mania" to showcase this music. I had Bruce and bassist Steve Harris on my show that year. WDHA wasn't playing their records very often (Maiden never had radio airplay in the United States then, or now), so they were grateful to be on the show and signed a copy of *The Number of the Beast* for me, which I still have.

I got to see Maiden for the second time on their 1982 tour. They were headlining three-to-five-thousand-seat venues across America. In New York, they played a smaller venue called the Palladium (which has since closed), and it would be the last time fans could see them in a venue of that size. Just a year later, they'd be playing arenas globally.

That night, people were lined up to get in. Everyone seemed to know that they were about to see something extraordinary: this band on the rise, just about to reach the top. Those were the days when fans had a strange need to throw firecrackers at rock concerts. During the opening band's set, someone in the upper level threw one that hit the soundboard. When it detonated, it took out one of the channels, which delayed the rest of the show. I'll never forget Bruce Dickinson coming onto the stage to yell at the audience. He told us to find the person who'd done it and beat the shit out of him. It really sent a message about how serious the members of Maiden were about playing. Where other bands might have sent a member of the crew to deliver the message, Bruce didn't care what

people thought of him. And fans have always appreciated the band's no-nonsense approach.

The band was phenomenal that night. Their stage show was also particularly memorable. The stage had two sets of stairs—one on either side, set up behind the band's amps—that met in the middle like a pyramid. They also had two guys dressed in devil costumes to look like the character on the cover of *Number of the Beast*. While the band played the album's title track, the devils began to climb the steps to meet at the peak in the middle and battle with their pitchforks. Taunting the crowd as they scaled the steps, one of the devils took a wrong step and fell off. From the audience, you could see his cape fluttering as he disappeared over the edge behind the amps and backdrop. With his nemesis gone, the other devil didn't know what to do, so he jumped off the stairs himself. It was hysterical.

A legendary part of Maiden's stage show is their instantly recognizable mascot, Eddie—a genius marketing device spawned from a drawing by artist Derek Riggs. Familiar to fans from his presence on every Iron Maiden album cover and most T-shirt designs, the rotting-corpse character was originally played by a roadie wearing a mask. As Maiden's stage shows evolved, Eddie did too. Eventually, he joined the band onstage as a giant mechanical robot and has remained with them in some form to this day.

DISCOGRAPHY

IRON MAIDEN (1980)

KILLERS (1981)

THE NUMBER OF THE BEAST (1982)

PIECE OF MIND (1983)

POWERSLAVE (1984)

LIVE AFTER DEATH [LIVE] (1985)

SOMEWHERE IN TIME (1986)

SEVENTH SON OF A SEVENTH SON (1988)

NO PRAYER FOR THE DYING (1990)

FEAR OF THE DARK (1992)

THE X FACTOR (1995)

VIRTUAL XI (1998)

BRAVE NEW WORLD (2000)

DANCE OF DEATH (2003)

A MATTER OF LIFE AND DEATH (2006)

THE FINAL FRONTIER (2010)

LEFT: Steve Harris at Hammerstein Ballroom, New York City, January 26, 2004

EDDIE'S PLAYLIST

IRON MAIDEN

1. PHANTOM OF THE OPERA
2. BLOOD BROTHERS
3. WASTED YEARS
4. THE PRISONER
5. CHILDREN OF THE DAMNED
6. REVELATIONS
7. HALLOWED BE THY NAME
8. KILLERS
9. WHERE EAGLES DARE
10. 2 MINUTES TO MIDNIGHT
11. FLIGHT OF ICARUS
12. MURDERS IN THE RUE MORGUE
13. THE TROOPER
14. GHOST OF THE NAVIGATOR
15. ACES HIGH

Another Iron Maiden constant is their undisputed leader and founder, Steve Harris. While the band's lineup has changed multiple times over the years, Steve is responsible for the consistent quality of the band's quintessential, classic British heavy metal sound. Harris is one of the most influential bass players in metal. The only other original member is guitarist Dave Murray, whose fluid playing helped develop Maiden's sound. (Harris and Murray are the only two band members who have played on every album.) But everyone will tell you that Iron Maiden is very much Steve's baby.

In a major blow to the band, Bruce Dickinson left in the early '90s to pursue a solo career. He was replaced for a couple of albums by Blaze Bayley of a band called Wolfsbane, but most Maiden fans would agree that this was a pretty major misstep in their career. Blaze didn't have the vocal range or the stage persona to come close to filling Bruce's shoes. The two studio albums recorded with Blaze went close to unrecognized in America. Their live show suffered, and their ticket sales dropped dramatically. So it was no surprise when Maiden reunited with Dickinson in 1999.

For a long time, I've been known as one of the few people who's consistently played Maiden's music on American radio (the band still continues to grow without having airplay or a hit single). Maiden knew of my support for them (their manager recently joked about how I keep messing up

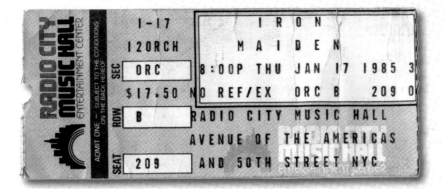

their marketing plan of never getting airtime in a major market), so they invited me to travel to England to interview them for a national radio special that would chronicle the making of their reunion album with Bruce, *Brave New World*. Needless to say, I accepted and was extremely excited to meet and hang out with the guys on their home turf. I interviewed each of them individually at the headquarters of Sanctuary, their management company. I got to watch them rehearse and then had beers with them in the lunchroom. (They had working beer taps there, and it was totally acceptable for employees to have a beer during the workday.)

With *Brave New World*, Maiden came back bigger and better than ever. It has all their signature elements: Bruce's massive voice, the tradeoffs and interplay of the three lead guitarists, and Steve Harris's machine-gun-style bass. The reunion ensured that the band would continue to sell out stadiums around the globe and keep their longtime fans happy. It's interesting to note that Iron Maiden has always had somewhat of a love-hate relationship with America. Clearly they love their fans here, but they do not like the fact that, unlike in other parts of the world, in America only their older material gets support. This has resulted in great controversy over their set lists every tour.

In 2006, the band shocked U.S. audiences when they played their most recent album at the time, *A Matter of Life and Death*, in its entirety at their shows. Maiden were defiant about it, saying that they would never be a nostalgia act by choosing to focus on only certain eras in their history. But in 2008, the band gave U.S. audiences what they really wanted with a set of classic material, and by re-creating the *Somewhere in Time* tour, which was actually called Somewhere Back in Time. This tour was a massive global success and was captured in a live album and documentary (which I make a brief appearance in) called *Flight 666*. In 2010, Maiden again created controversy with audiences by playing mostly music from their last three studio albums on tour. The tour was a success, but it left many Maiden fans wondering why they don't play a more balanced set. But if it's not broke, why fix it? In many ways the ultimate underground metal act, Maiden will continue to influence and inspire audience and fellow musicians alike, playing to generations of loyal fans around the globe in greater numbers than ever.

DID YOU KNOW

Singer Bruce Dickinson is an aviation fanatic and a licensed commercial airline pilot. In his spare time, Bruce flies commercial jets for fun and even flies Maiden on their private plane, *Ed Force One*.

Also, Steve Harris's daughter, Lauren, is an aspiring hard rock singer who released an album, *Calm Before the Storm*, in 2008 and has opened for Iron Maiden.

OPPOSITE TOP: Bruce Dickinson at Hammerstein Ballroom, New York City, January 26, 2004
OPPOSITE BOTTOM: Steve Harris at the Palladium, New York City, June 29, 1982

JUDAS PRIEST

After Black Sabbath, Birmingham, England's other great contribution to music history is Judas Priest, the second most important heavy metal band of all time. Their black leather biker style, powerhouse vocals, and brutal dual-guitar assault created what would become the holy grail for metal.

Priest's beginnings in the early 1970s really weren't very metal—the guys looked more like hippies than leather-clad badasses. Their first two albums, *Rocka Rolla* and *Sad Wings of Destiny*, have some strong moments and provided a glance at what they would become, but it wasn't until their major-label debut, *Sin After Sin*, that they found the vicious sound that would define them. Tracks like "Sinner" and "Dissident Aggressor" (which was later covered by Slayer and earned Priest a Grammy for their live version more than thirty years after its original release) feature the driving guitar riffs and trade-off solos of K. K. Downing and Glenn Tipton, as well as the groundbreaking vocal stylings of the one and only Rob Halford. No one had ever heard anything like his singing on a heavy metal record before.

CLASSIC LINEUP

K. K. DOWNING (GUITAR)

ROB HALFORD (VOCALS)

IAN HILL (BASS)

DAVE HOLLAND (DRUMS)

GLENN TIPTON (GUITAR)

AL ATKINS (VOCALS)

LES BINKS (DRUMS)

TIM "RIPPER" OWENS (VOCALS)

SCOTT TRAVIS (DRUMS)

OPPOSITE: K. K. Downing, Rob Halford, and Glenn Tipton at Convention Hall, Asbury Park, New Jersey, June 28, 1981

Appropriately dubbed the "Metal God," Rob Halford makes all the difference in Priest. With a vocal ability that has inspired awe in metal fans and influenced generations of musicians—from Bruce Dickinson to Geoff Tate—Halford set a standard that very few are able to duplicate. He's the Pavarotti of heavy metal, with a devastating vocal range and a powerful falsetto. Halford can sing and scream and put emotion into his lyrics in a way that very few can. Like the late Ronnie James Dio, Halford can range far beyond the style of the metal genre. Listen to the acoustic version of "Diamonds and Rust" or the great ballad "Before the Dawn" from *Hell Bent for Leather*. Halford can take you on a sonic journey with his voice. I also love how he stalks the stage and how when he hits a special note, he physically winds up for it, then releases his arms in the air, almost like a weight lifter after a heavy set on a bench!

Of course, Priest is more than just their remarkable singer. Tipton and Downing are one of the most underrated guitar duos in history and complement each other to perfection: Glenn is the precise technician, and K.K. the over-the-top, Hendrix-influenced whammy-bar guy. The unsung hero of Priest is bassist Ian Hill, who masterfully anchors the bottom end and hangs away from the spotlight. Priest has had many drummers, but none better than Scott Travis, who perfects the old material and powers the band's new recordings.

Priest's 1979 live album, *Unleashed in the East*, marks a turning point in the band's sound. Like many live recordings, the "liveness" of *Unleashed* has always been the subject of controversy. Although the band maintains it was recorded live, with the exception of a few touch-ups, rumors have been around for years that it was more of a studio creation—something not uncommon with many "live" albums of the day. But who cares? This record captures a band at its peak, onstage in Japan, with higher-energy versions of some of their best material to that point, including the definitive version of the all-time classic "Victim of Changes." The only thing that's not great about this album is that it's not a double!

With the success of that live album, Priest learned what they would have to aim for in the studio; it's no coincidence that some of their best and signature studio recordings came after *Unleashed*. Landmark records like *British Steel*, the underrated *Point of Entry*, *Defenders of the Faith*, *Painkiller*, and the near-masterpiece *Screaming for Vengeance*—which would finally break Priest into the U.S. charts with its hooky single "You Got Another Thing Comin'" and its video—captured more of the fire and adrenaline of Priest's live shows.

Judas Priest never apologized for being metal when it wasn't cool. Instead, they've always been proud of it, as they should be. They haven't drastically altered their sound or look or the bands they tour with, and they've never shunned the term "metal," going so far as to feature the word prominently in many of their song titles. This is an important point. Some forget how unfashionable it was to be a metal band in the '90s, but Priest always waved that flag. Defenders of the faith indeed!

Because of what Rob Halford brought to Judas Priest, it was a huge

ABOVE: Rob Halford at Capitol Theatre, Passaic, New Jersey, November 10, 1979

DISCOGRAPHY

ROCKA ROLLA (1974)

SAD WINGS OF DESTINY
(1976)

SIN AFTER SIN (1977)

STAINED CLASS (1978)

HELL BENT FOR LEATHER
(1979)

*UNLEASHED IN
THE EAST* [LIVE] (1979)

BRITISH STEEL (1980)

POINT OF ENTRY (1981)

SCREAMING FOR VENGEANCE
(1982)

DEFENDERS OF THE FAITH
(1984)

TURBO (1986)

PRIEST . . . LIVE! (1987)

RAM IT DOWN (1988)

PAINKILLER (1990)

JUGULATOR (1997)

'98 LIVE MELTDOWN
(1998)

DEMOLITION (2001)

LIVE IN LONDON (2003)

*ANGEL OF
RETRIBUTION* (2005)

NOSTRADAMUS (2008)

*A TOUCH OF
EVIL: LIVE* (2009)

*BRITISH STEEL
30TH ANNIVERSARY* [LIVE]
(2010)

shock for fans to learn that he was leaving the band after their 1988 album *Ram It Down*. The usual tensions and creative differences that happen over fifteen years of touring and recording drove the band apart. Halford decided to come out of the closet shortly thereafter. To be honest, his homosexuality was perhaps one of the worst-kept secrets for a long time—one of metal's premier singers and frontmen and he was never with girls. Add to that some suggestive lyrics and leather-and-bondage gear, and let's just say that his announcement was not a shock to many. It certainly gave new meaning to some of his lyrics for a lot of fans. Still, metal supporters didn't care; they loved their Metal God and always will. For this Halford and many metal fans do not get the credit they should. Rob was brave enough to come out, and metal fans (often thought of by the mainstream as not being particularly evolved) embraced him as much as ever.

Halford has some great material away from Priest, first with a band called Fight, which released two albums. He then moved away from metal a bit when he teamed up with Nine Inch Nails' Trent Reznor for a project called Two. This goth-industrial departure was not a highlight for metal fans. But Halford returned to classic form with a band simply called Hal-

ABOVE: K. K. Downing at
Brendan Byrne Arena, East Rutherford,
New Jersey, December 14, 1990

EDDIE'S PLAYLIST

JUDAS PRIEST

1. DELIVERING THE GOODS
2. FREEWHEEL BURNING
3. BEYOND THE REALMS OF DEATH
4. RIDING ON THE WIND
5. A TOUCH OF EVIL
6. JUDAS RISING
7. METAL GODS
8. PAINKILLER
9. RAPID FIRE
10. DEATH
11. THE GREEN MANALISHI
12. VICTIM OF CHANGES
13. SCREAMING FOR VENGEANCE
14. DESERT PLAINS
15. SOLAR ANGELS
16. DEVIL'S CHILD
17. ONE ON ONE
18. THE RIPPER
19. PROPHECY
20. THE RAGE

ford and released two great albums, *Resurrection* and *Crucible*. I remember being in England in 2000 to interview Iron Maiden when their band manager Rod Smallwood first showed me the cover for *Resurrection*, featuring a close-up of Halford driving his motorcycle. He was back.

Priest, in the meantime, did the unthinkable: They hired a new singer! That man's name was Tim "Ripper" Owens, and needless to say, he had some huge shoes to fill. Ripper came from Ohio and was discovered while singing in a Priest tribute band. (The 2001 Mark Wahlberg film *Rock Star* is loosely based on his story.) The Owens-fronted version of Judas Priest released two studio albums and two live albums in an attempt to quickly establish him with Judas Priest's fans. The albums were decent, but sales and the desire to see the band live had dimished. You could see how much Judas Priest wanted this new lineup to work at the time, and they would bristle when asked about Halford in interviews.

During the Ripper days, I remember the obvious tension in the air when I had Priest on my radio show and callers would ask whether Rob was ever coming back. Tim is a great guy and a remarkable singer, but I think that even he, as a Priest fan, knew that eventually Halford would return. The fans wanted it and the band needed it. Both Halford's solo project and the new Priest were doing OK in terms of business and art, but neither created what the classic Priest lineup could yield. So in 2003 Halford

returned to his throne as the Metal God to front Judas Priest once again. The band did a string of Ozzfest dates and then headed into the studio to record a new album called *Angel of Retribution*.

I'd had both personal and professional relationships with all the guys in the band for years by this point, so I was thrilled when I learned that Glenn, K.K., and Rob were going to shoot an interview with me at VH1 Classic. They decided to do something they had never done before: play acoustic in our studio. The trio performed a stunning version of the classic "Diamonds and Rust" and "Worth Fighting For" from the current album. It was a testament to the quality of their songs that they could play them this way, and hearing Halford's voice without any effects highlighted his incredible ability. Even though I am not a big acoustic fan, it was truly special to see this powerful metal band stripped down. Hopefully you caught this episode when it aired.

I've often said that Rob Halford is one of the classiest guys in the world of metal. He's a gentleman through and through and truly grateful for those who support his music. In early 2008, I had him in my radio studio to discuss some of his solo material. (Though he's a full-fledged member of Priest, he never stops working and still actively releases his own material.) We were having a conversation off-air about how long we had known each other, and he thanked me for always being there for him, his bands, and metal in general. We started trying to trace our history to recall when we'd first met, and I told him that I had been doing a metal radio show for twenty-five years. He looked at me and said, "That's amazing! You must do something to celebrate. Nobody does that for this long!" I jokingly responded, "You play the party and I'll throw it." He said he would talk to his bandmates and get back to me. I never really expected anything to come of it.

A few months went by and I got a call from the band's publicist, who said that Priest's manager, Jayne Andrews, wanted to meet with me in New York to discuss "the party." What party? I couldn't believe it was really possible, and if it was, I wouldn't have the money to support it! Jayne and I met at the Sony offices in New York, where she told me that

DID YOU KNOW

Throughout their history, Priest has rarely done cover tunes. However, two of their best-loved songs are covers: "Diamonds and Rust" by Joan Baez and "Green Manalishi" by early Fleetwood Mac. Two Priest classics written by bands not exactly known for metal.

Another piece of trivia is that Rob Halford is not the original singer of Judas Priest. There was a guy named Al Atkins who left the band just prior to the release of *Rocka Rolla*. Al has a writing credit on some of Priest's most classic songs.

LEFT: K. K. Downing, Rob Halford, and Glenn Tipton at PNC Bank Arts Center, Holmdel Township, New Jersey, August 9, 2008
OPPOSITE: Glenn Tipton at Brendan Byrne Arena, East Rutherford, New Jersey, December 14, 1990

ABOVE: Rob Halford at
Brendan Byrne Arena, East Rutherford,
New Jersey, December 14, 1990
OPPOSITE: The marquee for Eddie's
twenty-fifth anniversary party at the Hard
Rock Café, New York City, August 4, 2008

as a thank you for supporting Judas Priest and metal for many years, the band was offering me their services for a night, for a free private show. I was floored! I have worked with hundreds of bands, but no one had ever done anything like this before. She said that I would only need to cover any additional expenses and that Priest would use the show as a warm-up date for their next tour—no tickets sold to the public, my guest list only! As excited as I was, I was equally nervous. I didn't know how I could pull it off. I thought something was bound to backfire.

I called my friend John Pasquale, who runs special events for the Hard Rock Café in New York City, which had just moved to Times Square and had a proper stage for live performances. John has always been a good friend and supporter of mine, and we've done many great events together. Amazingly, he said he could get me the Hard Rock for the night. Then another friend and great supporter, Erik Luftglass, whom I'd worked with for a few years at VH1 Classic, stepped in. Erik said that he could secure sponsors for the night to offset expenses for Priest. Both John and Erik wanted this to be a special event and for me to be able to enjoy myself and not worry about every detail (even though anyone who knows me realizes that would be impossible). They took the idea and ran with it.

My twenty-fifth anniversary in radio party took place at the Hard Rock on August 4, 2008, with a performance by Judas Priest! I gave tickets

away on my radio show and to close friends and people who had supported me over the years. It was surreal, to say the least, to see my name with Priest's on the marquee in Times Square!

Erik and John surprised me with a video roast before the band played, featuring many members of bands like Black Sabbath, Aerosmith, Tesla, and Twisted Sister. My parents, wife, and brother were there, and we picked up my good friend Mike Piazza in the limo on the way. The VIP entrance was loaded with photographers and friends, and my current cohosts Don Jamieson and Jim Florentine were doing interviews on the red carpet for me, pre-*That Metal Show*. Geoff Tate and Scott Rockenfield from Queensrÿche flew in to attend, along with Anthrax, Overkill, Carmine Appice, Glenn Hughes, and all the members of Heaven & Hell, to name a few. Black Sabbath and Judas Priest in the same room to pay tribute to me? The night was an insane blur.

Before the show, Mike Piazza introduced me, and then I had the honor of introducing Judas Priest. I tried to take in every moment of their eight-song set. Just before their final song, Rob Halford called me onstage to thank me for supporting Judas Priest and heavy metal. He had me sing some of "You Got Another Thing Comin'" with him, and then Glenn offered me his guitar to play! What he didn't know is that I can't play a note. I have never regretted not taking lessons more than I did at that moment.

When the set ended, I found my mom and dad—who hadn't planned to stay long when the night started—in the dressing room having drinks with Judas Priest! That summed up what a special night this was. To this day, I am grateful and will forever be in debt to the Metal Gods for one of the best nights of my life. I'll also never forget when, a week later, Priest played a regular gig in New Jersey at the PNC Bank Arts Center. When they played at my event, they had dressed in casual street clothes—no leather or studs. But this night, I was standing on the side of the stage, about to introduce the band, when Halford lumbered up to me in full biker regalia. It was a blazing August night, and he looked at me and said, "Man, I wish I was playing your event instead of wearing this." Not only do Rob and all the guys in the band have a great sense of humor, but they are also icons and architects of a sound and image that will forever be synonymous with heavy metal.

It's disgraceful that, at the time of this writing, they haven't been considered for the Rock and Roll Hall of Fame. But true fans of metal know the importance of Priest, and Priest continues to make new music while celebrating their past. It was also fitting that Rob sat just behind me at the funeral for Ronnie James Dio. Ronnie and Rob have always been not only two of my favorite singers but also two of my favorite people. As the funeral ended that day and everyone lined up to pay final respects, Rob placed his hand on my shoulder, and we approached Dio's casket together. We supported each other through this tough time, and standing side by side, we said good-bye to our mutual friend and the rock legend. After Black Sabbath, there is simply no band as important in the history of metal than Judas Priest, and like Dio, no such vocalist and friend as Rob Halford.

KISS

When I was twelve years old, the music I knew was mostly limited to what I saw on TV (like on *The Partridge Family*) or heard on Top 40 radio in my parents' car. My best friend in junior high went to get the new Kiss album after school one day in 1976. I went with him and had no idea what he was buying. I remember him saying, "You've *never* heard of Kiss?" and then asking him which record I should buy to get to know them. He was clearly a fan, and since I was at that age when it was time to graduate to *real* bands, not pretend ones on TV, I decided to take a shot.

I bought *Destroyer* for about four dollars that day at his suggestion. When I got home, I took the album from its jacket and dropped the needle on the vinyl. I heard "Detroit Rock City" start with background noise, the sound of a car door and keys, and an engine revving, and then a driving guitar riff that exploded into the song. I was floored by the wash of guitars and the powerful drums that came from my speakers. I stared at the album cover, with its larger-than-life demons in leather and makeup, holding their fists in the air in some kind of revolt. It was like nothing I'd ever heard or seen before.

PETER CRISS
(DRUMS/VOCALS)

ACE FREHLEY
(GUITAR/VOCALS)

GENE SIMMONS
(BASS/VOCALS)

PAUL STANLEY
(GUITAR/VOCALS)

ERIC CARR (DRUMS)

BRUCE KULICK (GUITAR)

ERIC SINGER (DRUMS)

MARK ST. JOHN (GUITAR)

TOMMY THAYER (GUITAR)

VINNIE VINCENT (GUITAR)

OPPOSITE: Gene Simmons, Ace Frehley, Paul Stanley, and Eric Carr at the Palladium, New York City, July 25, 1990

OPPOSITE: Gene Simmons at Capitol Theatre, Passaic, New Jersey, October 3, 1975

The next day, I borrowed money from my mom so I could buy every other Kiss album. I found *The Originals*, a collection of the first three studio albums packaged as one. Like all Kiss records, they came with posters, which became the beginning of my collection. A few days later, I decided to get rid of the few other records I owned. Bobby Goldsboro, Bobby Sherman, and the 1910 Fruitgum Company couldn't even be filed anywhere near Kiss. It seemed like a hundred years ago that I'd listened to that other stuff, even though it had only been two days. The slate had to be cleared for the new kings of my world!

I became a Kiss freak. My bedroom walls were covered with Kiss posters. There was no other band to me. There could be no other band. Like so many kids in the world, I was consumed by Kiss, but I didn't get into the marketing machine as much as some. I never dressed up like the band members or had a Kiss lunch box or action figures. Outside of posters and magazines, I pretty much stayed with the albums, because for me, still to this day, that's what I like most about Kiss—and for some reason, that's what you hear about the least. All of their merchandise was simply a by-product of their popularity.

Kiss's golden years were 1975 to 1977. The guys were the stuff of legends. No one knew what they looked like without their makeup, if they were devil worshippers, or if they were another band in disguise! There were rumors about the blood Gene spit—that it was his own from biting his mouth or that it was cow's blood—and questions about whether his tongue was real or a sewn-on extension! People wanted to know how Ace Frehley made his guitar smoke when he played and if he was really from another planet. Kiss merged heavy rock with horror movies and comic books and blood and fire. They were larger than life. Nobody had ever taken theatrics to this level other than Alice Cooper. But there were just as many detractors as there were fans. As a Kiss lover, you became part of the Kiss Army and found yourself constantly defending them.

In addition to their recordings and their stage show, one of the best things about the original Kiss lineup was the fact that all four members had an equal role in the band. They all sang lead vocals in addition to playing their instruments, and each had his own fans. They modeled themselves as a hard rock version of the Beatles, one of the bands that was a huge influence on them.

People always talk about the fire, the costumes, and the makeup when it comes to Kiss, but they are rarely given credit for their music. Unfortunately, from their more than thirty records, only two or three Kiss songs are ever played regularly on the radio. I've made it my job to bring the unheard stuff to the mainstream. If you look at the band's musical history, you'll see, for better or worse, that they've always experimented and explored different sides of their writing abilities. At their core, Kiss is a hard rock band, but within that context, there's something in their catalog for everyone. They even have a song written by Lou Reed. They have plenty of pop, a little bit of disco and grunge, and full-on heavy metal. If you're a true Kiss fan, you love all of it, but if you don't know them at all, there's a lot to explore.

DISCOGRAPHY

KISS (1974)

HOTTER THAN HELL (1974)

DRESSED TO KILL (1975)

ALIVE! (1975)

DESTROYER (1976)

ROCK AND ROLL OVER
(1976)

LOVE GUN (1977)

ALIVE II (1977)

ACE FREHLEY (1978)

GENE SIMMONS (1978)

PAUL STANLEY (1978)

PETER CRISS (1978)

DYNASTY (1979)

UNMASKED (1980)

MUSIC FROM
"THE ELDER" (1981)

CREATURES OF THE NIGHT
(1982)

LICK IT UP (1983)

ANIMALIZE (1984)

ASYLUM (1985)

CRAZY NIGHTS (1987)

HOT IN THE SHADE
(1989)

REVENGE (1992)

ALIVE III (1993)

MTV UNPLUGGED
[LIVE] (1996)

CARNIVAL OF SOULS:
THE FINAL SESSIONS
(1997)

PSYCHO CIRCUS (1998)

KISS SYMPHONY:
ALIVE IV (2003)

SONIC BOOM (2009)

On December 16, 1977, I went to my very first concert: Kiss at Madison Square Garden. I was thirteen, and it was also one of my first trips to New York. My friend's older sister took us, and I remember everything like it was yesterday–the frenzy on the street in front of the venue and the people selling buttons and T-shirts. I bought a T-shirt from one of the bootleg sellers outside, and we went to our nosebleed seats. I wouldn't know what it was until years later, but I smelled pot everywhere.

Before the show, I remember the buzz in the air and wondering how the music would sound from our seats high up in the upper level. I remember how the stage looked so small and far away. But when Kiss came out and the bombs and flames went off, I could feel the heat of the fire. This was the *Love Gun/Alive II* tour, widely regarded by Kiss fans as having the best-ever stage show, featuring lighted staircases on either side of the enor-

EDDIE'S PLAYLIST

KISS

1. WHO WANTS TO BE LONELY
2. ANYTHING FOR MY BABY
3. LARGER THAN LIFE
4. WHAT MAKES THE WORLD GO 'ROUND
5. I'VE HAD ENOUGH
6. GOT TO CHOOSE
7. ROOM SERVICE
8. MAKIN' LOVE
9. MR. SPEED
10. SHOCK ME
11. CREATURES OF THE NIGHT
12. I STOLE YOUR LOVE
13. NOWHERE TO RUN
14. HIDE YOUR HEART
15. A MILLION TO ONE
16. FLAMING YOUTH
17. PSYCHO CIRCUS
18. 100,000 YEARS
19. MAGIC TOUCH
20. I WANT YOU
21. STRUTTER

mous drum kit, risers that elevated the members into the air on platforms (including a part where it looked like Gene was "flying" into the lighting rig), and many more Kiss trademarks. It was massive and mind-blowing, especially since it was my first concert! From then on, I was a loyal Kiss freak. Of course now, I'm much more objective as a fan, and I realize there are a lot of other bands in the world to love. But Kiss will always hold the most special place for me. They introduced me to heavy rock and roll and were the most extreme and theatrical act I had ever seen.

I discovered Kiss at the peak of their popularity. Only a year and a half later, the ride was over. They became a joke to many, and their fan base decreased and changed considerably. Suddenly, instead of being dark and dangerous, Kiss was a kiddie band. Their merchandise appealed to youngsters, and their more commercial sound prevented them from being taken seriously. When I saw them for the second time, in 1979, "I Was Made for Loving You" was a huge hit. It didn't sound the way a Kiss song was supposed to—it was more disco than rock and roll—but I found a way to accept it because I was such a loyal fan. Still, I had to admit that they were no longer the powerful heavy rock legends. They were more like characters from children's comic strips and coloring books.

In 1981, when I was in high school, there was no band on the planet less cool than Kiss. I was considered a total freak and an outcast because I had the audacity to wear Kiss T-shirts and put their stickers on my locker. I de-

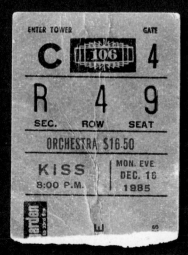

ABOVE: Gene Simmons at PNC Bank Arts Center, Holmdel Township, New Jersey, August 11, 2003

fended them and I went down with the ship. I was ridiculed and picked on constantly, and I didn't get invited to cool parties or have girlfriends. If I hadn't been six foot two and 270 pounds, I would've gotten my ass kicked on a regular basis. But I was a music fan. It was more important to me to stay true to what I liked and write music reviews for my school newspaper and work at the college radio station. I've never followed trends just to look cool. I maintained such a worship of Kiss that even in the '80s, when they were down and out in America and they had trouble getting a gig in New York City, my friends and I would drive wherever we had to so we could see them. Like most Kiss fans, we were superloyal.

When Kiss toured for *Creatures of the Night* in 1983, we decided to take a road trip to see them in Worcester, Massachusetts, at the Centrum. It was going to be my fourth Kiss show and I couldn't wait, because *Creatures* was heavier and more aggressive than anything they'd done before. Released in 1982, it was a commercial flop but now widely regarded as one of their best. This would also turn out to be their final tour in makeup for many years.

The night before we were supposed to leave, I didn't feel well. I had the worst stomachache, which kept me awake for hours. In the middle of the night, my parents decided to take me to the hospital, where I had to have emergency surgery to remove my appendix. I was devastated to miss Kiss. My friends went to the show without me, and I ended up staying in the hospital for four weeks with an infection!

ABOVE: Peter Criss at Spectrum, Philadelphia, September 9, 1979

My parents have always been so supportive of my love of music, and they knew how upset I was about missing my favorite band. I had no idea, but while I was in the hospital, my mom tracked down a management contact for Kiss and wrote them a letter. She told them about her poor son who had suffered this horrible surgery, infection, and a monthlong hospital stay but was most upset about not being able to see Kiss.

A while later, she got a response. The band's management said they were very sorry to hear about my ordeal and would give me backstage passes to meet the guys the next time they played in the area. But I was angry! At seventeen years old, I thought the last thing that seemed cool was for Kiss to hear from my mother. I thought they'd think I wasn't tough and that I was a momma's boy, so the letter became a controversy in my family. Of course, now I appreciate it, and a year later, when Kiss played the same venue in Worcester, I was only too happy that she had written to them.

I took the road trip I was supposed to have taken the year before and checked into a hotel across from the venue. My friends and I started to get ready for the show with some adult beverages and Kiss tunes on our boom box. We'd left the door open and were having a great time when into the room walked Eric Carr, then the band's drummer. He and the rest of the band were staying in rooms down the hall! He'd heard the music and just stopped in to say hello, hang out, and take photos with us. This is one of many things that made Eric so loved by the fans.

Later that night, I got to meet my heroes. It was a very brief interaction in which we were pulled into a hallway and given a quick autograph. The guys didn't stick around for long, but that wouldn't be my last interaction with them. A few years later, when I got my first music-industry job at Megaforce Records in 1986, I told Megaforce owner Johnny Z that bands like Metallica and Anthrax and Manowar were great but that we needed to expand and sell some records by someone who could actually get played on the radio. I suggested signing Ace Frehley, whose guitar playing was always one of my favorite elements of Kiss. He was never just a mindless, flashy player. His solos were like songs within songs, and his vocals—although not great in a technical sense—were loved by many. He had been out of Kiss for a few years and was considered to be somewhat of a recluse.

Johnny Z was cool with it, so we tracked Ace down through producer Eddie Kramer and signed him for four solo albums, which helped to relaunch his career. It was risky, since Ace was known as a real nightmare to deal with because of his dependency on drugs and booze. It was amazing to me that less than ten years after seeing my first Kiss concert, I was signing the lead guitarist of the band I'd worshipped. I would've never dreamed that the same twelve-year-old kid watching from the nosebleed seats at Madison Square Garden would help to reintroduce Ace Frehley to the world. And I would've never imagined that one day he'd come to my wedding or become one of my closest friends, as he is to this day.

A few years after signing Ace, I was introduced to Eric Carr again, but

this time on a professional level. I came to see that it was completely in his character to do something like stop by the hotel room of a bunch of fans. He always acted like a regular guy and never forgot where he came from. Eric still holds a special place with me, as he does with most Kiss fans, because of how down-to-earth he was. It was because of him that I got to introduce Kiss before their live show at the Meadowlands for the first time in 1990.

The guys were touring to support *Hot in the Shade*. They had the best lineup since the original band (Bruce Kulick on guitar, Eric on drums), as well as the best set list, and they had the coolest stage show they'd ever had when playing without makeup and costumes. Even back then, I was known as the radio guy who always played Kiss. (I'm still the only one in their home market of New York City who plays music other than "Rock and Roll All Nite.") At the Meadowlands, I went backstage to say hello to Eric. As I was leaving, he called me back and said, "You're the only guy who supports us or plays our records on the air. You should introduce us tonight." I didn't know what to say. I hadn't done much of that kind

ABOVE: Eric Carr at the Palladium, New York City, July 25, 1980
OPPOSITE: Paul Stanley at PNC Bank Arts Center, Holmdel Township, New Jersey, August 11, 2003

of thing before, but I couldn't say no. We walked toward the stage, and I could see fifteen thousand people in the crowd. When the lights went out and a spotlight came on for me, I was a nervous wreck.

Eric handed me a cup and told me to drink some water so my voice wouldn't crack, but it wasn't water. It was whiskey. He laughed and said, "That should take the edge off." He spun me around and then pushed me through the gap in the curtain. Everything happened so quickly. While I was standing onstage, I kept feeling something clipping my legs. Eric was throwing drumsticks and guitar picks at my back to mess with me while I was at the mic. Anyone who knew him knows that's classic Eric Carr–a total prankster. I don't really remember what I said or did that night, but I learned a valuable lesson that would come in handy in years to come: As long as you say the name of the headlining band a couple of times, people will applaud. If you say, "Are you ready for Kiss?" people will go nuts.

The Kiss member who has always been my favorite is also the one I've found the most difficult to get to know. Paul Stanley was one of the best frontmen I've ever seen. He could control an audience like no one else

and is one of the most underrated singers in the history of rock music. He had so much attitude and wrote some of the catchiest hooks and riffs. But Paul has always been very aloof with me. We've had some great moments and conversations, but there have been times where he's viewed me as a problem because of misinformation. The majority of my career has been devoted to promoting Kiss in positive ways, but for the small criticisms I've made over the years, I've been cast from the ship, so to speak. I've never known what triggered it: if it's because he's listened to others' versions of what I've said or because he's read stuff that's inaccurate online instead of just talking to me directly. Everyone knows how much I love Kiss, but it has always been very strange and frustrating to get a read on Paul, even though I have interviewed him for TV and radio several times and we have a ton of mutual friends in the business.

In 1992, I started to do the "Merry Kissmas" radio special. People made fun of me for doing it, but fans love it and the station continued my tradition even after I left to work elsewhere. I'm still known as "the Kiss guy" on the radio. I'm in my forties now, but my mom still calls me whenever any member of Kiss is on TV. That's how much they were a part of my childhood.

As much as I still love and respect the band's music, in 2007 it became very hard for me to remain a Kiss fan. The band opted to dress replacement members in the costumes and makeup of Ace Frehley and Peter Criss. I had no issue with Tommy Thayer or Eric Singer being in Kiss, but I could not watch people impersonating Ace and Peter. Kiss is known for having many tribute bands around the world, but when the band itself becomes one, it gets too hard to take. Still, I stand behind their records and my support for Kiss will never change on the radio—they are forever the band that started it all for me as a fan.

UNDERGROUND CLASSIC

There aren't many under-the-radar Kiss albums, unless you count *Carnival of Souls*, officially released with very little fanfare in 1997 after it leaked as a bootleg. The last album to feature the Singer-Kulick lineup, *Carnival of Souls* was shelved almost immediately after its recording in 1995 because Gene and Paul reunited the band's original members and started wearing makeup again—so they didn't want it to come out. In what seems to be Kiss's attempt at grunge, *Carnival* is an anomaly in the band's catalog. I really like songs like "Jungle" and "Rain," which show a different side of the band. The album also features the only lead vocal ever released by Bruce Kulick, on the song "I Walk Alone."

LEFT: Paul Stanley, Gene Simmons, and Bruce Kulick at Stabler Arena, Lehigh University, Bethlehem, Pennsylvania, April 1, 1986
OPPOSITE: Paul Stanley, Peter Criss, and Ace Frehley at Spectrum, Philadelphia, September 9, 1979

LED ZEPPELIN

As ridiculous as it sounds, Led Zeppelin was the enemy during my early high school years. Because I was such a blind-worshipping Kiss fan, I couldn't admit that Led Zeppelin's music was great. I couldn't even listen to them. In the late 1970s, there was no bigger threat to the mantle of Kiss than this English rock band. They were two of the biggest bands in the world, and it was always Kiss versus Led Zeppelin. For proof, just look at any *Hit Parader* or *Circus* magazine cover from 1977.

At my high school, Led Zeppelin was the band that everyone liked. They were eternally hip. Kiss, on the other hand, wasn't cool in the least. Even though I flew the flag hard for Kiss, I just couldn't avoid the power of Zeppelin. They were everywhere. Eventually, I decided to assess the enemy, so I bought *Physical Graffiti*. As my first introduction to the band, it was a pretty big undertaking. The music was structured around the concept of a full album rather than individual hits, and many of the songs were longer and more complex than Kiss's. It was a far cry from

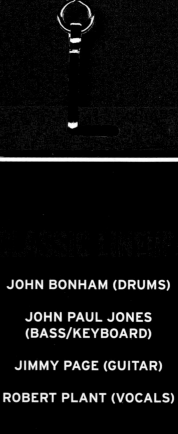

CLASSIC LINEUP

JOHN BONHAM (DRUMS)

**JOHN PAUL JONES
(BASS/KEYBOARD)**

JIMMY PAGE (GUITAR)

ROBERT PLANT (VOCALS)

OPPOSITE: Robert Plant and Jimmy Page at Madison Square Garden, New York City, February 3, 1975

DISCOGRAPHY

LED ZEPPELIN (1969)

LED ZEPPELIN II (1969)

LED ZEPPELIN III (1970)

LED ZEPPELIN IV (1971)

HOUSES OF THE HOLY (1973)

PHYSICAL GRAFFITI (1975)

PRESENCE (1976)

*THE SONG REMAINS
THE SAME* [LIVE] (1976)

IN THROUGH THE OUT DOOR
(1979)

CODA (1982)

HOW THE WEST WAS WON
[LIVE] (2003)

OPPOSITE: Robert Plant and Jimmy Page
at Madison Square Garden, New York City,
June 13, 1977

the basic three-minute rock anthems my makeup-wearing heroes were known for. But as much as the music and the very cool album art grabbed me, I still couldn't like Led Zeppelin more than Kiss. Yet I found myself returning to *Physical Graffiti* again and again, and the album took hold of me.

When I officially became a full-fledged convert to Zeppelin in 1980, the first record I bought was *In Through the Out Door*. I will never forget that day. I had my driver's permit and drove to my cousin's house so he could dub the album onto cassette. I had heard that Zeppelin would be touring in support of the album and was looking forward to seeing them live. I remember leaving my cousin's house and thinking that even though my friends had said I had to choose between Kiss and Led Zeppelin, maybe it was OK to like both.

On the drive home, I heard a radio announcement that John Bonham had died. It hit me like a ton of bricks. Tragically, this incredible drummer had died at a very young age, and I was angry with myself for resisting Zeppelin for all those years. I'd finally grown up and begun to embrace their magic, but I was never going to have the chance to see them play. It was then that I vowed to myself to be more open-minded to other bands. This vow has carried me through my entire career and helped me to explore more music. It has also driven me to help expose those great bands that don't get much airplay or media coverage.

When I started in radio, I realized that you truly just can't get away from Led Zeppelin, no matter what. They are arguably the biggest band of all time, and every few hours, one of their songs comes up on a playlist. People always want to hear them. There are so few bands whose early recordings hold up the way Led Zeppelin's do and sound as fresh and exciting, as innovative and groundbreaking, as they did years ago, every time you hear them. It's cliché to call Led Zeppelin's albums timeless, but they never sound dated. No matter if it's their softer acoustic passages or their bigger heavy riffs, Zeppelin embodies a swagger and groove that transports you every time. Whatever mood you're in, you can always find something in their catalog that captures it.

No other frontman has been so imitated as Robert Plant, thanks to his powerful charisma, wailing high vocals, and mystical lyrics. John Bonham's speed and strength made him one of the best drummers of all time—nobody laid down a pocket and hit the drums like the late Bonzo. John Paul Jones provided the soulful bass and keyboard lines that gave the band its groove, not to mention arranged some of the music. And Jimmy Page's bluesy style and captivating riffs drew from many genres of music. They have been copied by countless guitarists (as has his wizardlike aura).

Even though much of what Zeppelin initially did was derived from early blues recordings, they gave it a charge that laid the blueprint for what would become metal. Look no further than "Dazed and Confused" from the debut album. That song alone takes you on an amazing journey—with pounding drums and a blues melody that builds to a fast, screeching gui-

tar solo. Even though Zeppelin didn't embrace the metal image or tag, it's hard to imagine the genre without them. It was less than two years after that debut that Sabbath emerged, taking the darker side of Zep and truly creating metal.

I did get to see a version of the band years later. While I was working at Megaforce Records, Atlantic Records celebrated its fortieth anniversary in 1988 with a party at Madison Square Garden. The biggest buzz about the anniversary party was that Led Zeppelin was going to play a few songs. But seeing them play in the setting of an industry function was far from the true experience.

In 2007, Led Zeppelin reunited with John Bonham's son, Jason, on drums, for what was billed as a onetime tribute to the late founder of Atlantic Records, Ahmet Ertegun. It took place at the O2 Arena in London, and a ticket to the show was one of the most difficult to get in the world. I was offered a ticket, but I declined it because I was convinced that they were going to play in America. I thought I'd spend all the time and money to go to London only to have them announce a reunion tour. But I was wrong.

I'm not surprised that Robert isn't up for a tour. As the band's frontman, all the pressure is on him to hit every note and look as good as he did in 1973. He already has all the money he could ever want, and he's told me that he is constantly trying to move forward after Zeppelin. As much

EDDIE'S PLAYLIST

LED ZEPPELIN

1. HOTS ON FOR NOWHERE
2. WEARING AND TEARING
3. DAZED AND CONFUSED
4. ACHILLES LAST STAND
5. WHAT IS AND WHAT SHOULD NEVER BE
6. IN THE EVENING
7. CUSTARD PIE
8. THE ROVER
9. TRAMPLED UNDER FOOT
10. HOUSES OF THE HOLY
11. THE WANTON SONG
12. OUT ON THE TILES
13. THE SONG REMAINS THE SAME
14. NOBODY'S FAULT BUT MINE
15. NIGHT FLIGHT

as I would love to see a Zeppelin reunion, I think it's better to leave the legacy where it is, with Zeppelin simply being one of the greatest hard rock bands in history. Plant also wanted to try a different style of music, which he did with great success in 2008 when he teamed up with bluegrass singer Alison Krauss.

I've had the opportunity to interview Robert Plant for VH1 Classic twice. The first time, in 2005, was one of my early assignments when Plant was releasing a box set of solo recordings he'd done after Zeppelin. I went to England for the first time, and we met at some sort of holistic center. It was like a spa, with a juice bar and New Age music playing in the background, and I had to sit on a bunch of pillows. Robert entered without an entourage and seemed like a very unassuming, regular guy. Then he asked if the crew and I would wait for him for an hour so he could get a massage—only Robert Plant could get away with that. When he emerged from the room, ready to be interviewed, he ordered a salad sandwich and cucumber sandwiches with tea. The food in England might be awful, but that was the first time I'd ever heard anyone order something like that! Salad sandwich?

After our interview in the spa, my producer suggested filming another segment at an outdoor market. Plant and I walked through rows of tents where people were selling things and talked about music like old friends.

ABOVE: Robert Plant at the Atlantic Records fortieth anniversary party at Madison Square Garden, New York City, May 14, 1988
OPPOSITE: John Paul Jones and Jimmy Page at Madison Square Garden, New York City, February 3, 1975.

Surprisingly, he went largely unnoticed. A homeless man asked him for money, but otherwise, he wasn't bothered. When I mentioned it to him, he said, "At the end of the day, I'm just an old hippy."

In early 2007, I went to England again to interview both Ronnie James Dio, who was then recording with Black Sabbath, and Robert Plant, who was releasing another collection of solo material. I stayed in a castle that had been converted into a hotel in Birmingham—the birthplace of heavy metal. One of the most surreal experiences of my entire life was having a beer with Ronnie James Dio while I waited for Robert Plant. As a life-long rock fan who does this stuff every day, even I had to stop and take that moment in! Watching Plant's sports car drive up the castle's long, dirt driveway, I had to take a step back and pinch myself. I rarely ask to have my photo taken with musicians, but this was one time that I did. This photo of me, Dio, and Plant is one of my most cherished pieces of memorabilia.

For Robert's interview, someone had set a couple of chairs in front of a roaring fireplace in the castle's billiards room. When Robert saw the setup, he said, "No. This is no bloody good! I don't want the fire going—it looks like a greeting card in here. It will make me look like an old man!"

When we realized how hard it would be to put out the blazing fire, Robert said he would try to do the interview anyway. But the fire was burning our backs, and we were both pouring sweat. Robert got up and said, "The fire has to go!" We called some people from the hotel to remove the burning logs from the fireplace, but the guys burned their hands and dropped logs on the floor. I thought the whole place was going to burn down! Meanwhile, Robert took charge and started to douse the fireplace with bottles of mineral water. For some reason, while he poured out the water, he broke into "The Immigrant Song," singing, "I come from the land of the ice and snow . . . ." He smiled while steam filled the room. That moment is etched in my brain forever.

LEFT: Jimmy Page at Madison Square Garden, New York City, June 13, 1977
OPPOSITE TOP LEFT: John Bonham at Madison Square Garden, New York City, June 13, 1977
OPPOSITE TOP RIGHT: Robert Plant and Jimmy Page at Madison Square Garden, New York City, February 12, 1975
OPPOSITE MIDDLE: Jimmy Page, John Bonham, and Robert Plant at Madison Square Garden, New York City, June 7, 1977
OPPOSITE BOTTOM: Robert Plant, Eddie, and Ronnie James Dio in England, 2007

MEGADETH

I t still surprises me that there are metal fans who don't know what an important role Megadeth frontman Dave Mustaine played in Metallica's history, especially when you consider that so much of what Megadeth does is linked to Dave's time in Metallica. When people describe Megadeth, they talk about the anger and aggression in the music and the snarl in Mustaine's vocals. Much of that is a by-product of his bitterness over being kicked out of Metallica. Sure, it's pretty safe to say that much of it also has to do with Mustaine's personality to begin with, but harboring such hostility over that very bitter breakup is definitely what drives him.

When Mustaine was sent packing, a lot of people were surprised. Metallica was a band of drunks back then, but Dave apparently was the worst of them, so they let him go. They fired him one day when he woke up from a stupor while touring the East Coast. They just handed him a bus ticket back to the West Coast.

CLASSIC LINEUP

DAVID ELLEFSON (BASS)

DAVE MUSTAINE (GUITAR/VOCALS)

CHRIS POLAND (GUITAR)

GAR SAMUELSON (DRUMS)

ADDITIONAL MEMBERS

MARTY FRIEDMAN (GUITAR)

NICK MENZA (DRUMS)

AL PITRELLI (GUITAR)

JEFF YOUNG (GUITAR)

OPPOSITE: Dave Mustaine and David Ellefson at L'amour, Brooklyn, May 29, 1987

DISCOGRAPHY

*KILLING IS MY
BUSINESS . . . AND
BUSINESS IS GOOD!*
(1985)

*PEACE SELLS . . .
BUT WHO'S BUYING?*
(1986)

*SO FAR, SO GOOD . . .
SO WHAT!* (1988)

RUST IN PEACE (1990)

*COUNTDOWN TO
EXTINCTION* (1992)

YOUTHANASIA (1994)

CRYPTIC WRITINGS (1997)

RISK (1999)

THE WORLD NEEDS A HERO
(2001)

THE SYSTEM HAS FAILED
(2004)

UNITED ABOMINATIONS
(2007)

ENDGAME (2009)

**OPPOSITE: Dave Mustaine at L'amour,
Brooklyn, May 30, 1987**

Mustaine was a super talent, evidenced by the fact that some of his most legendary riffs are now, forever, a part of Metallica's catalog. Even though he'd asked them not to use his songs if he wasn't going to be in the band, they still incorporated what he wrote into their first few recordings. They knew it was too good not to use! As hard as it's been for him to reconcile, Dave's experience with Metallica is a large part of the reason that Megadeth is so loved by their fans—because Mustaine was the underdog who rose above defeat.

Even if the mainstream doesn't know Dave as one of the founding members of Metallica, the rivalry between him and the band will always be a part of his career in some way. But I've never been able to understand it. Once I said to him, "What went down between you and the guys from Metallica happened over twenty-five years ago, and you still harbor so much resentment. It's not like you didn't make it on your own. You didn't go from playing in Metallica to flipping burgers. *And* you're considered one of the founding fathers of thrash metal! Why do you still carry this with you when you're so successful?"

It's not like the accolades aren't there for Dave—Megadeth is one of the Big Four of thrash. But that doesn't stop him from carrying a deep-seated anger. If he didn't, Megadeth might not be what it is today. But when you put yourself in his shoes, you can see why he's upset: Megadeth may be considered an iconic band in the metal world, but every day Mustaine has to be reminded that most mainstream fans of Metallica—the band he helped to create, which has gone on to be one of the biggest bands in the world—don't even know who he is or that he was there in the beginning. That wound was deepened when Mustaine was not included in Metallica's induction into the Rock and Roll Hall of Fame in 2009. I attended that ceremony as a guest of Metallica. The band invited Mustaine to attend too, but he declined since he was not being inducted. (Only those members who'd played on the band's releases were inducted.)

After he was ousted from Metallica, there was huge interest in the metal community in what Dave Mustaine was going to do next. In 1985, when the first Megadeth record came out, I was working at a record store. Recorded on a shoestring budget, *Killing Is My Business . . . And Business Is Good!* was released on an indie label, which meant that the store wasn't able to get it very easily or through the proper distribution channels. A couple of copies came in and quickly sold out, but so many people were asking for it that I was told to drive to a distribution center in Queens to get a box of albums! Record stores across the country were inundated with the same demand, and the lack of distribution was a detriment to the band's success.

It became somewhat of a battle in those days between Metallica and Megadeth: Which band was heavier, bigger, and making better albums? Metal fans won in the end, because both bands were doing some of their best work. Like Metallica, which started on the indie label Megaforce and then went to the major label Elektra, Megadeth quickly jumped from Combat Records to Capitol Records. I'm not sure if it was because of Mega-

EDDIE'S PLAYLIST

MEGADETH

1. TRAIN OF CONSEQUENCES
2. KILLING IS MY BUSINESS
   . . . AND BUSINESS IS GOOD!
3. SWEATING BULLETS
4. HOOK IN MOUTH
5. WAKE UP DEAD
6. SYMPHONY OF
   DESTRUCTION
7. HANGAR 18
8. TRUST
9. IN MY DARKEST HOUR
10. HOLY WARS . . .
    THE PUNISHMENT DUE
11. ALMOST HONEST
12. RECKONING DAY
13. FORECLOSURE OF
    A DREAM
14. SLEEPWALKER
15. PEACE SELLS
16. MECHANIX

ABOVE: Dave Mustaine at the Izod Center,
East Rutherford, New Jersey,
August 12, 2010

deth's many lineup changes, marketing, or management, or Mustaine's own erratic behavior and substance-abuse issues, but despite some amazing Megadeth albums, Metallica managed to cross over to a much larger audience and clearly won the popularity battle.

A breakthrough year for both Metallica and Megadeth was 1986, when Mustaine released one of the heaviest albums of the era, *Peace Sells . . . But Who's Buying?* The album put the band on Capitol and into the public eye with the hit single and video for the title track. That song's iconic opening bass line actually became the theme for MTV's "newsbreaks." The album's first track, "Wake Up Dead," remains one of my all-time favorite Megadeth songs.

Though no one can possibly argue that Megadeth is anything but Mustaine's vehicle and vision, he has always presented it as a group effort. Mustaine's controversial lyrics—both political and personal—are his, but he's always given the amazing players he's worked with a chance to shine. The lineup is a bit of a revolving door, but it's consistently included some top-flight players: Chris Poland and Marty Friedman on guitar, David Ellefson on bass, and Nick Menza on drums, to name a few.

I've seen the band live through countless eras, lineup changes, and stages of Mustaine's substance abuse. No matter who has been in the lineup or whether their frontman has been sober or not, Megadeth has

always crushed it live. I've never seen a bad show. Part of what fans love about Megadeth is Mustaine's volatility—the idea that he's so angry he might go over the edge at any moment, and he has on many occasions. You never know if you'll see him as the lovable smart-ass or the angry guy. He's gotten wiser as he's aged, but there's still always a wild-card factor when it comes to him. And that's what people have come to expect.

Dave Mustaine's influence on metal cannot be understated. He was never a singer before he was kicked out of Metallica, but he turned himself into one. His voice is so distinctive and has so much personality; it really defines the sound of the band. Dave Mustaine showed that if you've got the talent and the drive, you can be successful by doing things on your own terms. Many of the Megadeth albums have some of the greatest metal ever created. The musicianship is always top-notch, the production is always strong, and the great riffs and guitar work are always a powerful element. Even though Dave is a great player in his own right, he has always had equally killer guitarists with him in the band to share the spotlight—Megadeth is known for long, trade-off guitar solos. It's very rare that a metal band with a player of Mustaine's caliber would add another equally strong player to the lineup. But that's all part of Dave's plan to try to make Megadeth better than the rest.

Mustaine was the ultimate underdog, but he picked himself up, dusted off, and was determined to create a band that was bigger and better than Metallica. (Megadeth are not bigger, and whether they're better is, of course, a matter of opinion.) He's also brutally honest about his feelings, often to his own detriment. As a guest on *That Metal Show*, he's been anything but politically correct. Mustaine totally marches to his own beat, and that, in and of itself, is a theme that's synonymous with metal. I've always respected him for it.

I've found Dave to be a warm, good person. Once he came to my radio show with a trail of about fifty fans behind him. He asked if it was OK to bring them into the studio for the entire hour-and-a-half interview because they'd been waiting outside in the cold to see him. He's the only person I've ever interviewed who's done something like that. He still has a great appreciation for the fans and people who have stood behind him. When organizing the metal package tour Gigantour, which he started in 2005, he always includes a stop to play a charity softball game to raise money for various causes. For all the negative stories about Mustaine, many warranted, there is much good that often gets overlooked.

In June 2010 it looked as if Dave and Metallica may have finally reconciled to some degree. Metallica, Megadeth, Slayer, and Anthrax—the Big Four of thrash—all performed together for the first time in Europe. The show was broadcast to movie theaters in America and around the world. In a moment most metal fans thought they would never see, Mustaine joined Metallica onstage with the other bands, hugged Lars, and jammed with the guys. It was truly historic, although something tells me that the anger in Dave's music will not go away. And let's face it—we would have it no other way.

DID YOU KNOW

In 1996, Dave Mustaine recorded an album under the name MD.45 called *The Craving*. It's a punk metal album he did to get a break from writing thrash, which was a struggling genre at the time. The original album was a collaboration with Lee Ving, singer of the L.A. punk band Fear. In 2004, when Mustaine reissued remixed versions of the entire Megadeth catalog, he also included *The Craving* in the series. On the reissue of the album, Ving's vocals have been wiped out and replaced by Mustaine's, something most fans had wanted when the album was originally released. Mustaine was unable to find the tapes with Ving's vocals, so he took the opportunity to let fans revisit a completely different version of the album.

METALLICA

Photo by Kevin Kane, courtesy of Wire Image/Getty Images

When I started doing radio at New Jersey's WDHA-FM in 1983, I was one of the first DJs in America to spotlight heavy metal. Even though WDHA was a smaller-market station, there was a lot of buzz across the country about my show. At the time, I often went to Rock n' Roll Heaven, a flea market music store owned and run by husband-and-wife team Johnny and Marsha Z. Johnny and Marsha were on top of everything in the early '80s metal scene, so their store became a real destination for metal fans who wanted to learn about the next big thing or buy metal magazines and albums.

Back then, Johnny got to know me as a customer and metal fan. When he found out about my radio show and realized that I had an audience, he started to give me records by bands like Raven, Manowar, and Exciter. If I liked them, I'd play them on the air.

CLASSIC LINEUP

CLIFF BURTON (BASS)

KIRK HAMMETT (GUITAR)

**JAMES HETFIELD
(GUITAR/VOCALS)**

LARS ULRICH (DRUMS)

KEY ADDITIONAL MEMBERS

DAVE MUSTAINE (GUITAR)

JASON NEWSTED (BASS)

ROB TRUJILLO (BASS)

OPPOSITE: Rob Trujillo, James Hetfield,
Lars Ulrich, Kirk Hammett, and
Jason Newsted at the Rock and Roll Hall
of Fame induction ceremony,
Cleveland, Ohio, April 4, 2009

DISCOGRAPHY

When Johnny started the record label Megaforce, he continued to give me records to play on my show. One night while I was in the studio, Johnny came to the door with a paper bag full of records. He said, "I just signed this band and put out their first record, but I can't get anyone to play it on the radio. No one understands it. Will you play a song just once and see what your listeners think?" I told him to leave the record and I'd listen to it. He said, "Eddie, you've got to trust me on this. Just play it right now and see what you think."

I asked him what the record was, and he pulled out Metallica's *Kill 'Em All*. I knew they were from the West Coast and had a cassette demo that had been generating some buzz, but I had never heard their music. So I played the track Johnny suggested, "The Four Horsemen," but I didn't like it at first. The music I loved up to that point was heavy, but it also always had a strong sense of melody—especially in the vocals—along with great production. Metallica sounded like they were from another planet! I had never heard anything so fast or heavy or abrasive.

Johnny thanked me for playing it and wrote on the album cover, "Ed, you were the first to play this band. Thank you, Johnny Z." On his way out, he explained that he was just starting Megaforce with Metallica and didn't know what was going to happen with either one of them. He really appreciated that I'd given the record a chance, and he told me if he could ever hire another employee at his label, he would hire me.

I would love to be able to say that I heard the future of metal that night—a band that would become one of the most famous in the world. But I didn't know what I'd heard. I couldn't decide if it was something great, something awful, or something in between. But my listeners seemed to like it. So, I started to get requests for Metallica, and slowly they began to grow on me.

The band came to New York and started playing on the East Coast, where fellow metal band and labelmates Anthrax took them in and gave them a place to stay and rehearse. I saw them a lot back then, opening for other groups that never went anywhere like Vandenberg and the Rods. (I have the ticket stubs to prove it!)

Metallica would come onstage—four guys in black leather jackets and T-shirts with their heads down—and bang the hell out of their instruments. They didn't care about image—they were hard, fast, loud, and extreme. Pretty quickly, they started to get a huge following in the metal underground. *Kill 'Em All* sold very well and their legend grew, and before anyone knew it, they were headlining shows everywhere. When their second album, *Ride the Lightning*, came out in 1984, more and more people started to discover Metallica. They weren't just this cult phenomenon anymore.

Soon enough, in the middle of the record's promotional cycle, the band broke their agreement with Johnny Z's Megaforce to join a major label, Elektra (which would reissue *Ride the Lightning*) and pick up new management. Though it was a blow to Johnny, the settlement that was reached to break Metallica's contract was very rewarding for him financially. With the

money he won, he was able to truly focus on Megaforce. Up to that point, he'd been running it out of his house with his wife and a family friend they called Metal Maria.

Johnny got in touch with me around this time to say he was taking the label to another level and wanted to make good on his promise to hire me. I was twenty-two years old and it was a no-brainer for me to leave the record store I was working at for a job at his label. It was partially due to my early support of Metallica that I got my first real job in the music industry—they had a huge impact on my life and career.

Though Metallica had left his label, Johnny felt a lot of pride about bringing the band's music to the world. I'd be lying, though, if I said there wasn't also an amount of resentment. We watched from the sidelines as Metallica's success changed the game for metal bands as well as the music business. Before Metallica, extreme metal bands had been relegated to indie labels and considered underground. But when *Master of Puppets* came out in 1986 (with a Megaforce logo on it as part of the settlement) and Metallica started to sell boatloads of records without a video or any mainstream radio play, major labels took notice. Suddenly bands like Anthrax, Megadeth, Testament, Overkill, Slayer, and Exodus—which never would have been seen as commercial pre-Metallica—were being signed to major labels.

Before *Master of Puppets*, I appreciated the power of Metallica's sound but I wasn't totally feeling it. When I heard that record, I fully grasped what they were doing. *Master of Puppets* had much better production, not to mention incredible riffs, and it showed that Metallica was really the best band in the genre. They started to appeal to a broader base of music fans, and before long, they were touring with Ozzy. Still, they remained very much a working-class band. They played hard and partied even harder.

Even as they got more and more famous, the guys in Metallica didn't act like rock stars. They didn't wear makeup or have wardrobes for the stage. They loved to drink beer and they loved heavy metal. They related to their audience as fellow music fans (drummer Lars Ulrich in particular), proudly showing their influences by playing covers onstage and writing in their liner notes about why the songs and artists (like the Misfits and Black Sabbath) are important to them. Indirectly, they've supported many other lesser-known metal artists this way too.

In the '90s, the band started to take heat for being followers instead of innovators. They cut their hair and got new wardrobes, and at the same time they stripped their songs of guitar solos, which was unheard of. With albums like 1996's *Load*, the 1997 follow-up *ReLoad*, and 2003's *St. Anger*, it seemed like they'd lost their way. Though I understand their need to evolve, I didn't always agree with it.

In 2008, Metallica reestablished themselves as metal gods by returning to what they do best. *Death Magnetic* is Metallica at their uncompromising best. Its first single, the seven-and-a-half-minute-long "The Day That Never Comes," shows that they were back to doing things on their own

TOP: Cliff Burton at Brendan Byrne Arena, East Rutherford, New Jersey, April 21, 1986
BOTTOM: James Hetfield and Kirk Hammett at L'amour, Brooklyn, January 2, 1985
OPPOSITE: Rob Trujillo at Madison Square Garden, New York City, February 1, 2009

EDDIE'S PLAYLIST

METALLICA

1. THE UNFORGIVEN
2. WELCOME HOME (SANITARIUM)
3. THE FOUR HORSEMEN
4. DON'T TREAD ON ME
5. ONE
6. BATTERY
7. THE THING THAT SHOULD NOT BE
8. DISPOSABLE HEROES
9. FIGHT FIRE WITH FIRE
10. RIDE THE LIGHTNING
11. CREEPING DEATH
12. FOR WHOM THE BELL TOLLS
13. 2X4
14. BROKEN, BEAT & SCARRED
15. THE JUDAS KISS

terms. Even after chasing trends, suffering lineup changes, and pissing off fans with a lawsuit over illegal downloads, Metallica endures. They've done what very few bands from the genre could—they've crossed over to the mainstream.

I've always known Lars the best. What I love most about him is that he's such a true fan of metal. He still gets excited about new bands and even older bands reuniting. Once, when he was doing a meet and greet after a show, Lars kept calling me over to see all the photos and patches people were bringing to him. He had the same excitement about other band logos and memorabilia as the fans did about his band. He truly gets what it means to be a music fan.

When *Death Magnetic* came out, I was critical of the fact that the production was awful. It was distorted and too compressed. I love the album and played it on air, but I was very vocal about my opinion of the recording. Most bands at Metallica's level would've been annoyed or banished me from their shows or from coming backstage for saying so. (I've had it happen many times.) But rather than shun me, Lars invited me to see the band play in New Jersey, leaving me backstage passes and great tickets. He also let me interview him for VH1 Classic. When I sat with him for my TV show, I brought up the fact that I'd been critical of the record. He listened to what I had to say and then told me how he felt—we talked about the record like honest fans would.

Lars also took a hell of a beating in the press and from fans when he led the band's lawsuit against Napster and others. He was accused of being greedy, but in retrospect it's interesting to consider that he actually foresaw a future problem for the record industry. Given the way record companies have suffered because of illegal music downloading in recent years, it seems Lars was looking out for them, but has never been given credit for it.

When Metallica was inducted into the Rock and Roll Hall of Fame in 2009, I was surprised to be invited to attend. They invited 150 friends and people who they felt were instrumental to their success in the early part of their career to Cleveland. I never knew they regarded me as important in their history because for many years we'd lost touch. So I was totally floored that a band of their stature thought it was important for me to be there for their biggest night.

They paid for my flight and hotel room, and I had a great weekend reuniting with people from the early days of my career: Johnny and Marsha Z, Metal Maria, DJs, and other early members of the band. I also got to take the stage at the band's private party before the induction ceremony to tell the story about Johnny Z coming to my radio show at WDHA with *Kill 'Em All* many years earlier.

For most Metallica purists, the essence of the band is revealed in their first three albums, but if you focus only on those, you're leaving a lot of great music on the table. Metallica may not have made albums that were completely solid from start to finish, but they have plenty of amazing moments. Over the course of their career, Metallica went from being one

of the most indigestible bands, completely ignored by radio and MTV, to being aired virtually every minute on rock radio and having their video for "One" become one of the most famous of all time. As pioneers on so many levels, Metallica bridged barriers to become a household name, always doing it on their own terms. They remain one of the biggest and most important bands in all of music. In the summer of 2010, Metallica played with fellow Big Four bands Anthrax, Slayer, and Megadeth for the first time ever at festivals across Europe. The event was so monumental that it was featured in movie theaters across America.

DID YOU KNOW

It's rare for Metallica members to play on any outside projects, but in 2005, guitarist Kirk Hammett joined Carlos Santana for a track called "Trinity" on Santana's album *All That I Am*. Hammett, like me, is a huge fan of classic UFO and Scorpions, and on the tour for *Death Magnetic*, he played those bands' riffs in some of his solos.

Bassist Jason Newsted had stints playing with several bands, including Canada's Voivod and a group called Echobrain, after leaving Metallica in 2001. Jason suffers from severe back pain due to years of onstage headbanging and now paints for creative expression. His work is often shown at galleries in the San Francisco Bay Area.

Kirk Hammett and Lars Ulrich at Madison Square Garden, New York City, February 1, 2009

MÖTLEY CRÜE

When I was just starting to do radio in the early '80s, one of the first promotional copies of a record I ever received was Mötley Crüe's debut album, *Too Fast for Love*. The copy I received wasn't the Elektra Records version that's widely available today; it was the band-financed recording from their own label, Leathur Records. It was hard, fast, loud, and dirty and reeked of the Sunset Strip. The songs— written mostly by the bass player, Nikki Sixx—were full of catchy hooks and melodies. The drummer was completely over-the-top, the singer's voice was totally distinctive, and the guitar tone was something you just didn't hear at the time. There was a live, raw feel to the playing and an almost creepy aura in the riffs and solos. I loved it. People talk about Guns N' Roses' *Appetite for Destruction* being so real and "street," but I felt that five years earlier listening to *Too Fast for Love*.

CLASSIC LINEUP

TOMMY LEE (DRUMS)

MICK MARS (GUITAR)

VINCE NEIL (VOCALS)

NIKKI SIXX (BASS)

RANDY CASTILLO (DRUMS)

JOHN CORABI (VOCALS)

SAMANTHA MALONEY (DRUMS)

OPPOSITE: Nikki Sixx and Vince Neil at Brendan Byrne Arena, East Rutherford, New Jersey, December 12, 1989

DISCOGRAPHY

OPPOSITE: Nikki Sixx and Mick Mars at
Brendan Byrne Arena, East Rutherford,
New Jersey, April 15, 1990

Not long after I got the promo, I saw the video for "Live Wire." The guys looked glam, but they sounded ruder and edgier than any glam band I'd ever heard. They were very visual and already theatrical: Bassist Nikki Sixx lit his boots on fire, and guitarist Mick Mars had blood dripping from his mouth.

As I came up in radio, Mötley made great strides in their career. I remember getting their second album, Shout at the Devil, when I was working in a record store in 1983. It was immediately obvious that they'd gotten some money, because the record's photos and packaging had improved drastically and they had more impressive clothes. They also went from being glam to something darker and more sinister. While Too Fast for Love was the work of a loose, fast, and kind-of-fun-sounding band, on Shout they'd suddenly become the devil! In leather bondage outfits and makeup, they looked evil, in an Alice Cooper way, with a huge pentagram in their logo. And the songs were a lot heavier, way more metal. I don't know if the money they got led to different, heavier drugs or what, but the band was darker. They were singing songs like "Shout at the Devil," "Bastard," and "Looks That Kill," and even had a great cover of the Beatles' "Helter Skelter."

I saw them on what would become one of their most legendary tours, for Shout at the Devil, when they opened for Ozzy Osbourne. You could see even then that it wouldn't be long before they'd be headlining their own arena shows because they were already drawing a crowd. It was around this time that I met them at a party after a show they'd played in New York.

So many times, I've seen bands whose onstage personas are different from who they are in real life. But the guys in Mötley Crüe were even crazier offstage. Like all the stories you've heard, they were truly hard-living, hard-partying, and clearly off the rails, out of their minds. They would do or say or screw anything, and there was a palpable element of danger around them. It felt like anything could happen: a fight might break out, a drug bust could take place, your wallet (or your girlfriend) could get stolen—you just didn't know. That feeling of danger was well perceived. Vince would later accidentally kill Hanoi Rocks drummer Razzle in a drunk-driving incident, and Nikki Sixx would overdose and be pronounced dead for two minutes but return to using heroin almost immediately afterward. The notorious stories go on, and many are documented in the band's bestselling book, The Dirt.

I've always been pretty levelheaded. I never got into over-the-top drinking and I never did drugs, so I didn't really hang out or get to know them very well back then. Personally, I was always more into their songs and records, although they are uneven. Like their live shows, Mötley's good records are really good and the ones that aren't are really bad. They'd be the first to tell you that.

With their third record, 1985's Theatre of Pain, Mötley tried to get "pretty" all of a sudden. They became so glam looking again, and so loaded with drugs and the excesses of the time, that they made a very bad

record. They were so heavily into substances that they didn't know what they were doing. Still, they managed to get something right, because the power ballad "Home Sweet Home" became a huge hit and earned a whole new group of fans.

The subsequent albums, 1987's *Girls, Girls, Girls* and 1989's *Dr. Feelgood*, brought the guys into a biker, street-gang version of rock that seemed to be their comfort zone. But Mötley's sound is always evolving. At the core, they're a snotty hard-rock band with an attitude, but they're always willing to take a chance.

Mötley Crüe's sound certainly contributed to what commonly became known as hair metal, but they are much more than that. They showcase the importance of having a strong look (with a good-looking singer up front for the girls) and of being able to write songs that appeal to a broad demographic—both men and women, people who like heavier music and people who like more melodic rock—yet are never so commercial that they lose the metalheads. This formula has been adapted by so many bands that have followed.

MOTLEY CRUE
BEACON THTR
74TH & B'WAY
NEW YORK CITY
JUN 3 1984
SUN 8:00 PM
NO REFUNDS - NO EXCHANGES
$13.50
ORCH DOOR 4
SEC.	ROW	SEAT
R-C	**D**	**24**

ORCH DOOR 4
R-C D 24
JUN 3 1984
$13.50 8:00 PM

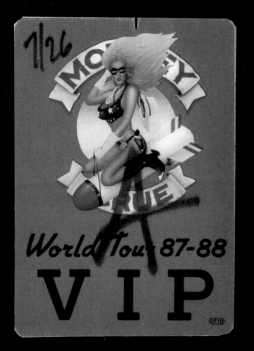

EDDIE'S PLAYLIST

MÖTLEY CRÜE

1. PIECE OF YOUR ACTION
2. DON'T GO AWAY MAD
3. HOOLIGAN'S HOLIDAY
4. ON WITH THE SHOW
5. PRIMAL SCREAM
6. CITY BOY BLUES
7. LIVE WIRE
8. WILDSIDE
9. KNOCK 'EM DEAD, KID
10. SHOUT AT THE DEVIL
11. KICKSTART MY HEART
12. TOO FAST FOR LOVE
13. LOOKS THAT KILL
14. DR. FEELGOOD
15. BASTARD
16. AFRAID

It's Mötley's level of celebrity that's served them best. All the wild things they've done have kept them in the spotlight when so many other bands of that era have a hard time finding traction. Their legend became larger than life. People who didn't care about their music knew that their bass player was going out with a girl from *Baywatch* or that their singer had killed a guy. If Tommy Lee hadn't been married to actress and former *Playboy* Playmate Pamela Anderson, and hadn't made a notorious sex tape with her, he probably wouldn't be as big of a star as he still is today. He's a tremendous drummer, but people only talk about who he's dating, the sex tape, or his run-ins with the paparazzi. The band's book, *The Dirt*, only helped to fuel the machine of gossip and excess.

In 2005, when the original lineup of Mötley Crüe reunited, I went to Los Angeles for VH1 Classic to attend the band's press conference. As we were setting up for an interview, Nikki told me to put him and Vince in front and Mick in the back because Mick wouldn't talk much. But I wanted to get Mick engaged. He'd always intrigued me for being the most under-the-radar guy in the band, and I went into that interview specifically wanting to hear what he had to say. I started by directly asking him questions and, as a result, really got him talking. He opened up a lot, joking about his status in the band, his various ailments, and his ability to make a single guitar sound like three guitars. He also had a great sense of humor, which

I had never seen come out before, and he seemed excited that someone had decided to include him so much in the conversation.

Afterward, Nikki said, "I've never heard Mick talk so much in an interview," and I asked him, "Has anyone ever tried to talk to him that much?" The other guys in the band are such characters that no one seems to focus on Mick. He's an original member, but he rarely gets a moment to shine if people don't engage him. And when they do, he has great stories. It's hard to make a band with one guitar player sound good live, but Mick does, and I think he is overlooked when people talk about Mötley.

Though Vince has been sober on and off, a funny moment I remember with him was when he was still drinking. We attend the same Super Bowl party in Las Vegas every year (I've seen him literally carried out of several!), so I always get a chance to talk to him. In Las Vegas, you can place bets on anything when it comes to the Super Bowl. That year, Vince came running up to me early in the night to show me that he'd bet on the length of time it would take to sing the national anthem. He said he thought it would take four minutes and twenty seconds. And it did! He won the bet. But by the time it happened, he didn't even remember he'd placed it! After the national anthem, I ran up to Vince to tell him that he won, and he had no idea what I was talking about. Even before kickoff he was on another planet! But Vince really is a nice guy and always the leader of the party.

Nikki writes some great songs, Vince's voice makes all those songs instantly recognizable, Mick plays some huge and consuming riffs, and Tommy is, by all means, a powerhouse drummer. (While the other guys have settled down, Tommy is still a maniac. If you're trying to stay sober, he's not the influence you want nearby.) But to me they have always sounded like supercharged elements of the bands I grew up loving, like Kiss, Aerosmith, AC/DC, and even the Raspberries, whose song "Tonight" Mötley covered. Still, they've managed to conquer music fans by walking a line between metal and pop with an attitude and a swagger that's never fabricated. And things did not come easy for them. They came from the streets, lived hard, paid their dues, and actually persevered.

These days Mötley continues to tour and record with their original lineup. In 2010 they performed some shows at Ozzfest, and a few years before that they launched their own traveling festival, Crüe Fest. Vince Neil released a new solo album in June 2010 called *Tattoos & Tequila* and actually has a tattoo parlor, a tequila line, and now his own cantina in Vegas. Tommy walks a line between his love of rock and hip-hop and often guest DJs at dance clubs around the country. He releases his own albums as well. These days Mötley Crüe has a whole new generation of fans who have come to see if all the stories they've heard are true. And although the guys of Mötley have grown up just a bit, they still put on one hell of a show.

UNDERGROUND CLASSIC

Prior to the Mötley Crüe reunion, Nikki Sixx put together a band called Brides of Destruction with Tracii Guns of L.A. Guns. Their debut, *Here Come the Brides*, was released in 2003 and has some really cool, punk-flavored hard rock. Even though Mötley reformed, the Brides did a second album without Nikki that was not as solid. Nikki also did an album based on his memoir, *The Heroin Diaries*, with a band called Sixx: A.M. in 2008, scoring a hit with a great track called "Life Is Beautiful." Vince Neil's solo band is also good and features Slaughter members Dana Strum and Jeff Blando, as well as the totally over-the-top and amazing drummer Zoltan Chaney. Even though their set is mostly Mötley classics, I enjoy this band's take on them.

OPPOSITE: Tommy Lee at Brendan Byrne Arena, East Rutherford, New Jersey, April 15, 1990

MOTÖRHEAD

Perhaps one of the most identifiable people in metal history is Lemmy of Motörhead. The Motörhead logo (which I assume is drawn from Lemmy's love of German war relics) is worn by many people who probably can't even name one of the band's songs yet consider it eternally cool. The same can be said for the ageless wonder who is the band's resilient leader, the one and only Lemmy Kilmister. Interestingly, this metal icon does not consider Motörhead to even be a metal band! I've had this talk with Lemmy many times, and he truly feels his group is just a really loud rock-and-roll band. And if you can get past the insane level of volume the band plays at, you can see where he's coming from.

CLASSIC LINEUP

"FAST" EDDIE CLARKE
(GUITAR)

LEMMY KILMISTER
(BASS/VOCALS)

PHIL "PHILTHY ANIMAL"
TAYLOR (DRUMS)

OTHER PERSONNEL

PHIL CAMPBELL (GUITAR)

MIKKEY DEE (DRUMS)

PETER GILL (DRUMS)

BRIAN ROBERTSON (GUITAR)

WÜRZEL
[MICHAEL BURSTON]
(GUITAR)

OPPOSITE: Phil Campbell,
Lemmy Kilmister, and Würzel at
Roseland Ballroom, New York City,
February 15, 1994

In many ways, Motörhead has followed the signature rock-and-roll approach of trailblazers like Chuck Berry, by taking a simple three-chord melody and turning it up to eleven. Most of the songs are short, sweet, and to the point, but with snarling vocals, reckless drums, superdistorted guitars, and rumbling bass. After four decades, if it ain't broke, don't fix it. To me, Lemmy is the Keith Richards of heavy rock, making him one of music's most legendary frontmen. Now in his sixties, he shows no sign of slowing down, continues to uniquely charm the ladies, and is as influential and relevant as he's ever been. He makes no apologies for his famous heavy-muttonchops look or his growly sound, which have served him well for years.

After a brief stint as a roadie for Jimi Hendrix, Lemmy first came on the music scene as a member of the quasi-psychedelic band Hawkwind. The classic version of Motörhead was formed in the mid-'70s and included guitarist "Fast" Eddie Clarke, Lemmy on bass, and drummer Phil "Philthy Animal" Taylor, who had an odd way of sitting seemingly fifty feet away from his drum kit when playing. Lemmy is also known for the trademark position of his microphone. With the mic angled high and tilted down, Lemmy seems to almost be straining upward to reach for that special gravel in his voice. Lemmy told me he places the mic like that because it's simply more comfortable for him and enables his voice to be more open. Once, when Lemmy was on *That Metal Show*, we placed the mic the same way, forcing the audience to ask questions Motörhead-style.

The lineup of Lemmy, Clarke, and Taylor recorded one of metal's all-time classic albums in 1980, *Ace of Spades*. To this day, the album and its title track are by far Motörhead's most well-known recordings. The song "Ace of Spades" is a bona fide anthem for metal fans and has influenced so many musicians. Motörhead is unique in that they've walked a line between rock, metal, and punk. They basically invented the thrash scene by combining speed and distortion along with gruff vocals that were not exactly Freddie Mercury–worthy, if you know what I mean. (Lemmy says that Motörhead could never replace him because they'd never be able to find someone who sings as bad as he does.) But Motörhead created their own sound and had an impact on a wide range of rock and metal artists. One could argue that without Motörhead, there would be no Metallica, Anthrax, Megadeth, or countless other thrash bands that took their cue from the no-frills, no-holds-barred attack of Lemmy. Hell, Overkill even took their name from a Motörhead album. There have been many different members in and out of Motörhead over the years, but remarkably the band always sounds the same, and that's because of their unstoppable leader. Motörhead always just sounds like Motörhead because Lemmy *is* Motörhead.

I've had the chance to spend time with Lemmy and to interview him on many occasions on both TV and radio. In all honesty, he's one of the tougher people to have as a guest. Don't get me wrong—he has great stories and is very interesting, but he often has fairly short and to-the-point answers and can be hard to engage. He's also sometimes hard to under-

DISCOGRAPHY

MOTÖRHEAD (1977)

OVERKILL (1979)

BOMBER (1979)

ON PAROLE (1979)

ACE OF SPADES (1980)

NO SLEEP 'TIL
HAMMERSMITH
[LIVE] (1981)

IRON FIST (1982)

ANOTHER
PERFECT DAY (1983)

NO REMORSE (1984)

ORGASMATRON (1986)

ROCK 'N' ROLL (1987)

1916 (1991)

MARCH OR DIE (1992)

BASTARDS (1993)

SACRIFICE (1995)

OVERNIGHT
SENSATION (1996)

SNAKE BITE
LOVE (1998)

WE ARE
MOTÖRHEAD (2000)

HAMMERED (2002)

INFERNO (2004)

KISS OF DEATH (2006)

MOTÖRIZER (2008)

stand, between his British accent and the constant swigging of booze. He lives the total rock-and-roll lifestyle—always with a different hot girl on one arm and a Jack and Coke in the other hand. Never in my life have I been with Lemmy and not seen him drinking.

The first time he came to VH1 Classic to be on a show I used to host called *Hangin' With*, he refused to come before three PM (Lem does not wake earlier) and asked that large bottles of Jack Daniel's and Coke be in the greenroom with plenty of ice. When he arrived, he went straight to the greenroom with a girl that had to be forty years younger, closed the door, and finally surfaced about an hour later, ready to tape the interview. But I'd have it no other way. In all his years of drinking, I've also never seen Lemmy out of control. Think about that for a second. This is a guy who lives in walking distance from his favorite bar, the legendary Rainbow Bar and Grill in Los Angeles, and can be seen there on any given night when not on the road. But you also never hear stories about him being fall-down drunk, out of control, or in some rehab joint. I asked Lemmy what the key to that was in 2009, and he told me it's all about knowing your limits and maintaining an even keel without ever going over the edge. He

ABOVE: Lemmy Kilmister, Eddie, and Rob Halford, 2010
OPPOSITE: Lemmy Kilmister at Roseland Ballroom, New York City, February 15, 1994

1. KILLED BY DEATH 2. ACE OF SPADES 3. TERMINAL SHOW
4. IRON FIST 5. OVERKILL 6. EAT THE RICH 7. ORGASMATRON
8. THE CHASE IS BETTER THAN THE CATCH 9. NO CLASS
10. MOTÖRHEAD 11. STAY CLEAN 12. LOVE ME LIKE A REPTILE

EDDIE'S PLAYLIST MOTÖRHEAD

also said that he drinks just enough to maintain the same buzz around the clock every day. So essentially, he knows no other way to exist but at his perfect balance of Jack, Coke, and smokes. He is simply a machine both onstage and off, and somehow he gets better with age.

All the stories of Lemmy's persona can often overshadow his brilliance as a musician. He has written some amazing songs for himself and others, including one of Ozzy Osbourne's biggest hits, "Mama, I'm Coming Home." He's also never been afraid to have a wide range of guest musicians on his albums, working with people like Slash, Dave Grohl, Steve Vai, and C. C. DeVille. I once asked Lemmy how it came to be that C.C. guested on a Motörhead album, thinking it was a bit of a strange pairing for a guy from a glam band like Poison to work with Motörhead, and Lemmy told me that's exactly why he did it: to keep people guessing.

While many will agree that Lemmy has achieved iconic status, it's a shame that so many don't really know much of the man's music outside of a few select Motörhead classics. I encourage all rock fans to explore the world of Motörhead and discover some real gems in their extensive catalog. The new music Lemmy is making with his band's current lineup (which Lemmy thinks is its best ever), with Phil Campbell on guitar and Mikkey Dee on drums, is right up there with classic Motörhead. It attests to why Lemmy is one of the most dedicated men in rock.

OPPOSITE: Lemmy Kilmister at Roseland Ballroom, New York City, February 15, 1994

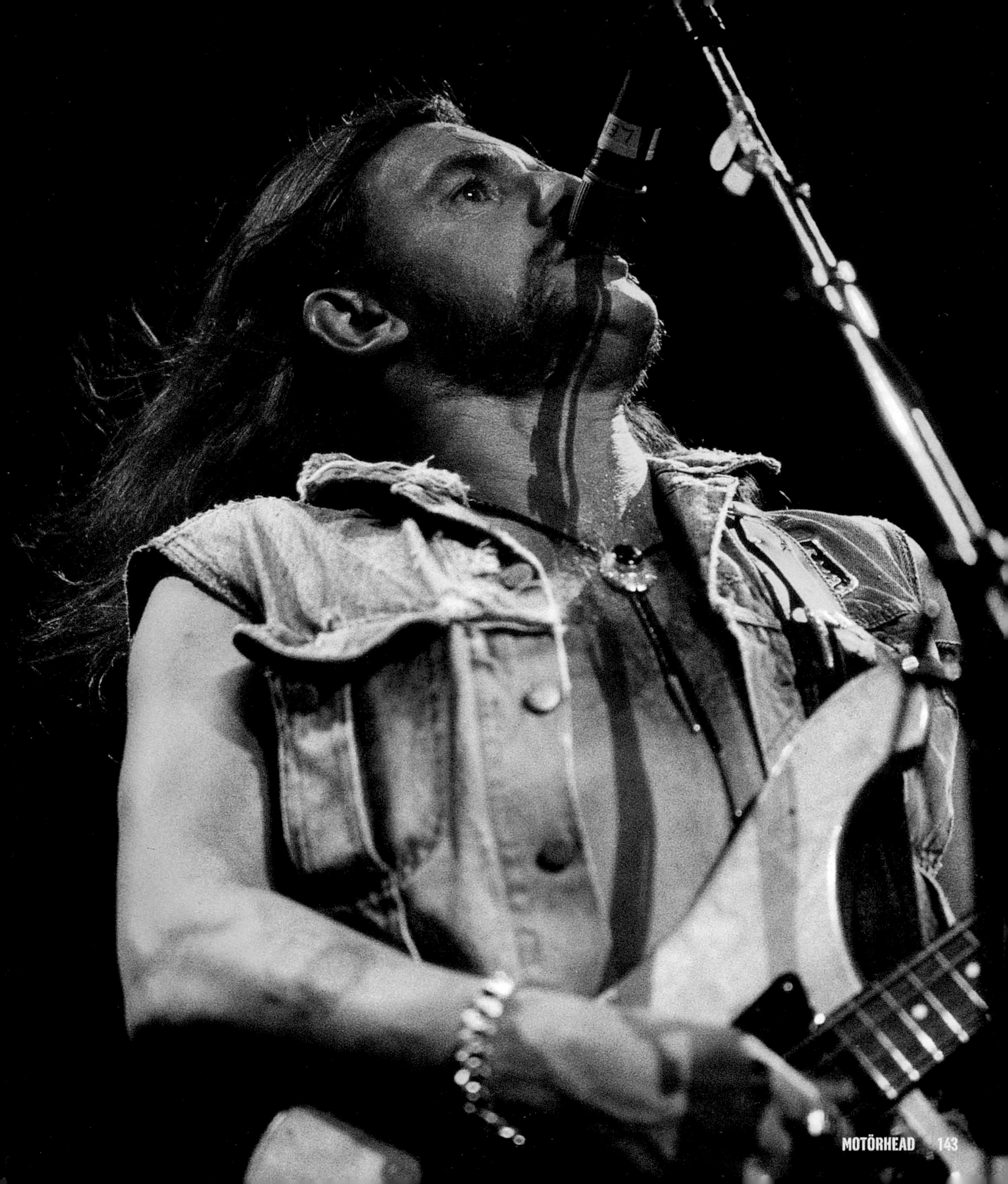

OZZY OSBOURNE

People tend to forget that after the original lineup of Black Sabbath dissolved in 1979, Ozzy Osbourne was considered a joke. He was yesterday's news. Not only was he kicked out of the band for being a drunk and a drug addict, but toward the end, he'd also become totally exiled and was no longer even fronting the band. When Sabbath played, Ozzy was literally off to the side of the stage while Tony Iommi stood in the center. Considering this history, it's remarkable to think of what he's evolved into as a solo artist.

It was a long road back after Sabbath. Ozzy was far from sober, his early solo gigs were poorly attended, and it was difficult for him to get bookings at venues. But he sounded more convincing on his own, like he knew he had more ownership over the music he was singing, and he was clearly able to reconnect with both Sabbath lovers and a whole new fan base as well. I've been critical of Ozzy's vocal abilities live. It's fairly obvious that he often has some "help" onstage, but he actually has a great, very listenable voice when recording in the studio, and the albums sound great.

CLASSIC LINEUP:

BOB DAISLEY (BASS)

LEE KERSLAKE (DRUMS)

OZZY OSBOURNE (VOCALS)

RANDY RHOADS (GUITAR)

KEY ADDITIONAL MEMBERS:

TOMMY ALDRIDGE (DRUMS)

RANDY CASTILLO (DRUMS)

GUS G. (GUITAR)

BRAD GILLIS (GUITAR)

JAKE E. LEE (GUITAR)

RUDY SARZO (BASS)

ZAKK WYLDE (GUITAR)

OPPOSITE: Ozzy Osbourne and Zakk Wylde at Brendan Byrne Arena, East Rutherford, New Jersey, December, 1988

DISCOGRAPHY

BLIZZARD OF OZZ (1980)

DIARY OF A MADMAN (1981)

SPEAK OF THE DEVIL
[LIVE] (1982)

BARK AT THE MOON (1983)

THE ULTIMATE SIN (1986)

TRIBUTE [LIVE] (1987)

NO REST FOR THE WICKED
(1989)

JUST SAY OZZY
[LIVE] (1990)

NO MORE TEARS (1991)

LIVE & LOUD (1993)

OZZMOSIS (1995)

DOWN TO EARTH (2001)

LIVE AT BUDOKAN (2002)

UNDER COVER (2005)

BLACK RAIN (2007)

SCREAM (2010)

Over the years outside of Black Sabbath, Ozzy Osbourne has become a household name. Plenty of people know him not as the frontman o Black Sabbath but as the star of the reality-TV show *The Osbournes*. think Ozzy's appeal as a solo artist changed radically with the success o his reality show and he was reinvented. He dropped the whole "prince o darkness" act and revealed himself as a father and a husband who ofter took orders from his wife. I give Ozzy credit for being so vulnerable or that show, and it earned him an entirely new group of fans. Instead of the crazy madman who bit the heads off bats, suddenly Ozzy was America's favorite bumbling husband and father. That's why I find it almost comi cal now when Ozzy is still marketed as a sinister figure. Those days have clearly passed, and Ozzy is now loved for his history, his persona, and his music.

What a lot of people don't recognize, though, is that Ozzy has neve been a major songwriter in his career. He didn't write lyrics for Sabbath and while he's a solo artist in name, he relies heavily on his backing band producers, and songwriters. Throughout Ozzy's solo career, his song: have only been as good as the musicians he has working with him, and many of them have gone largely unacknowledged. I don't mean to dimin ish Ozzy's power as a frontman, but it's also important that the people who've helped him to create his landmark recordings are given the credi they deserve. For me, there are three definitive periods in Ozzy's career each tied to his amazing guitarists: Randy Rhoads, Jake E. Lee, and Zakl Wylde.

The guy who gets the most credit for writing songs and playing with Ozzy—and rightfully so—is the late guitarist Randy Rhoads, who had previ ously been in Quiet Riot. On Ozzy's first solo record, *Blizzard of Ozz*, there

was obviously going to be an undeniable element reminiscent of Black Sabbath, but Rhoads's playing is what separated Ozzy from his past. Born of the new school of Eddie Van Halen followers, Rhoads had a style that was urgent and immediate. It had more melody, flash, and speed than Tony Iommi's and incorporated classical influences as much as modern ones. Rhoads sounded like three guitar players at once, and his riffs were incredibly huge and heavy, something that Iommi no doubt influenced. Where Sabbath was darker and a little gloomier at times, Rhoads added a brighter and more uplifting feel to Ozzy's voice. On his first two records, backed by Rhoads, Osbourne sounds reinvigorated. To the general rock fan, Ozzy's most famous hits are songs like "Crazy Train," "I Don't Know," and "Over the Mountain"—all written by Ozzy, Rhoads, and bassist Bob Daisley (a hugely important contributor). But there's so much more to Ozzy the solo artist than Ozzy and Randy Rhoads.

When Rhoads died tragically in a plane crash in 1982, it was not easy for Ozzy to find a replacement. He had enormous shoes to fill! After brief stints playing with Bernie Torme and Brad Gillis (who would later leave to form Night Ranger), Ozzy found another budding L.A. guitar hero in Jake E. Lee. He was a phenomenal player—someone who could play with the same flash as Rhoads but who clearly had his own style. Lee made Ozzy's songs relevant to what was happening in music and guitar playing at the time, and he was nonstop energy onstage. Ultimately, Lee did a great job not only in bringing his own style to the music while paying respect to what Rhoads had created before him but also by helping to write two of the most successful records of Ozzy's career: 1983's *Bark at the Moon* and 1986's *The Ultimate Sin*.

Tensions in the band led to Lee's departure and the addition of New Jersey native Zakk Wylde. I remembered seeing Zakk (or Jeff Wielandt, before Ozzy renamed him) playing on the Jersey club scene with a band called Zyris. Very much a descendant of Iommi and Rhoads, Wylde joined Ozzy's band for the 1989 album *No Rest for the Wicked*. The opening riffs to "Miracle Man" quickly identify Wylde as the best combination of the two defining guitarists of Ozzy's career. Wylde was able to merge their styles, which made for a long and productive partnership with Ozzy and created some hugely successful moments in his career. Zakk became a larger-than-life persona and also launched his own band, Black Label Society. In 2009, Zakk was replaced by a young Greek player named Gus G., whose debut as Ozzy's newest guitar discovery was on an album called *Scream*, released in June 2010.

In 1984, I was just starting to do a heavy metal radio show in New Jersey when I was approached by Ozzy's record label about being a part of his upcoming gig at the Meadowlands with Waysted and Mötley Crüe. As part of the live act, Ozzy needed an "assistant"—someone dressed as a monk—to come onto the stage and hand him a drink in a big goblet. There would be roles for my friends too, and we were all thrilled at the chance to be part of the show.

When we got to the Meadowlands that night and went backstage into a

dressing room, we were given black hooded robes to wear. They smelled disgusting—like dirty rags and body odor—and I quickly realized that they were being used in every city on the tour but never being washed. When you're eighteen years old, though, and getting ready to go onstage with Ozzy in front of twenty thousand people, you've gotta suck it up! So we put them on and were taken to a staircase that led to the side of the stage.

I was instructed that in the middle of the show, when they were performing "Center of Eternity"—which has a very long gothic intro with bells ringing and monks chanting—I was to walk up the stairs with a huge goblet filled with some Ozzy elixir and deliver it to him. He was supposed to take it from me, and I was supposed to turn around and walk back down the stairs. I was told to keep my head down and not look at the audience. It was nerve-racking! The crowd was going crazy, the arena was dark, the band was playing, and the awful smell from the robes was in my nose. When the spotlight hit Ozzy and I got my cue to start walking, my feet got stuck in the robe. I started to stumble, and someone grabbed me and helped me, but my knees were knocking. I started looking everywhere—exactly what they'd told me not to do.

As I walked across the stage, I tripped again, this time on Jake E. Lee's guitar cord. Just as I started to stumble, Jake grabbed me and moved the cord out of the way. He saved me in front of that huge crowd!

On my way back to the stairs, I remember being struck by the fact that I could hear the crowd but couldn't see past the first five rows. I was also amazed that the stage was littered with so much stuff. There were wallets, watches, somebody's crutch, car keys, chewing gum . . . I wanted to stop and pick everything up!

I've had Ozzy on my radio show by phone a few times, and my experiences with him have always been great. I think he's genuinely nice, and it's

UNDERGROUND CLASSIC

It's hardly underground, but I think the live record *Speak of the Devil* is especially cool. For those who might have missed it, it was the first album Ozzy made after the passing of Randy Rhoads. Recorded at the old Ritz in New York City, this is an album of classic Sabbath tunes performed by Ozzy's band at that time. Randy was supposed to do the record but was very much against it, as the story goes, because he didn't want to do an album of cover material.

Brad Gillis—who'd spent time in Ozzy's band but never made a studio album with him—briefly replaced Rhoads on guitar before leaving to form Night Ranger. I call Gillis "King of the Whammy Bar" and love his playing and tone on this record. The band also featured Rudy Sarzo on bass and Tommy Aldridge on drums. It's a killer lineup with some really electric versions of great Sabbath material!

Also, check out a song called "You Said It All." It was a B-side from *Blizzard* and one of the few Ozzy-Randy tracks that wasn't properly released. Lastly, I want to call attention to guitarist Joe Holmes. Joe never did a studio recording with Ozzy either, but played with him for a few years starting in 1995. He is a great player who is often forgotten in the history of those who worked with Ozzy.

cool to see someone who is so famous never seeming to take himself or the industry too seriously. But I do worry that he's staying at the party too long. It has seemed for a long time that Ozzy doesn't want to be performing anymore. It was clear for the world to see on *The Osbournes* that on many occasions Ozzy went on the road kicking and screaming. The man is a legend and an icon in the genre, but it's tough to watch someone get up there and not be able to really deliver the songs the way he once did. Just like athletes, musicians cannot keep doing it forever, and as much as it's great to see him, you wonder when he will truly say he's done. People forget that Ozzy did a farewell tour in 1996!

It's pretty obvious that Sharon calls all the shots and has carved out her own career as a reality-TV star or talent judge. Keeping Ozzy in the public eye helps her greatly. I've been vocal about this and other things that have struck me as strange in the Ozzy world. As a result, Sharon won't let him do interviews with me anymore. She's also restricted my access to him because I've spoken out about what a travesty it is that the currently in-print editions of Ozzy's first two solo records do not feature the original bass and drum tracks. They've been rerecorded by other players for financial reasons. To me, this is sacrilege. It would be like Led Zeppelin rerecording the bass and drums on their first two records! Obviously I was right, because in Ozzy's book, *I Am Ozzy*, he mentions how much it bothered him, and in 2010, special editions of both *Blizzard* and *Diary* were issued with the original bass and drums restored. I do not know Ozzy or Sharon personally, but I would hope that in her new role as a TV talent judge, whose job it is to be critical, she can now appreciate and respect that I give my honest opinion on how I feel about things. I have the utmost respect for Ozzy and his incredible legacy, but I also have respect for my audience and I simply call things as I see them.

The story of Ozzy is a remarkable one: a man who was down-and-out and reborn through the help of amazing musicians, Sharon, and die-hard fans. What he created outside of Sabbath is in some ways even more popular than what he created during his time in that groundbreaking band.

ABOVE: Rudy Sarzo, Tommy Aldridge, Ozzy Osbourne, and Randy Rhoads at Capitol Theatre, Passaic, New Jersey, April 24, 1981
OPPOSITE: Ozzy Osbourne at Capitol Theatre, Passaic, New Jersey, April 24, 1981

PANTERA

heard about Pantera from my friend, guitarist Marc Ferrari of the '80s band Keel, while I worked at Megaforce Records around 1988. Marc had started writing songs for other artists (he'd recently written "Five Card Stud" for Ace Frehley's third solo album after I put them together) and told me about a band from Texas he'd been working with called Pantera. They were aiming for a major-label deal after several indie releases, and Marc had cowritten a song or two on their album *Power Metal*, so he sent me a copy. I thought it was decent—a little glam and Van Halen-esque—but it didn't strike me as anything extremely special. I played it around the Megaforce offices, and the consensus was that Pantera was good, but not a band we were jumping to sign to the label.

PHIL ANSELMO (VOCALS)

REX BROWN (BASS)

DIMEBAG DARRELL (GUITAR)

VINNIE PAUL (DRUMS)

TERRY GLAZE (VOCALS)

OPPOSITE: Rex Brown and Dimebag Darrell at the Meadowlands, East Rutherford, New Jersey, June, 1992

DISCOGRAPHY

ABOVE: Vinnie Paul and Eddie, 2008
OPPOSITE TOP: Phil Anselmo at the
Meadowlands, East Rutherford,
New Jersey, June, 1992
OPPOSITE BOTTOM: Dimebag Darrell at
the Meadowlands, East Rutherford,
New Jersey, June, 1992

Flash forward just two years to their next album, *Cowboys from Hell*, Pantera had become a totally bruising metal band. Their level of growth from the previous record was incredible. They were much heavier, their songs had gotten so much better, and it was hard to believe that they were the same band at all. Instead of wearing their influences on their sleeves, Pantera came into their own as songwriters on *Cowboys* and threw away the glam rock. I was blown away and knew that they were quickly going to become a metal force to be reckoned with.

I started to play songs like the title track and "Cemetery Gates" on my radio show. When they toured, I went to see them at a small club in Asbury Park, New Jersey, called the Fast Lane. It was hardly packed, but they came out and played like they were headlining Madison Square Garden. I was impressed by their guitarist, then known as Diamond Darrell (aka Dimebag Darrell), and remember thinking, "This is a band that's going to up the ante in metal." Most of what was happening at the time was glam—not nearly as aggressive as Pantera's music and emphasizing style over substance. But there was Phil Anselmo, prowling and growling on that small stage. Phil was anything but pretty, Dimebag just shredded, and drummer Vinnie Paul and bassist Rex Brown locked in on some insane grooves. Pantera was able to draw a diverse fan base. They captured fans of extreme heavy metal but also somehow attracted fans of more mainstream hard rock, who were drawn to the other sides of the group's sound by mellower songs like "Cemetery Gates" and "This Love." From then on, they always walked that line and even had a decent female following for a metal act.

In 1992, Pantera went on the road opening for Skid Row on their "Slave to the Grind" tour. By then, Pantera was known as a pure power-metal band. The fact that they opened for a very commercially successful '80s hard rock band is a great example of how they appealed to both worlds. That tour served both bands well. It brought Pantera to Skid Row's more mainstream audience, and it gave Skid Row a level of credibility with metal fans that they probably wouldn't have had otherwise after being such fixtures on MTV.

Like the guys in Skid Row, the members of Pantera were all enormous rock music fans. They never stopped being fans when they became rock stars. They enjoyed all sorts of music—Southern rock, hard rock, thrash metal, glam, punk. It wasn't unusual for Dimebag or Vinnie to jam with Slayer one night and show up onstage with Poison the next. Beyond their songs, I've always really respected that about them.

But what about those songs? The best thing about Pantera's style is the groove. It's insanely heavy at times, but it always has a riff that immediately gets your foot tapping. A great example is a song like "Walk"—it's superheavy but with a guitar and a drum line you just can't help but bang your head to. It seems like almost every Pantera song has a moment that captures you in that way (and made for some unreal mosh pits at their live shows). The late Dimebag Darrell gets much of the credit for Pantera's power because of his killer guitar work—deservedly so—but I've al-

ways thought of Vinnie Paul as one of the key elements in the band. He's a monster drummer, and when he locked in with his brother Dimebag's riffs, he set the Pantera standard. He also knows a thing or two about recording and producing and put his imprint on that part of the band's career as well. Phil Anselmo was the perfect frontman. At times, Phil could sound menacing, like he was torturing someone. But he could convey softer, subtler emotions too, with a voice that could range from a howl to a falsetto. When Pantera was firing on all cylinders and relatively sober, they were a metal machine that was truly awesome.

It's pretty amazing how well their music has held up over time. With the production of their records, their playing, and Phil's voice, Pantera was always pushing it to become louder, faster, and heavier, right up to the end. They found the perfect balance of heaviness on 1992's *Vulgar Display of Power*, which is their definitive album for me and many other fans.

Pantera's live shows were also great. Anselmo brought a no-bullshit, punk attitude that seemed to promise the band would take your head off. Dimebag—not only a brilliant guitar player but also the ultimate party host—was his partner in crime, and they were an incredible mix. Their audiences were always completely appreciative and over-the-top. I saw Pantera play at Ozzfest one year, and it was incredible to watch this sea of people responding to every drum fill and each command Anselmo shouted. The band had a level of power and intensity and connection with the crowd that was different from anything I'd ever seen before.

Whenever any of the guys from Pantera released new music, I knew it would be of a certain quality. After Pantera's nasty breakup in 2003, Dime and Vinnie started a band called Damageplan. One night, they had just completed recording and mastering an album in New York, and I got a call saying that they were dying to hear it on the radio. I was asked if I'd be willing to have the whole band in the studio that night. They wanted to take the album right from the mastering studio to my radio show. Of course I wanted to premiere their new music! And I knew my radio listeners would want to hear it.

According to their record label, we were only supposed to play one song from the album. The guys were so excited, though, that they kept asking me to play more. Much to the chagrin of the label, by the end of the night we'd played five songs from the new album, months before it came out.

Everyone knows the incredible history of Vinnie's and Dime's partying. They brought a case of beer and various cocktails to my radio show, and it wasn't long before they were asking for more booze. I usually don't have alcohol in my studio, but I'd had Dimebag's extremely close friend Zakk Wylde on the air a couple of weeks prior. He'd brought me a bottle of Jack Daniel's, which he'd finished half of, so I offered the rest to Dime as long as he didn't mind Zakk's backwash. He finished the bottle and signed it with a note that said, "Thanks Eddie and Zakk for your backwash." Normally, I would've thrown something like that away, but for some reason, I stuck the bottle back in the cabinet that night. After Dime's senseless murder, I was so happy I'd kept it. It's a great reminder of that night for

1. COWBOYS FROM HELL 2. CEMETERY GATES 3. DOMINATION 4. BECOMING 5. 5 MINUTES ALONE 6. I'M BROKEN 7. GODDAMN ELECTRIC 8. REVOLUTION IS MY NAME 9. DRAG THE WATERS 10. A NEW LEVEL 11. WALK 12. THIS LOVE

EDDIE'S PLAYLIST PANTERA

me, as well as the fact that someone can be here today and gone—very quickly—tomorrow.

Dimebag Darrell's murder, which is a tragedy of incredible proportions, has been much discussed. (Dimebag was shot and killed while onstage in 2004 playing with Damageplan.) I know it's cliché to say that after someone dies, their memory lives on. But Dime really seems to be around more now than he's ever been, years after his murder. The companies that endorsed him still run the same ads for his instruments with his photos and continue to keep his brand in stores. He still appears in countless magazine articles, and Pantera's music has never been played or exposed more than it is now. He had such a love of life (and a love for Kiss—he was even buried in a Kiss casket and had Ace Frehley's face tattooed on his chest) that no one is willing to let him go. His brother Vinnie is doing his part to keep Dime's memory alive by putting out previously unreleased music and videos.

Phil Anselmo had tremendous problems with heroin and battled various addictions. He also had chronic back pain that led him to use painkillers, which have thrown him off the wagon. When he was in Pantera, his drug use was a detriment to the band. Eventually, he drifted musically and personally from the other guys in Pantera to the point that they rarely spent time together unless it was onstage. Vinnie and Dime did their best to keep the band together, but it was bound to unravel.

After the official breakup, the guys would snipe at each other in the press. In an interview, Phil said something to the effect that Dimebag needed a serious beat down, and the battle lines became clearly drawn. There are theories that the guy who eventually killed Dimebag had read those harsh comments from Anselmo and was acting on them. But no matter how nasty their fight got, Phil would've never wanted that to happen. Unfortunately, at this time, the division between Phil and Vinnie is still very great. But there have been encouraging signs that one day

they'll make some peace. When I've spoken with Phil or read interviews with him, it's clear that he's still hurting very much over Dime's death, and I hope that over time there will be a way for the guys to reconcile.

As the successor of Metallica, Megadeth, and Anthrax, Pantera was the next great metal band. I always viewed them as the ones who would carry the torch and lay the groundwork for the next wave of metal. It's a tragedy that we will never have new music from them. When you listen to '90s crossover metal acts like Korn or Limp Bizkit and pay attention to their riffs and drum lines, it's clear that many borrowed heavily from Pantera, whose influence lives on.

ABOVE: Dimebag Darrell and Ace Frehley at the Ritz, New York City, May 1, 1993
OPPOSITE: Eddie and Phil Anselmo, 2010

POISON

I clearly remember getting a copy of the first Poison album on an independent label called Enigma. The year was 1986, and I was still living at home. I tossed the album on my parents' kitchen table, and later my dad asked, "Who is that band Poison with those four great-looking girls on the cover?" True story. Poison was as glam as glam could be when they burst on the scene, and nobody could blame my father for thinking that. I'm sure he wasn't the only one at the time. But as I would also learn, you can never judge a band by its album cover. Heck, as a Kiss fan, I knew all too well how people wrote them off for looking silly and thought they couldn't play. So I cranked up that first album, *Look What the Cat Dragged In*, and loved what I heard. It's hard rock with a pop edge—huge hooks and choruses, loud guitars, and just a fun-loving sound. To this day, *Look What the Cat Dragged In* is by far my favorite Poison album.

BOBBY DALL (BASS)

C. C. DEVILLE (GUITAR)

BRET MICHAELS (VOCALS)

RIKKI ROCKETT (DRUMS)

RICHIE KOTZEN (GUITAR)

BLUES SARACENO (GUITAR)

OPPOSITE: C. C. DeVille, Bret Michaels, Rikki Rockett, and Bobby Dall at Brendan Byrne Arena, East Rutherford, New Jersey, November 17, 1990

Poison came to Los Angeles in the mid-'80s, from Pennsylvania, in search of success. They became legendary on the Sunset Strip for their work ethic, image, and festive live shows, complete with streamers and balloons. There was even a segment in the show when each member would introduce himself, something a young unknown player by the name of Slash couldn't bring himself to do when he auditioned for the band at the time! Poison built a buzz and a following, and a record deal soon followed. Over the years and decades, Poison's look, like that of many bands from the '80s, evolved to become much less glam—Bret Michaels is now known for his bandannas and cowboy hats. But regardless of the fashion, the band has always been part of that Hollywood '80s scene and proud of it.

I remember being in Los Angeles when their first album started to break. I was in the studio with the band White Lion, who were good friends and being produced by legendary engineer and producer Michael Wagener. Wagener had mixed Poison's album too. Since Poison was an indie band and had no money, he made a deal that paid him a percentage on every copy sold. It was a good time to be around Michael. As each day passed, with the album selling more and more, Michael would take me and the White Lion guys for more and more extravagant dinners, cruises around L.A. in his Rolls-Royce, and shopping sprees to Tower Records on Sunset to buy one copy of every album that had just come out. I didn't know the Poison guys yet but had no problem enjoying their success through their mix engineer!

Look What the Cat Dragged In was just edgy enough to play on my metal show, and I was very much an early supporter. Even though thrash metal was really starting to explode, Poison offered a fun alternative to my music mix on the radio, and I've always prided myself on bringing my audience a variety of hard rock and metal and presenting it equally without prejudice. Being a Kiss fan, I also enjoyed hearing their influence Poison. And it was clear that Poison was a real band, not a manufactured label product. They worked their asses off to get an album out, and they received rare commercial success for their indie-label debut. Soon Capitol Records came along and signed them to a long-term deal.

I have as much respect for them as any band of that era because they delivered what they promised: good live shows, great videos, and a party all the time. Are they the greatest players in the world? No. They would even tell you that. But rock and roll is also about writing catchy songs. How can you forget that opening riff on "Talk Dirty to Me"? And how many hearts were won with "Every Rose Has Its Thorn" or "Something to Believe In"?

Over the years I've become good friends with all the guys in the band. The differences between Bret Michaels, C. C. DeVille, Rikki Rockett, and Bobby Dall are well documented—they are far from the best of friends offstage—but somehow they keep it together the best they can because they know they are better as a unit than apart. Even though they travel on separate buses and have individual dressing rooms backstage, they still

DISCOGRAPHY

LEFT: Bret Michaels at
Brendan Byrne Arena, East Rutherford,
New Jersey, November 17, 1990
OPPOSITE: Rikki Rockett, Eddie, Bobby
Dall (back row), Bret Michaels, and C.C.
DeVille (front row), 2006

1. BLAME IT ON YOU 2. #1 BAD BOY 3. CRY TOUGH
4. LOOK WHAT THE CAT DRAGGED IN 5. I WON'T FORGET YOU
6. LOVE ON THE ROCKS 7. RIDE THE WIND 8. FALLEN ANGEL
9. STAND 10. LIFE GOES ON 11. SOMETHING TO BELIEVE IN

EDDIE'S PLAYLIST POISON

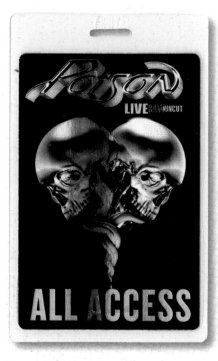

have love in their hearts for each other and respect what each member brings to the band. I've been backstage on a few occasions and have literally been caught in a tug-of-war over which member's bus I was going to hang out on after the show.

One of the most telling stories of the Poison wars happened in 2006. The band was on their twentieth-anniversary tour when Bobby and Bret actually fought onstage. The fight, and the show, ended with Bobby hurling his huge bass at Bret's head. That was how Poison celebrated twenty years of being a band!

Later that year, I was sent to L.A. to interview the band for VH1 Classic. They were making an all-covers album called *Poison'd!* and that interview was one of the first times they'd all sat together in the same room since the fight onstage. (For those who don't know, many bands do not record in the studio at the same time.) I couldn't help but ask what the hell had happened that night that had caused the band to almost break up. What I watched unfold was pretty amazing. It was as if an intervention started to take place among the band members. I quickly realized that they had never addressed the issue before and were now being forced to. Once we got into it and peeled away the layers, it turned out that Bret and Bobby themselves weren't even sure why it escalated to violence that night. Something to do with Bret's mic onstage and Bret thinking Bobby had sabotaged him. These guys fight like brothers, so once the air was clear, everyone's guard came down and the rest of the interview went well. I think, at the end of the day, the guys in Poison had just grown apart. I truly believe they love each other deep down, but they are all very different people with different interests outside the band.

I've always been closest with Bret over the years. He is a relentless worker, and I've had some of my favorite radio interviews with him in my studio. It's just nonstop fun and laughs when we get together, have a

few drinks, and crank our favorite tunes on my radio show. We are also both die-hard football fans (he's a Steelers fan; I'm all about the Giants) and love to get into sports talk as well. I've also hosted countless Poison shows, and Bret has even thanked me from the stage at times for supporting the band. It's become clear, however, that a new storm has been brewing in the Poison world, and that storm is the emergence of Bret as far and away the biggest celebrity in the band. And this is not by mistake. It seemed pretty obvious toward the end of the 2000s and as Poison entered a new decade that Bret's focus was on Bret, not so much Poison. Yes, he tours from time to time with the guys, but he's much more interested in being a solo artist. That is what drives his songwriting and what turned him into a reality-TV star with *Rock of Love* and *The Celebrity Apprentice*.

I was one of the few people who could not watch *Rock of Love*. I love Bret, but the show just seemed ridiculous (then again, I feel that way about most reality TV). However, it succeeded in doing exactly what Bret wanted—exposing him to a whole new fan base. Soon my seventy-year-old aunt was calling me, asking if I really knew Bret Michaels! Yeah, for like twenty years! Why did she care all of a sudden? The next time I went to see Poison I realized why. Among the rockers, the audience was full of housewives and their daughters, who'd come not so much to hear Poison but to see Bret. Everything had changed. The balance of power in any band always falls to the frontman, but this was a massive shift. Bret ran toward his new celebrity like an Olympic sprinter, leaving C.C., Bobby, and Rikki to wonder if they would ever have Poison again.

That question remains unanswered. Bret loves attention and press, and a tragic event in May 2010 gave him more press than ever when he almost died of a brain hemorrhage. As horrible as this was, it also added to his celebrity status. Now he was on *Oprah* and in *People* magazine. Bret did so much press from his deathbed that some even accused him of faking it! Thankfully, he recovered, but outside of a possible twenty-fifth-anniversary tour with Poison, his total focus is on Bret solo.

But no matter how big Bret gets, there are still more fans to be had with a Poison reunion. We have seen throughout history that often the band name is bigger than any one single member. Do you think Guns N' Roses would be playing arenas with Axl Rose as the only original member if the act was billed as "Axl Rose" and not "Guns N' Roses"? So there is still some life left in Poison if they can keep from killing each other onstage and off. They are all good guys who I have enjoyed long friendships with—and they've had a string of huge hits and been one of the few bands to come from the '80s hair metal scene that can still draw a crowd. It takes more than makeup and bandannas to get people to still crave the raunchy, glam band with the party songs that Poison epitomizes. Without tunes that stand the test of time, even the best-looking bands fade away.

DID YOU KNOW

Poison had a couple of replacement guitarists in the '90s when C.C. was forced out of the band because of substance abuse. By far the greatest musician to have ever been in Poison is guitarist Richie Kotzen, who appeared on the album *Native Tongue*. Kotzen is an incredible player, writer, and singer (check out his solo albums *Go Faster*, *Into the Black*, and *Peace Sign*), and the one album he did with the band was a huge evolution for Poison. Sadly, Kotzen was booted from the band after a few years for having an affair with Rikki's girlfriend on the road, but you can only wonder what a new Poison would have been like going forward with a guy of his talent. C.C. is the best guy for Poison because he captures the band's spirit and energy so well, and he played on all the classic Poison songs, but check out Kotzen and you will be blown away.

QUEEN

How could a book on essential hard rock and metal not include Queen? Although the band was commercially successful in the States, their fame overseas was unparalleled. Unfortunately, Queen's importance—like that of Thin Lizzy, Deep Purple, and others—is not as fully recognized here in the United States. Don't get me wrong—in the mid- to late '70s, Queen had strong U.S. arena tours, but overseas they often played to much bigger crowds in stadium venues. Robert Plant, lead singer of Led Zeppelin, once told me that, in his opinion, Queen is the most beloved British rock band of all time in the U.K. Queen was proud to be British, and they sounded British too. They were a hard rock band at the core but one with a high level of majesty and theatricality that delivered a little something for everyone.

CLASSIC LINEUP

JOHN DEACON (BASS)

BRIAN MAY (GUITAR)

FREDDIE MERCURY
(VOCALS)

ROGER TAYLOR (DRUMS)

KEY ADDITIONAL MEMBER

PAUL RODGERS (VOCALS)

OPPOSITE: Freddie Mercury and Brian May at Madison Square Garden, New York City, February 5, 1977

DISCOGRAPHY

QUEEN (1973)

QUEEN II (1974)

SHEER HEART ATTACK (1974)

A NIGHT AT THE OPERA (1975)

A DAY AT THE RACES (1976)

NEWS OF THE WORLD (1977)

JAZZ (1978)

LIVE KILLERS (1979)

THE GAME (1980)

FLASH GORDON (1981)

HOT SPACE (1982)

THE WORKS (1984)

A KIND OF MAGIC (1986)

THE MIRACLE (1989)

INNUENDO (1991)

LIVE AT WEMBLEY '86 (1992)

MADE IN HEAVEN (1995)

Queen was a pioneer in the rock world. Their early music was incredibly heavy for its time, and they influenced many metal bands with their mammoth guitar sound, Brian May's intense riffs, and incredible lead vocals by the late, great Freddie Mercury. Mercury and May's harmonies, bassist John Deacon, and drummer Roger Taylor, created an awesome vocal symphony that cannot be matched. Queen's choruses—often achieved with multilayered vocal tracks and overdubs—were as massive as the sound of Brian's guitar, and to me, that is the true signature sound of the band. It's what makes them one of the most identifiable bands of all time. Listening to the opening of "Somebody to Love" or the huge sing-along chorus in "Tie Your Mother Down" is all the proof you need that this band's vocal ability is one of its many trademarks.

Queen's first two albums, *Queen* and *Queen II*, were dark and heavy—strongly influenced by heavy metal and progressive rock. But it wasn't until their third album, 1974's *Sheer Heart Attack*, that America took notice. (Metallica later covered "Stone Cold Crazy" from this record as a homage.) It was on *Sheer Heart Attack* that they started to incorporate a vaudeville element alongside the hard rock, and they perfected this combination on their next record, *A Night at the Opera*. Released in 1975, *A Night at the Opera* was at the time the most expensive recording ever made. It featured long instrumentals and the mind-blowing "Bohemian Rhapsody," which became one of the bestselling singles of all time.

Queen continued to push boundaries and include many styles in their music. While still drawing on their prog, metal, and glam roots, they created a gospel choir with their voices on "Somebody to Love," wrote the ultimate stadium anthem with "We Will Rock You," incorporated rockabilly in "Crazy Little Thing Called Love," and even introduced synthesizers and disco in "Another One Bites the Dust." What other band has used so many styles while playing and singing them so well? The production and performances on each of Queen's albums were also groundbreaking. Performers from all these genres took note and emulated Queen's layered vocal tracks and big guitars. Every Queen recording captured a certain grandeur that consumed listeners and set the bar for the whole rock world.

I was very young when the power of Queen's music hit me. It was even before I discovered Kiss. I was in elementary school during the mid-'70s, and the smash hit "Bohemian Rhapsody" was all over the radio. Even at an early age, I knew I was hearing some pretty mind-blowing stuff. All these complicated, haunting vocals over the piano, and then, the best part, when the guitar and band kicked in and it ROCKED!

For my fifth grade talent show, I proposed to a group of friends that we should perform "Bohemian Rhapsody." The show was just a few weeks away, and even though I was in the school band and could play the bass drum, performing a Queen song was way beyond my talent range. Rather than actually singing and playing, we decided we would simply lip-synch the song and act out its parts. That would be our talent—acting like rock stars but not really playing a note (something some real rock stars have

actually been caught doing over the years). Queen was always great live and really made their shows a spectacle, so to stay true to the band, we needed some sort of light show for our performance. When more friends asked to join our group, I decided I would step out from my role as performer and assume the job of running the lights. To the side of the stage in the school gym, just out of sight, was a giant panel with switches for a few different colored lights recessed in the ceiling. The plan was that the performance would start with one guy at the piano playing Freddie's part, and then the curtain (which I was responsible for raising) would go up to reveal the band when the heavy part kicked in. When the day of the performance arrived, nerves were high. I had also taken on a stage manager-type role, making sure everyone knew the song and which places to chime in with their fake instruments. Everything went off without a hitch: Just when the heavy part of "Bohemian Rhapsody" kicked in, I raised the curtain with one hand and flicked the light switches at a feverish pace with the other. Even though there were only green, red, and blue lightbulbs, I thought it was the greatest light show ever. I remember

ABOVE: John Deacon, Freddie Mercury, and Brian May at Madison Square Garden, New York City, February 5, 1977

EDDIE'S PLAYLIST

QUEEN

1. GET DOWN, MAKE LOVE
2. SHEER HEART ATTACK
3. I'M IN LOVE WITH MY CAR
4. WHO WANTS TO LIVE FOREVER?
5. HAMMER TO FALL
6. DRAGON ATTACK
7. OGRE BATTLE
8. FAT BOTTOMED GIRLS
9. SPREAD YOUR WINGS
10. STONE COLD CRAZY
11. TIE YOUR MOTHER DOWN
12. BRIGHTON ROCK
13. NOW I'M HERE
14. ONE VISION
15. LIAR

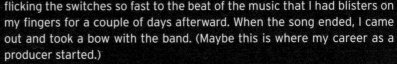

ABOVE: Roger Taylor at Madison Square Garden, New York City, February 5, 1977

flicking the switches so fast to the beat of the music that I had blisters on my fingers for a couple of days afterward. When the song ended, I came out and took a bow with the band. (Maybe this is where my career as a producer started.)

Many years later, in 2006, I saw Queen and Paul Rodgers in Las Vegas. I was hired as a producer for an awards show called "Rock Honors" that VH1 was doing, and Queen was being given a tribute, along with Judas Priest, Def Leppard, and Kiss. Obviously, Queen without Freddie will never be the same, but Rodgers did a solid job. I remember taking a walk around backstage and watching while all the bands that were playing the event rolled in cases and cases of gear, amps, guitars, effects, and more. Then I saw where Brian May's area was. There was only one guitar case, and in it, a single guitar. It was the guitar that May had used to create the essential Queen sound. My friend and I simply stood there in awe. It was almost like that scene in *Spinal Tap*—we were expecting someone to come over and say, "Don't even look at it." Later that night, I met May for the first time. It was obvious that he was not only a brilliant musician but also a brilliant person in general, with interests and knowledge far beyond music. That was proved in 2009 when he earned a Ph.D. in astrophysics. Not your average rock star by any means.

In the summer of 2009, I met May again. I was in England at the Down-

load Festival taping for *That Metal Show*. My cohosts and I heard that Brian was backstage and that he had come to see our friends, the members of the band Dream Theater, who are massive Queen fans and had just covered one of their songs. Brian came over and recorded almost thirty minutes with us on our set. He was a total gentleman, and it was an honor to talk with him again. There's always seemed to be a certain level of class to whatever Queen did or does, and I can't help but think that extends directly from Brian May. Their albums and songs are truly timeless, and because of the incredible strength of their material, when Brian May and Roger Taylor perform together as Queen, they are still able to draw stadium-size audiences around the world. And they somehow manage to retain that classic Queen sound.

DID YOU KNOW

Freddie Mercury was a guest on albums by a number of artists, including Billy Squier. Billy opened several shows for Queen, and Freddie provided a guest vocal on a great song called "Love Is the Hero" on Squier's *Enough Is Enough* album.

LEFT: Brian May at Spectrum, Philadelphia, November, 1978

RAINBOW

ainbow's two definitive lineups are very different from each other. It was actually the second incarnation of the band—the '80s-era group fronted by Joe Lynn Turner—that I first came to know when I won *Difficult to Cure* at a boardwalk stand on the Jersey shore. I was curious about the band's strange and mysterious guitarist, Ritchie Blackmore—the virtuoso who'd also played with Deep Purple—and drawn to the image of guys in surgical scrubs on the cover. When I listened to the record, the idea that this dark, elusive guitarist was playing commercial hard rock was a strange contrast that I wasn't prepared for. But with a singer as powerful and tremendously melodic as Turner, Rainbow was easy to like.

CLASSIC LINEUP:

JIMMY BAIN (BASS)

RITCHIE BLACKMORE (GUITAR)

TONY CAREY (KEYBOARD)

RONNIE JAMES DIO (VOCALS)

COZY POWELL (DRUMS)

KEY ADDITIONAL MEMBERS:

GRAHAM BONNET (VOCALS)

JOE LYNN TURNER (VOCALS)

DOOGIE WHITE (VOCALS)

OPPOSITE: Ritchie Blackmore at Spectrum, Philadelphia, June 29, 1982

DISCOGRAPHY

OPPOSITE: Joe Lynn Turner at
Spectrum, Philadelphia, June 29, 1982

It wasn't until a few years later that I realized what I'd come to know as Rainbow's sound wasn't really indicative of the band's roots. A friend told me to check out their albums from the '70s with Ronnie James Dio on vocals. On early albums like 1975's *Ritchie Blackmore's Rainbow* and 1979's *Down to Earth*, Rainbow was a radically different-sounding band. Outside of Blackmore, there were none of the same players and with Dio on vocals, the lyrics and sound were a lot more in line with what I'd initially expected from this band.

It may have been the '80s era of Rainbow that I discovered and saw countless times live, but it's the '70s version with Dio on vocals that holds up in retrospect. I still enjoy the melodic Joe Lynn version, but the music made with Ronnie really captures the majesty of Rainbow. Dio's songs are far less commercial than Turner's and more adventurous. With all respect to Joe, who has been a good friend over the years, I think the Dio records are more innovative and timeless.

With Dio on vocals, Rainbow had more elements of Deep Purple—a versatile, exceptional singer and longer songs with the possibility for free-form jams. Live, this version of the band would do incredibly long improvisations of their songs. The 1977 live album *On Stage* captures this: It has only six songs! And Dio's Dungeons and Dragons-style lyrics and imagery suited Blackmore's mystique.

What I've always loved about Ritchie's playing is the way he wove his notes between the rhythms and how he led the song through the verses. He could rip with the best of them, but there was always a certain texture and style to his riffs that went beyond his solos. With the Dio lineup, the late Cozy Powell was always one of my favorite drummers. His powerful drumming always takes you somewhere when you hear it.

When Dio parted with Ritchie, to replace Ozzy Osbourne in Black Sabbath, Rainbow made an album with Graham Bonnet on vocals, *Down to Earth*, which is actually a really good record. Though it was the only album Rainbow recorded with Bonnet, its songs, like "Since You've Been Gone" and "All Night Long," got more radio play in America than anything from the Dio era. Though the Dio-fronted Rainbow is the most revered among metal fans and the most popular globally, with Bonnet on vocals, Blackmore was finally able to crack the U.S. market.

For Blackmore, this taste of U.S. commercial success made him look for an American singer with American sensibilities—someone who could help Rainbow gain more radio play in the States. Joe Lynn Turner has told me many times that his mandate from Blackmore was very simple: "Get me on the radio in America." And Joe did exactly that. Though there was initially a lot of backlash from fans who were appalled at the legendary European rock band's transition to playing four-minute tracks sung by an American—and lots of middle fingers from the audience at live shows—the formula worked. For the first time in the band's history, they became an arena act and scored what are still considered classic rock standards with songs like "Street of Dreams," "I Surrender," and "Stone Cold."

Though this version of the band was viewed as a sellout by many, I liked

it because it was my introduction to them. And Turner was even from my home state of New Jersey! While the music was much more commercial, there was still an element of danger and mystery when you saw them live. Blackmore was such a wild card that you never knew what you were going to get with him—whether he would storm offstage because the sound wasn't right or because someone was wearing a T-shirt he didn't like. You just never knew what kind of a mood he'd be in when he came onstage.

Over the years, both of Rainbow's most well-known lead singers, Dio and Turner, became very close friends of mine. I've mentioned Ronnie in other chapters of this book, but Joe is a lot of fun to talk to and hang out with too. He still lives in New Jersey, and we've done countless interviews together. Unfortunately, Joe has never been able to capture the level of success he had with Blackmore and Rainbow in the '80s. He's spent much of his career trying to recapture that, singing with Yngwie Malmsteen (who is very much a disciple of Blackmore's) and forming a version of Rainbow with Blackmore's son called Over the Rainbow. He's also released a string of solo albums and tours regularly around the world. Outside the United States, Joe has a very loyal following, mostly generated from his days with Ritchie Blackmore. Joe would no doubt love to reunite Rainbow, but Blackmore has been reluctant.

After a short-lived lineup with singer Doogie White, Rainbow broke up for good in 1997. The band has never reunited. When Blackmore met a younger woman named Candice Night, who would become his wife, she pulled him into the world of Renaissance music and he abandoned hard rock completely. Ritchie has always had that style in his playing, so the move wasn't totally out of left field, but I'm not the only fan who wishes he would fire up that Strat and play a little hard rock again.

I've never met Ritchie Blackmore, but he lives on Long Island. My radio show reaches that market, and I know for a fact that he has heard many of his former bandmates on the air with me discussing how they'd love to reunite with him. I know he's also heard me saying how much I want to see him do Deep Purple or Rainbow again. I've received offers to have him on my show—of course, I'd be honored to—but they've always come with conditions. For example, I could only discuss his current project, Blackmore's Night, and wouldn't be allowed to mention Rainbow or Deep Purple. As someone who does a hard rock show, I can't pretend they don't exist! And needless to say, Blackmore's Night is a stretch for what I do.

The reason Blackmore doesn't want to be interviewed about those bands has more to do with past business than a push to sell his current project. The majority of the time, the decision making in the history of any band can be traced back to money and contracts and other business dealings. Apparently Ritchie signed some bad deals with the companies that managed Deep Purple and Rainbow, and outside parties ended up owning a big stake in those bands' catalogs. Blackmore's refusal to acknowledge those bands has been a way to shun the people who wronged him with those shady deals.

I had been railing on radio for years that Ritchie needed to stop pretend-

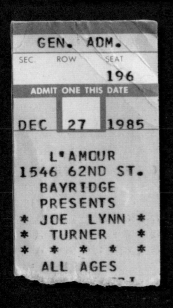

EDDIE'S PLAYLIST

RAINBOW

1. LONG LIVE ROCK 'N' ROLL
2. CATCH THE RAINBOW
3. GATES OF BABYLON
4. MAN ON THE SILVER MOUNTAIN
5. JEALOUS LOVER
6. I SURRENDER
7. STARGAZER
9. DEATH ALLEY DRIVER
10. EYES OF THE WORLD
11. CAN'T LET YOU GO
12. ALL NIGHT LONG
13. TAROT WOMAN
14. KILL THE KING
15. STONE COLD
16. POWER

ing that he worked at Medieval Times and rock again. At an event where I was doing a meet and greet, a woman came up to me and introduced herself as Candice Night—Ritchie Blackmore's wife, the woman who'd turned him on to medieval music and who was all too aware of the things I'd said. To her great credit, she was very cool and told me she understood where I was coming from, but that I ought to listen to what they were doing now because it was much more rock-based than I was giving it credit for.

Unfortunately, her sales job was ineffective with me. I went back, at her request, and listened to Blackmore's Night again. I tried to find something to like or connect with, but I'm still searching. I've never claimed to be an eclectic fan of music, but I just cannot get into what they're doing. I still hold out hope that Blackmore will come back to hard rock, even if it's just for one show, but by all accounts, I shouldn't hold my breath. Regardless, of whether we see a reunion or not, the music Ritchie created with both Deep Purple and Rainbow is something to truly cherish.

DID YOU KNOW

The current lineup of Billy Joel's touring band features two former members of Rainbow from the '80s lineup: drummer Chuck Burgi and keyboardist David Rosenthal.

Graham Bonnet, who sang on the Rainbow album *Down to Earth*, never really set out to be in a metal band. He had done some session work in England that led him to the gig, which explains why he never looked the part with his short hair and skinny-tie style.

Ritchie Blackmore at Spectrum, Philadelphia, June 29, 1982

RUSH

grew up listening to WDHA-FM, the New Jersey radio station where I would eventually get my first job in radio. On weeknights, it would play full albums, and sometimes I would record them on tape. If I really liked something, I'd go out and buy it on record. One night in 1980, the station played *Permanent Waves* by Toronto's Rush. It was the first time I'd ever heard them.

The album's opening track, "Spirit of Radio," sucked me in immediately. It sounded completely fresh. Its great guitar solo, adventurous drumming, crisp production, and incredibly distinct, high-pitched vocals made it obvious that Rush was much more accomplished musically than a lot of the bands I had been listening to. I listened to the record from start to finish on the air. Then I rewound the tape I had just made and listened to the whole thing again. From the powerful first track to the moody last song, "Natural Science," with its beachy sound effects, the album was an all-consuming experience.

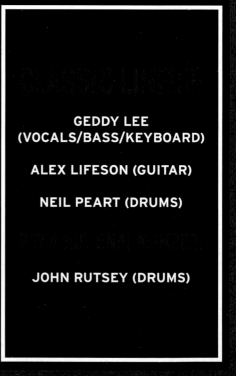

GEDDY LEE
(VOCALS/BASS/KEYBOARD)

ALEX LIFESON (GUITAR)

NEIL PEART (DRUMS)

JOHN RUTSEY (DRUMS)

OPPOSITE: Alex Lifeson, Neil Peart, and Geddy Lee at the Palladium, New York City, May 11, 1980

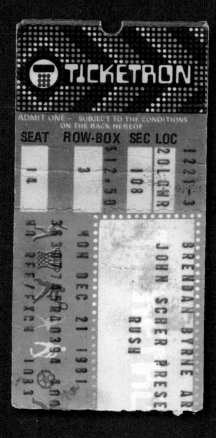

I didn't know that Rush had released a bunch of records before *Permanent Waves* because the band never had hit singles or got any kind of major radio play or media coverage. With epic concept songs, progressive instrumental arrangements, and interesting time changes, they were anything but commercial. To get caught up on their catalog, I bought *Chronicles*, their first three albums packaged together. I quickly learned how dynamic this band was. Their songs were guitar-driven but their subject matter was really unusual. Bassist Geddy Lee sang lyrics written by drummer Neil Peart about science fiction, fantasy, poetry, and other things that were so "out there" that I sometimes wondered if he even knew what he was singing about. (Geddy would later tell me that he often didn't!) They also had twenty-minute-plus songs, which I had never encountered before. Rush's ambitious music took some time to sink in, but when it did, they became one of my favorite bands.

In their early days, Rush was influenced by a lot of the blues-inspired British hard rock bands of the time, like Led Zeppelin, Cream, and the Yardbirds. And as a result, their music took on much of that flavor. But when original drummer John Rutsey was replaced by Neil Peart after their first album, Rush became a whole other entity with a completely different approach. Neil is one of the greatest drummers of all time, and his musical ability is well known, but he is also extremely well read. Not only did he shape the band's sound by his playing, but when he took over writing lyrics, he changed their direction too.

DISCOGRAPHY

RUSH (1974)

FLY BY NIGHT (1975)

CARESS OF STEEL (1975)

2112 (1976)

ALL THE WORLD'S
A STAGE [LIVE] (1976)

A FAREWELL TO KINGS
(1977)

HEMISPHERES (1978)

PERMANENT WAVES (1980)

MOVING PICTURES (1981)

EXIT . . . STAGE LEFT
[LIVE] (1981)

SIGNALS (1982)

GRACE UNDER PRESSURE
(1984)

POWER WINDOWS (1985)

HOLD YOUR FIRE (1987)

A SHOW OF HANDS
[LIVE] (1989)

PRESTO (1989)

ROLL THE BONES (1991)

COUNTERPARTS (1993)

TEST FOR ECHO (1996)

VAPOR TRAILS (2002)

RUSH IN RIO
[LIVE] (2003)

SNAKES & ARROWS (2007)

SNAKES & ARROWS
LIVE (2008)

CLOCKWORK ANGELS
(2011)

It's sometimes hard to comprehend that Rush's big sound is created by only three players. Of course, there is some multitasking going on. Geddy Lee plays keyboards in addition to providing his classic, deep bass sound and unique singing style. Neil Peart sounds like five different drummers at once, though he never overplays, and he brought many diverse percussion instruments, including electronic drums, to the band's songs. And Alex Lifeson is such a unique player that you can easily forget that the band has only one guitarist.

Rush's earliest albums—those from the '70s to the early '80s—are still my favorites. After 1981's *Moving Pictures*—the last of their albums that I love from start to finish—the band changed too much for my taste. They started to introduce a lot of multilayered synthesizers and place less emphasis on Lifeson's guitar playing. That's where they lost me. The song "New World Man," from the album *Signals*, was the first warning that they were becoming something a young metalhead like me wouldn't be interested in. The song opens with a gurgling synth sound, without the usual Rush edge, and with its reggae flavor, it sounds more like something by

ABOVE: Neil Peart at Madison Square Garden, New York City, March 8, 1994
OPPOSITE: Alex Lifeson and Geddy Lee at PNC Bank Arts Center, Holmdel Township, New Jersey, August 14, 2004

EDDIE'S PLAYLIST

RUSH

1. SOMETHING FOR NOTHING
2. DISTANT EARLY WARNING
3. LA VILLA STRANGIATO
4. WHAT YOU'RE DOING
5. FINDING MY WAY
6. LAKESIDE PARK
7. IN THE END
8. CYGNUS X-1
9. THE TREES
10. ANTHEM
11. BU2B
12. 2112

13. CLOSER TO THE HEART
14. THE SPIRIT OF RADIO
15. JACOB'S LADDER
16. RED BARCHETTA
17. BASTILLE DAY
18. STICK IT OUT
19. ENTRE NOUS
20. IN THE MOOD
21. HERE AGAIN
22. CARAVAN
23. XANADU
24. YYZ

the Police than the blazing power trio I had loved. They retained some of the quintessential Rush qualities—that incredible musicianship and Geddy's unmistakable voice—but they weren't the same band I'd grown up with. Though I soured on them for pretty much *all* of the '80s and into the early '90s, I've always loved what Rush did as a progressive-leaning hard rock band. Even if I wasn't into it, I respected them for taking chances and evolving.

Known for their live shows, Rush has released multiple live albums. My favorite is still the first one, the 1976 album *All the World's a Stage*. It's the sound of a young, not-so-polished band—not perfect, but that's why I like it. It truly captures the raw energy of the live experience of some of my favorite material. Interestingly enough, in their very early days, Rush toured with one of my favorites: Kiss. Although I was too young to see those early shows, I often imagine what it would have been like to see those two young and hungry bands together on the road. Both Ace Frehley and Peter Criss have told me stories about how much fun those tours were, as have Geddy and Alex.

Perhaps what is most remarkable about Rush is the fan base they've accumulated. Despite fairly limited radio play, Rush maintains some of the most passionate and loyal fans I've ever seen. Predominantly male, Rush fans seem to see themselves in Geddy Lee, Neil Peart, and Alex Lifeson—

ABOVE: Geddy Lee at Continental Airlines Arena, East Rutherford, New Jersey, December 15, 1996

they are such anti-rock stars. Beyond the music, a large part of their appeal is the type of people they are. The way they talk and dress and act is a lot more like guys who grew up reading sci-fi than guys who made great progressive hard rock records. Their fans can say that the Rush guys probably didn't go to their proms either, but look where they ended up. In any city the band tours, their audience averages twenty thousand a night. Having fans who stick with them has given Rush the freedom to experiment and create things the way they want to, evolving musically without fear of commercial backlash.

When Geddy Lee released a solo album called *My Favorite Headache* in 2000, he called into my radio show from Canada for an interview. My great friend Mike Piazza, who was playing for the New York Mets at the time, was in the studio with me. Geddy is an enormous baseball fan and couldn't believe that this baseball star was on the other end of the phone. Mike is a huge Rush fan, so he said to Geddy, "I see you in the stands at

ABOVE: Neil Peart at the Palladium, New York City, May 11, 1980

all of the spring training games in Florida. Why don't you ever come and say hello?" Geddy said, "I can't do that! *You're* Mike Piazza!" Mike had the same response: "*You're* Geddy Lee from Rush! I can't say hello to you!"

I've interviewed Geddy and Alex Lifeson—who handle all the press for the band—several times for VH1 Classic. They've told me that they always enjoy doing interviews with me because I know their history, and most people who interview them don't go beyond the bio and their most well-known songs, like "Limelight" and "Tom Sawyer." Neil Peart has always been reclusive. In the late '90s, Peart endured a tragic period when his wife and daughter died just ten months apart. It nearly broke him and the band, he took a break for five years and checked out of all press and band-related activities. He's since remarried, but he's remained the guy who no one gets to talk to. So it was pretty incredible when, in 2006, I got a call from a publicist who said that Neil was interested in doing an interview with me—and only me—for VH1 Classic to promote a book he'd just written. He'd seen the interviews I'd done with Geddy and Alex over the years, and he liked my style. I was incredibly flattered, and it's still one of the things I'm asked about all the time.

When an artist comes to the TV studio, they usually arrive with all sorts of handlers: managers, publicists, record label people. And they often have demands, like certain drinks or food in the greenroom, that no still photos be taken, or that they will only come at a certain time of day. Neil showed up by himself and with only a backpack. He just rang the doorbell to be let in. The intern who answered the door thought he was there to deliver food! The icon of rock just strolled in off the street without any entourage or demands—he was friendly to everyone and even hung out after the show to take photos with people. The only time I saw Neil recoil was when people made a big deal about him being there. He's notoriously shy, so when people made a scene, it made him visibly uncomfortable. As long as he was treated like one of the guys, he'd stay and talk forever. This is true for many artists: If you geek out in front of them, they're going to pull back. But Neil and I spent over an hour on the street in front of the studio after the interview, chatting as all of New York City walked by. No one knew who he was, and that's what Neil loves most.

In 2007, VH1 Classic's studio closed temporarily and many people were let go. Rush's record label called me to see if I was working anywhere in TV, because Geddy and Alex wanted to do an interview with me for their album *Snakes & Arrows*. I told them that I wished I could do the interview, but I didn't have anywhere to do it. They told me to come to the Atlantic Records offices and they would produce a video interview themselves. Geddy and Alex were loyal and adamant about continuing their interview streak with me. The interview was included on a DVD and a download for the special editions of that album.

Though I don't stay in regular contact with the guys, I have a great working relationship with them. When I started doing the first season of *That Metal Show* in 2008, I was booking most of the guests myself. At that time, the show had never aired. No one had seen it, or knew what it was,

so the guests had to trust me. I told my producer that I wanted to take a shot at booking Rush, but nobody thought I could pull it off. I called their management in Canada and let them know about the new show. I was told that the message would be relayed to the guys and that they'd get back to me, but I knew this was a long shot. We didn't even have a budget to fly people to New York or put them up in a hotel! But the next day, I got a call saying that Geddy and Alex would love to be on my show and would pay their own way to New York, the day after a major Canadian holiday.

They were great on the show. My cohosts, Don Jamieson and Jim Florentine, are comedians, and though Rush is considered to be a thinking man's band, Geddy and Alex held their own and showed their great sense of humor. I told them that I couldn't thank them enough for doing the show when they didn't even know what it was, and they said, "We'd do anything for you, Eddie. We trust you, and we feel like we owe you." Having that kind of connection with legends like Rush was and is amazing.

In 2010 I was invited to the premiere of the Rush documentary *Rush: Beyond the Lighted Stage* in New York City. Geddy and Alex came out to introduce the film and then left because they couldn't stand to see themselves on a movie screen. At the after-party, I had a great time talking to the guys. Alex told me that I would love the new music they were making because it was heavy and more like their old power-trio sound. I'm happy to say that he was right! What I didn't know was that Alex Lifeson had been right there with me all those years, fighting to get his guitars louder and bigger-sounding on the Rush albums I didn't like! It was a relief to know that he'd been thinking the same thing as me in a battle with Geddy to bring back the edge. Songs like "BU2B" and "Caravan" are some of the best Rush songs in more than thirty years. In a day and age when most bands retain only one original member and are living off nostalgia, Rush remains classic in every way—accomplished and innovative musicians who have remained true to each other and their fans. They are simply one of the greats.

DID YOU KNOW

When Rush tours, Neil Peart often rides his motorcycle to the band's next gig instead of taking the tour bus. Neil loves to ride and see whatever country he's traveling through up close. He takes back roads and often stops to chat with people who have no idea who he is. It's not unusual for Neil to get right on his bike after the last note rings out at a show, hit the road, and not be seen by his bandmates until a few hours before they take the stage again.

ABOVE: Don Jamieson, Eddie, Ace Frehley, Geddy Lee, Alex Lifeson, Jim Florentine, and Ron "Bumblefoot" Thal backstage at *That Metal Show*, October 15, 2008
OPPOSITE: Alex Lifeson at PNC Bank Arts Center, Holmdel Township, New Jersey, August 14, 2004

SCORPIONS

I didn't know Scorpions until I won a copy of 1980's *Animal Magnetism* on the Jersey Shore boardwalk when I was fifteen. Back then, I chose my music by album cover—not the best policy, but it served me well, since many of the albums I chose were not being played on the radio. Since Scorpions have a long history of using bizarre and controversial album art (1976's *Virgin Killer* features a naked, prepubescent girl behind shattered glass), it's not surprising that I was struck by the provocative cover of *Animal Magnetism*. It features a woman kneeling on the beach and looking up at a man whose back is to the camera as he holds a beer—while a Doberman pokes its head into the frame. It's total *Spinal Tap*! I wasn't sure what was going on in the *Animal Magnetism* cover photo, but it was strange enough that I wanted to hear the album. And with its superpowerful rock, catchy riffs, and great guitar playing by Matthias Jabs, *Animal Magnetism* instantly made me a huge fan of this German band.

CLASSIC LINEUP:

FRANCIS BUCHHOLZ (BASS)

MATTHIAS JABS (GUITAR)

KLAUS MEINE (VOCALS)

HERMAN RAREBELL (DRUMS)

RUDOLF SCHENKER (GUITAR)

KEY ADDITIONAL MEMBERS:

JAMES KOTTAK (DRUMS)

ULI JON ROTH (GUITAR)

MICHAEL SCHENKER (GUITAR)

OPPOSITE: Rudolf Schenker and Klaus Meine at Brendan Byrne Arena, East Rutherford, New Jersey, April, 1991

Many of Scorpions' covers were designed by a company called Hipgnosis, which had done numerous popular and artsy covers for bands like Pink Floyd and UFO, to name a few. Hipgnosis specialized in images that made you scratch your head but immediately got your attention. Scorpions got into trouble, however, for the covers that seemed to denigrate women. The original cover for the 1979 album *Lovedrive* features a woman and a man in the back of a limo, with his hand attached to her bare breast by a string of chewing gum. Just crazy stuff. The cover of *Lovedrive*, like that of *Virgin Killer*, was later changed in the United States.

Soon after winning *Animal Magnetism*, I discovered Scorpions' back catalog of multiple albums from the '70s. I realized, with the 1978 double live album *Tokyo Tapes*, that Scorpions had a huge, longstanding global following. I wondered how I'd never heard of them! It wasn't until a few years later, in 1982, that Scorpions broke stateside with their album *Blackout* and its hit "No One like You." Ironically, "No One like You" was an old song that the band had written years earlier. It was a hit only in America—nothing more than an album track everywhere else in the world—and rarely played live outside the United States.

Though I prefer the later Matthias Jabs era for its more contemporary production and interesting hooks, the early albums recorded with Uli Jon Roth on guitar have some of the band's best material. Very much a disciple of Hendrix in all ways—with a similar onstage persona and hippy clothes—Roth is highly regarded by other guitar players for his groundbreaking style. He helped to shape the stomping, militant precision of the very German Scorpions sound. Anyone who saw Metallica on their 2009 Death Magnetic tour heard Kirk Hammett break into an Uli riff from "The Sails of Charon" mid-solo. Kirk has often said that Uli (along with Michael Schenker, who was briefly the guitarist in Scorpions) is one of his biggest influences. Uli had a very distinctive style that seemed to weave in and out of the songs in a way that's hard to explain. His riffs were as interesting as his solos, and when he played he looked as if he was channeling some spirit of Hendrix or another guitar god. Uli departed Scorpions on good terms in 1978, wanting to play different styles of music and expand his vision. He also wanted to do instrumental work, something he does to this day. He had a desire to break free from the confines of a hard rock band but still pops up from time to time as a guest with Scorpions.

When Uli left, the band enlisted Michael Schenker to play lead on the *Lovedrive* album. Rudy's younger brother had played on the band's debut, *Lonesome Crow*, as a teenager and had just left UFO for the first time. Michael's second stint with the band was short-lived, and he was permanently replaced by Matthias Jabs, who holds the job to this day. Jabs was a big Hendrix fan too, but his playing is sharper and more radio-friendly than Uli's. In a 2010 interview I did with Matthias, I pointed out the coincidence that both he and Uli were such big Hendrix fans. Matthias quickly clarified that, unlike Uli, he loved Hendrix's playing but didn't think he actually *was* Hendrix! Jabs, injected the contemporary flash and attention to melody that Scorpions needed to make Americans take notice.

DISCOGRAPHY

LONESOME CROW (1972)

FLY TO
THE RAINBOW (1974)

IN TRANCE (1975)

VIRGIN KILLER (1976)

TAKEN BY FORCE (1978)

TOKYO TAPES [LIVE] (1978)

LOVEDRIVE (1979)

ANIMAL MAGNETISM
(1980)

BLACKOUT (1982)

LOVE AT FIRST STING
(1984)

WORLD WIDE LIVE (1985)

SAVAGE AMUSEMENT (1988)

CRAZY WORLD (1990)

FACE THE HEAT (1993)

LIVE BITES (1995)

PURE INSTINCT (1996)

EYE II EYE (1999)

MOMENT OF GLORY:
THE SCORPIONS WITH THE
BERLIN PHILHARMONIC
[LIVE] (2000)

ACOUSTICA [LIVE] (2001)

UNBREAKABLE (2004)

HUMANITY: HOUR 1 (2007)

STING IN THE TAIL (2010)

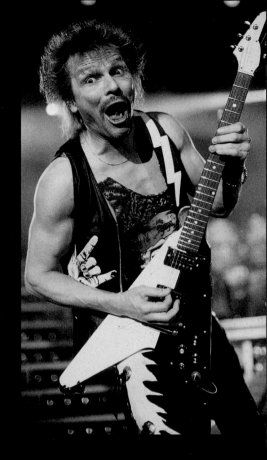

They had their Eddie Van Halen in Jabs, and suddenly Scorpions were constantly on MTV and the radio. They released *Blackout* and *Love at First Sting* and were viewed as a new '80s band in the United States, when in fact they had been around for more than fifteen years.

Scorpions were and still are best known for their live shows. Anyone who's seen them knows that they're one of the most powerful live bands imaginable. With antics like forming a human pyramid onstage, they're also really fun. Scorpions' energy and effort, not to mention their tight sound, are unbelievable. Klaus Meine is a small man but a big presence onstage. He never stops moving—even when the band is jamming, Klaus stays out onstage hitting a cowbell or dancing around. The guitar duo of Rudolf and Matthias works so well together, with Jabs smiling and soloing and Rudy sprinting around the stage pumping out the riffs. James Kottak is also a powerhouse drummer who drives the band. Outside of the energy of the live shows, which sometimes last for more than two hours, the band's real power, I think, comes from the music and songs themselves. Sometimes they sound even better live than they do on their records. Like a lot of bands, Scorpions struggled throughout the 1990s. Instead of do-

ABOVE: Rudolf Schenker at
Brendan Byrne Arena, East Rutherford,
New Jersey, April, 1991
OPPOSITE: Matthias Jabs, New Haven,
Connecticut, June 10, 1984

EDDIE'S PLAYLIST

SCORPIONS

1. THE SAILS OF CHARON
2. WE'LL BURN THE SKY
3. LOVING YOU SUNDAY MORNING
4. ANOTHER PIECE OF MEAT
5. VIRGIN KILLER
6. BLACKOUT
7. THE ZOO
8. SLAVE ME
9. ALWAYS SOMEWHERE
10. ANIMAL MAGNETISM
11. HE'S A WOMAN– SHE'S A MAN
12. CATCH YOUR TRAIN
13. COMING HOME
14. CHINA WHITE
15. LOVEDRIVE
16. IN TRANCE
17. HOLIDAY

ing what they do best, they got caught up in trends and scrambled to stay afloat. No matter what went on in the studio, though, or how they suffered commercially, there were still few bands that were better or more consistently powerful live.

In 2007, Scorpions released *Humanity: Hour 1*. It was the first sign that they were returning to their roots as a blazing hard rock band. The band worked with producer and writer Desmond Child (the man behind huge hits for bands like Bon Jovi, Aerosmith, and many others), and their new material was closer to what everyone wanted to hear. That year, they headlined the German festival Wacken and released a DVD called *Scorpions Live at Wacken*. If you want to see what I mean by their live power, just watch it. It is one of the greatest live DVDs I've ever seen. You'll also get to see them bring many former band members onstage for a song or two.

For a band that initially had trouble cracking the American market, Scorpions' songs are now part of pop culture. Their chainsaw guitar sound is easily recognizable, and "Rock You like a Hurricane," from 1984's *Love at First Sting*, even appears in Coors beer commercials (which the guys told me they weren't aware of during a 2010 visit to my radio show!). But when you listen to songs like "Animal Magnetism" (which is featured prominently in Marisa Tomei's strip scene in the 2009 Mickey Rourke film

DID YOU KNOW

Current Scorpions drummer James Kottak joined the band in 1996 at the suggestion of original drummer Herman Rarebell, who saw him perform when he was a member of the band Kingdom Come. Both bands played together on the Monsters of Rock tour in the mid-'80s. James is married to Tommy Lee's younger sister, Athena, who is also a drummer and plays in her husband's side band, simply called Kottak.

The Wrestler) or "China White," you hear a whole other side to Scorpions—haunting, heavy riffs that show some real darkness and a bit of why they've been influential to a lot of metal bands. The Scorpions also have some epic ballads like "Lady Starlight" and "Holiday" and scored massive hits with "Still Loving You" and "Wind of Change." While at their core they're a slamming European-sounding rock band, they have something for everyone.

In 2010, Scorpions announced their retirement with a farewell tour and album called *Sting in the Tail*. It's their best album in decades. Around this time, I spent an evening with them over drinks in Los Angeles. They'd been in town promoting their new record and had just put their handprint in Guitar Center's Hollywood RockWalk. Most bands do farewell tours because they've run out of steam, they don't really like each other, or they feel that their creative well has run dry. But what I saw that night was that the guys in Scorpions are still very good friends. Despite being in their sixties, they looked great and had written their best material in twenty years. So I asked them why they were packing it in. They said that regardless of how they looked, their choice to quit was simply about being realistic. They know the standard they've set for themselves as a live act and by recording top material like *Sting in the Tail*, so they just couldn't imagine going through another cycle of touring and recording at over sixty years old, which would be the case for founding members Klaus and Rudy. Unlike so many bands that do farewell albums or tours only to reform and go for another cash run, Scorpions are sincerely calling it a day for the right reasons. Not only are they one of the best bands I've ever encountered live, but they're also one of the classiest.

When you listen to their music and hear how well it holds up—how timeless it is—it's no surprise that Scorpions have been such a global force. After all these years, I can still get excited when I think about seeing them live. Their last record and tour are a perfect finish to their incredible career.

ABOVE: Francis Buchholz, Rudolf Schenker, Klaus Meine, and Matthias Jabs at Buffalo Memorial Auditorium, Buffalo, New York, July 3, 1982
OPPOSITE TOP: Klaus Meine at Brendan Byrne Arena, East Rutherford, New Jersey, April, 1991
OPPOSITE BOTTOM: Rudolf Schenker at Merriweather Post Pavilion, Columbia, Maryland, June 19, 2010

SKID ROW

New Jersey's Skid Row remains, to this day, one of my favorite bands of the 1980s. Instead of chasing radio and TV play by making a more accessible album after their hugely successful debut (which most bands would have done), the Skids got meaner and heavier and saved their credibility. They earned the respect of groups like Pantera and Alice in Chains (who opened for them) by moving out of the hair-band world.

As a Jersey native, I was aware of the band from very early in their career. They were great self-promoters in those days, taking out ads for shows in the local music papers and even holding softball games to build buzz in different ways and make personal connections with potential fans. They were a good band with good songs and good players, but they were missing something to make them "great." No one was jumping out of their skin to go see them. Founding members guitarist Dave "Snake" Sabo and bassist Rachel Bolan worked with a couple of different singers back then, but it wasn't until the arrival of Canadian import Sebastian Bach in 1988 that people really started to take notice. How could you not?

CLASSIC LINEUP

ROB AFFUSO (DRUMS)

SEBASTIAN BACH (VOCALS)

RACHEL BOLAN (BASS)

SCOTTI HILL (GUITAR)

DAVE "SNAKE" SABO (GUITAR)

KEY ADDITIONAL MEMBERS

DAVE GARA (DRUMS)

JOHNNY SOLINGER (VOCALS)

PHIL VARONE (DRUMS)

OPPOSITE: Rachel Bolan and Sebastian Bach at Brendan Byrne Arena, East Rutherford, New Jersey, March, 1992

DISCOGRAPHY

SKID ROW (1989)

SLAVE TO THE GRIND (1991)

B-SIDE OURSELVES (1992)

SUBHUMAN RACE (1995)

40 SEASONS:
THE BESTOF SKID ROW (1998)

THICKSKIN (2003)

REVOLUTIONS PER MINUTE
(2006)

There was nothing subtle about Sebastian. At over six feet tall with long, blond hair and chiseled features, he demanded attention with his good looks and boisterous, monster energy, and his voice was incredibly powerful. He could scream as loud as Rob Halford or slip into a dirty growl, but he could also sing in a soft falsetto. With Sebastian as their frontman, the Skids were playing the same songs they'd always played, but with a completely different, much more aggressive attack and unforgettable vocals. Bach hit the stage and didn't stop moving. He was a swirl of energy and he gave the other guys a kick. Suddenly, everyone in New Jersey and beyond was talking about Skid Row.

I remember going to a club in Newark, New Jersey, called Studio One to see the band with Bach for the first time and there was a string of limos out front—not a common sight at that venue or in that area of New Jersey! Execs from all the major record labels were coming to see the band and their new star. A bidding war began between Geffen and Atlantic Records to sign them. With additional support from Snake's longtime buddy Jon Bon Jovi (who took them on the road to open stadium tours), things really went supernova.

Atlantic ended up signing Skid Row, and the band quickly traveled to Wisconsin—where they couldn't get into trouble—to record their self-titled debut. It was around this time, in 1988, that I first started getting to know them. I was working for Megaforce Records and attended Atlantic Records' fortieth-anniversary event at Madison Square Garden. Skid Row was the newest band at the label and still relatively unknown. We hung out for a bit in the VIP area, and the guys learned that I had just signed Ace Frehley, who hadn't been heard from in several years, to Megaforce. Being huge Kiss fans, they begged me to tell Ace about them, so we went to a pay phone and I got Ace to talk to Bas (Sebastian) and Snake. They were blown away. The fact that we were around the same age, into the same music, and from the same scene created a bond between us that we have to this day. As a matter of fact, some of the Skid Row guys ended up singing backing vocals on Ace's album *Trouble Walkin'* in 1989, not long after I introduced them.

Of all the guys in the band, Snake and I have always been the closest. When he came back from recording in Wisconsin, he asked me to stop by so he could play me some of the finished album. They were struggling to decide on a first single and he wanted my input. The choices were album-opener "Big Guns" or "Youth Gone Wild." We sat in a production studio at my old radio station WDHA and I had a listen. As soon as I heard the line in "Youth Gone Wild" where the band sings, "It's just SKID ROW," I looked at Snake and said, "That's got to be it!" "Youth Gone Wild" ended up being the world's introduction to the band a few months later. The album would spawn several hits, including modern classics "18 and Life" and "I Remember You," and would sell more than two million copies in the United States alone. Even though the money and fame started rolling in, they always appreciated their fans and acted like the same buds from Jersey.

Between records, Skid Row evolved very quickly and showed tremen-

Photo by Mark Weiss

dous growth as players and writers—the Skids just had better songs than most other bands of the time. Bach became a monster figure in the world of heavy rock. Snake and Rachel never pumped out filler or wrote disposable "I love you, honey—let's go screw in the backseat" kinds of songs. They told stories with thoughtful lyrics on tracks like "Quicksand Jesus." They had the substance to back up their edgy, from-the-streets look.

Album two, 1991's *Slave to the Grind*, is even louder and heavier than their debut—something no band with big radio support would have done at the time. I remember being at Nassau Coliseum, where they were opening for Aerosmith, and Snake taking me into the tuning room. He played the beginning of "Monkey Business" on his guitar and said it was something new they were working on. Even hearing it in that primitive form, I knew it would be massive, and it was when *Slave* was released a few years later. Killer songs like "Quicksand Jesus," "In a Darkened Room," "Wasted Time," "Psycho Love," and the title track still blast on my iPod all the time. Even though it didn't have a hit at the level of "18 and Life" or "I Remember You," the album was still very successful and showed Skid Row to be a real major player, not a one-trick pony. *Slave* also became the first heavy metal album to enter the *Billboard* charts at number one.

It was fun hanging out with the guys in Jersey at the time. Snake purchased a big house with a studio in the basement and had a pet pig named Buttlick that he kept in a crib. Crazy rock-and-roll times! We would get some beer and listen to old Kiss and UFO. I still love remembering those days. But the good vibes around the band started to go as quickly as they'd arrived. Sebastian had become the focus and face of Skid Row, and that, coupled with his controversial behavior, started to weigh on the band. Needless to say, when *Rolling Stone* put only Sebastian on its cover in a 1992 issue, it didn't sit well with some. The other guys wanted recognition as the key founding members and songwriters, but generally the

ABOVE: Rob Affuso, Dave "Snake" Sabo, Scotti Hill, Eddie, Ace Frehley, Rachel Bolan, and Sebastian Bach backstage at Brendan Byrne Arena, East Rutherford, New Jersey, 1989

1. SWEET LITTLE SISTER 2. HERE I AM 3. MAKIN' A MESS
4. QUICKSAND JESUS 5. IN A DARKENED ROOM 6. FIRESIGN
7. MUDKICKER 8. EILEEN 9. FROZEN 10. BREAKIN' DOWN
11. GHOST 12. BORN A BEGGAR 13. LAMB 14. NOTHING

EDDIE'S PLAYLIST SKID ROW

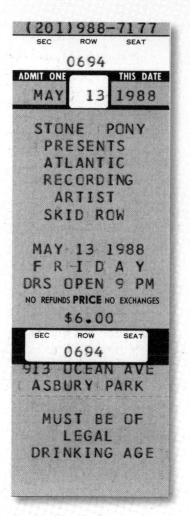

(201) 988-7177

SEC	ROW	SEAT

0694

ADMIT ONE		THIS DATE

MAY 13 1988

STONE PONY
PRESENTS
ATLANTIC
RECORDING
ARTIST
SKID ROW

MAY 13 1988
F R I D A Y
DRS OPEN 9 PM

NO REFUNDS **PRICE** NO EXCHANGES

$6.00

SEC	ROW	SEAT

0694

913 OCEAN AVE
ASBURY PARK

MUST BE OF
LEGAL
DRINKING AGE

ABOVE: Sebastian Bach,
Alex Lifeson, and Eddie, 2010

public doesn't care who wrote or produced the music, just who they see singing it. And Bas was every bit the star. A power struggle started, with Bach wanting more of a say in the band and a role in the songwriting, while Rachel and Snake wanted to continue to control that end.

The stress continued as the band started their third full-length album in 1995, *Subhuman Race*. It's the final album with the original lineup. If *Slave* is heavy, *Subhuman Race* takes it to a whole new level. This is Skid Row as an all-out metal band. To this day, I think it's one of the great, somewhat overlooked classics in metal. Produced by Bob Rock, the album is heavy as hell, with Bas just screaming his head off—it's more aggressive than anything he's ever sung. There are totally heavy, crushing riffs and guitar trades from Scotti Hill and Snake, and the best-ever drum performance from Rob Affuso. *Subhuman* may be the sound of a band imploding, but I still love it. Though it didn't have any hits, there's tons of amazing material.

Tensions got worse on the tour for the album, and the breaking point came in 1996. Kiss had offered Skid Row a slot opening for them on their reunion tour at the Meadowlands. This was a dream come true for Sebastian, but the other guys weren't feeling up to it at the time. They needed some time off, and they were not rehearsed and ready for the gig. The vote was to pass on the date. This did not sit well with Bach, who called Snake and blasted him and the rest of the band on his answering machine for ruining his dream. It was at that point, Snake told me, that he made the decision to pack it in with Bach once and for all. The original lineup of Skid Row pretty much ended that day.

Snake, Rachel, and Scotti started a new band called Ozone Monday, which actually did open for Kiss, further rubbing salt in the wounds! Sebastian started a solo career and also made a name on Broadway in *Jekyll and Hyde* and *The Rocky Horror Picture Show* and on TV as an actor, singer, and host. Skid Row launched a new version of the band in 2000 with a new singer, Johnny Solinger, from Texas. Because Skid Row was so

identified with Bach, Solinger had huge shoes to fill. He does a great job vocally, but he's not the maniac frontman Bach was. The band to date has released two albums with Johnny on vocals: the very strong *Thickskin* and the poorly received *Revolutions per Minute*. I actually like both albums, though, *RPM* suffers from fewer contributions by Snake.

I have been very vocal that the band should reunite. Both Sebastian Bach and Skid Row still tour heavily, and with all due respect to Johnny, the time is now for this band to get the original lineup back together and kick some ass once again.

UNDERGROUND CLASSIC

I can't recommend *Subhuman Race* enough. Although it didn't have a hit, it is such a killer album, loaded with heavy grooves and riffs. Some of my all-time favorite songs are on this album, such as "Firesign," "Eileen," "Frozen," "Breakin' Down," and so many more. I'll never forget sitting in the back of Sebastian's Jaguar outside the Stone Pony in Asbury Park, New Jersey, while he cranked out the demo for "Frozen" and sang every word an inch from my face. Every time I hear the song, that image comes to me. Classic Bas!

Dave "Snake" Sabo and Sebastian Bach at the Chance Theater, Poughkeepsie, New York, January, 1989

SLAYER

This chapter should really be called "Fuckin' Slayer," because that seems to be their real name. If you've ever gone to a Slayer show, then you know that's all you can hear being screamed from the top of every set of lungs. I've introduced Slayer many times, and I know better than to stay out on the stage too long. My friend, baseball great Mike Piazza, once told me he would lend me his catcher's gear when I went out to intro Slayer in case stuff was thrown at me from the crowd. (And I'm one of the few who actually plays the band on the radio!) Slayer shows are that intense. The audience is a sea of rabid animals and the red meat is Slayer. Fans have even been known to rip out seats bolted down to the floor! Early in Slayer's career, no band ever succeeded in opening for them; the fans just wanted "Fuckin' Slayer"!

CLASSIC LINEUP

TOM ARAYA (VOCALS/BASS)

JEFF HANNEMAN (GUITAR)

KERRY KING (GUITAR)

DAVE LOMBARDO (DRUMS)

KEY ADDITIONAL MEMBERS

PAUL BOSTAPH (DRUMS)

JOHN DETTE (DRUMS)

OPPOSITE: Tom Araya at the Izod Center, East Rutherford, New Jersey, August 12, 2010

DISCOGRAPHY

PPOSITE: Jeff Hanneman at
NC Bank Arts Center, Holmdel Township,
ew Jersey, July 16, 2004

The band has some of the most loyal, hard-core fans in metal history. Why? Because Slayer are heavier than anyone else and they don't care at all what others think or what the trends are. They are also totally outspoken about how they feel about anything you ask. You will never get a politically correct answer from these guys. They march to their own beat and sound, and if you don't like it, step aside. I once heard my good friend Scott Ian of Anthrax describe Slayer's music as "the soundtrack to hell," and that's a great way to sum it up. Slayer plays some of the fastest, meanest thrash metal ever created, with touches of punk, hardcore, and even death metal thrown in. Dueling guitarists Jeff Hanneman and Kerry King, lead screamer and bassist Tom Araya, and superdrummer Dave Lombardo (perhaps metal's finest) make up the band's classic and original lineup. Few bands, if any, embody speed-thrash metal better. Toss in some satanic visuals for effect and controversial, violent lyrics and you have the ultimate metal band.

Aside from their heaviness and speed, what's truly remarkable about Slayer is their fan base. Early on, it was a bunch of angry dudes in denim and leather, but somehow, without any airplay or hit singles, they added a whole new generation of fans and, shockingly, a huge female fan base as well. I'll never forget seeing Slayer shows in the 2000s and noticing there were almost as many women as men in the audience. The albums are one thing for Slayer, and they have some great ones, but this band does most of its damage on the live stage. It's just a relentless assault of lights, guitars, and drums (and even some blood) at warp speed for nearly two hours. It's not out of the norm to see fans leaving a Slayer show injured. Those who venture into the pit often leave bloodied or with broken bones. It's that intense.

Slayer's music has had a huge influence on many of the new-school metal bands from the '90s and beyond. Through classic albums like *Reign in Blood* (many argue over which is the masterpiece of thrash, *Reign in Blood* or Metallica's *Master of Puppets*) and *South of Heaven*, their moodier follow-up, they've proved that you can make the music you want and perform it how you want without compromise and still have a huge level of success. If Slayer didn't have the balls to do it their way and break so much new ground when they came on the scene, metal never would have evolved like it did. Slayer has made a huge mark, especially in the death metal world. With the Rick Rubin–produced *Reign in Blood*, they unleashed one angry, ten-track blast that continues to influence extreme artists to this day.

To hang postshow with Slayer is almost as dangerous as going into the pit. This is a band with a Jägermeister endorsement, after all, and your liver will take a pounding should you enter into their dressing room. I once attended a Slayer show with Mike Piazza while he was playing with the Mets. He had a game the next day but was still brave enough to come backstage with me and say hi to the guys. Kerry was in a dark corner, mixing some shots and pouring them into Slayer shot glasses. It is not an option to deny having a shot with Slayer. Problem is, it's often many,

DID YOU KNOW

Pantera was one of the many bands influenced by Slayer, and guitarist Kerry King even appears on the Pantera song "Goddamn Electric." His guest guitar solo was recorded in one take in a bathroom backstage at a Pantera gig.

ABOVE: Tom Araya at
PNC Bank Arts Center, Holmdel Township,
New Jersey, July 16, 2004

EDDIE'S PLAYLIST
SLAYER

1. SEASONS IN THE ABYSS
2. EYES OF THE INSANE
3. PSYCHOPATHY RED
4. ANGEL OF DEATH
5. DEAD SKIN MASK
6. WAR ENSEMBLE
7. BLOODLINE
8. WORLD PAINTED BLOOD
9. MANDATORY SUICIDE
10. SOUTH OF HEAVEN
11. RAINING BLOOD
12. PIECE BY PIECE
13. KILLING FIELDS
14. DISCIPLE

many shots! As Kerry handed Mike and me shots of his special brew, Mike was caught in a bad spot. He didn't want to seem like a wimp, but he also had no idea what was being mixed up by Kerry and could not risk being hungover and having to catch nine innings in hundred-degree heat the next day. Each time Kerry would look away, Mike would toss his shot over his shoulder into a potted plant in the corner. Kerry seemed impressed at how Mike handled his booze, having no idea the plant in the corner was going to die from alcohol poisoning the next day. I was not so smart and ended up in almost as bad a shape as the plant.

In 2009, I came up with the idea to do celebrity record reviews on an episode of *That Metal Show*. But the segment would only work if the reviewers were brutally honest and didn't worry about what they said. Who could we get? The answer was easy: Slayer! Don Jamieson, Jim Florentine, and I shot the segment at a dive bar in New York City with Kerry and Dave, and man, did they deliver. They were critical and outspoken about albums by Metallica and many others, even tossing some CDs on the floor in disgust. Metallica's latest album, *Death Magnetic*? "Nice attempt." Stryper's *Soldiers Under Command*? Smashed against the wall. Of course, there were plenty of albums that earned high praise as well, but the opinions were honest and flowing like the beers in front of us that day.

Slayer are rightfully acknowledged as one of the "Big Four" of thrash

metal. Because they are so outspoken, they often find themselves at war with other bands of the genre. Issues between Slayer and Dave Mustaine of Megadeth have been around forever, but finally, at the end of 2009, a peace was reached. (I never could really put my finger on the trouble between these guys. Much of it came from the press and the fact that both Mustaine and Slayer speak their minds with no filter or politically correct answers.) The guys were older and wiser and knew that continuing an old feud was a waste of time. Slayer also knew that playing with a band like Megadeth would be something fans of both bands would like to see, so they sucked it up and played some shows together in Canada.

In early 2010, it was announced that the Big Four would play on a bill together in Europe at the massive Sonisphere Festival. The peace between Slayer and Mustaine was an uneasy one, but in the interest of metal fans, everyone agreed to make it work. In April 2010, I was in L.A. doing some interviews on the red carpet for a metal awards show called the Golden Gods. When Kerry and Dave joined me, Don, and Jim at the press podium, we were no sooner into the Slayer conversation when a clearly wasted Dave Mustaine literally came stumbling into the shot and onto our stage. You could see the expressions on Kerry's and Dave's faces change instantly—tension you could cut with a knife. By Slayer standards, they did everything they could to bite their tongues but were clearly pissed. Mustaine was feeling no pain and had no idea. Kerry told me several times later that night how angry he was and how close Slayer came to ending the truce with Dave right then and there. He wasn't happy that Dave crashed their party during the interview on camera. But if there is such a thing as a kinder, gentler Slayer in their older age, Kerry took the high road and let it go. As a result, the Big Four did play Europe in June 2010 in an event that was simulcast back to American movie theaters. Megadeth and Slayer continue to tour together.

Nobody in his or her right mind could argue the importance of Slayer to metal. Love them or hate them, they are true pioneers of the thrash genre with a fury all their own. They are the most intense metal band to ever come on the scene.

ABOVE: Kerry King at
PNC Bank Arts Center, Holmdel Township,
New Jersey, July 16, 2004

BILLY SQUIER

Some may be surprised by the inclusion of Billy Squier in a book on hard rock and metal, but to me, he has been an immensely important influence on the hard rock world for a variety of reasons, both personal and professional. You see, technically, Billy was the first artist I ever saw live and the first artist I ever truly championed on the radio.

My first concert was Kiss at Madison Square Garden on December 16, 1977. I was thirteen, and the experience set me on my path to be consumed not only by Kiss but also by rock music in general. The band that opened that show was called Piper, a group I had no knowledge of at the time. So officially, Piper was the first band I ever saw perform. I remember watching from my seat high up in Madison Square Garden (in "Blue Heaven," as the upper seats are known, both for their blue color and for being so far away from the action) and feeling the energy as a real live rock band took the stage. I was amazed that I was so far from the stage yet the music was still so loud! I wondered how guitars could be amplified like that (remember, I was thirteen). I would later find out about amplification, and also about Piper, led by Billy Squier.

BOBBY CHOUINARD (DRUMS)

MARK CLARKE (BASS)

JEFF GOLUB (GUITAR)

BILLY SQUIER
(GUITAR/VOCALS)

ALAN ST. JON (KEYBOARD)

DOUG LUBAHN (BASS)

OPPOSITE: Billy Squier at Giants Stadium, East Rutherford, New Jersey, June 12, 1989

DISCOGRAPHY

Piper was a band with a three-guitar attack. Billy Squier wrote all the songs, sang lead, and was very much its leader. They were a hard rock band but also had elements of power pop—melodic but with hard-hitting guitars. To this day, I still love some power pop, and the two albums Piper released in the late '70s, *Piper* and *Can't Wait*, are real gems. I went and picked them up after seeing Piper open for my heroes at MSG and still listen to them now. Piper never made it, but Billy struck out on his own, releasing his debut solo album, *Tale of the Tape*, in 1980. The album sounds very similar to Piper's releases, and why not? After all, it's the same songwriter and singer steering the ship. I loved *Tale of the Tape* and reviewed it favorably when I started writing for my high school newspaper that year. Even though the album failed to make Billy a star, it has some great songs—some of which were sampled by hip-hop giants like Jay-Z, Run DMC, and others years later. It also has a remake of a great song from Billy's Piper days called "Who's Your Boyfriend (I Got a Feelin')." Though rare for an artist to cover his own song, it's cool to hear this more straightforward, harder version.

As great as it was having Billy as my own personal discovery in the rock world, 1981 brought the release of his second album, *Don't Say No*, full of hard rock classics that were loved by the masses. I was about to enter my senior year in high school, and since I was known as the class music geek, I was asked, along with a small group of other students, if I wanted to learn about radio. My high school didn't have a radio station, but my hometown of Madison, New Jersey, had three colleges, including Drew University. Drew University had a small, ten-watt station on campus that the students wanted to keep running during the summer break. I was only too happy to volunteer and learn about radio, as it was another way to share the music I loved with many people (or in the case of a ten-watt college station, about ten!). On my first day of training I was asked to cue up an album track to play. The guy showing me how to do it directed me to the mail that had just come in that day. It contained lots of new releases, so I grabbed the box on top and opened it, and there was the radio-ready *Don't Say No*. I was excited to have one of the first tracks I played on any radio station be from Billy Squier, an artist I was already a fan of and knowledgeable about, so I cued up the first song, "In the Dark." I still remember how great it sounded: Opening with a swell of synthesizer (a sign of the times), it kicked into ringing guitars and power chords. In my short time at Drew University's WMNJ, I made sure to play something from *Don't Say No* every time I was on the air. My interest in radio was ignited by that brief experience, and soon Billy Squier's career would explode.

Don't Say No quickly became a smash hit. Tracks like "In the Dark," "Lonely Is the Night," "Too Daze Gone," "The Stroke," and "My Kinda Lover" became the soundtrack to 1981 and are still staples on classic-rock radio today. I think Billy's success and his signature combination of melody and a heavy rock edge had a major influence on the artists that came after him, especially those in the mid-'80s hair metal scene and many pop-rock acts. People tend to forget just how big Billy was. Bands

Jon Bon Jovi and Billy Squier
at Brendan Byrne Arena,
East Rutherford, New Jersey,
March 10, 1989

OPPOSITE: Billy Squier at Brendan Byrne Arena, East Rutherford, New Jersey, August 9, 1982

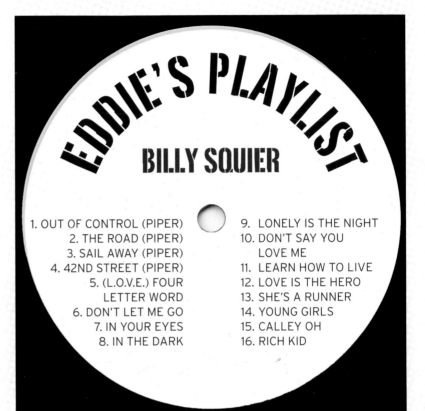

EDDIE'S PLAYLIST

BILLY SQUIER

1. OUT OF CONTROL (PIPER)
2. THE ROAD (PIPER)
3. SAIL AWAY (PIPER)
4. 42ND STREET (PIPER)
5. (L.O.V.E.) FOUR LETTER WORD
6. DON'T LET ME GO
7. IN YOUR EYES
8. IN THE DARK
9. LONELY IS THE NIGHT
10. DON'T SAY YOU LOVE ME
11. LEARN HOW TO LIVE
12. LOVE IS THE HERO
13. SHE'S A RUNNER
14. YOUNG GIRLS
15. CALLEY OH
16. RICH KID

like Ratt and Def Leppard were opening for Billy in arenas at the time. He reached a male and female audience equally and wrote some incredible songs, memorable hooks, and albums that still hold up well today. And his strong voice could range from a Robert Plant wail to a soft falsetto. To me, many of Billy's best songs are not his hits. I've always felt he is a great and somewhat underrated songwriter and lyricist who's never received the credit he should have. There is so much brilliant music deep in his catalog other than "The Stroke." Right up until his final rock album, *Tell the Truth*, Billy has at least a half dozen great songs on every release.

I've seen Billy countless times over the years after my formative Madison Square Garden experience. Especially memorable was the album-release party for *Hear & Now* at the China Club in New York City. The album wasn't out yet, but someone at Capitol had given me an advance cassette. My buddy Bill and I were a few rows from the front of the stage, and when Billy played the then-new material, we sang along to every word. We could see Billy looking at us while he sang these unreleased songs. After performing a new track from *Hear & Now*, Billy said right from the stage, "Hey, how the hell do you guys know the words to these songs?" Billy acted like he was kind of pissed but then laughed it off, and at the end of his set he invited us to join him onstage to sing the chorus for "The Stroke" with some other fans.

DID YOU KNOW

Billy had one of the best record deals of the time back in the mid-'80s. Coming off of hit albums like *Don't Say No* and *Emotions in Motion*, he renegotiated his contract to get a massive advance. Billy was incredibly smart on the business end. He held on to his publishing rights—a gold mine for any successful songwriter—and also had a special arrangement so that his label, Capitol Records, could not recoup money from his advance if an album underperformed. Essentially, he had guaranteed money for a long string of albums and a contract that prevented him from being dropped by the label. When Billy's sales started to diminish, Capitol wanted to offer him reduced advances and asked him to contribute his own marketing costs. A settlement was reached in which, instead of receiving future large advances, Billy would gain the rights to his catalog and ownership of it would revert to him after a few years. Billy Squier now owns his catalog and publishing completely—something that's extremely rare for an artist. With his songs being sampled and appearing in various commercials and TV shows, he's financially secure in a time when most artists struggle greatly once they're out of the spotlight.

TESLA

will never forget the first time I heard Tesla. I was working for Megaforce Records, which was run out of the label owner's house. MTV had a request hour in the afternoon, and one of my duties was to watch the channel, dial the request line, and see if I could log votes to get our artists to chart in the countdown. Much of what was on MTV at the time was overproduced pop garbage. Many of the hard rock bands it did play lacked substance and only made the countdown because they had good-looking singers all the girls wanted to see. When the VJ announced a debut from a California band called Tesla and showed the video for "Modern Day Cowboy," I was blown away.

Here was a no-bullshit, straight-up hard rock band. No contrived image, no makeup, just denim and T-shirts. They looked like me and my friends. And their song kicked ass—with dual trade-off guitars, a vocalist with an amazing range and a bluesy delivery, and a killer pocket drummer. I was immediately a fan and called Geffen Records for an advance of *Mechanical Resonance*, Tesla's first album.

FRANK HANNON (GUITAR)

JEFF KEITH (VOCALS)

TROY LUCCKETTA (DRUMS)

TOMMY SKEOCH (GUITAR)

BRIAN WHEAT (BASS)

DAVE RUDE (GUITAR)

OPPOSITE: Tommy Skeoch, Frank Hannon, and Jeff Keith at Brendan Byrne Arena, East Rutherford, New Jersey, March, 1992

DISCOGRAPHY

ABOVE: Jeff Keith at
Brendan Byrne Arena, East Rutherford,
New Jersey, March, 1992

To this day, I get pissed when Tesla gets lumped into the glam scene. Instead, they were a breath of fresh air in the mid-'80s, when hair metal was at its peak. They never got lost in the hairspray or image. The band felt genuine and relatable because they seemed to care more about what they were creating than the way they looked. Who needs fancy clothes or styled hair when the guitars and vocals are that strong and soulful? Their songs are as no-nonsense as their look.

Tesla has never made a bad album. They've never gone for the obvious hits and never written songs specifically to get on the radio. Instead, they've written with albums in mind—records you can listen to from start to finish and love every track; there's no filler. These guys also deserve great credit for inspiring the whole "unplugged" trend (which, for the most part, was never a fan of) when they released a live acoustic album called *Five Man Acoustical Jam* and scored a huge hit with a cover of Five Man Electrical Band's "Signs." Their records have always sounded live, like the band was just setting up and playing—with no layered vocal effects, giant choruses, or overproduction that would require samples to re-create onstage.

Like many bands of the era, Tesla broke up for a while in the 1990s, but they reunited in 2000 and released the album *Into the Now* in 2004. Instead of trying to be hip and connect with the musical flavor of the moment, they stayed true to their own sound, just like they did in the '80s. They used the band's original lineup, they kept the same look, and they wrote a record that sounds just like you want it to—like a Tesla record.

Over the years, I've had a great friendship with all the members of the band. One of my fondest memories is from the period when *Into the Now* came out. The guys wanted to do my radio show in NYC but were told by their label, Sanctuary, that I was booked and unable to have them on the show. Sanctuary didn't want to upset another radio station (that wasn't even playing the band's record) and decided to send me Nikki Sixx instead, who was promoting a band called Brides of Destruction. Tesla's singer, Jeff Keith, called me to say he was bummed that they couldn't come on the air with me, and it hit us quickly that the label was lying to us both and just pushing Nikki's new band. So Jeff went to the nearest Rent-A-Wreck and got a car to drive from Long Island to NYC to do my show that night. The label was furious, but that's typical Tesla—down-to-earth guys who stand by the people who support them. I've introduced the band almost every time they play in the New York area. Whether it's tossing a football backstage, talking UFO and Thin Lizzy, or busting balls and having beers, it's always a fun time with Tesla.

A recent, favorite Tesla story of mine revolves around the 2009 Download Festival in England. I was there to tape a *That Metal Show* special for VH1 Classic. All three days of the festival my cohosts, Don Jamieson and Jim Florentine, and I were looking for a band that would let us introduce them so our VH1 crew could shoot us in front of fifty thousand crazy Brits and show it on TV back home. Because of the tight schedules they were keeping onstage, we couldn't get the shot. Once I saw Tesla was on

the bill, I knew they would let us introduce them, and they did. But they never told the stage manager. When he saw three guys who weren't in Tesla take the stage, the stage manager was outraged. Nobody was at the soundboard, so the mic was dead and suddenly three idiots from New Jersey, who nobody came to see, were cutting into Tesla's playing time!

While the band was waiting to go on, the stage manager was chasing us around the massive stage yelling, "This is bullocks," and trying to grab the mic from Jim, who wouldn't give it up. "The intro is off!" he yelled as Jim circled the stage and tapped the top of the mic to see if it was live. Once it came on, Jim ran to the front of the stage and started his shtick, like the bulldog that he is. He passed the mic to Don, then to me, and I announced, "Please welcome TESLA!" And then we ran.

We started walking down the back stairs of the stage, back to our broadcast spot, when suddenly I felt a tap on my shoulder. Was it the stage manager ready to deck me? No, it was JEFF KEITH! Jeff was running after me while his band was onstage playing to a crowd of fifty thousand waiting fans because I still had his microphone in my back pocket! Most times when anyone does a stage introduction, it's with a backup or monitor mic, not the one about to be used by the singer! But I had Jeff's only mic, and I had left him essentially naked onstage. He grabbed it from me and ran back in time to make the first verse of "I Want to Live." It was a hysterical moment that we all still joke about.

If I had to pick one Tesla album to start with—and like I said, I don't think there's a bad one among them (including the underrated *Bust a Nut*, which was their first album without a bona fide hit or single)—it would be their second release, *The Great Radio Controversy*. By the time it came out, the guys had toured for a couple of years and had become better players, but the trappings of success hadn't yet started to creep in. This record is as dynamic as their amazing debut, but it's tighter and packs more punch.

UNDERGROUND CLASSIC

While Tesla was broken up, singer Jeff Keith and now former Tesla guitarist Tommy Skeoch made an album called *The World Is a Freak* (2000) under the name Bar 7. It was released on a small label and quickly went away, but it's a great record that features some really solid songs. I always loved what Skeoch brought to Tesla—an aggressive guitar. He was the punk and raw edge in the band (who also had the biggest issues with drugs and booze, which resulted in his departure more than once). The Bar 7 album not only shows how strong Tommy is as a player and writer but also captures the attitude of his heavy metal approach to the stage. It highlights what's missing from this great band when he's not in it.

ABOVE: Tommy Skeoch and Frank Hannon at Brendan Byrne Arena, East Rutherford, New Jersey, March, 1992

THIN LIZZY

Photo by Fin Costello, Redferns, courtesy of Getty Images

When I was a kid, the first song I heard from Dublin's Thin Lizzy was "Jailbreak," from the album of the same name. If you've heard it, you know that it starts with a huge open note—a big sting before the groove kicks in that forces you to take notice. The riff that follows is classic Thin Lizzy, but it was singer Phil Lynott's storytelling, and his fantastic vocals, that held my attention. Lynott was the hard-rock poet. His way with words and images is something that few people in hard rock have been able to duplicate, and it cements Thin Lizzy's importance in the world of rock. Songs like "Cowboy Song" paint vivid pictures like a movie script, and "Emerald" tells a harrowing war story. "Black Rose" is a sweeping epic, while "The Boys Are Back in Town" is about getting the guys together for a night out.

CLASSIC LINEUP:

BRIAN DOWNEY (DRUMS)

SCOTT GORHAM (GUITAR)

PHIL LYNOTT (VOCALS/BASS)

BRIAN ROBERTSON (GUITAR)

KEY ADDITIONAL MEMBERS:

ERIC BELL (GUITAR)

VIVIAN CAMPBELL (GUITAR)

GARY MOORE (GUITAR)

JOHN SYKES (GUITAR/VOCALS)

RICKY WARWICK (VOCALS)

DARREN WHARTON (KEYBOARD)

SNOWY WHITE (GUITAR)

OPPOSITE: Brian Robertson, Phil Lynott, and Scott Gorham at Wembley Empire Pool, United Kingdom, June 22, 1978

DISCOGRAPHY

It was pretty consuming for me as a kid to hear one of my favorite rock bands put such effort into their lyrics—not always a strength in hard rock and metal. Soon after, when I heard "The Boys Are Back in Town," I realized that Thin Lizzy had another great signature: the playing of not just one great guitarist but two, who, in most cases, traded off solos and rhythms and played in harmony unlike any other band I'd ever heard.

I was inspired to explore their whole catalog and excited to find that they'd released a number of albums before *Jailbreak*. Though *Jailbreak* is known as their definitive record, there are plenty of other great ones to check out. I wouldn't say every one of them is a masterpiece, but Thin Lizzy has enough great moments to justify being included in this book, not to mention their obvious influence and impact on so many bands over the decades.

While Thin Lizzy's music has only grown in stature throughout the years, it remains absolutely tragic that most people in America aren't aware of them beyond "The Boys Are Back in Town." In many other countries, Thin Lizzy has had more than a dozen bona fide hits throughout their career. In fact, their 1978 album, *Live and Dangerous*, is considered to be one of the greatest live recordings ever made in England. For whatever reason, though, they've never been able to break through with anything else in America.

In an interview I did with him for the 2009 release, *Still Dangerous: Live at Tower Theatre Philadelphia, 1977*, I spoke with guitarist Scott Gorham about why he feels America has been so stubborn when it comes to learning about Thin Lizzy's catalog. He attributed this lack of attention to bad timing, saying that whenever they started to gain momentum through U.S. touring, they had to stop and go back to England. They were also crippled by Phil Lynott's drug addiction and related illnesses while on tour. They had to cancel several shows over the years, and when they did play, Scott said, they weren't always as good as people expected them to be. Drug abuse and the excesses of the time really took their toll on the band, as did a nonstop work schedule. He also never felt the production of many of the band's albums was at the level it should be and expressed an interest to me in completely remixing the catalog someday to give the songs the kick he thought they lacked on the records.

Regardless, Thin Lizzy has written some incredible songs and albums throughout their history. Their dual-guitar playing style had such a significant influence on hard rock and heavy metal of the late '70s and early '80s that it can be heard in bands from Iron Maiden to Metallica. Many of the bands that were influenced by them have actually helped Lizzy gain some new stature in America. Metallica's cover of "Whiskey in the Jar" was much more popular than Lizzy's version. Anthrax covered "Cowboy Song," Def Leppard did "Don't Believe a Word," and Bon Jovi was one of many bands that covered "The Boys Are Back in Town."

If "The Boys Are Back in Town" is all you've heard from this great band, you should know that there's much more to discover, right up to the band's final studio statement, the 1983 release, *Thunder and Lightning*. It's one of

my favorites. Metal fans should take note that this is their hardest-rocking album, which is mostly due to the arrival of young hotshot guitarist John Sykes, who breathed new life into the band. He also inspired them to get out on the road to do one more tour. The more than fifteen years of hard living had started to weigh on Phil, who was looking to shelve the band for a while, but Sykes came with a new energy and helped keep the band alive for a bit longer. Some say Lizzy with Sykes was "too metal," but to me it was perfect!

The band's final tour with Phil was in 1983. By this point, many in the group were battling addiction, none more seriously than Phil, who by then was a full-blown heroin addict. He recorded a few albums in the years after Lizzy broke up, but he was considered too much of a risk and could not score a proper record deal. Tragically, on January 4, 1986, Phil died from organ failure and pneumonia, all brought on by drugs. He was just thirty-six years old.

I never got to see the band play while Phil was still alive, but I did get to see them with a different lineup, formed in 1999, that included Sykes on guitar and vocals. Although a lot of people felt it was crazy to have a version of Thin Lizzy without Phil Lynott, I saw it as more of a celebration of their songs. Many of them are so solid that even without the band's classic frontman singing, it was still fun and moving to hear them live. John did an amazing job capturing Phil's style and delivery. It's always made me wonder what direction the band would've taken had Phil lived. From their ballads to their hard-rock tunes to their Celtic-flavored songs, they could have gone anywhere. Scott Gorham said he thought that if Phil were still alive, he'd be onstage with Thin Lizzy or writing and recording for some other project. He thought that Phil would've gotten a kick out of how their music had found its way into American pop culture through video games like *Rock Band* and beer commercials and other bands' covers of Thin Lizzy songs.

Phil Lynott was one of rock and roll's all-time greatest songwriters, as evidenced by how many people can sing along to "The Boys Are Back in Town" and recognize its melody instantly. A lot of hard rock and metal lyrics are disposable, but Lynott's memorable characters and stories would've made perfect videos for the MTV generation.

In 2009, John Sykes announced his departure from Thin Lizzy. Scott Gorham formed a brand-new lineup of the band in 2010 featuring Ricky Warwick on vocals, the return of original Lizzy drummer Brian Downey, and Def Leppard guitarist Vivian Campbell (a huge Lizzy fan) on second guitar. The Lizzy legend rolls on, and regardless of who is playing the songs, the strength of Phil's material shines through.

EDDIE'S PLAYLIST
THIN LIZZY

1. JAILBREAK
2. DON'T BELIEVE A WORD
3. COLD SWEAT
4. THUNDER AND LIGHTNING
5. BAD REPUTATION
6. STILL IN LOVE WITH YOU
7. COWBOY SONG
8. SUICIDE
9. WAITING FOR AN ALIBI
10. HOLLYWOOD
11. THE ROCKER
12. EMERALD
13. CHINATOWN
14. BLACK ROSE

DID YOU KNOW

On Thin Lizzy's classic 1978 live album, *Live and Dangerous*, a then relatively unknown Huey Lewis (credited as Bluesy Huey Lewis) appears as a guest on harmonica! The band also had a big hit covering the Bob Seger classic "Rosalie."

TWISTED SISTER

Twisted Sister's inclusion in this book goes way beyond my respect and appreciation for their music; it's also about their key involvement in an event that's one of the proudest moments of my career. In the early '80s, when Twisted Sister first came on the scene, I thought the band was from England, not New York. I never read about them in my local papers, but they were always featured in the British magazines I bought. Factor in that their first few records had to be purchased on import because they didn't have a record deal in the United States and that their debut, *Under the Blade*, was produced by one of my heroes, Pete Way of UFO, and you can see why I thought they were anything but New Yorkers.

CLASSIC LINEUP

JAY JAY FRENCH (GUITAR)

MARK MENDOZA (BASS)

EDDIE OJEDA (GUITAR)

A. J. PERO (DRUMS)

DEE SNIDER (VOCALS)

JOE FRANCO (DRUMS)

OPPOSITE: Jay Jay French, Dee Snider, and Mark Mendoza at NY Steel, Hammerstein Ballroom, New York City, November 28, 2001

DISCOGRAPHY

Twisted Sister had a huge following on the New York and New Jersey club scene during the '70s and early '80s. The stories of the band's rowdy club days are legendary in my New Jersey stomping grounds. But I missed all of it because I was too young—as cool as my parents were, there was no way I was allowed to hang out at a bar at age fourteen. So, as a kid, I started getting into the band through their original songs and recall buying an EP at the time with the track "Shoot 'Em Down," still one of my Twisted Sister favorites. Since I was a Kiss fan, the theatrical aspect of Twisted Sister caught my attention right away, and rumor had it that guitarist Jay Jay French was *almost* in Kiss at one time. After a couple of independent releases, Twisted Sister scored a deal with Atlantic Records and exploded with the 1984 release of *Stay Hungry*.

I recall working in a record store and selling boxes of *Stay Hungry* at the time. Suddenly, Twisted Sister was everywhere, but nowhere more than on MTV. The band hit just at the right time—when music videos were coming into their own and having a major impact on record sales. Their mix of hard-rock stadium anthems with their over-the-top look of wild hair and makeup was a match made in metal heaven for MTV programmers. We're Not Gonna Take It" and "I Wanna Rock" became known as much for their videos and the actors in them as for the songs themselves. Even though the guys in Twisted Sister looked like transvestites, they were tough and had a gang mentality when they took the stage—"bikers in drag," if you will. The ringleader was singer Dee Snider. Dee had a powerful voice, was a top showman, and could also write great anthems. He's the sole songwriter on almost every Twisted Sister song, which would later become a problem with the rest of the band.

After *Stay Hungry*, Twisted Sister crashed as quickly as they'd hit it big; that album had been such a success that a backlash was almost inevitable. The follow-up album, *Come Out and Play*, did not have a single hit. Suddenly, instead of seeing Twisted Sister as a heavy rock band, people started to view them as a bit of a joke. The next album, *Love Is for Suckers*, tanked even more, and Twisted Sister was in free fall. This was compounded by the fact that Dee, as the band's main songwriter, was getting wealthy from the royalties rolling in, while the other guys were struggling, with some working day jobs. This created great tension in the band and resulted in the group's demise. I've noticed that money and control are consistently the biggest things that cause bands to break. Dee was the face of the band, was making all the money, and was even on the cover of *Stay Hungry* by himself—which some of the other band members still haven't recovered from. By the late '80s, the band was finished.

I respect Twisted Sister for personal reasons as well as musical. Like everyone, I was extremely impacted by the events of September 11, 2001. As I watched everything happen, I was blown away by the bravery of the military, cops, firefighters, and emergency medical workers. Police officers and firefighters were among some of the first people to support my radio show when it began in New York City—they work crazy hours, and since my show was on late at night, they really looked forward to it while

out on duty. So when 9/11 charities started to be announced, I was hoping to see some heavy metal benefit shows included, especially since I knew how many people in these lines of work loved my radio show. Needless to say, nothing close to a metal show was being arranged. To make matters worse, some radio ownership groups issued a mandate that certain songs shouldn't be played because of their sensitive nature and how they thought people were feeling at that time. This mandate made no sense to me, and not surprisingly, there was a bunch of hard rock music on the list. People rely on music to get them through tough times, so I didn't think some suits should decide what should or shouldn't be played. I have always fought against the stereotypes and misconceptions about hard rock and metal music, so on my first radio show after 9/11, I made a point to play every song on that banned list that anyone requested.

I wanted to do something more to help my police and firefighter fans, so I decided to plan a benefit for the New York Police and Fire Widows' and Children's Benefit Fund to aid those who had lost loved ones. I contacted some friends I had worked with at a promoter called Metropolitan Entertainment Group and told them I wanted to get a venue. The Hammerstein Ballroom in New York City had just opened; it held 3,500 people, and Metropolitan arranged for me to have it for free. This was a huge break, but the only condition was that I needed to get a bill together that would fill the place—in the months after 9/11, people were not exactly flocking to New York City. I immediately called on some of my closest friends in the

ABOVE: A. J. Pero, Eddie Ojeda, Jay Jay French, Eddie, Mike Piazza, Dee Snider, and Mark Mendoza backstage at NY Steel, Hammerstein Ballroom, New York City, November 28, 2001

EDDIE'S PLAYLIST
TWISTED SISTER

1. COME OUT AND PLAY
2. THE KIDS ARE BACK
3. I AM (I'M ME)
4. YOU CAN'T STOP ROCK 'N' ROLL
5. SHOOT 'EM DOWN
6. WHAT YOU DON'T KNOW (SURE CAN HURT YOU)
7. DESTROYER
8. UNDER THE BLADE
9. BURN IN HELL
10. THE PRICE
11. STAY HUNGRY
12. COME BACK
13. 30

business who lived in the New York area and wouldn't need budgets for travel and hotels. Everyone would have to check their egos at the door and show up ready to play. I quickly assembled a lineup consisting of Ace Frehley, Anthrax (who were under the gun to change their name at the time because of recent events), Overkill, and Sebastian Bach (who would open the show, play three songs, then run next door to perform on Broadway, where he was starring in *The Rocky Horror Picture Show*). My cohost for the event would be my close friend Mike Piazza, one of the most popular baseball stars for the Mets, a major metal fan, and a frequent guest on my shows. I took this bill to the people at Metropolitan, and they liked it but still felt it needed a stronger hook to assure a sellout. I needed a New York–based band that people would want to see and that would be something truly special.

In the years prior, members of Twisted Sister had been on my show to talk about their different projects or reissues from the band's catalog. Jay Jay French was the guy I had become closest to, and he managed the band's affairs. I'd always sensed that Jay wanted to play again, but it had been thirteen years since the band's breakup, and the members, especially bassist Mark Mendoza, were still bitter about the royalties and various other issues. I knew there was still tension, but I also knew some of the guys were looking to play again if it was the right reason to bury the hatchet. And what better reason for a New York band than a 9/11 charity? I called Jay Jay, who said that he was interested but admitted that he had no idea if he could assemble the other band members in the same room. A few days later, he called back and said they would do it. I knew it could blow up at any point, so I held my breath and told Metropolitan that I had reunited Twisted Sister for the first time in thirteen years to close the benefit show. The date was locked in for late November, and we put tickets on sale a week after Twisted Sister confirmed.

At that time, my radio shows were on the now-defunct WNEW in New York. It was an FM talk-show station, and my shows were its only music-based broadcasts. It was all on me to get the word out about this event, outside of a few print ads. But the word spread quickly, and in just a few weeks the show was sold out! Twisted Sister decided to play the show without their trademark makeup and costumes, which they didn't feel would be appropriate, and Dee wore a T-shirt that said "Fuck Osama." Twisted Sister put on a hell of a show, as did all the other bands, and we all raised over $200,000 for the fund. Also we were able to shine a positive light on the power of heavy metal and to challenge misconceptions. To this day, NY Steel (as it was called) is the single event I am most proud of putting together in my career.

Twisted Sister reunited as a onetime deal. They had no intention of continuing as a band and didn't even know if they would speak to one another again afterward. But as the 2000s started to roll in and the band's music started to show up in sports arenas and TV commercials, they decided to become active again. Dee has always been the tough nut to crack. If it was up to the other four guys, they would be out playing all the time. But Dee

is reluctant unless the opportunity is right. He has many outside projects and has said many times that he doesn't want to be an old guy fronting a band like Twisted Sister. But Dee is still very good, and even though he goes onstage kicking and screaming at times, Twisted Sister now plays about a dozen shows a year around the world. Because they only do a handful of dates, they draw in decent crowds at U.S. shows and are still even bigger in Europe, where they headline festivals. I am bonded forever with Twisted Sister. I gave them the reason to become a band again, and they gave me the chance to do something I will forever be very proud of.

Dee Snider at Pier 84,
New York City, July 15, 1984

DID YOU KNOW

Though Twisted Sister hasn't made a new album of original material since reforming for NY Steel, they have reissued some very interesting projects, including a rerecorded version of *Stay Hungry* called *Still Hungry* and a DVD of their classic MTV live show from 1985. They also orchestrated a Twisted Sister tribute album and recorded *Twisted Christmas*. Released in 2006, the band's collection of holiday favorites was an unexpected hit. As a result, Twisted Sister plays a theater in Times Square every year with an elaborate Christmas-themed stage show. A twenty-fifth anniversary edition of *Stay Hungry* was also released, and as a bonus it features one new original track called "30"—the only new material the band has issued since reforming.

UFO

My love of UFO has been well documented over the years on my radio and TV shows. They are one of the most criminally underrated bands in rock history, and I have done my best to let people know about how amazing they are, however and whenever I can. It seems to have paid off to some degree, since I constantly get e-mails from listeners and viewers asking where they should start when buying one of UFO's many recordings. There is something about the band's sound that is just timeless for me. It takes me back to my days in high school, trying to score beer for a weekend party or sitting in my friend's basement cranking UFO on his stereo, which had a poster of Michael Schenker in a black leather jumpsuit above it, Flying V guitar and all!

CLASSIC LINEUP

PHIL MOGG (VOCALS)

ANDY PARKER (DRUMS)

PAUL RAYMOND (KEYBOARD/GUITAR)

MICHAEL SCHENKER (GUITAR)

PETE WAY (BASS)

KEY ADDITIONAL MEMBERS

MICK BOLTON (GUITAR)

NEIL CARTER (GUITAR/KEYBOARD)

PAUL CHAPMAN (GUITAR)

ATOMIC TOMMY M. (GUITAR)

VINNIE MOORE (GUITAR)

OPPOSITE: Neil Carter, Pete Way, and Paul Chapman at Radio City Music Hall, New York City, February 27, 1981

I never have to be in the mood to hear UFO. For as many amazing records as this band has produced, though, there are also a few clunkers, due to the various lineups they've had over the decades. Contrary to what many people believe, the founding members are bassist Pete Way, drummer Andy Parker, and vocalist Phil Mogg, who has remained the sole original member through all eras of the group. The many changes in UFO's lineup are a big part of this band's story.

UFO got their start in England in the late '60s, when those three founding members started a band that played "space rock." More psychedelic than heavy, the band recorded two studio albums that went largely unnoticed except for some interest in Japan. It wasn't until 1973, when a young German guitar wizard by the name of Michael Schenker joined the band, that UFO really solidified their sound and began to make an impact on the world of heavy rock. Michael had been playing with his brother, Rudolf Schenker, in Scorpions, and even though he was several years younger than the rest of the guys in UFO and barely spoke English, he made a huge imprint on their direction. With his stunning playing on a Flying V guitar and his incredible writing abilities—he cowrote almost every song that's considered to be a UFO classic—Schenker gave the band a bona fide guitar hero.

Through the '70s, Schenker had an amazingly volatile relationship with his British bandmates. Drinking, drugs, the language barrier, and Michael's painfully shy nature all played a role in the band's battles, which at times even got physical. It was so bad during the late '70s that UFO would often have a second guitar player, Paul Chapman, waiting in the wings at live gigs in case Schenker decided not to show (which wasn't uncommon). Whatever issues may have existed, though, each album recorded with Schenker has great music. While the production may sound a little dated, with Mogg's incredibly soulful vocals, Parker's rock-solid backbeat, and the lunatic Way's rumbling sliding bass, their songs are timeless. Schenker left UFO for the first time in 1979, following what many (including me) feel to be the band's defining album, *Strangers in the Night*. Probably my favorite live album of all time, this double set recorded in Chicago (still a UFO stronghold to this day) showcases the band's definitive lineup and gives their best material an energy and feel that can only come from a live show. It's the album I tell anyone looking to explore UFO to start with.

After this landmark recording, Schenker was permanently replaced by his stand-in, Paul Chapman, whose first studio effort with UFO was the 1980 release *No Place to Run*. The unlikely pairing of producer George Martin, aka the "fifth Beatle," with these musicians resulted in a great album. Even though some refused to embrace UFO without their star ax man, the great songs and sound remained in place, and UFO released a string of awesome albums. Chapman may have been a different player, but the material he wrote is as good as anything they had done with Schenker to that point. *The Wild, the Willing and the Innocent*; *Mechanix*; and *Making Contact* all proved UFO was much more than just Schenker's

OPPOSITE: Phil Mogg at Starland Ballroom, Sayreville, New Jersey, 2010

DISCOGRAPHY

UFO 1 (1971)

UFO 2: FLYING (1971)

PHENOMENON (1974)

FORCE IT (1975)

NO HEAVY PETTING (1976)

LIGHTS OUT (1977)

OBSESSION (1978)

STRANGERS IN THE NIGHT
[LIVE] (1979)

NO PLACE TO RUN (1980)

*THE WILD, THE WILLING
AND THE INNOCENT* (1981)

MECHANIX (1982)

MAKING CONTACT (1983)

MISDEMEANOR (1985)

AIN'T MISBEHAVIN' (1988)

*HIGH STAKES &
DANGEROUS MEN* (1992)

WALK ON WATER (1995)

COVENANT (2000)

SHARKS (2002)

YOU ARE HERE (2004)

SHOWTIME [LIVE] (2005)

THE MONKEY PUZZLE
(2006)

THE VISITOR (2009)

band. Pete Way once told me he considered Chapman to be a "reckless" and flashy guitarist compared with Schenker's more focused and precise approach, and that really sums it up best. They were both brilliant in their own way.

After years of nonstop touring and the various vices that come with it, UFO started to crash in the early '80s. Prior to the recording of *Making Contact*, Pete Way left the group, with Paul Chapman not far behind. What followed was a string of subpar albums with lineups that featured only Mogg as the original member. The songs and production weren't good, and it began to seem like Phil was just trying to keep the name alive. For the first time, UFO was making music that didn't match their legacy as a world-class hard rock band.

Fortunately, things began to turn around—though it wasn't until 1993, when the *Strangers* lineup reunited. The resulting album, *Walk on Water*, and the tour that supported it showed what UFO was still capable of. But the usual infighting started again and this reunion was short-lived. Schenker continued to drift in and out over the years, releasing average albums like *Covenant* and *Sharks* with UFO and less-than-stellar albums with his Michael Schenker Group (MSG). But it seemed at this point they were all just going through the motions. Inevitably, Schenker left for good, but

Photo by Kevin Hodapp

EDDIE'S PLAYLIST

UFO

1. *STRANGERS IN THE NIGHT* (WHOLE ALBUM, TOP TO BOTTOM!)
2. STOP BREAKING DOWN
3. CAN'T BUY A THRILL
4. PROFESSION OF VIOLENCE
5. CHAINS CHAINS
6. MAKIN' MOVES
7. BABY BLUE
8. TERRI
9. DOING IT ALL FOR YOU
10. SLIPPING AWAY
11. WE BELONG TO THE NIGHT
12. NO PLACE TO RUN
13. BELLADONNA
14. LET IT RAIN
15. LONG GONE
16. ANYDAY
17. VENUS

ABOVE: Michael Schenker at Starland Ballroom, Sayreville, New Jersey, 2010
OPPOSITE: Phil Mogg at Radio City Music Hall, New York City, February 27, 1981

UFO was reborn for a third time with the arrival of American guitarist Vinnie Moore in 2003.

Moore had a reputation as a "shredder" with a string of solo instrumental albums, so I was very apprehensive when I heard he had joined UFO, because their sound has always been about melody first and foremost. To his tremendous credit, Moore brought new life to the band, playing brilliant melodies that ended up being exactly what the band needed. He added some flash but was respectful of the material he was interpreting. With Moore, UFO created what was by far the best studio music they'd made since 1996. Albums such as *You Are Here*, *The Monkey Puzzle*, and *The Visitor* all showed UFO back in top form and even bluesier in their older age. When anyone asks me how to navigate the UFO catalog, I always say, "You're safe with anything featuring Schenker, Chapman, or Moore on guitar." After forty years, UFO continues to record and tour, and they still make some of the best hard rock known to man. Just ask the guys in Iron Maiden, who for more than two decades have started every show by playing the UFO classic "Doctor Doctor" over the PA.

I first met Phil Mogg in the mid-'80s, when the band released *Misdemeanor*, their final album for Chrysalis Records. I interviewed him at the label's office in New York while writing for a New Jersey paper called the *Aquarian Weekly*. I had heard stories of the band's pranks over the years,

so I was not surprised to find out that some of the guys had spiked the watercooler and their label's office with tasteless grain alcohol that day, making for an interesting time for any employee who took an innocent drink. For those who don't know, Phil and the UFO guys have an incredible, very British sense of humor.

I've continued to interview the band throughout my career, and I've gotten to know them pretty well. They were aware that in New York I was pretty much their lone support system. In 2008, I was almost duped into getting a UFO tattoo! We were shooting a field segment for *That Metal Show* at a tattoo shop, and I was told that a viewer was going to get the *That Metal Show* logo inked on himself (something that has since happened for real, more than once). It turned out that it was all a setup to pressure me into getting my first ink: a UFO tattoo. Mike Portnoy of Dream Theater even made a surprise appearance since he knew of my love for the band. I'd once told him that if I ever did get a tattoo, I would consider UFO's logo.

I stood my ground that day and today I remain ink free, but I almost went through with it. The guys in UFO heard about the stunt when it aired on TV and teased me about it pretty good. To this day I'm stopped often by fans of my show and asked, "Did you ever get that UFO tattoo?" For me, UFO still holds an extra-special place in my heart for many reasons, but above all for their music and how it still continues to move me like it did when I first heard it. There are few bands that conjure that same charge and emotion when I hear them after all these years. I'm proud to know that I have helped expose this incredibly underrated band to so many who have thanked me for it over the years. If you're reading this and don't own any UFO, please go buy *Strangers in the Night* today and

VAN HALEN

I've had some arguments with friends over the years when they ask, "Will there ever be another Led Zeppelin?" Because my answer is yes, and they're called Van Halen. To me, the music of Van Halen is *that* essential and timeless. Listen to any of the David Lee Roth–era Van Halen recordings today and they sound as fresh and groundbreaking as they did when they first came out in the late '70s and early '80s. Just like the Led Zeppelin albums, those Van Halen records never sound dated.

Back in 1978, when the first, self-titled Van Halen album came out, I was in high school and still very much a card-carrying member of the Kiss Army. For me at that time, any other band was a threat to my heroes Gene, Paul, Peter, and Ace, and I would argue constantly with Zeppelin fans that Kiss was a better band. (I usually lost that one.) At Madison High School in New Jersey, I was lucky enough to have the "cool" teacher for history. Mr. Chemerka—or Mr. C as we called him—knew music and loved how fanatical I was about it even then. One day, during my freshman year, Mr. C told me

CLASSIC LINEUP

**MICHAEL ANTHONY
(BASS/VOCALS)**

DAVID LEE ROTH (VOCALS)

ALEX VAN HALEN (DRUMS)

EDDIE VAN HALEN (GUITAR)

KEY ADDITIONAL MEMBERS

GARY CHERONE (VOCALS)

SAMMY HAGAR (VOCALS)

**WOLFGANG VAN HALEN
(BASS)**

OPPOSITE: David Lee Roth and
Eddie Van Halen at Convention Hall,
Asbury Park, New Jersey, August 11, 1979

DISCOGRAPHY

he'd found the band that would eclipse Kiss in my book, a band with better guitar playing, performances, and songs. He was talking about Van Halen. I had to explore this band right away, so I ordered the first album through one of those record clubs advertised in *TV Guide*.

When it arrived and I dropped the needle on it for the first time, the opening sounds of "Running with the Devil" made me nervous. I knew that this was a whole new level of rock and roll—something beyond Kiss— and I had never heard anything like it before. At the time, no one had! Eddie Van Halen's playing—his finger-tapping technique on the neck of the guitar—was totally groundbreaking. The entire band sounded massive! Van Halen were heavier and meaner than a lot of what I was listening to at that point. I couldn't believe it.

I quickly got a hold of myself and realized that this Van Halen was a threat to Kiss's throne. Even though I knew Van Halen was great, I still had to fight for my favorite band. I could never be a traitor to the makeup monsters on my wall. So I argued with Mr. C every day, and he continued to torment me as Van Halen got bigger and bigger. But one day I noticed on the back of Van Halen's album cover that the first person named on their "thank you" list was GENE SIMMONS! I was shocked. Gene knew Van Halen! I confronted Mr. C and, after doing some digging, found out that it was Gene who'd discovered Van Halen. He also produced and financed their demo. As if anointed by the gods, with my loyalty no longer in question, I was then fully willing to embrace VH—and, man, did they ever deliver!

RIGHT: Michael Anthony and Sammy Hagar at Brendan Byrne Arena, East Rutherford, New Jersey, August, 1986

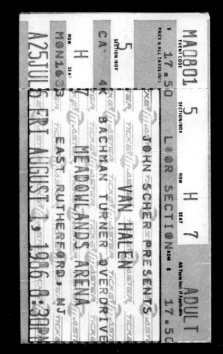

The band's next three albums—*Van Halen II, Women and Children First*, and *Fair Warning*—are still incredible. Eddie's innovative guitar playing is at the core of every song, but the rest of the band is equally amazing. With his blues influence, David Lee Roth's raspy-to-wailing vocals are always exactly the perfect accompaniment to the music. Bassist Michael Anthony is not only a great player, but his high vocal harmonies also add a whole other layer to Roth's style. Additionally, Alex Van Halen is a totally powerful drummer in his own right. The band evolved within a hard-rock context, continually turning out their in-your-face sound and timeless songs.

I often went to see VH back in the day, but to be honest, I was never in love with their live shows. The band always sounded sloppy, and David Lee Roth was sometimes more of a circus clown than a singer. He'd drive me nuts when he'd do nothing but stand with his arms out just soaking in applause. Or when he'd do karate moves and gymnastics while waving around a sword with scarves dangling from it for five full minutes. I'd think, "Hell, I could be hearing two more songs!" But I realize that many would disagree with me, as Van Halen was considered one of the best live acts at the time.

When 1984—also the name of their album released that year—rolled around, I was working as a clerk in my local record store. I still remember rushing to the turntable and cranking the stereo the day Van Halen's new single "Jump" arrived. I was shocked at what came out of the speakers: KEYBOARDS! A huge synth-sound and a poppy melody? On a Van Halen song? The only guitar I could hear was in the solo. While this crossed the line of what was appropriate in hard rock for me, I was again in the minority, because "Jump" became a major hit, as did the whole album when it came out.

When Sammy Hagar replaced Roth in 1986 for Van Halen's next album, *5150*, I was actually thrilled. I was already a fan of Hagar's old band, Montrose, as well as his solo work, and I was excited to see what a singer of his

ABOVE: David Lee Roth and Eddie Van Halen at Convention Hall, Asbury Park, New Jersey, August 11, 1979

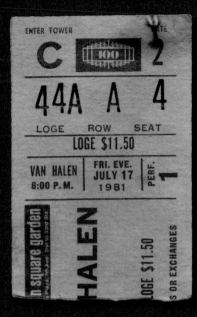

EDDIE'S PLAYLIST
VAN HALEN

1. HEAR ABOUT IT LATER
2. JUDGEMENT DAY
3. GOOD ENOUGH
4. SOMEBODY GET ME A DOCTOR
5. LOVE WALKS IN
6. ATOMIC PUNK
7. ON FIRE
8. IN A SIMPLE RHYME
9. ROMEO DELIGHT
10. LIGHT UP THE SKY
11. LITTLE DREAMER
12. GIRL GONE BAD
13. POUNDCAKE
14. FOOLS
15. D.O.A.

range would bring to the band and how his writing would work with Eddie's. I loved *5150* and many of the Hagar-era releases—they're definitely different from Roth's over-the-top approach, but equally cool and, to me, more musical. David Lee Roth is a great frontman for sure, but no one would necessarily call him a great live singer. Sammy, on the other hand, is a powerhouse vocalist—his capabilities widened the musical possibilities for Van Halen, allowing them to evolve in a way they wouldn't have been able to with Roth's vocal limitations.

I saw VH countless times with Hagar, and even had the chance to meet and interview them. I loved when the band would let Sammy do some of his solo material or even jam on old Montrose songs. Hagar related to the audience in a much more down-to-earth way, and Hagar-era Van Halen was more about the music and less about the circus act. These days, however, I prefer the Van Halen albums from the Roth era. Back then, the band may have been limited by Roth's voice, but they were more consistent as a band and the albums have held up over time. Yet, I'm not someone who thinks the Hagar era should be brushed over—*For Unlawful Carnal Knowledge* and *5150* are great albums.

I've only met Eddie Van Halen once, during the tour for *Van Halen III*—which featured the short-lived and much-maligned lineup with former Extreme singer Gary Cherone on vocals. The guys were playing Madison

Eddie Van Halen at Spectrum,
Philadelphia, May 9, 1980

Square Garden, and ticket sales were not strong. The program director at the radio station where I was working told me Eddie would be calling in to my show in thirty minutes to plug the Garden show live. I didn't have much time to prepare, but I didn't need it. This was Eddie Van Halen! On the air, Eddie encouraged the fans to come out and see Gary as the new singer. I was a fan of Gary's old band, Extreme, and knew his history well. Eddie seemed generally impressed that I knew my stuff and wasn't just reading from some provided bio. So he asked me if I would come to the show and meet him.

I went to the Garden that night not really expecting to meet the legendary Eddie Van Halen. I thought he was just being nice to the local radio guy and would leave me some tickets at the door. But I got there to find front-row seats and backstage passes in an envelope under my name. Shortly after I sat down, a road manager came to my seat and said, "Ed wants to say hi." Sure enough, the man had kept his word. I walked back to the Madison Square Garden dressing rooms and into a room marked "Tuning." There, standing alone, fiddling with a guitar, with a cigarette hanging from his mouth, was the one and only Eddie Van Halen! I played it cool, as I always would, but inside I was saying "Holy shit!" We chatted for a bit, he complimented me on the interview and talked about the band's new album and tour, and I left him to prepare for the show that night. I've made a rule to never ask musicians to take photos with me, since I think it changes the dynamic of the potential relationship, but that was one night I wish I had broken my own rule! (Years later, I was told by Eddie's wife that the two of them watched *That Metal Show* at home and got a kick out of it, which made me proud.)

Now that a Van Halen reunion with David Lee Roth has taken place (2008), I think it's also time for a Hagar-era reunion. There would be a huge demand to hear Hagar sing those songs again. For me, the Roth reunion was lacking because I missed the Hagar-era songs and also be-

ABOVE: Eddie with Michael Anthony at the Borgata Hotel, Casino & Spa, Atlantic City, New Jersey, May 6, 2005

RIGHT: Wolfgang Van Halen, David Lee Roth, Alex Van Halen, and Eddie Van Halen at Madison Square Garden, New York City, May 23, 2008

OPPOSITE: Eddie Van Halen at Madison Square Garden, New York City, March 31, 1984

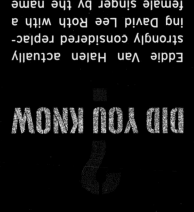

DID YOU KNOW?

Eddie Van Halen actually strongly considered replacing David Lee Roth with a female singer by the name of Patty Smyth from the band Scandal. Imagine how that might have sounded!

EDDIE TRUNK'S
ESSENTIAL
HARD ROCK AND
HEAVY METAL

WITH ANDREA BUSSELL
FOREWORD BY ROB HALFORD
PHOTOGRAPHS BY RON AKIYAMA

ABRAMS IMAGE, NEW YORK

CONTENTS

Everybody wants a backstage pass.

All metalheads and rock and rollers want to know what goes on in dressing rooms, tour buses, and hotels. We are intrigued, fascinated, and eager to hear the real stories.

In these pages you will find stories about some of the most memorable moments in rock from the illustrious Eddie Trunk—metal's living, breathing backstage pass. In chronicling such events and exposing such environments, as well as documenting rock-and-roll history, attention to detail is everything—and Eddie is the master. His passion for hard rock and metal has not only secured him fans around the globe but has also blessed him with a superhuman memory. Whenever our paths cross, be it on his TV or radio shows, Eddie will talk, on and off air, with amazing accuracy about this band or that musician and what they have going on. His knowledge of hard rock is unmatched.

There is a strong difference between gossip and reality, and while Eddie may indulge in the former, he only deals with the latter. His honest and loyal reputation precedes him, and Eddie will not let anyone diminish its value. So Eddie's recollections are genuine and, I believe, important. We get to hear the real facts and the real tales from a source who commands a style all his own, which sets this book apart.

It's time more people had the chance to get into Eddie's crazy world—into his adventures with famous and infamous people—to learn about his essential music, and to see it all through the eyes that revel, record, and then recount. It's time to go backstage.

Rob Halford, 2010

ABOVE: Rob Halford and Eddie at the
Q104 studio, New York City, May 7, 2010
OPPOSITE: K. K. Downing and
Rob Halford at Convention Hall,
Asbury Park, New Jersey, June 25, 1981

E. TRUNK

ABOVE: Ace Frehley and Eddie at the Q104 Studio, New York City, 2009

About Me . . .

My first job in music was writing for my high school newspaper in Madison, New Jersey. It was 1981, and my music column was called "Sharps & Flats." What was I writing about back then? The greatness of bands like UFO! (As you can see, truly very little has changed.) I started writing not because I thought I was a great wordsmith, but for the same reason I went into radio a few years later: to share the music I loved with others and to spread the word about all those underappreciated bands out there. It's that same principle that's driven me in everything I've done professionally, from radio to record label A&R to television.

I've lived my entire life in New Jersey and spent almost all of my years in love with rock music. When I was a kid, it was pretty much all I cared about (which was unfortunately reflected in my grades at school). I didn't even go to college, other than a year at the local community school, because I landed a job in a record store, which was, at that point, my dream gig. Working in a record store for years was great. In order to sell music, you need to know about all styles, so I was forced to educate myself about pop, R&B, country, and more. People are always surprised when I throw out some knowledge about other genres, but even though rock and metal are my passion, if you want to work in music, you need to learn as much as you can about it.

When I got the record store gig, I found out my boss had an illegal radio station in his basement in Staten Island. He was into Top 40 and all the big-echo voice announcer stuff that I wasn't. (For me, radio was never about how you sounded on the mic, but what you had to say and play—a platform to share and debate.) He could fire up the transmitter only at certain times of the day to avoid getting busted as a pirate broadcaster. The request line was the local phone booth down the street. But his station allowed me to make a demo tape that would land me my first radio job right out of high school at WDHA in Dover, New Jersey.

I'd grown up listening to WDHA, and I will never forget cracking the mic there for the first time. I was so nervous that my hands shook at the controls. I turned on the guest mic across the console by accident, and nobody heard my first-ever station break. Sixty seconds of dead air is how my career in radio started! Thankfully, they gave me another shot, and my show was born. Many believe the *Metal Mania* radio show in 1983 was the very first specialty metal show. I was able to convince the station bosses to let me play heavy metal only because I told them how many metal records I was selling in the shop across the street. I worked at WDHA on the weekends while working full-time at the record store for nine years. Since it wasn't a major-market station, I couldn't support myself on my DJ salary alone. (For a stint I was also vice president of Megaforce Records, the label that discovered Metallica, but more on that in the other chapters of this book.)

I had always dreamed of cracking New York City radio, the number-one market in the country. I loved WDHA, and it will always be a part of me, but when a classical radio station changed formats in 1992 and became Q104.3, "New York's Pure Rock," I dropped a tape in, hit Record, and sent in an air check (your resume in the radio world). I was shocked to get a call offering me the seven-to-midnight slot on Sunday. It was an honor to get the job and have the opportunity to broadcast into the tristate area—New York, New Jersey, and Connecticut. Suddenly, by making the short drive to Manhattan from New Jersey, I went from a local 3,000-watt station to 50,000 watts! While I never did my own programming at Q104, I was thrilled just to be a part of the station in the big city that played hard rock. The Pure Rock format was canned one year later, but I managed to stay at Q104 until 1998 as a classic rock DJ.

Then I got a call from the legendary New York City station WNEW. The management was making changes and hired me. I begged them to let me do a metal show, and my dream came true: I was on NYC radio, the biggest market in the country, saying and playing what I wanted. Suddenly, I had an audience and was known for something other than a nice voice be-

TOP: Dave Mustaine, Eddie, and Don Jamieson on the set of *That Metal Show,* 2009
BOTTOM: Jake E. Lee, Ron Akiyama (photographer of this book), and Eddie, 1984

TOP: Tommy Lee, Eddie, Slash, Scott Ian, Rob Zombie, Ace Frehley, and Gilby Clarke at the VH1 Rock Honors show, 2006
MIDDLE: Vinny Appice, Eddie, Rob Halford, and Geezer Butler, 2010
BOTTOM: Eddie signing Ace Frehley with Marsha Zazula and Johnny Zazula, 1986

tween records. I stayed at WNEW until it folded in 2003, and that's when Q104 saved me. The people at my old station had seen what I'd created in the four years I'd been gone, so they let me bring my specialty metal show to Q104 on Friday nights at eleven PM where it still sits today. At the same time, I got a call from an old friend from MTV and VH1, Rick Krim, who told me about a new VH1 channel called VH1 Classic and said I should audition to be a television host. Amazingly, I got the gig and became one of VH1 Classic's first-ever hosts, playing metal, alternative, soul, and rock videos and interviewing artists from Carly Simon to Robert Plant on a show called *Hangin' With*.

In 2002, I was also hired by XM satellite radio to do one of the few live shows on a music channel and spread my love of heavy metal music. Howard Stern has always been a huge influence on me, and even though I do a different style of radio, he taught me that it's OK to be honest and have an opinion—everyone won't always like it, but hopefully they will listen. To this day, thanks to the merger with Sirius, *Eddie Trunk Live* is on both XM and Sirius radio on Mondays six to ten PM EST on the Boneyard channel, and I am playing and saying what I want, just down the hall from Howard! It's great to have this weekly live national platform to interview artists and talk to listeners who call in. In addition, my website, www.eddietrunk.com, has grown to become a major destination for news and information for the metal community.

I pitched having my own heavy metal TV show many times, and in 2008, after much development and delay, *That Metal Show* was born. I introduced my friends Don Jamieson and Jim Florentine, both comics, to the channel. Being friends, fellow metal fans, and frequent guests on my radio show, our chemistry was instant. I pitched them as my cohosts and away we went. At the time of writing, we have completed the sixth season of *That Metal Show*, which has been one of the most popular shows in the channel's history. It broadcasts around the world, and I couldn't be prouder to bring my favorite hard rock and heavy metal to such a huge audience.

About the Book . . .

This book touches on some of the bands that are most important to me. Some bands made the book simply because I'm such a huge fan or for other selfish reasons, and others because they were vital to the evolution of hard rock and metal in the '70s and '80s. It was very hard deciding where to cut off the list—every time I said I was done, another band would hit me, and I would say, "They have to go in!" Many bands I love are not included, but who knows, maybe I'll get to write another book on them one day.

I've often toyed with writing an autobiography, and while this book isn't it, I think you'll see that it's certainly autobiographical. I've loaded the chapters with tons of fun personal stories and photographs. While I didn't rehash every gory detail of the times I've spent with these bands and

of my years in the music industry, I have included much that I've never talked about before. Instead of dishing too much dirt, this book walks the line between insights and opinions, with a little band history and lots of suggestions for listening.

While I'm very aware of the many subgenres of metal (death metal, black metal, thrash metal, glam metal, etc.), this book focuses only on heavy metal and hard rock in the broader sense. Just like on *That Metal Show*, I distinguish between hard rock and heavy metal. While they are connected, they are different. To some, the blanket term "heavy metal" can mean Poison; to others, Slayer. To me, metal is darker and heavier in its sound and delivery—and even in the band's look. Hard rock is loud guitars but with a strong melody in place. Led Zeppelin = hard rock. Judas Priest = metal. Guns N' Roses = hard rock. Megadeth = metal.

Please note that there were considerable space limitations for some of the aspects of this book. I felt strongly about including bands' classic lineups, but I had to limit the number of key additional members mentioned, since some lists could go on for pages. Musicians who have contributed greatly to some of these bands are not mentioned simply because of space constraints, and I mean no disrespect to these band members. Similarly, I had to limit the number of songs on my personal playlists. I love many more songs from these bands, but I had to draw the line. The "More Essentials" chapter could be expanded into a book of its own, and many of the bands I include there could have received the same in-depth treatment as the top thirty-five bands covered, but again, pages were limited and it's a reason to write a sequel. I listed the main studio discographies for the selected bands, along with a few live recordings that I consider hallmark records. I purposely left out bootlegs, most compilations, and live recordings that didn't necessarily receive band support or that the label put out to make a quick buck.

I hope that you enjoy the photos (many of which have never been published before) and the stories, and that this book inspires you to take the time to discover some new artists or some new music from the artists who have the same songs (over)played on the radio. I do not go one day without realizing how lucky I am to have simply been a rock fan who found a way to make a living by sharing my passion for this music. I am truly grateful to each and every one of you for listening, watching, and now reading about the music that I love and for giving me such incredible support over the last decades. I look forward to many more to come.

—Eddie Trunk, 2010

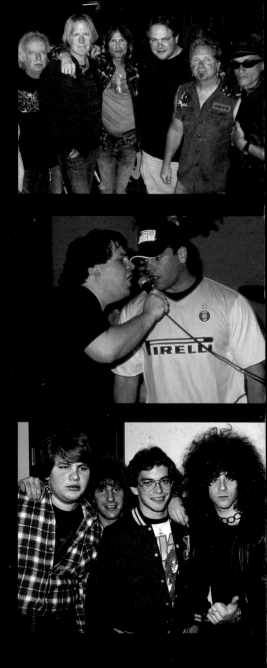

TOP: Brad Whitford, Tom Hamilton, Steven Tyler, Eddie, Joey Kramer, and Joe Perry, 2006
MIDDLE: Eddie and Mike Piazza, 2006
BOTTOM: Eddie and friends

AC/DC

grew up an hour from Seaside Heights, one of the major shore towns with a boardwalk in New Jersey (where Bon Jovi filmed most of their video for "In and Out of Love"), and went there every summer. Along the beach, there were stands with games where, for a quarter, you could spin a wheel. If it landed on the number you'd chosen, you would win a prize. Like a lot of bands I discovered as a kid, I first heard AC/DC after winning one of their albums playing this game on the boardwalk. I chose *Highway to Hell* the way I chose most of the records I won there—because I thought the cover looked cool. It showed a bunch of guys—one with devil horns coming through his hat—looking crazy and mischievous, which is all it took to win me over as a kid.

From the first thirty seconds of the album's title track—that raw, dirty sound that I would come to know as unmistakably, certifiably AC/DC—I was a fan. Their singer, Bon Scott, had a sleazy snarl. He sounded like a guy you'd want to hang out

PHIL RUDD (DRUMS)

BON SCOTT (VOCALS)

CLIFF WILLIAMS (BASS)

ANGUS YOUNG (GUITAR)

MALCOLM YOUNG (GUITAR)

MARK EVANS (BASS)

BRIAN JOHNSON (VOCALS)

CHRIS SLADE (DRUMS)

SIMON WRIGHT (DRUMS)

OPPOSITE: Malcolm Young, Angus Young, and Cliff Williams at Roseland Ballroom, New York City, March 11, 2003

DISCOGRAPHY

OPPOSITE TOP: Brian Johnson and Angus
Young at Madison Square Garden, New
York City, July 12, 1991

OPPOSITE BOTTOM: Malcolm Young and
Angus Young at Madison Square Garden,
New York City, July 12, 1991

with because you knew you'd get into trouble. "Walk All Over You" and "Girls Got Rhythm" are two more reasons why *Highway to Hell* is still my favorite AC/DC record.

Highway to Hell was AC/DC's first inroad to success in America. As an Australian band, their build had been slow. Previous albums hadn't done well (their first wasn't even released in America), and when they'd played stateside, they were only an opening act. *Highway* was their last recording with Bon Scott, who died of alcohol poisoning in 1980.

When Brian Johnson replaced Scott as their singer, I—like most fans—was skeptical of whether AC/DC could carry on or have any level of success. Replacing someone as iconic as Bon Scott was no small task, but their fan base in America wasn't yet so huge that losing him would be debilitating. To many in the mainstream, AC/DC was still unknown.

As tragic and crazy as it was, Bon Scott's death brought AC/DC notoriety—and news coverage—that they didn't have before. At the same time, they were writing some of their best material ever. They knew that if they were going to make a record that would honor their original singer, they had to come up with the goods! Obviously they did. Their next recording, *Back in Black*, remains one of the greatest-selling records of all time and made AC/DC a global success. They were launched to a whole other stratosphere.

I stayed with AC/DC through their future records but was never completely consumed by them the way I was with other bands. I enjoyed them, I saw them play, and I bought the new records, but they were never on my top-tier list, like Kiss and Aerosmith and Sabbath and Rush. I'm not sure why. As much as I love a lot of their songs and albums, I've never been a psycho fan, but I've always recognized their incredible importance to rock and metal. What they've created and what they continue to accomplish have transcended any tags or genres. They take very basic catchy riffs, a rock-solid simple drumbeat and groove, and wailing vocals and make loud hard rock that's instantly catchy. AC/DC is almost danceable at times. Look no further than guitarist Angus Young's constant motion onstage for proof. The minute AC/DC starts playing, feet start tapping. Some people call them metal, but I've always thought of them as a very loud blues-rock band.

There's never been more of a recipe for "if it ain't broke, don't fix it" than AC/DC. Though some say they were bluesier and jammed a little more with Bon Scott, you always know exactly what you're going to get with one of their records: gritty, mischievous, gargled-with-razor-blades vocals and that distinctive groove. Angus's supercharged, heavy blues riffs are enormously powerful, and they are given exactly the space they need by the rhythm section of Cliff Williams and Phil Rudd—an overlooked part of the AC/DC sound.

Most attention certainly goes to Angus—who still wears his schoolboy uniform even though he's pushing sixty—but without his brother Malcolm's rhythm playing to hold things down, AC/DC's sound wouldn't be the same. The band's backing vocals are also rarely talked about. Bassist

Cliff Williams helps to create some of the best melodies, with sing-along choruses on songs like "Rock 'N Roll Train." As in many bands, the guys from AC/DC who are rarely interviewed or on magazine covers are just as important as the guys who are always in the spotlight.

When I landed my first job as a host for VH1 Classic—way before *That Metal Show* existed—one of the interviews I was told I was going to do was with AC/DC. (Obviously, that's a pretty cool first TV gig!) It was 2003 and they were being inducted into the Rock and Roll Hall of Fame. Angus and Malcolm Young and Brian Johnson came to the studio to talk about it. All the members of AC/DC are known to be pretty short in stature, and I'm much taller than they are, so when we sat down to talk, it looked like I was a father with his three kids! We had to arrange boxes on the set to stagger our heights, because otherwise it would have seemed like they came up to my waist. They all chain-smoked in unison like I've never seen anyone do before or since.

Angus and Malcolm can be a little hard to understand—they have a tough Australian accent—and Brian talks like a pirate, but they are such nice and sincerely genuine people. One of the biggest things about AC/DC is the energy of their live shows—Angus, for instance, is known for his insane stamina while he runs and spins around the stage—but interestingly, off the stage they are just reserved, relaxed guys who like to sit back and enjoy a cup of tea with a cigarette.

We had a great time that day. I remember telling Brian—who was a lot of fun, with a great sense of humor—that I also did a radio show in New York and would love for them to come on the air. Everybody at every level of the media was trying to get them on radio and TV shows to talk about being inducted into the Hall of Fame, so when he said, "Sure. I'll see what I can do," I took that to mean, "It's not going to happen in a million years."

The politics of the music industry are such that if the lead singer of AC/DC does the Eddie Trunk show but doesn't visit all the other rock stations too, people get pretty upset. Over the years, one of the biggest obstacles to getting AC/DC on my radio show had been Howard Stern's perceived ownership of them in New York. In addition to being a big fan, Howard had featured the band in his film *Private Parts*, and he was known to get pissed if they did any other show. I've said many times publicly that I'm a huge fan of Stern's and that he's been my biggest influence as a radio host. I never thought I had a drop of the impact that he did, but when it comes to music, I have something unique to offer. Howard isn't a huge music guy and doesn't usually know everything in a band's history. His interview would be pretty different than mine, and I think the guys in AC/DC recognized that. (Plus, I actually play their music all the time on my shows.)

The next afternoon, as I was getting ready to go to my radio studio, Brian Johnson called my cell phone. He said, "Eddie, me son," which is what he calls everyone, "tell me where I'm headed tonight. I'm looking forward to seeing you later." He skipped the handlers and publicists and came to my show, that night, on his own without an entourage. Brian was

EDDIE'S PLAYLIST

AC/DC

1. ROCK 'N ROLL TRAIN
2. FLICK OF THE SWITCH
3. WALK ALL OVER YOU
4. WHOLE LOTTA ROSIE
5. LET THERE BE ROCK
6. NIGHT OF THE
   LONG KNIVES
7. HIGH VOLTAGE
8. EVIL WALKS
9. SIN CITY
10. GIVIN THE DOG A BONE
11. DOWN PAYMENT BLUES
12. SHOT DOWN IN FLAMES
13. KICKED IN THE TEETH
14. I PUT THE FINGER
    ON YOU
15. TOUCH TOO MUCH
16. PROBLEM CHILD
17. HELLS BELLS
18. RIFF RAFF

open and outspoken about everything. We had a great hour-long conversation on the air. He even called my show again the following week so that he could personally thank an Italian restaurant where he'd had dinner on Staten Island while in town. I mean, who does that? It was my first experience getting to know a member of the band, and I always look forward to talking to him. Brian is unlike any other lead singer, in that he is very unassuming about his role in the band. It's like he still feels that he's the new guy after thirty years! He is fully aware that the Young brothers steer the AC/DC ship.

Brian is also so honest about his role in life and his opportunity to be in AC/DC. He told me that after he recorded vocals for *Back in Black* at a studio in the Bahamas in 1980, he walked out to a pier behind the building, lit a cigarette, and thought about what he was going to do for a living. He was completely convinced that once the record label heard the album, they would wipe all of his vocals and the band would be forced to find a new singer. He knew he was replacing an icon, and when he first heard the album, he had absolutely no sense of the overnight success it would have. Considering what a hit that record was, it's pretty remarkable that he had any doubts about his vocal tracks.

Brian is now in his sixties and a little older than the other guys in the